1,000,000 Books

are available to read at

www.ForgottenBooks.com

Read online
Download PDF
Purchase in print

ISBN 978-1-331-35087-3
PIBN 10177927

This book is a reproduction of an important historical work. Forgotten Books uses state-of-the-art technology to digitally reconstruct the work, preserving the original format whilst repairing imperfections present in the aged copy. In rare cases, an imperfection in the original, such as a blemish or missing page, may be replicated in our edition. We do, however, repair the vast majority of imperfections successfully; any imperfections that remain are intentionally left to preserve the state of such historical works.

Forgotten Books is a registered trademark of FB &c Ltd.
Copyright © 2018 FB &c Ltd.
FB &c Ltd, Dalton House, 60 Windsor Avenue, London, SW19 2RR.
Company number 08720141. Registered in England and Wales.

For support please visit www.forgottenbooks.com

1 MONTH OF FREE READING

at
www.ForgottenBooks.com

By purchasing this book you are eligible for one month membership to ForgottenBooks.com, giving you unlimited access to our entire collection of over 1,000,000 titles via our web site and mobile apps.

To claim your free month visit:
www.forgottenbooks.com/free177927

* Offer is valid for 45 days from date of purchase. Terms and conditions apply.

English
Français
Deutsche
Italiano
Español
Português

www.forgottenbooks.com

Mythology Photography **Fiction** Fishing Christianity **Art** Cooking Essays Buddhism Freemasonry Medicine **Biology** Music **Ancient Egypt** Evolution Carpentry Physics Dance Geology **Mathematics** Fitness Shakespeare **Folklore** Yoga Marketing **Confidence** Immortality Biographies Poetry **Psychology** Witchcraft Electronics Chemistry History **Law** Accounting **Philosophy** Anthropology Alchemy Drama Quantum Mechanics Atheism Sexual Health **Ancient History Entrepreneurship** Languages Sport Paleontology Needlework Islam **Metaphysics** Investment Archaeology Parenting Statistics Criminology **Motivational**

DOCUMENTS ON THE STATE-WIDE
INITIATIVE, REFERENDUM, AND RECALL

THE MACMILLAN COMPANY
NEW YORK · BOSTON · CHICAGO
SAN FRANCISCO

MACMILLAN & CO., LIMITED
LONDON · BOMBAY · CALCUTTA
MELBOURNE

THE MACMILLAN CO. OF CANADA, LTD.
TORONTO

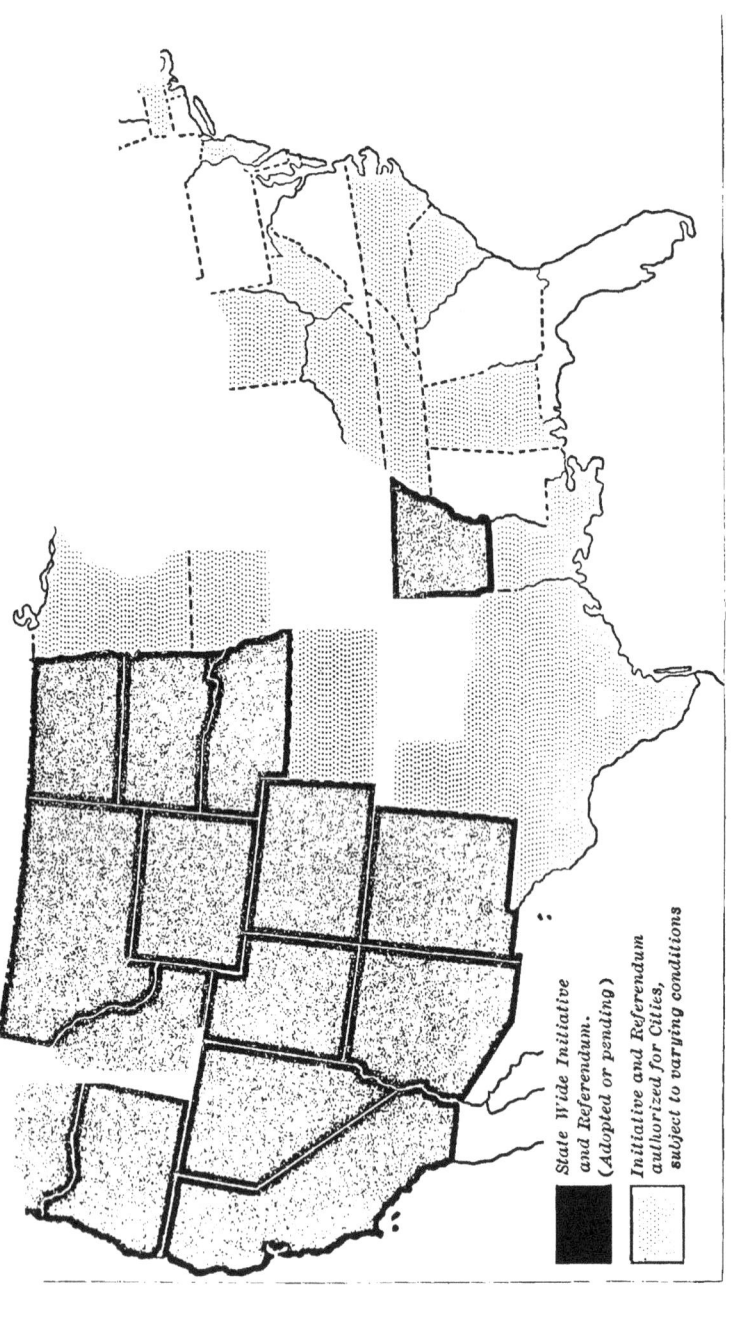

MAP SHOWING THE INITIATIVE AND REFERENDUM, STATE AND MUNICIPAL.

NOTE: New Mexico and Nevada have the referendum only. Initiative and referendum are pending adoption in Washington, Arizona, North Dakota, Wisconsin, Nebraska, Wyoming, and Nevada (initiative). See Table, pages 1-2.

DOCUMENTS ON THE STATE-WIDE

INITIATIVE, REFERENDUM AND RECALL

BY

CHARLES A. BEARD

ASSOCIATE PROFESSOR OF POLITICS IN COLUMBIA UNIVERSITY

AND

BIRL E. SHULTZ

INDIANA SCHOLAR IN POLITICAL SCIENCE
IN COLUMBIA UNIVERSITY

BOSTON UNIVERSITY
COLLEGE OF LIBERAL ARTS
LIBRARY

New York
THE MACMILLAN COMPANY
1912

All rights reserved

COPYRIGHT, 1912,
By THE MACMILLAN COMPANY.

Set up and electrotyped. Published January, 1912.

Norwood Press
J. S. Cushing Co. — Berwick & Smith Co.
Norwood, Mass., U.S.A.

PREFACE

THIS volume includes all of the constitutional amendments providing for a state-wide system of initiative and referendum now in force, several of the most significant statutes elaborating the constitutional provisions, all of the constitutional amendments now pending adoption, six important judicial decisions, and certain materials relative to the state-wide recall. While no attempt has been made to go into the subject of the initiative, referendum, and recall as applied to local and municipal government, some illustrative papers showing the system in ordinary municipalities and commission-governed cities have been included.[1] We have published as an appendix the complete scheme of government suggested by Mr. W. S. U'Ren and a committee of Oregon citizens. This is one of the most suggestive documents to be found in recent American political literature, and it will be read with profit in connection with the chapters of Mr. Herbert Croly's *Promise of American Life* dealing with state government and administration.

It is obvious that this volume will soon be partially out of date if the several projects for the initiative, referendum, and recall now pending are adopted. It is hoped, however, that new editions may be issued from time to time so that students of government may have readily accessible the primary materials for the study of these new institutional devices.

We are indebted to Mr. H. H. Jones, of the Columbia Graduate School, for valuable aid in reading the proof. We have

---

[1] Extensive documentary material on the initiative, referendum, and recall in commission-governed cities may be found in Beard, *Digest of Short Ballot Charters*.

followed the exact language of the official document in every case, and must disclaim responsibility for the atrocious grammar and painful obscurities to be found in the texts, which (it is worthy of note) are, with few exceptions, legislative, not initiative, measures.

C. A. B.
B. E. S.

COLUMBIA UNIVERSITY,
  August, 1911.

TABLE OF CONTENTS

I. INITIATIVE AND REFERENDUM

		PAGE
PREFACE	. . . .	v
INTRODUCTORY NOTE	. . . .	1
I.	SOUTH DAKOTA	70
II.	UTAH	78
III.	OREGON	79
IV.	NEVADA	121
V.	MONTANA	125
VI.	OKLAHOMA	137
VII.	MAINE	162
VIII.	MISSOURI	168
IX.	MICHIGAN	178
X.	ARKANSAS	180
XI.	COLORADO	181
XII.	CALIFORNIA	184
XIII.	WASHINGTON (Proposed)	191
XIV.	NEBRASKA (Proposed)	195
XV.	IDAHO (Proposed)	200
XVI.	WYOMING (Proposed)	201
XVII.	WISCONSIN (Proposed)	206
XVIII.	NORTH DAKOTA (Proposed)	210
XIX.	ARIZONA (Proposed)	230
XX.	NEW MEXICO (Proposed)	234
XXI.	ILLINOIS (Public Opinion Law)	238
XXII.	TEXAS (Party Initiative)	240

II. THE STATE-WIDE RECALL[1]

		PAGE
XXIII.	OREGON	242
XXIV.	ARIZONA (Proposed)	244
XXV.	CALIFORNIA	264
XXVI.	IDAHO (Proposed)	271
XXVII.	NEVADA (Proposed)	272

III. INITIATIVE AND REFERENDUM IN MUNICIPAL GOVERNMENT

XXVIII.	OHIO	274

IV. INITIATIVE, REFERENDUM, AND RECALL IN COMMISSION GOVERNMENT

XXIX.	IOWA	280
XXX.	NEW JERSEY	285

V. JUDICIAL DECISIONS

XXXI.	LUTHER v. BORDEN	291
XXXII.	KADDERLY v. PORTLAND (Oregon)	304
XXXIII.	STATE v. PACIFIC STATES TELEPHONE AND TELEGRAPH COMPANY (Oregon)	310
XXXIV.	KIERNAN v. PORTLAND (Oregon)	314
XXXV.	Ex parte WAGNER (Oklahoma)	330
XXXVI.	BONNER v. BELSTERLING (Recall in Texas)	337

VI. APPENDIX

THE PROPOSED OREGON SYSTEM	349
BALLOT TITLES FOR OREGON ELECTION, 1910	384
INDEX	391

[1] For North Dakota, see pp. 210, 221.

DOCUMENTS ON THE STATE-WIDE INITIATIVE, REFERENDUM, AND RECALL

DOCUMENTS ON THE STATE-WIDE INITIATIVE, REFERENDUM, AND RECALL

INTRODUCTORY NOTE

The Initiative and Referendum

THE initiative and referendum are no longer of mere academic interest. The two devices, in one form or another, have been adopted for state-wide purposes by nearly one-fourth of the commonwealths of the Union; and if the system is approved in the other states where it has become a serious political issue or is already submitted to popular approval, the next decade will see it in force in more than one-half of the states. The evidence afforded by the following table shows that the initiative and referendum have been taken out of the realm of speculation and made subjects of practical consideration for students of government and men of affairs.

I. *South Dakota.* — Complete system of initiative and referendum (1898). Machinery finally constituted on March 3, 1899.

II. *Utah.* — An amendment establishing the initiative and referendum submitted by a fusion legislature and adopted on November 6, 1900. The statute has not been provided for carrying the amendment into effect because the legislature passed into the control of Republican leaders, who repudiated the principle which had been approved at the polls.

III. *Oregon.* — Constitutional amendment adopted June 2, 1902.

IV. *Nevada.* — Adopted November 8, 1904. Provision was made for the referendum only; but an initiative and recall amendment is now being submitted to popular vote.

V. *Montana.* — Adopted November, 1906.

VI. *Oklahoma.* — System embodied in the constitution under which the state was admitted to the Union, in 1907.

VII. *Maine.* — Adopted September 14, 1908.
VIII. *Missouri.* — Adopted November 3, 1908.
IX. *Michigan.* — The new Michigan constitution which went into effect in 1909 included a system of initiative and referendum applicable only to constitutional amendments and subject to such restrictions as to be well-nigh unworkable. Referendum on laws at the option of the legislature.
X. *Arkansas.* — Adopted September 12, 1910.
XI. *Colorado.* — Adopted November 8, 1910.
XII. *California.* — A constitutional amendment providing for the initiative, referendum, and recall submitted to the voters at a special election on October 10, 1911, and adopted.
XIII. *Washington.* — Constitutional amendment passed in January, 1911, to be submitted to popular vote in November, 1912.
XIV. *Nebraska.* — Initiative and referendum amendment approved by the governor March 24, 1911, to be submitted to popular vote in November, 1912.
XV. *Idaho.* — To be submitted to the voters at the next general election — November, 1912.
XVI. *Wyoming.* — To be submitted to the voters at next general election — November, 1912.
XVII. *Wisconsin.* — Constitutional amendment passed by the legislature in 1911, but must be approved by the next legislature before being submitted to popular vote in the election of 1914.
XVIII. *Arizona.* — Complete system of initiative and referendum included in the constitution under which admission to the Union was sought.
XIX. *New Mexico.* — The constitution under which New Mexico sought admission to the Union makes provision for the referendum only.
XX. *North Dakota.* — Initiative, referendum, and recall passed by the legislature in 1911; to be submitted to 1913 session for approval previous to reference to popular vote.
XXI. *Illinois.* — A public opinion bill making provision for securing popular expression on questions of public policy was adopted in 1901, and the initiative and referendum have become practical issues.
XXII. *Texas.* — Party referendum provided by law.

In view of all these facts the desirability of coming to some conclusion concerning the principles upon which the initiative and referendum rest is surely apparent, although it can hardly be said that the experience thus far gained in the actual operation of the system is sufficient to warrant many dogmatic conclusions. Certainly it is useless to dismiss the theme on the ground that the proposed devices are a hybrid growth grafted upon an ancient system of Anglo-Saxon institutions by short-sighted reformers. It is likewise useless to take the doctrinaire position that representative government is a sacred thing, invariable in its forms and limitations from the time of Simon de Montfort's Parliament down to the last session of the Illinois legislature.

The fact is that representative government has been in the process of transformation in the United States from the first assembly of burgesses in Virginia in 1619; and during the nineteenth century state legislatures have been steadily declining in popular esteem. This is not a matter of speculation, for the proof of the statement is to be found in the successive constitutions and constitutional amendments in nearly every important state.

We began our history with a substantially omnipotent legislature. Our eighteenth-century constitution-makers distrusted the executive power on the one hand, and feared the extension of the suffrage on the other. Accordingly, they generally vested the power of electing the governor in the legislature, fixed his term at one year, and seldom gave him the veto power. In New York, where the governor was elected by the freeholders for a term of three years under the constitution of 1777, his veto power was shared by a Council of Revision and his appointive power could be exercised only in conjunction with a special Council of Appointment. The legislatures created new offices at will and elected the incumbents if they pleased; they granted charters to public and private corporations; and they laid taxes and incurred debts at their pleasure. Only a few limitations were imposed upon their law-making authority, for the early constitutions were generally brief documents constructing the frame of government and intrusting to the representatives full political power. And further to demonstrate public confidence in the legislature, it was stipulated that sessions should be frequent.[1]

This state of legislative omnipotence did not last long, however, because, in far too many cases, "the representatives of the people" betrayed their trust; and, having fallen into the evil habit, they found it difficult to throw off the tradition. Those who had been first in their advocacy of legislative supremacy began to repudiate their own doctrine. Constitutional convention after constitutional convention left behind it a record of distrust in the competence and common honesty of legislatures, and exhausted its ingenuity in devising methods for restricting the power of the lawmakers for evil. The conventions, being elected for the particular purpose and usually composed of more disinterested citizens than the ordinary legislature, gave special attention to building defences against the unscrupulous manipulators who were sure to find their way into the state assemblies.

The contest between the convention and the legislature reminds one of the struggle now going on in the field of preparation for naval warfare. A new high-powered gun and a particularly dangerous projectile are invented; and straightway the makers for armor plate exert their wits in discovering some material that will resist the new engine of destruction. When the satisfactory armor is invented the makers of guns and projectiles labor unceasingly until they have found a still more terrible instrument. And so the seesaw goes on. Thus in politics, one state convention devises a new constitutional limitation designed to thwart a certain kind of corrupt and vicious legislation; the succeeding legislature finds a way through, for, as Mr. Dooley remarks, a stone wall is often a triumphal arch to the eye of

[1] For many illustrations given here I have drawn upon my *American Government and Politics*.

the experienced. A new convention is called and new constitutional limitations are invented; but the legislature proves to be as ingenious as ever.[1]

It is not hazardous to say that in every state constitutional convention since the opening of the nineteenth century, the theme of limitation upon legislative prerogative has been extensively discussed. In the convention of Kentucky in 1890, Mr. Carroll exclaimed, "It is a well-known fact that one of the prime causes for the calling of this convention was the abuses practised by the Legislative Department of this State; and I venture the assertion that, except for the vicious legislation and the local and special laws of all kinds and character passed by the Legislatures that have met in Kentucky for the past twenty years, no proposition to call a constitutional convention could ever have received a majority of the votes of the people of Kentucky. The people of Kentucky are more in danger from abuses by the Legislative Department than they are from abuses of any other department of the State Government." [2]

To checkmate legislatures in bartering away, negligently and corruptly, charters, franchises, and special privileges, the constitutions of our important states now generally either forbid the legislatures to create corporations by special act, or otherwise limit this exercise of legislative power. The present constitution of Virginia vests in the corporation commission, appointed by the governor, the power to grant all charters and amendments of charters for domestic and foreign incorporations. Delaware stipulates that general and special incorporation laws must have the approval of two-thirds of all the members elected to both houses of the legislature.

To secure publicity in legislative matters, and prevent sinister

---

[1] It is largely through this contest for popular supremacy over legislative incompetence and dishonesty that our state constitutions have grown in bulk — conventions have embodied statutes in the constitutions because they have been unwilling to trust the state legislatures.

[2] Beard, *Readings in American Government and Politics*, p. 445.

influences from working by secret methods, our newer constitutions contain provisions controlling legislative procedure. As was stated, for instance, in the New York constitutional convention of 1894, it was a common thing, which happened at every session of the legislature, for an apparently insignificant amendment to be offered on the third reading of a bill, and after being adopted in the hurry and confusion of the moment, turn out to be a vicious proposition.[1] This practice is the source of that section of Article III of the present New York constitution, which provides that no bill shall be passed or become a law until it shall have been printed and on the desk of the members at least three calendar legislative days prior to its final passage, unless the governor or the acting governor shall have certified to the necessity of its immediate passage.

Legislatures cannot be given a free hand in laying taxes, incurring debts, and making appropriations. This nearly all of our states have learned by bitter experience; and they have now written in their constitutions limitations on the extent of the taxing power and on the amount of debt which may be incurred. For example, the constitution of New York limits the ordinary debt of the state to a million dollars, and provides for a popular referendum on debts incurred in excess of that amount, excepting debts necessary to suppress insurrection and defend the state in war. A study of the limitations to be found in the several state constitutions now in force reveals the most astounding ingenuity in the devices employed to check legislative extravagance and dishonesty.

In local and special matters our legislatures have been particular offenders, and it is now the practice for state constitution-makers to include in the fundamental law of the commonwealth a long list of subjects on which the legislature is forbidden to pass local and private bills.

While shearing the legislature of its power, our constitution-makers have been gaining faith in the executive as the respon-

---

[1] Beard, *Readings in American Government and Politics*, p. 466.

sible functionary on whose integrity and decent respect for the opinions of mankind the public may more safely rely. We have seen how the early governors were designedly servants of the legislature; and even a casual survey of our state constitutions to-day shows their changed position. In every commonwealth in the Union, save North Carolina, the governor enjoys the veto power, and in an increasing number of instances he is given the power to negative particular items of appropriation bills so that he may be the "watch-dog of the treasury." In other ways the governor's powers have been constitutionally extended, but the limits of his authority are by no means set in the letter of the constitutions.

There can be no doubt that the most popular state governors of recent years, — Roosevelt, Hughes, Folk, La Follette, Wilson, — whatever may be their individual merits, owe their positions to the free way in which they have coerced and checkmated the legislatures. It need not be said that their popularity has been due altogether to corrupt practices on the part of the respective legislatures over which they wielded their sway. The fact is that there has been growing up the notion that the legislature is inherently unfitted for some of its most important work.

This notion was voiced by Mr. Gamaliel Bradford in an article published in the *Evening Post*[1] in 1908: —

Consider how our legislatures try to govern. When they meet in session there are two houses in each state, varying from fifty to three hundred men, all representing different districts and all precisely equal. There is nobody there representing the state as a whole or the state administration. The only duty of each member is to get all he can for his constituents, and he would be regarded as impertinent if he interfered with the schemes of any of the others. Every member can propose as many measures as he pleases upon any subject he pleases, and they are all thrown on an equal footing into a number of committees made up by the Speaker, who is elected for that purpose, at his discretion; while the legislature, with little discussion, passes what the committees

[1] Reinsch, *Readings in American State Government*, p. 18.

recommend. It is an ideal system for corruption. It was the origin of the lobby, that is, a power which, by corrupt methods, can induce a mass of conflicting atoms to act together for private ends; and out of the lobby is evolved the boss. What the government of the state is, that will be the government of the cities.

In addition to these unquestionable proofs that there is a decline in public confidence in legislative ability and honesty, attention may be drawn to some passages in current history. While no one would deny that a great amount of conscientious, serious, and honorable work is done in our state legislatures, it must be admitted that there is a vague feeling abroad to the effect that one can never be certain that any particular legislature is engaged in the faithful discharge of its duties. Almost within the last year the legislatures of New York, Ohio, and Illinois have been smirched by exposures and scandals which, in spite of the exaggerations, contain a distressing amount of established fact. The Republican legislature of New York was hopelessly discredited by the revelations of 1910, and its Democratic successor, which went into office under the ancient slogan "Peace, Retrenchment, and Reform," by its devotion to party and private interests speedily lost the confidence of that portion of the public that derives no advantage from the distribution of the spoils of office.

Even such a conservative and respectable paper as the New York *Times*, in an editorial of July 3, 1911, makes the following observation concerning the law-making body of the Empire commonwealth:—

The "combine" — the term has a definite and ugly connotation — between the Tammany machine in control of the majority of the Legislature and the Old Guard, with a solid block of Republican votes, is not novel. Partnerships of that sort have been a reliance for Tammany for many years. Tweed ran one of amazing efficiency in the Legislature forty years ago, and its wild excursions culminated in his exposure and downfall. It was but an extension of the business arrangement he had formed in this city, which made "Tammany Republicans" a hissing and a byword in our political history. The present conspiracy against the rights and interests of the public is probably not nearly so formidable or so bad, and will undoubtedly be broken up at the polls next Fall, but in morals it is the same sort of odious and mischievous thing.

What is particularly bitter and disappointing in the actual situation at Albany is that it is the outcome of an honest effort by the independent voters of the State to drive bad men from the Legislature and put in good ones. And the most unfortunate result of this betrayal of the hopes and aims of honest men is that it tends strongly to discourage like attempts in the future. Respectable and well-meaning men all over the State, and especially in this city, are going about saying: "What is the use? You only replace one lot of rascals by another, generally worse." And there is no denying that the facts give a good deal of support to that weary plea. A Legislature under the thumbs of the worst Republican managers could hardly have done anything worse in its line than the Levy Election bill, or so bad as the City Hall Park invasion bill, the finance bills, and the New York Charter that will pretty surely be jammed through in the next ten days.

Even if one does not agree entirely with the editor of the *Times* in his severe strictures upon the New York legislature, he must admit that opinions of this character are widespread and do not spring from any mere partisan prejudices. It is incontrovertible that the popular estimate of the ability and common honesty of legislators is by no means high. That the popular judgment is often unjust and based upon an exaggeration of the facts in any particular case will be conceded. It is needless, however, to argue the point as to whether the judgment is altogether just and righteous; it stands nevertheless. And as a psychological fact it must be reckoned with by those who contend that no fundamental alterations should be made in our representative system.

If we turn from the state legislatures to the legislative bodies of our cities, we find the same growing distrust of the representative principle. This distrust is likewise to be found recorded in legal instruments, as well as in the more or less vague and fluctuating public opinion of our cities.

Our new charters, like our state constitutions, are generally formidable instruments covering the whole domain of municipal organization and restraining on every side the power of municipal councils. The great principle of checks and balances, which some thought was realized in the bicameral system, has proved a flat failure, and most of our larger cities — New York, Chicago, Cleveland, and Cincinnati, for example — now have councils composed of only a single chamber.

The Boston Finance Commission in 1907 declared that while in the double-chambered council the mistakes of one body might be corrected by the other and the unwise exercise of the borrowing power by one branch had sometimes been negatived by the other, yet "much more frequently improvident loans desired by one branch have been added to the similar loans desired by the other and incorporated into a single bill and passed."

Even the single-chambered system which it was hoped would give more simplicity and responsibility in municipal government has been by no means unqualified in its success, and in some cities, notably in New York, the council has been stripped of all its important powers over finances and franchises. It may be truly said that in New York City the real government is in the hands of the Board of Estimate and Apportionment, composed of the mayor, the comptroller, the president of the board of aldermen, and the presidents of the five boroughs into which the city is divided. In Boston, under the new charter, the budget is originated by the mayor, and city finances are scrutinized by a commission appointed by the governor. In Ohio cities the mayor makes up the budgets from estimates furnished by the departments, and the council may omit or decrease items but cannot increase the total.

The limitations placed upon municipal councils by charters and statutes, similar in character to the constitutional limitations imposed upon state legislatures, have by no means rehabilitated the councils in the public mind. The widespread adoption of the system of commission government for cities is an evidence that a considerable portion of the American people have come to the conclusion that one way of getting rid of the abuses of "representative" government is to abolish the council altogether, and substitute for it a commission of a few men elected at large and endowed with full legislative and executive powers.

No further testimony needs to be adduced than that afforded by the dry legal record to be found in statutes, charters, and constitutions, to demonstrate the general dissatisfaction with the simple uncontrolled representative system of government. It cannot be said, however, that the reaction against legislative abuses at once took the form of a movement for direct popular control over the legislatures through the initiative and referendum. On the contrary, it led at first to a long series of experiments in electoral reforms, in addition to the constitutional limitations just described.

In some quarters the disrepute into which representative government had fallen was attributed to the wide extension of the suffrage; but it was found impossible to replace restrictions once removed. A number of schemes, however, were devised to secure a greater purity at the ballot box: registration laws, official elections, bi-partisan election boards, judicial control over electoral procedure, and the like.

In other quarters it was thought that the Australian ballot, printed at public expense, would destroy the boss, and improve the quality of our legislatures. The cost of printing ballots, it was argued, deterred independent men from entering into politics and made it impossible for new political organizations opposed to the rings in power to get a foothold in politics. The Australian ballot was to be the instrument for the elevation of legislatures; the machine would be put out of business and could no longer nominate its corrupt henchmen for the legislatures; and at length, as Ostrogorski remarks, the politicians, entrenched in assemblies, were intimidated into granting the reform.

But the Australian ballot did not prove to be the Wonder-working Providence which its advocates had prophesied; and almost immediately the cry went up for legislative regulation of party organizations. At once there began to come from our state legislatures a series of statutes regulating at first the minor features of party organization and operation, then extending in every direction — culminating in a complete system incorporating the political party in the legal framework of government, making the direct nomination of candidates obligatory, and even, in some instances, defraying a portion of party expenses from the public treasury.

Nearly all of the proposals designed to checkmate legislative abuses have been based upon the assumption that the hope for better government lay in more democracy rather than in less. Indeed, the decline of legislative assemblies has been marked by a steady extension of democratic principles; and some writers have assumed that a corrupt and ignorant electorate based upon universal manhood suffrage is responsible for the evil days into which we have fallen. As a matter of fact, however, the connection between the growth of corruption and the extension of the suffrage is difficult to establish. Corruption in legislatures is older by far than manhood suffrage. Long before the franchise had been generously widened in the United States, malodorous practices in legislatures had attracted the attention of political chroniclers; and, while it cannot be doubted that in some instances the purchase of the poor and ignorant vote has been responsible for the election of corrupt legislators, there is absolutely no reason for believing that, had the earlier property qualifications on the suffrage been retained, our legislative record would have been essentially different so far as honesty is concerned.

It seems not unreasonable to argue that the corruption and malpractices in our state legislatures which have discredited them in the public mind have been due rather to the increased opportunities for exploitation offered by the advance of the country in material wealth than to the extension of the suffrage. At all events it cannot be shown that corruption is inherent in democratic as contrasted with aristocratic institutions; for, turning to English experience, we find that the reform of Commons and the elimination of the bribery and corrupt practices that characterized Parliament in the eighteenth century, have been accomplished since the extension of the suffrage.

However one may view the matter, it is now hardly worth while to argue it. We are committed to the great democratic principle of a widely extended suffrage, and the history of the nineteenth century has been largely a record justifying the extension of popular power.

At the beginning of our history the propertied classes were everywhere dominant. The Fathers, notwithstanding the rhetorical flourish in the Declaration of Independence, did not believe that the right to vote should be given freely to all men regardless of the amount of property they owned or the religious opinions they entertained. And as for woman suffrage, they doubtless held with Blackstone that woman was specially favored by the generous provisions of the law which turned over all of her earnings and property to her husband, and merged her personality in his. At the close of the eighteenth century, in nearly every state, the suffrage was limited by the constitution or laws to property-owners, generally freeholders and taxpayers. The conservative thinkers of the time regarded the owners of land as the only safe depositories of political power. Doubtless most of them agreed with Mr. Dickinson, who exclaimed in the Federal Convention of 1787 that the freeholders were the best guardians of liberty, and the restriction of the suffrage to them a necessary defence "against the dangerous influence of those multitudes without property and without principle with which our country like all others will in time abound."[1]

In spite of the prophecies of dire evils to come, the suffrage was steadily extended in the United States until on the eve of the

[1] Farrand, *Records of the Federal Convention*, Vol. II, p. 202.

Civil War the principle was well-nigh universally adopted that every adult male of reasonably settled habitation should be entitled to share in political power by exercising his right to vote. And since the Civil War the principle has been further extended in six states so as completely to enfranchise women. The movement which secured to woman educational advantages, opened the professions to her, gave her control over her own property and her earnings, and won recognition for her before the law as an independent personality, culminates logically in the extension to her of that equality in the field of politics which she now commonly possesses in the domain of civil rights.

While no one can be blind to the evils which have been associated with democracy in the United States and in the Old World, no serious student of history, when he compares the long train of abuses, brutalities, and disorders connected with the rule of kings, priests, and nobles, can doubt for an instant that as between democracy and the outworn systems of the past there can be no choice. Every branch of law that has been recast under the influence of popular will has been touched with enlightenment and humanity. Compare the brutal criminal codes of old Europe with the still imperfect but relatively enlightened codes of our own time. Compare the treatment of prisoners, women, and children, the education of the youth, and the public institutions devoted to general welfare, with those existing before the age of democracy. Mr. Bryce's remark that evidences of philanthropy and humanitarianism are mingled in our state politics with folly and jobbery "like threads of gold and silver woven across a warp of dirty sacking" is true, and yet when one looks for evidences of philanthropy and humanitarianism in the folly and jobbery that characterized aristocratic and monarchical institutions in the old régime, one does not even have the satisfaction of getting the gleam of gold and silver across the dirty sacking. As Desmoulins declared concerning the excesses of the French Revolution, "The blood shed in the cause of liberty was as nothing to that spilt by kings and prelates for maintaining their dominions and satisfying their ambitions." With all its faults, and they need not be glossed over, democracy is justifying itself, and every student of history who devotes himself to the investigation of institutions and social conditions will find encouragement in the record of mankind under democratic government, such as it is.[1]

Correlated with the development of the democratic principle in the suffrage there has been a steady extension in the political activities of the voters. In the beginning of our history as an independent nation the voters were practically restricted to the single function of choosing representatives and electing officers, except in town-meetings. But step by step their functions have been enlarged until in nearly every state in the Union they participate in determining public policy in matters great and small.

Even the principle that state constitutions should be subject to popular ratification was not accepted by our first lawmakers. Only three of the constitutions adopted before 1800 were submitted to the voters for their direct approval or rejection. The Federal Constitution was ratified by conventions chosen by the voters in the several states, — this method of ratification by conventions being in Chief Justice Marshall's opinion "the only manner in which they can act safely, effectively, and wisely on such a subject." [2]

Nevertheless the vague idea was in the air that constitutional provisions should receive popular approval in some form or another. For example, the Pennsylvania legislature, in calling a new constitutional convention in 1789, declared: "It would be expedient, just, and reasonable, that the convention should publish their amendments and alterations for the consideration of the people, and adjourn at least four months previous to confirmation." This recommendation was followed by the

[1] See a brilliant essay by my colleague, Professor James Harvey Robinson, "The Spirit of Conservatism in the Light of History," Journal of Philosophy, Psychology, and Scientific Methods, May 11, 1911.
[2] McCulloch v. Maryland, 4 Wheaton, 316.

constitutional convention, and although, as Professor Dodd remarks,[1] these proceedings cannot be regarded as equivalent to a formal submission to the people, they do recognize the necessity for popular participation. The constitutions of Massachusetts (1780) and New Hampshire (1783) were submitted to direct popular vote; and in drafting her new constitution in 1792, New Hampshire followed the earlier precedent.

In spite of these examples, however, the idea of popular ratification was slow in taking root, especially outside of New England, where it is supposed that the referendum was received more favorably because of the practical experience which the people had gained in law-making in town meetings. It was not until 1821, when New York submitted her constitution to popular vote, that the referendum appeared in any state outside of New England. Before the opening of the Civil War, however, the principle of popular ratification had won favor throughout the country. Every constitution adopted between 1840 and 1860 was submitted to popular approval.[2] The principle was also accepted by Congress in passing Enabling Acts for new states. "The earlier enabling Acts did not require submission, and their language not only seems to indicate that popular approval was not considered necessary, but actually precluded submission." It was not until the joint resolution of March 1, 1845, admitting Texas to the Union that Congress showed any inclination to approve the principle of popular ratification; and it was not until 1857 that popular ratification was specified in an Enabling Act — the Act for Minnesota passed on February 26, 1857. At length, however, so widely adopted was this principle of popular ratification that it led the distinguished authority on state conventions, Judge Jameson, to declare that submission of constitutional provisions to popular ratification was a fundamental principle of American public law.

[1] Dodd, *Revision and Amendment of State Constitutions*, p. 63.
[2] *Ibid.*, p. 65. The details here are taken from this excellent work.

While Judge Jameson's conclusion is somewhat sweeping, it must be admitted that the later exceptions to the uniform practice have been due rather to peculiar circumstances than to any abandonment of the general doctrine. Five constitutions adopted since 1890 have not been submitted to popular approval — Mississippi (1890), South Carolina (1895), Delaware (1897), Louisiana (1898), and Virginia (1902); but in the case of four of these states the reason of this departure from accepted principles is obvious. As Professor Dodd remarks, "The failure to submit constitutions to the people in Mississippi, South Carolina, Louisiana, and Virginia may perhaps be explained as a necessary part of the plan to disfranchise the colored population of these states, and may on this account be treated as exceptional." The reasons for the action in Delaware are not so apparent, but it can hardly be said that the single unexplained violation of the principle of the referendum would indicate any weakening in the doctrine as it is now accepted in the United States.[1]

At the same time the principle of popular ratification was being worked out, easier methods of securing the expression of popular will in the amendment of constitutions were being devised. When the sovereignty of the British Crown and Parliament was thrown off, the Revolutionists naturally declared that the popular will was the basis of all government. The right of the people to alter or abolish, and to institute new forms of government on such principles and with such powers as might to them seem most likely to effect their safety and happiness was laid down in the Declaration of Independence. Notwithstanding this, it was a long time before the state constitution-makers came to see that, according to this great democratic theory, every fundamental law ought to provide for a simple mode of amendment through which, from time to time, the electorate might alter or reconstruct the government. A number of the early state constitutions

---

[1] The constitution of Kentucky (1891), after it had been approved by popular vote, was changed by the convention. But this can hardly be regarded as overthrowing the general principle.

made no provisions whatever for amendment, and nearly all of them were put into operation without being submitted to popular ratification. This was due to the confusion of the Revolutionary days during which the constitutions were drafted, to a failure to distinguish between constitutions and statutes, and to the generally prevailing notion that a convention composed of delegates chosen by the electorate had the sovereign power to frame new governments. And, as a matter of practice, amendments were made from time to time, and new constitutions were drafted by conventions summoned on the mere call of the legislatures without any higher sanction. This seems to have been recognized as a regular method; for, with the exception of the Vermont constitution of 1793, none of the constitutions framed before the opening of the nineteenth century provided that amendments, whether made by the legislature or a special convention, should be submitted to popular vote.

It was therefore only by a gradual process that our constitution-makers arrived at anything like the complete and elaborate system of amendment to be found in the most carefully prepared fundamental laws of our day, such, for example, as that of New York. This process, according to Professor J. W. Garner, has four stages. In the closing decades of the eighteenth century it was the common practice to make no provision at all for amendments: (1) during the first half of the nineteenth century the method of amendment by convention was fairly well developed; (2) immediately preceding and following the Civil War the more simple method of alteration through a legislative enactment ratified by the voters was widely adopted; (3) during the three or four decades immediately following the Civil War the system of double amendment through periodic conventions and legislative enactments popularly ratified was worked out; and (4) within the last decade has come the still more complete and democratic system of amendment through the popular initiative and referendum.

The principle of popular ratification is by no means confined to constitutional provisions. As has been noted above, in placing restrictions upon the financial powers of the legislatures, many of our state constitutions provide that exceptions to the restrictions may be made if the matters are referred directly to popular vote. For example, in New York, the total debt of the state is fixed at one million dollars, and additional debts, except those incurred to repel invasion, suppress insurrection, and defend the state in war, can be contracted only when authorized by a special law passed by the legislature, submitted to the people, and approved by a majority of all the votes for and against it. The practice of referring local laws of a special character, such as those of selecting county seats or changing county boundaries, was early adopted in our history.

Even if we regard the reference of some statutes as highly exceptional, it must be remembered that the difference between statute and constitutional law is by no means easy to determine. The mere fact that a provision is in a constitution does not make it constitutional in character. A comparison of our state constitutions shows that there is absolutely no concensus of opinion in the United States on the principle of discrimination between statute and constitutional law.

The law controlling public service corporations is statutory in New York and constitutional in Oklahoma; the salaries of judges and high officers are, in some states, fixed by the constitution, and in other states left to the legislature; such an important matter as civil service reform is in some states statutory and in New York constitutional. Any one, therefore, who accepts the principle that constitutions should be ratified by popular vote — and, as we have seen, in spite of the exceptions noted, this principle has become a fundamental part of our public law — is compelled to admit that the practice of referring statutes to popular ratification constitutes no real breach in our legal traditions.

With this brief survey of our institutional development, we may now turn with more understanding to a consideration of the place of the initiative and referendum in our public law; but at the very outset of our inquiry into this extension of older principles, we are confronted by the fact that the system of initiative and referendum is by no means a simple, definite, and invariable thing which must be adopted in a stereotyped form. In fact, a survey of the various schemes now in force or seriously proposed in the United States (to say nothing of the possible combinations which one might conjure up in his imagination) shows that there are a score or more of forms in which the system may be constructed.

Defined in general, the initiative is a scheme whereby a small percentage of the voters may initiate a law and secure its adoption upon ratification by popular vote; and the referendum is a plan whereby a small percentage of the voters may require the reference of any act of the legislature to the electorate for approval or rejection. But these general principles may be worked out in a variety of special forms: —

I. The initiative may be separated from the referendum, as in Michigan, where constitutional amendments only may be initiated by petition and the referendum can be employed only when the legislature sees fit to refer one of its acts to the voters.

II. The initiative or referendum may be restricted to statutory enactments, leaving judicial control under the state constitution unaffected.

III. The initiative or referendum may be employed only in the case of constitutional provisions.

IV. The referendum may be exercised alone at the option of the legislature, as is the case in Michigan.

V. The referendum may be set in motion by an initiative petition, — by five per cent of the voters or twenty-five per cent.

VI. The referendum on constitutions and constitutional amendments may be compulsory, as is well-nigh universal in the United States to-day.

VII. The initiative may be coupled with a provision that the legislature may submit in addition to any initiated measure an optional provision, giving the voters a choice between the proposal of the private parties and that which has been debated and digested in the legislature.

VIII. The initiative may be coupled with a provision that any measure initiated which may be adopted by the state legislature in due form shall become a law, unless on a petition of the voters a referendum is required.

IX. The number of voters necessary to initiate a constitutional amendment may be fixed at a definite sum or a percentage of the voters, and a larger number may be required to initiate a constitutional amendment than is required to initiate an ordinary statute. For example, in Oklahoma, eight per cent of the voters may initiate a legislative measure, while fifteen per cent are required to propose amendments to the constitution by petition.

X. A differentiation may be made between the number necessary to initiate a new measure and the number required to sign a referendum petition on an act already passed by the legislature.

XI. A large number of variations may be made in the number of votes necessary to the enactment of any particular provision into law. It may be a simple majority of all those voting for or against the measure. It may be a simple majority of those voting for and against the measure, provided that majority is equivalent to a certain percentage of all the votes cast for some particular officer at a general election. A difference may be made between the vote required for the approval of an initiated measure and that required on a legislative enactment referred to the voters on petition; as, for example, in Oklahoma, where a measure referred to the people by the initiative can go into force only when approved "by a majority of the votes cast in such election," while a legislative measure referred to the people by a referendum petition need be approved "by a majority of the votes cast thereon and not otherwise."

XII. The initiative may be restricted, as in the proposed Wisconsin constitutional amendment, by a provision to the effect that it can apply only to measures which have been introduced in regular form in the state legislature — the design of this being to secure a certain amount of legislative consideration of any measure referred to popular approval.

XIII. The initiative and referendum may be accompanied by provisions designed to secure general publicity and to educate the voter, as is the case in Oregon.

XIV. Finally, the initiative and referendum may take the milder form of a public opinion bill such as is provided by the Illinois law of 1901 authorizing the submission of any question to popular vote on the initiative of a certain percentage of voters, with the understanding that popular approval of the proposal constitutes merely a pious recommendation to the legislature.

It is obvious from this by no means exhaustive table of variations that any one who dogmatically approves or disapproves the initiative and referendum will have to define his terms before he becomes intelligible. No one in harmony with the spirit of American institutions could flatly declare that he was opposed to the referendum in any form. Indeed, it can hardly be said that a system of initiative and referendum embodies many definite principles that can be intelligently discussed without any reference to the concrete forms in which it appears. One may expound the Maine system or the Michigan system or the Oregon system, and give his reasons for approving or disapproving it.

Nevertheless there are certain general propositions which are worthy of consideration as forming the bases of criticism and discrimination in considering any concrete form of initiative and referendum, and it seems worth while to call them to mind, although an exhaustive survey cannot be given here.

In the first place, a provision which authorizes the initiation of measures by voters or allows a certain percentage of the electorate to require a popular referendum on a legislative measure is undoubtedly a limitation upon representative government, if by representative government we mean that all laws should be made simply by representatives duly chosen by the voters. And it is one of the most common objections urged against the initiative and referendum that they mark the beginning of the end of representative government.

It is natural for the opponents of any proposition to devise arguments by driving it to its logical conclusion in every direction, and in the case of any principle, this immediately produces innumerable incongruities and absurdities. Now, as one reprobates the fanatic who ignores practical considerations and carries his doctrines to extreme lengths, so one should reprobate that type of reasoning that opposes the initiative and referendum on the ground that it will produce every possible absurdity that can be conjured up in the imagination, including the ultimate destruction of representative government. To argue that because one happens to be going in a given direction at a particular moment he is certain to arrive at a point infinitely distant is to ignore the fact that neither in daily life nor in the formation of institutions does mankind advance continuously in one direction. Indeed, the very notion of direction as applied to the development of institutions is false and misleading, because in the evolution of its institutions a nation may be going in several "directions" at the same time!

The initiative and referendum, indeed, no more necessarily imply the complete overthrow of the representative principle than does judicial control or the executive veto. It is no more a violation of that principle to stipulate that the legislature may refer any measure to popular approval than it is to provide, as does the New York constitution, that every financial measure involving a public debt beyond a certain limit must be submitted to popular vote. It is a matter of degree. Moreover, a study of the history of the initiative and referendum in those states where they have been in vogue shows that representative government is not destroyed. In most states the system has scarcely been applied at all, and remains in abeyance to be used whenever any considerable portion of the voters think that the legislature has failed to do its duty; and even in Oregon, where the system has been most extensively used, the legislature has been by no means abolished, or even set on the way to destruction.

The conclusion seems to be therefore warranted that anxiety for the preservation of representative institutions need not lead any one into the extreme view that the initiative and referendum are incompatible with them. They do not destroy representative government; neither is there any indication nor anything in the nature of things showing that they can destroy such government. In view of the fact that the fruit of the average representative body in America is a thousand or two thousand statutes a session—a fruit which even the defenders of representative government are by no means proud of—it hardly seems possible that the necessity of making a livelihood will allow the voters of a state to give enough time to law-making to assume the entire burden. The real danger is not that representative institutions will perish, but that law-making will not receive that critical deliberation and technical attention which it is supposed to receive in legislative assemblies.

Before descending, however, into more concrete particulars it seems worth while also to examine that other objection to the initiative and referendum which is frequently advanced by those who fear the violation of the representative principle, namely, that it is contrary to that clause of the federal Constitution which provides that the United States shall guarantee to every state in the Union a republican form of government.[1] While it need not be supposed that any person convinced of the soundness of some form of initiative and referendum will discover in them any violation of the federal Constitution, persons already convinced of their unsoundness will very probably draw to their support the constitutional argument, for it so happens that, owing to the uncertain language of that great instrument, a variety of constructions, according to one's temper or interests, is generally possible. When the Northern states were pressing the protective tariff upon the South, the Virginia legislature resolved in 1826 "that the imposition of taxes and duties by the Congress of the United States for the purpose of protecting and encouraging domestic manufactures is an unconstitutional exercise of power";[2] and Pennsylvania later replied, it is not strange to find, by a resolution "that the Constitution of the United States authorizes acts of Congress to protect manufacturers, and that the actual prosperity of the country attests to the wisdom of such acts." Calhoun in his later years was firmly convinced that a

---

[1] See below, pp. 291 ff., for judicial decisions.
[2] Ames, *State Documents on Federal Relations*, p. 142.

protective tariff was a violation of the letter and spirit of the Constitution, "a violation by perversion, — the most dangerous of all because the most insidious and difficult to resist"; while Clay felt certain of the constitutionality of protection.

Every other big issue in American politics — internal improvements, slavery in the territories, the income tax, and control of our dependencies — has involved questions of constitutionality; and men have differed in their views, sometimes on account of their party affiliations, sometimes because of the interests they represent, and not often, it may be surmised, because of any theoretical expositions of the Constitution. It is only natural, inasmuch as the Constitution is held in great reverence and esteem by the people, that every one who has a cause to oppose or defend should seek shelter under the protection of that historic and invincible instrument. It takes the place, in our political ethics, of "the Throne and Altar" in Great Britain.

In any inquiry into the meaning of the term "republican," as used in the clause in the Constitution which guarantees that form of government to each state, we are compelled to resort for light to the debates in the Federal Convention and to the writings of the men who framed the federal Constitution, for the Supreme Court, the final interpreter of questions of American federal law, has not yet spoken on this point.[1] The proposition does not seem to have been extensively discussed in the Federal Convention. It appeared in the Virginia plan of a constitution introduced by Mr. Randolph on May 29 in the form of a resolution that a republican government and the territory of each state ought to be guaranteed by the United States to each state.

Inasmuch as Madison was the author of this particular plan, it is important to inquire into his views concerning the nature

[1] For several details on this point I am indebted to an article by Mr. Herbert S. Swan on "Arizona and Republican Government," *The Nation*, May 18, 1911. A case on this point is now pending in the federal Supreme Court — Pacific States Telephone and Telegraph Co. *v.* Oregon.

of the terms "republican" and "democratic." Fortunately, an answer to this inquiry is speedily found. Madison repeatedly defined republicanism in terms of representative government. He was perfectly clear also in his distinction between representative institutions and what we now call "direct government." In the Number 10 of *The Federalist*, written to demonstrate the danger of majority rule and the necessity of checking democracy at every point, he sharply defined the two systems. By "a pure democracy," he said, "I mean a society consisting of a small number of citizens who assemble and administer the government in person"; and such democracies, he adds, "have ever been spectacles of turbulence and contention; have ever been found incompatible with personal security or the rights of property; and have been in general as short in their lives as they have been violent in their deaths." He then went on to define a republic as "a government in which the scheme of representation takes place." This type of government, he declared, promised the cure for which they were seeking — that is, the evils of majority rule. While it must be admitted from the context of this number of *The Federalist* that Madison did not have in mind any form of initiative and referendum as now conceived, it cannot be denied that representative government was in his mind the essential feature of a republican government.

This idea was further elaborated in Number 39 of *The Federalist,* in which he said: —

If we resort, for a criterion, to the different principles on which different forms of government are established, we may define a republic to be, or at least may bestow that name on, a government which derives all its powers directly or indirectly from the great body of the people, and is administered by persons holding their offices during pleasure, for a limited period, or during good behavior. It is *essential* to such a government, that it be derived from the great body of the society, not from an inconsiderable proportion, or a favoured class of it; otherwise a handful of tyrannical nobles, exercising their oppressions by a delegation of their powers, might aspire to the rank of republicans, and claim for their government the honourable title of republic. It is *sufficient* for such a government that the persons administering it be appointed, either directly or indirectly, by the people; and that they hold their appointments by either of the tenures just specified; otherwise every government in the United States, as well as every other popular government that has been or can be well organized or well executed, would be degraded from the republican character.

It is not apparent, however, that Madison's views on this subject were the accepted views of his contemporaries. Indeed, John Adams declared that Madison's distinction between a republic and a democracy could not be justified, and added that in his opinion "a democracy is as really a republic as an oak is a tree, or a temple a building." [1]

Others among Madison's contemporaries differed from him as to the essential elements of republican government. Mr. Randolph in discussing the proposition in the Convention seemed to consider monarchical government as the system with which republican government should be contrasted. He said: "A republican government must be the basis of our national union; and no state ought to have it in their power to change its government into a monarchy." [2] This was also apparently the view of Mr. Gorham, who said: "An enterprising citizen might erect the standard of monarchy in a particular state, might gather together partisans from all quarters; might extend his views from state to state, and threaten to establish a tyranny over the whole and the general government be compelled to remain an inactive witness of its own destruction." [3] In Mr. Wilson's view the object of the clause was "merely to secure the state from dangerous commotions, insurrections, and rebellions." [4]

Of the several members who spoke on the subject in the Convention no one seemed inclined to go into any detail as to what constituted republican government. The practice of referring

---

[1] *Life and Works*, Vol. X, p. 328.
[2] Farrand, *Records of the Federal Convention*, Vol. I, p. 206.
[3] *Ibid.*, Vol. II, p. 48.   [4] *Ibid.*, p. 47.

state constitutions to popular vote had been begun in Massachusetts and New Hampshire, and no member of the Convention seems to have mentioned that as objectionable, although Gouverneur Morris was unwilling to guarantee some of the laws then existing in Rhode Island, and Mr. Houston entertained serious objections to the constitution of Georgia.

It is idle to speculate, however, whether they would have regarded a system of initiative and referendum, such as that now existing in Oregon, as repugnant to the republican form. They were not called upon to consider any such a proposition.

Nevertheless from the tone of the Convention one may reasonably infer that they would have looked upon such a scheme with a feeling akin to horror. Everywhere in the laconic record of the proceedings of the Convention preserved by Madison there are evidences that one of their chief purposes in framing the federal Constitution was to devise a system of checks and balances which would effectively prevent direct majority rule in any form. Elbridge Gerry declared that in his opinion the evils they suffered flowed "from the excess of democracy," adding that he had been "too republican: he was still however republican, but had been taught by experience the danger of the leveling spirit."[1] Alexander Hamilton believed that the mass of the people "seldom judge or determine right," and advocated as a check on their representatives a Senate holding for life.[2] Mr. Randolph at the beginning of the Convention observed that "the general object was to provide a cure for the evils under which the United States laboured; that in tracing these evils to their origin every man had found it in the turbulence and folly of democracy."[3] Madison doubtless summed up the views of the Fathers when he said that to secure private rights against majority factions and at the same time to preserve the spirit and form of popular government was the great object to which their inquiry had been directed.[4]

[1] Farrand, *op. cit.*, Vol. I, p. 48.   [2] *Ibid.*, p. 299.   [3] *Ibid.*, p. 51.
[4] *The Federalist*, Number 10.

In the face of such evidence, which may be easily multiplied by citations from the records of the Convention, *The Federalist*, and other writings of this period, no one has any warrant for assuming that the founders of our federal system would have shown the slightest countenance to a system of initiative and referendum applied either to state or national affairs. If some state had possessed such a system at that time, it is questionable whether they would have been willing to have compromised with it, as they did with the slave states, in order to secure its adherence to the Union. Democracy, in the sense of simple direct majority rule, was undoubtedly more odious to the most of the delegates to the Convention than was slavery.

When the judges of the Supreme Court are called upon to interpret the "republican" clause of the Constitution as applied to a system of initiative and referendum, it is evident they cannot discover what was the intention of the Fathers, for the latter can scarcely be said to have had any intention about a matter which had not yet come within their ken in anything approaching the form which it has now assumed. If the court, however, wishes to apply the spirit of the federal Constitution as conceived by its framers, it can readily find justification in declaring a scheme of statewide initiative and referendum contrary to the principles of that great instrument.

Nevertheless in view of the principles laid down in the case of Luther *v.* Borden and the recent decision of the Oregon court in the cases of Kadderly *v.* Portland and Kiernan *v.* Portland,[1] it seems hardly possible that the Supreme Court of the United States will declare the system of state-wide initiative and referendum unconstitutional. In the case of Luther *v.* Borden, which grew out of Dorr's Rebellion in Rhode Island, the court had to consider that clause of the federal Constitution under which republican government is guaranteed to the states, and Chief Justice Taney said: —

[1] These cases are printed below, pp. 291 ff.

Under this article of the Constitution it rests with Congress to decide what government is the established one in a State. For as the United States guarantee to each state a republican government, Congress must necessarily decide what government is established in the State before it can determine whether it is republican or not. And when the senators and representatives of a State are admitted into the councils of the Union, the authority of the government under which they are appointed, as well as its republican character, is recognized by the proper constitutional authority. And its decision is binding on every other department of the government, and could not be questioned in a judicial tribunal. It is true that the contest in this case did not last long enough to bring the matter to this issue; and as no senators or representatives were elected under the authority of the government of which Mr. Dorr was the head, Congress was not called upon to decide the controversy. Yet the right to decide is placed there, and not in the courts.

Following this interpretation, Congress, in allowing the representatives and senators from states having the initiative and referendum to take their seats, has recognized the governments in those states as republican in form; and this recognition is binding upon the courts.

On the particular issue as to whether a system of initiative and referendum is contrary to republican government, we have the well-reasoned opinion of an Oregon court, which upheld the new scheme. The court said in part: —

Now, the initiative and referendum amendment does not abolish or destroy the republican form of government or substitute another in its place. The representative character of the government still remains. The people have simply reserved to themselves a larger share of legislative power, but they have not overthrown the republican form of the government or substituted another in its place. The government is still divided into the legislative, executive, and judicial departments, the duties of which are discharged by representatives selected by the people. Under this amendment, it is true, the people may exercise a legislative power, and may, in effect, veto or defeat bills passed and approved by the legislature and the governor; but the legislative and executive departments are not destroyed, nor are their powers or authority materially curtailed. Laws proposed and enacted by the people under the initiative clause of the amendment are subject to the same constitutional limitations as other statutes, and may be amended or repealed by the legislature at will.

In the Kiernan case the same court declared that responsibility directly to the people constituted the essence of republican government, and that the system of initiative and referendum contributed toward the establishment of such responsibility.

Monarchical rulers, said the court, refuse to recognize their accountability to the people governed by them. In a republic the converse is the rule; the tenure of office may be for a short or a long period, or even for life, yet those in office are at all times answerable, either directly or indirectly, to the people, and in proportion to their responsibility to those for whom they may be the public agents, and the nearer the power to enact laws and control public servants lies with the great body of the people, the more nearly does a government take unto itself the form of a republic — not in name alone, but in fact. From this it follows that each republic may differ in its political system, or in the political machinery by which it moves, but so long as the ultimate control of its officials and affairs of state remains in its citizens, it will, in the eye of all republics, be recognized as a government of that class. Of this we have many examples in Central and South America.

It becomes, then, a matter of degree, and the fear manifested by the briefs filed in this case would seem to indicate, not that we are drifting from the secure moorings of a republic, but that our State, by the direct system of legislation complained of, is becoming too democratic, advancing too rapidly toward a republic pure in form. This, it is true, counsel for petitioner does not concede; but under any interpretation of which the term is capable, or from any view thus far found expressed in the writings of the prominent statesmen who were members of the Constitutional Convention, or who figured in the early upbuilding of the Nation, it follows that the system here assailed brings us nearer to a State republican in form than before its adoption.

Coming now to less theoretical considerations, we may inquire what are the precise objections advanced by those who believe that law-making by a representative assembly is so far superior to occasional law-making by popular vote as to warrant the unhesitating rejection of the latter. We may preface this inquiry by a sketch of what may be deemed the theory of representative government, which is more or less unconsciously assumed to be its practice by those who have set themselves against the new system.

A representative assembly consists of delegates apportioned among compact and contiguous districts containing as nearly as practicable an equal number of inhabitants. Each delegate represents a majority of the electors in his district. Thus in the legislature of the state is reflected the will of the dominant majority for the time being. In this legislature each member is free to introduce such bills as he believes to be to the interest of the state in general or his constituents in particular. These bills are taken up one after the other for careful deliberation, debated and scrutinized according to their merits, recast under the influence of the light thrown upon them from various angles, and finally solemnly engrossed as the mature expression of the legislative will. Such is the theory of representative government; and as so conceived it would be difficult to imagine a more admirable instrument for popular government and scientific law-making.

Unfortunately, the practice of representative government is in general so far removed from this theoretical ideal as to make it scarcely worthy of consideration in discussing the desirability of a supplementary system of initiative and referendum. Without bringing under review the gross abuses practised in every state in the Union in the distribution of representation, and the wholly disproportionate results accruing from the district system of election, we may inquire at once as to what are the general methods in the average state legislature.

Every one knows that a considerable portion of our recent important state laws have not been drafted in the legislatures at all, but have been prepared at the instance of governors, and often forced through the legislatures under executive pressure. A large number of the bills which do not originate in the executive chamber are drafted by private parties, sometimes the members of societies organized for beneficent purposes, and sometimes by the agents of other societies organized as corporations particularly for private gain. It would be interesting to have a true history of all the bills passed in our state legislatures in the past decade, in order that we might know exactly how much legislative wisdom had been exercised in their preparation!

Fortunately, as to debates on legislative measures the public has access to them, and it is not too much to say that critical, searching debate, designed not for partisan display, but for the illumination of the subject, is a rare exception. Every one knows about the rapid and ill-considered fashion with which legislation is driven through in the last few days of the session under gavel rule, simply because the organization leaders of the assembly have agreed that the job must be done. The truth is that the voters of no commonwealth have any opportunity for discovering exactly who determines the legislative program in their state assembly.

When considering, therefore, a system of initiative and referendum, it is the *practice* of representative government as it now prevails in the United States, rather than its *theory*, which should be the basis of making contrasts. Furthermore, in the study of the system, its actual operation and reasonably certain potentialities should be considered rather than any extreme vagaries to which it might lend itself. If one were looking for imaginary horrors, one could construct them out of the representative idea as well as out of the direct legislation idea.

What are the requirements of good legislation? They are that any particular bill should be timely, technically drafted so as to secure the will of the electorate, and properly adjusted to the social and economic conditions — the habits and aptitudes of the particular community to which it is applied. In general, a law should be the expression of the matured and deliberate will of a clearly ascertained majority of the voters. But everybody knows that this is an ideal rather than a real condition of affairs. The actual process in the adoption of any important reform begins with a few interested and enlightened persons who draft the project of law; it is then more or less intelligently accepted by a small group of the voters in the state; and then it finally secures the legislative majority necessary to its enactment, largely by the tacit consent of those who know little or nothing about it. If, in real practice we should demand the deliberate and carefully formed will of a majority of all the voters of a commonwealth or their representatives on every important measure, progressive and enlightened legislation would be difficult indeed to secure. All that we can ask of a law, in a democracy, in addition to the qualities of form and adaptation to the social medium mentioned above, is that it shall be reasonably acceptable to that vague thing which we call public opinion.

Now, is there anything inherent in the plan of initiating legislation by groups of private parties which precludes satisfactory expertness in the drafting of measures, or at all events an expertness equal to that commonly secured in the average state legislature? Undoubtedly one may imagine a group of ignoramuses drawing together and drafting a legal monstrosity; but in view of the fact that, under the initiative and referendum, private persons do not initiate bills unless they are deeply interested in the success of their particular measures, there is every reason for supposing that they will take proper precautions to employ that legal talent which is necessary to secure technical formality. Of course, the instance of a measure initiated in Oregon without an enacting clause is often cited as an evidence of the inherent stupidity of popular initiators; but one swallow does not make a summer, neither does a considerable group of them, and if bad legislation on its technical side were an evidence of stupidity, representative government would have to stand with a shamed face at the bar of reason. It seems fair to assume that under a system of direct legislation where the initiators are bound to run the gantlet of opposition and criticism in the public discussion of their particular measures, special precautions will be taken to secure a satisfactory legal form. All that talent and enterprise which is now employed extra-legally in the drafting of bills for legislatures may be drawn upon in the drafting of bills for popular initiation. No doubt mistakes will be made and have been made under a system of popular initiative, and several ludicrous blunders have already been called to public attention. But the fact remains that the technical side of legislation may be handled in practice quite as well under popular initiation as under legislative initiation.

It must be acknowledged, however, that were the theory of the representative system — searching debate and illuminating discussion — actually carried out in practice, it would be difficult to imagine a system so well adapted to technical perfection in law-making. But in the world as one finds it, there seems to be as much hope for technically acceptable legislation from groups of public-spirited private citizens as from the committee rooms of state legislatures where two or three men—generally mediocre in character — usually do most of the work that is done there, and assume little or no responsibility for their measures.

Admitting as one must nevertheless, that there are grave dangers lurking in the possibility of initiation by irresponsible groups of private parties, the case for the initiative need not be given up as hopeless. Methods may be devised to assure more attention to the drafting of bills referred on popular petition. The publication of the names of those who actually drafted any bill referred by the initiative might be required and reliable sponsors secured. Or again, the Wisconsin plan for confining the initiative entirely to bills actually introduced in the legislature might help to obviate some of the objections laid against the indiscriminate drafting of laws.

Granting that the technical side of law-making may be taken care of by the initiative, a measure may not have behind it such an effective demand as to warrant its submission to the voters. It is certain that, where no precautions are taken to control the method of securing signatures the initiative petition may not represent any serious opinion on the part of those who sign it. Wherever the initiative is in force, a new trade, that of getting signatures, develops.

At all times these "signature-getters" keep busy, writes Mr. Hendrick, though they are most active during the April and May following a legislative session. They are found in practically every part of the State. They invade the office-buildings, the apartment-houses and the homes of Portland, and tramp from farmhouse to farmhouse. Young women, ex-book-canvassers, broken-down clergymen, people who in other communities would find their natural level as sandwich-men, dapper hustling youths, perhaps earning their way through college — all find useful employment in soliciting signatures at five or ten cents a name. The canvasser bustles into an office, carrying under his arm a neat parcel of pamphlets, the covers perhaps embellished with colored pictures of the American flag. He gives his victim a few minutes to read the printed matter, and then, placing his finger on a neatly ruled space, says, "Sign here." Very likely the person approached will demur. The proposed law is foolish, unnecessary — the work of a group of hare-brained cranks. Perhaps a protracted argument takes place which may ultimately ramify into the fundamental principles of constitutional government. Everywhere that the canvassers go there is a flood of talk. There is no State in the Union so perpetually argumentative and voluble as Oregon. This is especially true when the solicitors are not paid workers, but enthusiasts. And at times these workers do not receive a cordial welcome; there are plenty of Oregonians who regard the whole system as a nuisance and treat its representatives accordingly. In other instances people sign petitions thoughtlessly — sometimes without reading the measures or even understanding their contents. "I could easily get ten thousand signatures to a law hanging all the red-haired men in Oregon," one cynic on popular government remarked to the writer. It is not at all unlikely that he could. The business of getting names, as everybody knows, depends more upon the individual than upon the merits of the particular case at issue. This new profession in Oregon has its well-recognized experts; and not infrequently one group of canvassers will return disheartened, having absolutely failed in pushing a particular measure, only to have another group go out and return with all the signatures the law requires.[1]

In view of the facts here disclosed, which are corroborated by experience in securing signers for direct primary petitions, the number of signatures required for an initiatory petition should be large enough to offset the results of the professional name-hunters.

It should be observed also that the advantages which the representative system affords in initiation may be combined with those of popular initiative, as in the case of Maine, where the recognition of the necessity for discussion and technical work in good law-making led to the adoption of a scheme whereby the legislature may enact a measure of its own to submit to popular approval along with the proposal initiated by private enterprise. This device, it has been said, "enables the legislature to correct faults in proposed legislation. The substitute bill will undoubtedly be far superior to the initiative bill." The possible objection here is that the bill advanced by the legislature may not be any better than the initiated measure, and may contain "jokers" which are not apparent to the public eye. Furthermore it may introduce an element of confusion. Nevertheless it does give the legislature an opportunity to point out errors in an initiated measure and propose corrections.

It is not on the technical side of bill-drafting that the initiative and referendum are open to the most serious objections. The other criterion of a good law — adaptation to social and economic environment — is not easily met if a measure may be initiated by a small group of persons and then put into effect by a minority of voters not truly representative of the public opinion of the community. Experience with the reference of constitutional amendments has revealed an inertia and indifference on the part of the electorate which make possible legislation by insignificant minorities where the principle is accepted that a measure shall go

[1] *McClure's*, August, 1911, "Law-making by the Voters," B. J. Hendrick.

into effect on receiving a majority of the votes cast for and against it.

This lack of intelligent interest, it is said, is amply demonstrated by the statistics of the vote on constitutional referenda.[1] Indeed, it is easy to give a number of "horrible examples" of constitutional amendments adopted by insignificant fractions of the electorate. An instance commonly cited is the Louisiana election of 1906, in which a number of important constitutional amendments were carried into effect by a vote of only one-sixth of the electors. This, of course, is exceptional; but it frequently happens that only thirty or forty per cent of the electors take the trouble to vote on constitutional amendments, which often means that twenty or twenty-five per cent of the voters enact constitutional amendments into law.

At first glance, these facts would seem to indict not only the initiative and referendum, but the practice of referring any measure whatever to popular vote. But, as is usually the case in statistics, a little analysis is necessary in order to ascertain the significance of the figures. According to Dr. Dodd's estimate, 472 questions were submitted to the voters of the several states during the period 1899 to 1908, and of these about 410 were *not* of fundamental and state-wide importance, being in many instances special and local legislation. Much of this petty constitutional tinkering is due to the practice of including in the constitution of the state a mass of detail which really belongs in statutes. One is not surprised to find that in Washington in 1904, for example, only about nineteen per cent of the electors took the trouble to vote on a constitutional amendment authorizing the state legislature to appoint chaplains for state penal and reformatory institutions; or that only about twenty-five per cent of the voters of New York in 1905 cared to express an opinion on a constitutional amendment permitting a justice of the appellate division to serve in a supreme court.

[1] See the exhaustive tables in the Appendix, Dodd, *The Revision and Amendment of State Constitutions.*

Introductory Note 39

Indeed, the smallness of the vote in many instances indicates not a lack of interest, but a high degree of intelligence, on the part of the voters. It often shows that the voters are aware of the fact that they do not know enough about some particular or local matter to warrant their expressing an opinion one way or another. What does a voter in a lumber camp in the Adirondacks know about the advisability of exempting certain bonds in New York City from the operation of the debt limit? Or what does the voter on West 72d Street in New York City know about the desirability of increasing the number of judges in a judicial district in a western part of the state? It is evident, therefore, that in order to ascertain the significance of popular voting upon referenda, every case must be examined on its merits.

A general survey shows that for every instance of popular neglect another can be discovered of striking popular interest. Indeed, a careful examination of the figures in the tables cited above reveals an astounding amount of interest in a large number of the important proposals referred to popular vote; and this in spite of the fact that little or no systematic attempt is made on the part of state authorities to bring the significance of the amendments to the attention of the voters previous to election day. As Professor Dodd remarks, usually there is almost no newspaper discussion of amendments of minor importance which always constitute the greater portion of the referenda; and "the voter hardly knows that there are amendments to be voted upon until he reaches the polls, and after the election is over the result is hardly of sufficient interest to be reported."

Moreover, the proportion of the vote cast on a popular referendum is ascertained in most cases by comparing it with the total vote of the officer who stood highest at the election in which the voting on the referendum occurred — often the vote with which the referendum total is compared is that cast for President of the United States. Now, to any one even casually acquainted with the methods of American politics, this is obviously an unfair comparison. Everybody knows the strenuous efforts which are brought to bear "to bring out the vote" by beating the highways and byways and using carriages and automobiles to gather in the lame and the blind and the halt. The popular vote for elective offices is by no means an indication of the amount of intelligent discrimination which is made on the part of the voters. It would be interesting to know just what proportion of the electors would come to the polls if the leaders of the political parties should make a compact to bring no pressure whatever, monetary or otherwise, upon them. It is not surprising that, in a spectacular fight over personalities, on the results of which depends the distribution of the spoils of office and the revenues accruing from the sale of political privileges, an extraordinarily large vote is polled. Instead of being discouraged at the smallness of the vote cast on more or less remote questions of constitutional law, the friends of democracy really should be encouraged at the surprisingly large number of instances in which sixty and seventy and eighty per cent of the voters take advantage of their opportunity to express an opinion on questions referred to them for consideration.

There is, moreover, no magic significance about having one more than one-half of the voters in favor of a legislative proposition. Many of those who oppose the initiative and referendum on the ground that it may permit legislation by a minority are not celebrated as advocates of the principle of simple majority rule. In too many cases they proclaim the doctrine of majority rule when criticising the initiative and referendum, but overlook the principle when they come to reviewing election of United States senators by state legislatures, judicial control of legislation, and the executive veto.

Any one who is prayerfully solicitous for a majority vote in favor of every measure enacted into law will have to do some searching of his heart when examining the vote in our state legislatures. What assurance is there that any particular measure passed by a state legislature would, if submitted to popular vote, receive the approval of more than fifteen or twenty per cent of the electorate?

Every one at all familiar with the operations of American legislatures is too painfully aware of the ways in which measures are rushed through under the party whip, or passed as the result of group trading in which members vote for measures to which they are personally opposed and which are not supported by their constituents, in order to receive support from the other side for some particular measures of their own.

Surely it needs no lengthy demonstration to show that there is nothing sacred about percentages in elections. Nevertheless, legislation by small minorities is, of course, highly undesirable, and if a system of initiative and referendum necessarily made possible such legislation, it would be open to grave objections. In point of fact, however, it is possible to establish, in connection with the initiative and referendum, a safeguard against legislation by small minorities. For example, in Washington, the constitutional amendment to be submitted to the voters in 1912 provides that "any measure initiated by the people or referred to the people as herein provided shall take effect and become the law if it is approved by a majority of the votes cast thereon; provided that the vote cast upon such question or measure shall equal one-third of the total vote cast at such election and not otherwise." Obviously this proportion may be increased, if it is thought necessary, in order to secure a still wider expression of popular opinion; but in view of the practice of submitting unimportant and special questions, upon which the vote must obviously be small, it is undesirable to make too high the percentage necessary to carry an amendment into effect.

The ingenuity of the advocates of the initiative and referendum is by no means exhausted in the creation of rules as to the proportion of the votes necessary to enact a measure into law. Believing that the ideal of American government is the creation of a great democratic brotherhood on a high plane of intelligent coöperation, they prefer rather to establish a scheme of popular education in connection with the initiative and referendum. In Oregon, for example, the most noteworthy feature of the system is the recent statute providing for the publication and distribution of arguments for and against the propositions submitted to the decision of the voters. Under this law the supporters and opponents of any particular measure may prepare their arguments at length; these arguments are printed by the state (at the expense of the private parties concerned), together with the measures to be referred to the voters; and a copy is sent to every voter in the commonwealth. It is contended by the friends of this system that it has an immense educational value in arousing the interest of the people, in securing the consideration of each measure on its merits, and in turning the search-light of publicity and discussion upon all the important political issues in the state. In 1910 the measures referred to the voters and the arguments favoring and opposing certain of them constituted a booklet of 208 pages, a copy of which was sent by the secretary of state to every voter. The arguments are kept within a reasonable compass by the provision that whoever prepares them must pay for their publication at a regular rate.[1]

Doubtless other instrumentalities might be devised by which the public interest could be engaged in referenda, and a reasonably sober and deliberate judgment secured upon any particular proposal — a judgment which will satisfy those who do not expect mathematically correct results in the domain of politics. Moreover, if we take the actual vote on referenda in Oregon, where the most advanced system of publicity is now in force, we must admit that the proportion of votes is as a rule satisfactory to the most exacting. In the election of 1910 the vote cast for the several measures and constitutional amendments ranged from sixty to eighty-seven per cent of the total number of ballots cast in that election. The average totals cast for the four state offices, governor, secretary of state, state treasurer, and attorney-general, was 110,895, or ninety-two per cent of the entire number of ballots cast in the election. In drawing comparisons, therefore, between the vote on proposals and that cast for candidates, this

[1] See below, p. 94, for illustrative extracts from this pamphlet.

average should be taken as a basis. Thus the vote cast on referenda ranged from sixty-six to ninety-five per cent of the average vote cast for the four most important state offices.

A study of the following table giving the vote on all of the measures submitted in Oregon under the initiative and referendum, including the election of 1910, reveals a wide variation in the extent of popular interest in the several propositions but a reasonably satisfactory interest in all of them.

1904	Yes	No
1. Direct primary law with direct selection of United States Senator [1]	56,205	16,354
2. Local-option liquor law [1]	43,316	40,198
1906		
3. Omnibus appropriation bill, state institutions [2]	43,918	26,758
4. Equal suffrage constitutional amendment [1]	36,902	47,075
5. Local-option bill proposed by liquor people [1]	35,297	45,144
6. Bill for purchase by State of Barlow toll road [1]	31,525	44,527
7. Amendment requiring referendum on any act calling constitutional convention [1]	47,661	18,751
8. Amendment giving cities sole power to amend their charters [1]	52,567	19,852
9. Legislature authorized to fix pay of state printer [1]	63,749	9,571
10. Initiative and Referendum to apply to all local, special, and municipal laws [1]	47,678	16,735
11. Bill prohibiting free passes on railroads [1]	57,281	16,779
12. Gross-earnings tax on sleeping, refrigerator, and oil car companies [1]	69,635	6,441

[1] Submitted under the initiative.
[2] Submitted under the referendum upon legislative act.

1906	YES	NO
13. Gross-earnings tax on express, telephone, and telegraph companies [1]	70,872	6,360
1908		
14. Amendment increasing pay of legislators from $120 to $400 per session [3]	19,691	68,892
15. Amendment permitting location of state institutions at places other than the capital [3]	41,971	40,868
16. Amendment reorganizing system of courts and increasing supreme judges from three to five [3]	30,243	50,591
17. Amendment changing general election from June to November [3]	65,728	18,590
18. Bill giving sheriffs control of county prisoners [2]	60,443	30,033
19. Railroads required to give public officials free passes [2]	28,856	59,406
20. Bill appropriating $100,000 for armories [2]	33,507	54,848
21. Bill increasing fixed appropriation for state university from $47,500 to $125,000 annually [2]	44,115	40,535
22. Equal suffrage amendment [1]	36,858	58,670
23. Fishery bill proposed by fish-wheel operators [1]	46,582	40,720
24. Fishery bill proposed by gill-net operators [1]	56,130	30,280
25. Amendment giving cities control of liquor selling, poolrooms, theatres, etc., subject to local-option law [1]	39,442	52,346
26. Modified form of single-tax amendment [1]	32,066	60,871
27. Recall power on public officials amendment [1]	58,381	31,002

[1] Submitted under the initiative.
[2] Submitted under the referendum upon legislative act.
[3] Submitted to the people by the legislature.

1908	Yes	No
28. Bill instructing legislators to vote for people's choice for United States Senator [1]	69,668	21,162
29. Amendment authorizing proportional representation law [1]	48,868	34,128
30. Corrupt-practices act governing elections [1]	54,042	31,301
31. Amendment requiring indictment to be by grand jury [1]	52,214	28,487
32. Bill creating Hood River County [1]	43,948	26,778
1910		
33. Women's taxpaying suffrage amendment [1]	35,270	59,065
34. Bill for purchase of Eastern Oregon Insane Asylum [3]	50,134	41,504
35. Act calling a constitutional convention [3]	23,143	59,974
36. Amendment providing for single legislative districts [3]	24,000	54,252
37. Amendment providing that the power of taxation be not contracted away [3]	37,619	40,172
38. Amendment for state and municipal ownership of railways [3]	32,844	46,070
39. Amendment for uniform rule of taxation [3]	31,629	41,692
40. Bill increasing salary of judge of 8th District $1,000 [2]	13,161	71,503
41. Bill creating Nesmith County [1]	22,866	60,951
42. Bill maintaining Oregon Normal School at Monmouth [1]	50,191	40,044
43. Bill creating Otis County [1]	17,426	62,016
44. Bill annexing parts of Clackamas to Multnomah County [1]	16,250	69,002
45. Bill creating Williams County [1]	14,508	64,090
46. Amendment allowing counties to regulate taxes [1]	44,171	42,127

[1] Submitted under the initiative.
[2] Submitted under the referendum upon legislative act.
[3] Submitted to the people by the legislature.

1910	YES	No
47. Amendment giving municipal local option on temperance [1]	53,321	50,779
48. Bill extending the liability of employers [1]	56,258	33,943
49. Bill creating Orchard County [1]	15,664	62,712
50. Bill creating Clark County [1]	15,613	61,704
51. Bill maintaining Eastern Oregon State Normal School [1]	40,898	46,201
52. Bill annexing portion of Washington to Multnomah County [1]	14,047	68,221
53. Bill providing for maintenance of South Oregon State Normal [1]	38,473	48,655
54. Amendment providing for state prohibition of liquor [1]	43,540	61,221
55. Bill prohibiting sale and governing shipment of liquor [1]	42,651	63,564
56. Bill creating a commission to examine employers' idemnity [1]	32,224	51,719
57. Bill prohibiting fishing on Rogue River, except by angling [1]	49,712	33,397
58. Bill creating Deschutes County [1]	17,592	60,486
59. Bill providing for creation of new towns, counties, and municipal districts by a majority vote within boundaries of proposed municipality, and that 30 per cent within such territory may petition for such election [1]	37,129	42,327
60. Amendment permitting counties to incur indebtedness beyond $5000 to build permanent roads, election to settle question [1]	51,275	32,906
61. Bill extending direct primary to presidential nominations [1]	43,353	41,624
62. Bill creating Board of People's Inspectors and providing for the publication of an official state magazine [1]	29,955	52,538

[1] Submitted under the initiative.

Introductory Note

1910	YES	No
63. Amendment increasing "Initiative and Referendum" and Recall powers of people; 25 per cent may recall entire legislature; Speaker and President of Senate to be elected from outside of members; ten dollars fine for unexcused absence from roll-call; oath of office to provide against legislative log-rolling [1]	37,031	44,366
64. Amendment providing for three-fourths of jury verdict in civil cases; expediting court procedure and increasing powers of supreme court [1]	44,538	39,399 [2]

[1] Submitted under the initiative.

[2] A study of these tables shows that of the 64 measures, 48 or 75 per cent have been proposed by initiative petition, and 25 of them passed. Since 31 of the 64 measures passed and 25 of the 31 were proposed by initiative petition, 80 per cent of the successful measures never had the approval of the legislature. Moreover, 25 of the 64 measures were amendments to the state constitution, *i.e.* 39 per cent have been amendments and 61 per cent bills and acts. Of the 25 amendments 12 (48 per cent) were approved. From the time of the adoption of the Oregon Constitution, 1859 to 1902, it was not amended. Since 1906, or in four years, it has been amended 12 times. The process formerly took four years. It can now be done in four months. Of the 39 bills 19 (48 per cent) were approved. Further, of the 25 amendments 17 (68 per cent) were by initiative petition, and the other 8 were referred to the people by the legislative assembly. Of the 12 amendments approved 10 (83 per cent) were of the 17 proposed by initiative petition. In other words, 10 out of 17, or 58 per cent of the measures the people proposed got through, whereas only 2 of the 8 (25 per cent) proposed by the legislature (they must refer them to the people, being amendments) met with the approval of the voters. The submission of a total of 39 measures at three different elections in Oregon cost the state $25,000, or an average of about $780 for each measure. At the election in 1908, 19 measures were submitted at a cost to the state of $12,362, or an average of about $651 each. Five of these 19 measures were submitted without argument. Upon the other 14 measures there were 19 arguments submitted, for which the authors paid the cost, amounting to $3,157. The state election in 1910 cost the state $22,610.61 to submit 32 measures, or an average of $706.56 to the measure. For this year, the "publicity pamphlet" cost each registered voter 20 cents in taxes.

What proportion of these voters acted after careful examination of the measures on which they expressed an opinion, it is impossible of course to estimate, just as it is practically impossible for the citizen to know to what extent any particular bill has been deliberately considered in the legislature which passed it. There is no reason, however, why a fairly sound and deliberate judgment on all important questions of public policy may not be reached by the voters during the period in which the measures are pending before them for their consideration. The case for this view is thus put in short form by the advocates of the system in Oregon, in a pamphlet entitled *People's Power and Public Taxation:*—

As to the alleged burden of measures upon the minds of the voters, when submitted to popular vote, and the little time in which the voters have to study such measures, compare this with the corresponding burden upon the legislature. Of the nineteen measures submitted on the ballot at the election in 1908, four were submitted by the Legislature of 1907 a little more than 15 months before they were voted on; four were sent to the voters by referendum petition a little more than 12 months before the election; and eleven were submitted by initiative petition — all of them four months before the election and some of them more than six months before election; say, an average of five months, or 150 days. For the initiated measures, then, the voters had an average of fourteen days and a half to study and discuss each measure; and a much longer time for each of the referendum measures. Such was the "great burden" upon the minds of the voters. Now, take the records of the legislature, and compare the burden upon the minds of the legislators:

In 1909 the state senate was actually in session 28 days of the regular session, in which it had to consider 12 veto messages from the Governor of bills vetoed after the Legislature of 1907 adjourned; 262 senate bills; 201 bills passed by the house and sent to the senate; 104 senate resolutions and 27 resolutions passed by the house; 10 senate memorials and 10 house memorials; making 626 measures, without counting the reading of petitions and necessary action upon the Governor's vetoes of bills passed at the session of 1909. That is, 626 measures in 28 days, or an average of a little more than 22 measures a day, as against the "great burden" of fourteen days and a half to a measure, which the voters had for the measures submitted in 1908.

Similarly, in the 28 days they were in session, the members of the house of representatives had 681 measures to consider, or an average of more than 26 a day.

The experience with the initiative and referendum in South Dakota has not been so extensive as that in Oregon, and conclusions are not so readily drawn as to popular interest in direct legislation. The following table of the votes on referenda submitted to voters of that State at the election of November, 1910, shows that eleven out of the twelve propositions submitted were defeated. A keen observer of the campaign on these propositions thinks that this result is largely due to the activity of certain parties, especially interested in the defeat of one or two propositions, who filled the newspapers with advertisements and plastered the fences with billboards advising the electors to "Vote No." The figures are: —

	YES	No
Renting Lands	48,152	44,220
Salary, Attorney-General	35,932	52,397
Equal Suffrage	35,289	57,709
Debt Limitation	32,612	52,233
Revenue Amendment	29,830	52,043
New Institutions	36,128	47,625
County Option	42,416	55,372
Electric Headlights on Locomotives	37,914	48,938
"Czar" Law	32,160	52,152
Embalmers Law	34,560	49,546
Congressional Districts	26,918	47,893
Militia	17,852	57,440 [1]

One of these measures, the law requiring electric headlights for locomotives, was a bill passed by the state legislature on which

[1] Beard, *Digest of Short Ballot Charters*, folio 75,503. The total vote for governor was 105,801.

the railroads invoked popular referendum. The legislature, convinced that the defeat of the proposition at the polls did not represent the deliberate judgment of the people, reënacted the measure at the session immediately following, and it will again be submitted to a referendum. Thus, an apparently salutary measure, even if it is adopted by the people at the next election, will be deferred for at least four years. Opponents of the initiative and referendum will doubtless find no little consolation in such an example of public folly; but it can be duplicated many times over by instances in which legislatures have failed to enact laws demanded by popular opinion and sound policy.

If any conclusion on the wisdom of popular voting on laws is drawn from an examination of the "yea" and "nay" vote shown in the tables above, it will depend almost entirely upon one's view of what constitutes wise and sound public policy. Obviously, there is no scientific ground upon which contemporary political questions can be mathematically and precisely determined. In such matters one's conviction is not so much the result of ratiocination as of interest and feeling. Whether the voters of Oregon have voted wisely on questions referred to them, the reader must determine for himself by examining the following list of principles which have been established in that state since direct government was introduced:[1] —

1. That they will not tolerate a return to anything like the convention method of making nominations, but will retain their direct-primary system until something better is offered.

2. That they will enforce election by the legislature of that candidate for United States Senator in Congress who receives the highest number of the people's votes.

3. Complete prohibition of railroad passes for all persons except employees of the railroads.

4. Abolition of the power of city councils to give away public franchises.

5. Abolition of the temptation and opportunity to buy or sell votes in the legislature.

[1] Formulated by a group of initiative and referendum advocates.

6. That the people of every city or town shall have power to make and amend their city charters on all local matters at their own pleasure, absolutely free from special acts by the legislature.

7. That they will retain the initiative and referendum in law-making.

8. That they will have power to recall any elected public officer, from constable to governor, including judges of the courts.

9. That they approve the principle of election of members of the legislature by proportional representation, though they have not yet agreed on the method.

10. That they will provide liberally by taxes for support of higher education in the State University.

11. That they will maintain one efficient normal school. At the same election they voted to abolish two others created by the legislature some years ago.

12. That corporations having little or no tangible property should pay a gross income and license tax.

13. That the expenditures of any candidate for public office shall be limited to practically one-fourth of one year's salary of the office he seeks, and the State will provide the greater part of the expense for publicity of the merits of candidates and of political parties.

14. That edible fish, especially salmon, shall be conserved in the navigable rivers of the State.

15. That measures of chiefly local interest will be rejected if submitted to the voters of the whole state.

16. Abolition of convention system of electing delegates to national conventions, establishing direct election of such delegates by the voters of the great parties and permitting expression by the voters of their choice for party candidates for President and Vice-President.

17. That three-fourths of a jury shall be able to render a verdict in all civil cases, and court procedure shall be so simplified as to discourage appeals to the supreme court for delay and new trials because of technical errors, if substantial justice has been obtained in the lower court.

18. That they do not approve state-wide prohibition of the manufacture and sale of liquor.

19. That they have established and will maintain local option on the liquor question.

20. That they require a reasonable measure of employers' liability for workmen's accidents.

21. They have granted the people of each county power to exempt from all taxation any class or classes of property, subject to any general laws approved by the people of the State.

22. That no citizen shall be tried in a circuit court for crime unless accused by a grand jury.

23. That general election shall be held in November, when most other States vote, instead of in June.

24. That the public credit shall not be used to aid, build, or operate private or Government railroads.

25. That counties may issue bonds to build permanent railways.

26. That private schemes for looting the public treasury cannot be worked by the initiative method.

The Recall

The movement for the recall has grown out of a lack of confidence in administrative officials akin to that distrust of legislatures which was largely responsible for the establishment of the initiative and referendum. The principle upon which it is based is simple, namely, that elected officers are merely the agents of popular will, and that the electors should have an opportunity at all times to pass upon the conduct of their representatives. By this system, its advocates expect to establish that steady popular control over the administration which was fondly hoped would result from the popular election of public officials.

While apparently simpler than the initiative and referendum, the recall really involves problems of organization which go to the very root of public administration, already notoriously inefficient and irresponsible in the United States. A complete analysis of the implications of the system is therefore impossible in a cursory survey, to which this introduction is necessarily limited. A few of the elements of the problem, however, may be stated.

No discrimination has yet been made in the popular mind in the United States between those offices which may properly be made elective and those purely routine offices which have nothing to do

Introductory Note 53

with the formulation of public will into policies. The system of popular election, all right within limits, has already been carried to such an extreme as to defeat its very purpose. The theory itself is engaging enough : a number of men are candidates for a public office. Each of these candidates entertains certain notions of policy with regard to the office he is seeking, and each of them has his own standards of efficiency and integrity. The voters select the one who most accurately reflects the prevailing public sentiment and seems most likely to realize the dominant public desire. If he does not carry out the policy which he is expected to support, or fails to come up to the standards set by his constituents, he is turned out at the expiration of his term (which ought theoretically to be a short one in order to give the people a chance to express their judgment on the officer with great frequency), and some one who more nearly represents the electorate is chosen in his stead. Thus in the long run representative democracy triumphs and popular control is maintained. To question the essential soundness of this view is deemed petty treason by most politicians, and the doubter is met with the firm assertion that the people may be trusted to elect any officer, local, state, or national — an assertion which quite overlooks the fundamental fact that electing all of them together is an entirely different matter from electing any one of them.

As a matter of record, the theory of popular control through a multiplicity of elective offices does not work in practice. In the case of a large number of officers there is no question of policy involved, because their functions are purely ministerial, prescribed by statutes, and their discharge of these functions is enforceable through the ordinary processes of law. No one has been able to discover up to this time why we should select a Republican state treasurer to serve with a Socialist state veterinarian ; and it is because the results of state elections, so far as most of the offices are concerned, are of slight importance to anybody except the political experts, that the public is largely indifferent to the qualifications of the minor candidates. The real failure of the democratic theory, however, is due to the fact that it is absolutely impossible to discriminate wisely among candidates for a large number of offices. It is a matter of common knowledge that in almost every state election the only candidates who are seriously discussed in the press — in other words, the only candidates upon whose qualifications and record any light is thrown — are those seeking the office of governor, and, in the case of municipal elections, that of mayor. The candidates for the minor state offices, and, what is infinitely more important, the candidates for the city council and the legislature, are generally left in the same fog which envelopes the candidates for the position of coroner or clerk of the municipal district court. There are of course exceptions to this rule, but it applies quite generally throughout the United States.

Now to suppose that adding a system of recall to such a complex of public offices — already so large as to bewilder the voter — will advance public control over administration, is surely flying in the face of what may be reasonably called the plain teachings of American political experience. It seems useless to expect popular control through the recall when the inevitable development of political machines has defeated popular control in the selection of officers.

This does not mean, however, that with a simplified ballot and the concentration of large responsibility in the hands of a few elected officials some form of recall would not only be workable, but highly desirable. It would undoubtedly permit a considerable increase in the terms now conceded to public officials, for the electors would certainly be willing to relinquish the right of frequently passing upon the conduct of their agents at regular elections if, at any time, a special election could be called on the demand of a considerable portion of the voters. Indeed, the possibility of lengthening the terms of public officers, a thing highly desirable for the sake of efficient administration, will doubtlessly commend the recall to the consideration of many students and men of affairs who would otherwise be opposed to it in any form.

The recall of judges, however, rests upon a different basis. The most "interesting" function of the judges from the point of view of the electorate is that of fixing public policy. Judges in the United States, unlike the judges of England for instance, are not restricted merely to the settlement of disputes between private parties; they are policy-determining officers, because they have the power to declare null and void, on principles of constitutional law which are scarcely more than general moral precepts, acts passed by legislatures and by the initiative and referendum. During the period of seven years from 1902 to 1908 the supreme courts of the several states declared unconstitutional about five hundred statutes. The theory upon which they act, of course, is that in declaring a law invalid they are merely interpreting the higher law or the supreme will of the people as expressed in the state or federal Constitution.

Now, as Lincoln pointed out in his first inaugural address, nearly all the big questions of constitutional law cannot be settled at all by reference to the plain letter of the law, and when judges declare statutes unconstitutional they usually (except in plain and flagrant cases of violation by legislatures) make constitutional law — in the sense that they read into the constitution their view of what the popular will was supposed to be in the enactment of that constitution. The theory here is that a court of five or seven men can more nearly interpret the public will expressed in the supreme law than can the members of the legislature elected by the people. Whatever the theory, the judges, as long as they continue to exercise this policy-determining function, will be drawn directly into politics; and it must be expected that the same pressure which is brought to bear on other officials to secure more popular control will be brought to bear upon them.

The question of the recall of judges was the subject of such an elaborate discussion in Congress, occasioned by the demand for the admission of Arizona, that it seems worth while to state the case for and against the system in the language of the men who may be said fairly to represent the present state of public opinion in the country.

Those who opposed the recall in general took the ground that the judiciary should be considered entirely apart from the executive and legislative branches of the government, and should not be regarded at all as a policy-determining or a political branch of the government. Mr. Pickett of Iowa [1] sharply distinguished the judiciary from the executive and legislative branches: "Candidates for legislative and executive offices go before the people on platforms embodying the principles for which they stand, and besides they make declarations as to the policies and laws which they will favor or oppose," and thus the people determine their legislative and executive policy. Judges, on the other hand, he declared, "are not elected on an expression in advance as to how they will hold in a certain case, how they will construe a constitution or a statute, or whether they will or will not support a certain law, be it popular or unpopular." The judges, he continued, are not elected to represent the people in the sense in which that word is applied in the case of legislative and executive officers; but are chosen "to expound, construe, and interpret the law and apply it to the facts before them," irrespective of popular favor or disfavor. In his opinion, the judges are the arbitrators between the people on the one hand and the individual on the other, it being their duty "to protect under the law the minority or the single individual even though he stands alone against the whole people. It is their duty to protect the people against the people themselves when they overstep the limitations created for their protection."

This view that the judiciary is the only department of the government to which the minority can constantly look for protection against all majorities, no matter how great, was likewise advanced in a speech by Mr. Legare of South Carolina, on May 16, in which he said the judiciary "is the only branch to which the minority can turn for preservation at all times. The executive

[1] *Congressional Record*, June 23, 1911.

and legislative are supposed to represent the majority, and loudly do they proclaim this fact; but the judiciary is the harbor of refuge to which the minority can flee when pursued by the majority or by the servants of its making. Destroy this branch of the government, and you destroy the only hope of the minority, and at the same time you remove all restraint from the majority and leave them to be glutted with an unholy and uncontrollable power with which they will eventually destroy themselves and the country." [1]

Indeed, most of the opponents of the recall in Congress seem to have felt so strongly on the point of protecting the minority that they could hardly restrain the violence of their emotions in order to give the appearance of deliberation and reasonableness to their arguments. In running through the speeches, especially of Mr. Legare of South Carolina and Mr. Littleton of New York, one is struck with the resemblance between the dire prophecies made as to the outcome of the recall and the prophecies made half a century ago as to the effect of popular election on the judiciary. In the opinion of Mr. Legare and Mr. Littleton the recall, especially as applied to the judiciary, means the enthronement of the mob, the degradation of the bench, the destruction of safeguards of private rights, and the spread of wreck and ruin.

Both of these gentlemen held that the old form of impeachment was sufficient to control judges who went astray, and more commendable because it guarantees to the judges a fair trial by an intelligent jury. In the exercise of the recall, they seem to see mobs of "thugs and bums and loafers and sneak thieves and criminals" — "a howling mass of men drunk with power bent upon doing him [the judge] mischief" — to use the language of Mr. Legare, dragging judges from the bench at their sweet will. The very thought of recalling an officer without trial, continued Mr. Legare, was repugnant "to every sense of human decency. It is the rankest kind of political heresy. It is the result of the

[1] *Congressional Record*, May 17, 1911.

blatant, selfish, unreliable, and dangerous teaching of the demagogue. It is radicalism run rampant; it is socialism gone mad. . . . Once convince an excited populace — and I am speaking plainly to you gentlemen of this House — that through the means of this recall of the judiciary absolute control of the judges is placed directly within their hands, and no human agency can prevent their using that power rashly and recklessly at times, and there is danger that they will steer the old ship of state direct into the maelstrom, and this will mean rebellion and revolution, bloodshed and anarchy."

Mr. Legare then drew upon history for the illustration of the principles thus laid down; and exclaimed that George Washington, Abraham Lincoln, William McKinley, and Grover Cleveland would have been recalled in their day — "shorn of power, degraded, ruined, and damned for all time, if they had held office subject to this recall law."[1]

Mr. Littleton thought that the substitution of the recall for impeachment would transform an orderly process of regulated justice into "a sporadic assault born of hate and disappointment." He believed that the judge would be intimidated, and, instead of doing justice without fear and favor, would always be "scanning the ugly faces of an angry mob" and wondering whether "among the warring factions" there is the fatal percentage which may arraign him before the country. "Suppose," exclaimed the speaker, "the recallable judge is sitting to determine a controversy between employer and employed. Suppose on one side is organized labor, and on the other side organized capital. Does he meet the grave, economic, and legal questions as the great and dauntless minister of justice? Does he summon to his aid the juridical learning of the ages, and invoke the spirit of passionless justice to guide him? Or does he see in the grim and earnest faces of the contestants the imminence of a recall which will put him to shame before his neighbors?"

Mr. Littleton saw in the recall an opportunity to enlist "mis-

[1] *Congressional Record*, May 17, 1911.

guided malignant passions" against "a stainless judge"; and he presented a long list of the elements in the community that would be enrolled against the integrity of the judiciary: —

The lying litigant, he urged, baffled in his mendacious effort to subsidize the court to make secure his fabricated cause, lays his unscrupulous hand upon his ruthless weapon to strike from public esteem the upright judge.

The culpable confederates of the convicted criminal, audacious in that freedom which has foiled detection, and angered at the thought that tardy justice has overtaken one of their members, can assemble and foment the necessary and irresponsible fraction to put on trial the conservator of public honor. The corporate bandit, marauding through the legitimate fields of honest commerce, and finally condemned by the firm hand of an incorruptible court, can turn its passive chagrin into active revenge and summon sufficient of its dependents to write a recall.

The agrarian agitator, whose uplifted hand is always against the substance and the symbols of order, unable to write his crooked creed into the court's decrees, will call for venal volunteers to rebuke the judge who dared deny his loud protestations.

The reformer, whose righteous zeal and unbalanced judgment make him at once the most attractive and most dangerous of men, will find the courts archaic and too rigid bound to serve the elastic purpose of his pretentious program, and his honest wrath will stir the souls of his faithful followers to issue a recall in the name of all political virtue.

The "boss," who in the flush of full success sits in the shadow of the throne, and who even in defeat still reigns a mighty ruler in the empire of intrigue, will touch the mysterious sources of his unjust powers with deft and secret sign, and swarms of satraps will rise in mockery of the voice of an outraged community to indict the fearless judge.

The daring demagogue, whose eager ear catches the first sound of discontent, and whose strident voice swells it into a volume of protest against oppression, whose whole platform is the appropriated grievances of the community, will make of the recall a recurring opportunity to put himself in flexible adjustment with the superficial sentiment of the community.[1]

[1] *Congressional Record*, May 29, 1911.

Then, after portraying the delivery of Christ by Pilate to the chief priests, the rulers, and the people, Mr. Littleton concluded, in a somewhat strained figure, "God forbid that the sanctuaries of justice in this country of America shall ever be ravished by the sibilant hiss of a mob crying, Crucify him! Crucify him!"

Those members of Congress who favored the recall even in its application to the judiciary refused to accept the principle that a judicial officer differed in any respect from an ordinary administrative officer. In fact, they took the view expounded by Professor Goodnow in his *Politics and Administration* that there are really only two branches of government, legislative and executive, and that the function of the judiciary is at bottom merely executive. They furthermore emphatically applied the principle that a judicial officer was to be regarded as the agent of his constituents. "As an abstract proposition," said Senator Chamberlain, "why should a judicial officer any more than any other public official be independent of the wishes of his constituents?" He went on to argue that the democratic view of government is that the people do their own thinking and that the agent of the people, whether he is a judicial or an executive officer, is simply bound to reflect the popular will; and added that any conception of government which placed a representative in a position to be indifferent to the wishes of his constituents was aristocratic in its character.[1] Mr. Hardy of Texas shared this view,[2] and in support of it cited the famous declaration of Jefferson: "A judiciary independent of an executive or king alone is a good thing, but independence of the will of the nation is a solecism, at least in a republican government."

The advocates of the recall also sought to show that it was no innovation in our political practices, but merely a logical outgrowth of that constitutional principle, in vogue in several of the states, which authorizes the legislature to remove judges. Mr. Chamberlain devoted considerable attention in his speech to this branch of the argument, opening it with a quotation from the

[1] *Congressional Record*, April 20, 1911.   [2] *Ibid.*, June 1, 1911.

Maryland constitution of 1776 which stipulated that "the chancellor and judges shall be removed for misbehavior on conviction in a court of law, and may be removed by the governor upon the address of the general assembly: *Provided*, That two-thirds of all the members of each house concur in such address" — a provision which has continued to be a part of the fundamental law of Maryland to our time. Mr. Chamberlain also cited similar provisions in the Georgia constitution, in the several Virginia constitutions since 1830, and in the constitutions of Texas, Delaware, Connecticut, and other states. The senator then concluded his survey by inquiring whether this system of removing judges, which in some instances does not even provide for a hearing, has destroyed the integrity and independence of the judiciary of the states in which it is in force. The Texas Constitution orders the governor to remove the judges of the supreme and district courts on the address of two-thirds of each house of the legislature for "wilful neglect of duty or other reasonable cause"; but, inquires the senator, has the tendency of this system been "to compel the judiciary of that commonwealth to decide controversies between citizens to suit the whims of the legislative assembly, or to destroy the independence of the judiciary?"

On the basis of these facts, Mr. Chamberlain contended that the power of the recall as applied to the judiciary was not a new thing in the history of our public law, and "differs only in the Arizona constitution from the constitutions of other states in that there is a transference of the power of recall from the legislature to the people. The principle is the same. If the transference of this power to the people tends to destroy the independence of the judiciary, may it not also be claimed that the power to exercise it in the case of the legislature tends to destroy that independence? Recent developments tend to show that some legislative bodies at least are influenced by the corruptest motives, and if they may be corrupted to secure the enactment or the defeat of laws, or to secure the election or defeat of senators, may they not be influenced by the same corrupt instrumentalities to unseat the judges? It is safe to say that the tenure of a judge, whether appointive or elective, is more secure in the hands of the people than in the average legislature of to-day." [1] Indeed, Mr. Cullop went so far as to declare that there was more danger in removal by the legislature than in removal by the recall: "In one case you go to a partisan legislature to be tried by a partisan tribunal, instead of going to the whole people where your case can be passed upon without prejudice or partiality." [2]

Senator Owen favored the recall of the judiciary particularly on the ground that it would restrict the tendency of judges to enact law under the color of interpretation.[3] "Restoring the active right of recall of judges," he said, "will go far toward making democratic the Constitution of the United States, and for that reason I strongly favor it. When Congress or the people have a legal right to recall judges, the judges will respect public opinion and general welfare. They will not set aside state or federal laws nor legislate under the color of judicial decisions, and they will so conduct themselves that the use of the recall will be unnecessary." [4]

In support of a similar contention Mr. Hardy of Texas quoted the following passages from the vigorous dissent of Justice Harlan in the Standard Oil case:—

In the now not a very short life that I have passed in this capital and the public service of the country, the most alarming tendency of this day, in my judgment, so far as the safety and integrity of our institutions are concerned, is the tendency to judicial legislation, so that, when men having vast interests are concerned, and they cannot get the law-making power of the country which controls it to pass the legislation they desire, the next thing they do is to raise the question in some case to get the court to so construe the Constitution or the statutes as

[1] *Congressional Record*, April 20, 1911. [2] *Ibid.*, May 18, 1911.
[3] In 1911, Senator Owen introduced an amendment to the federal Constitution providing for the recall of federal judges by resolution of Congress.
[4] *Congressional Record*, June 20, 1911.

to mean what they want it to mean. That has not been our practice. . . . The court, in the opinion of this case, says that this act of Congress means and embraces only unreasonable restraint of trade in flat contradiction to what this court has said fifteen years ago that Congress did not intend. . . . Practically the decision of to-day — I do not mean the judgment — but parts of the opinion, are to the effect, practically, that the courts may, by mere judicial construction, amend the Constitution of the United States or an act of Congress. That, it strikes me, is mischievous; and that is the part of the opinion that I especially object to.[1]

Mr. Hardy was especially strong in his condemnation of impeachment as a method of removing judges. He cited Jefferson's statement that impeachment was "not even a scarecrow," and did not check the judges in the usurpation of legislative functions. Furthermore, impeachment blackens the character of the man impeached, while the exercise of the recall does not injure a man's reputation any more than a defeat at the polls. Impeachment is a cumbersome and often ineffective instrument for the removal of officers who have not committed grievous wrongs, but who are on the whole undesirable. "I have seen jury trials," remarked Mr. Hardy, "where, were I on the panel, I would render the Scotch verdict of 'Guilty, but not proven,' and I would acquit the defendant but not keep him in my employ. And so we have cases where you cannot properly impeach, where you cannot get the evidence to impeach, where through the courts full inquiry is blocked, where the servant is so powerful he can prevent full investigation; in such cases must we keep the servant?"

In going carefully through the arguments in Congress on both sides of the recall, particularly as applied to the judiciary, one cannot help discovering that the clear line of cleavage is on the question of how far the judges are to be bound by the will of the majority and how far they are to be independent in order to defend rights of person and property which are deemed more

[1] *Congressional Record*, June 1, 1911, p. 1674.

fundamental than constitutions themselves. Democratic senators, like Mr. Chamberlain and Mr. Owen, frankly declared that they favored democratizing the federal Constitution and instituting the principle of majority rule; and the latter especially is fully aware that this is a radical departure from the real spirit of American government. He declared in his speech of June 12 that the Constitution was not thoroughly democratic, but "was so drawn by Madison and those who were in the Constitutional Convention as to allow an unfair power to vest in the hands of the minority, and this principle is shown from one end of the Constitution to the other."

The Constitution of the United States, he continued, is not, and was not then (1789) in accord with the democratic constitutions of the various States as they existed at the time of the making of the Constitution of the United States.

One of the great differences which I will call the attention of the Senate to — and I am not going to detain the Senate long — is in the matter of the judiciary. Hamilton made the argument that the Federal judiciary ought to be appointed for life, and he made the argument and backed it up with a fallacious theory, which seems to have been quite generally acquiesced in by those who have written upon this subject. He based his argument for a life judiciary upon the theory that this would be in substantial accord with the English system, when, in point of fact, it was nothing of the kind. It is true, in the English system the judges were appointed for life, but it is also true that the right of recall of the English judges was provided for by memorial or resolution or address of the Parliament of Great Britain as far back as 1688. The judiciary of Great Britain does not legislate nor declare acts of Parliament null and void. It is responsible to Parliament, and not an entirely independent and irresponsible power. There is no recall for the Supreme Court of the United States, as in Great Britain, and on some more suitable and convenient occasion I will undertake to present to the Senate the reasons why I think it unwise to have a judiciary entirely independent of Congress and of the great public opinion of the United States. I do not believe in nine men, no matter who they are, being put in a position where they can disregard the will of the people of the United States and of their representatives in Con-

Introductory Note 65

gress with comparative impunity. It is one of the ways in which the right of the majority to control this country is denied; it is one of the ways in which the Constitution of the United States was made undemocratic.

In advocating the recall as an instrument for democratizing this constitution, Mr. Owen declared that he was merely recurring to the more liberal principles embodied in the several constitutions existing at the time of the adoption of the new federal system.[1]

Mr. Saunders of Virginia was likewise aware of the departure which the recall made from the principles of the Fathers.[2]

The gentleman from New York, he said, and other gentlemen from older States of the East, who apparently think that no good thing, in the way of new and progressive legislation, can come out of the West, quoted at length from the fathers of the Republic, from Hamilton, Marshall, and others of the same school, to show that the recall was not in the contemplation of these statesmen, and if offered to them, as a substantive proposition, would have been rejected. Granted. There are many modern innovations that these statesmen would reject. Undoubtedly they would view with extreme distrust the application of the recall to the judges, and the Oregon plan would be a chamber of horrors to them. It would be anathema maranatha to Hamilton or to Marshall. But the Member from New York, or the Member from any other State which elects the judges by popular vote, should hesitate to cite these gentlemen as authority against the recall. For with equal propriety, they may be cited as authority against an elective judiciary. In the contemplation of those statesmen it was an abhorrent, almost an unthinkable proposition, that a judge should hold his office, at what they deemed would be the caprice of the electorate, and at stated intervals be required to submit his claims for reëlection, to a popular vote. The rock upon which they builded the system of the Federal judiciary was an appointive judiciary with a life tenure. In no other way did they conceive that a fearless, self-respecting, upright, and efficient body of judges could be secured. But contrary to the anticipations of our forefathers, that plan

[1] *Congressional Record*, June 20, 1911.   [2] *Ibid*.

has not been followed. A radically different system of selection has been approved in many Commonwealths. In a number of States, notably New York, the judges are elected for fixed terms by popular vote.

The advocates of the recall in Congress found outside support in Mr. Roosevelt, who declared that time and circumstance might warrant the adoption of the recall, although, under normal conditions, it was inadvisable to apply the principle to the judiciary. In his opinion the Massachusetts system, under which judges may be removed by the two branches of the legislature and on assignment of reasons, was to be preferred to the popular recall. However, he thought "the difference between a judicial system under which judges are appointed for life and are removable only after impeachment, and a system under which judges are elected for short terms, is infinitely greater than the difference between the latter system — that is, a short-term, elected judiciary without a recall — and the proposed Arizona system for a short-term, elected judiciary with a recall."

He then added the caution that after all the essential thing to consider was not merely the name "recall," but the actual working of the system.

If in any given state the system of an elective or an appointive judiciary without a recall has proved in actual practice to work badly (as it certainly proved to work badly in California), then practical reformers who are working for the betterment of popular conditions are quite right in trying to substitute for it some other system. The all-important thing is the spirit in which the system is administered. If in any State the adoption of the recall was found to mean the subjection of the judge to the whim of the mob, then it would become the imperative duty of every good citizen, without regard to previous prejudices, to work for the alteration of the system. If, on the other hand, in any State the judiciary yields to improper influence on the part of special interests, or if the judges even, although honest men, show themselves so narrow-minded and so utterly out of sympathy with the industrial and social needs brought about by changed conditions that they seek to fetter the movement for progress and betterment, then the people are not to be excused if, in a servile spirit, they submit to such domination, and fail to take any measures necessary to secure their right to go forward along the path of economic and social justice and fair dealing. If our people are really fit for self-government, then they will insist upon governing themselves. In all matters affecting the Nation as a whole this power of self-governing should reside in the majority of the Nation as a whole; and upon this doctrine no one has insisted more strongly than I have insisted, for in such case "popular rights" becomes a meaningless phrase save as it is translated into National rights.[1]

The men who made the ablest argument against the recall were under no delusions as to the real function of the judiciary in the United States as the defender of the rights and privileges of property against the assaults of majorities. Mr. Howland of Ohio cited the famous speech of Marshall in which that great jurist declared that the judge "should be rendered perfectly and completely independent with nothing to control him but God and his conscience."[2] In reply to the "demagogue" who cries, "You are afraid to trust the people to choose their own judges," Mr. Howland recalled the argument made by Rufus Choate in the Massachusetts Constitutional Convention of 1853 against a short tenure of office: —

It seems to me that such an argument forgets that our political system, while it is purely and intensely republican, within all theories, aims to accomplish a twofold object, to wit, liberty and security. To accomplish this twofold object we have established a twofold set of institutions and instrumentalities — some of them designed to develop and give utterance to one; some of them designed to provide permanently and constantly for the other; some of them designed to bring out the popular will in its utmost intensity of utterance; some of them designed to secure life and liberty and character and happiness and property and equal and exact justice against all will and against all power.

[1] *The Outlook*, June 24, 1911, p. 378.
[2] *Congressional Record*, May 18, 1911.

It is obvious from these passages that a complete discussion of the recall as applied to the judiciary would involve an exhaustive analysis of the origin and nature of government which cannot be made here. Nevertheless, it is apparent that Mr. Choate's doctrine that the individual has fundamental personal and property rights which are beyond the reach, not only of the majority but of the state itself, can be sustained on no other theory than that of anarchy. It rests upon a notion as obsolete and indefensible as the doctrine of natural rights, and it is as unacceptable as the opposite conclusion that fundamental rights of person and property should be subject to the will of an incoherent and transient majority.

The judiciary in the United States is in fact, in view of its power over the constitutionality of laws, a political body, and it has, in a large number of unquestionable cases, assumed legislative power. If the judiciary is to retain this veto over legislation, it can hardly expect to escape that movement which is everywhere steadily and irresistibly making for direct popular control over all policy-determining instrumentalities in government.[1]

The most fundamental objection to the recall is not to its inherent potentialities, but its addition to an already burdensome and complicated system of election which has defeated its own purpose of securing popular control over administration. If the number of elective offices were reduced to those which are "important enough to attract and deserve public examination," — if the principle of the short ballot were introduced and administrative authority concentrated into fewer hands, so that genuine responsibility could be secured, the recall, applied under proper safeguards as to the number of petitioners, the percentage necessary for removal, and the period which must elapse before its exercise can be invoked, may commend itself not only to believers in direct democratic government, but also to many who at first thought are unutterably opposed to the so-called "progressive movement."

[1] See Goodnow, *Social Reform and the Constitution*, p. 357 (1911).

At all events, in view of the dire prophecies which have been made in times past concerning proposals which have proved advantageous, or at least harmless, "hard-minded persons," to use Professor James' phrase, will not be disposed to view with distress the introduction of these new devices — the initiative, referendum, and recall. That they will go as far toward solving our political problems as the simplification of representative government and the introduction of centralized responsibility on the part of public officials is certainly open to serious question. That representative government, where responsibility and deliberation are secured, is the best instrument for legislative work yet devised is scarcely open to argument. Nevertheless, the initiative and referendum, especially in important matters, have undoubtedly found a permanent place among our institutions. That longer terms of office and a freer range of discretion are conducive to administrative efficiency is everywhere accepted, and the recall seems to offer to democracy the proper safeguards against usurpation which will warrant the granting of longer terms and larger powers to executive authorities.

CHARLES A. BEARD.

I. THE INITIATIVE AND REFERENDUM

I. SOUTH DAKOTA

Constitutional Amendment[1]

[The following constitutional provision was passed by the legislature in 1897. The amendment was ratified at the general election held November 8, 1898. The Supreme court of South Dakota held the amendment constitutional in the case of State ex rel. Lavin et al. vs. Bacon et al., 14 S. D. 394. On March 3, 1899, the legislature elaborated the machinery for working the system. These laws provide for state-wide and local use of the initiative and referendum.]

§ 1. The legislative power shall be vested in a legislature which shall consist of a senate and house of representatives. Except that the people expressly reserve to themselves the right to propose measures, which measures the legislature shall enact and submit to a vote of the electors of the state, and also the right to require that any laws which the legislature may have enacted shall be submitted to a vote of the electors of the state before going into effect (except such laws as may be necessary for the immediate preservation of the public peace, health or safety, support of the state government and its existing public institutions).

Provided, that not more than five per centum of the qualified electors of the state shall be required to invoke either the initiative or the referendum.

This section shall not be construed so as to deprive the legislature or any member thereof of the right to propose any measure. The veto power of the executive shall not be exercised as to

---
[1] Constitution of South Dakota, *Revised Codes of South Dakota*, 1903, p. 1.

The Initiative and Referendum

measures referred to a vote of the people. This section shall apply to municipalities. The enacting clause of all laws approved by vote of the electors of the state shall be: "Be it enacted by the people of South Dakota." The legislature shall make suitable provisions for carrying into effect the provisions of this section.

Elaborating Law — State-Wide [1]

§ 21. All measures proposed to the legislature under the initiative shall be presented by petition, which petition shall be signed by not less than five per cent of the qualified electors of the state, and each elector shall add to his signature his place of residence, his business, and his post office address. The petition shall be filed in the office of the secretary of state, and upon the convening of the legislature the secretary of state shall transmit to the senate and house of representatives certified copies of all of said petitions which may be on file in the office of the secretary of state at the convening of said legislature, and whenever a measure is proposed during the session of the legislature it shall be transmitted by the secretary of state forthwith to the senate and house of representatives, and the legislature shall enact and submit all of such proposed measures to a vote of the electors of the state at the next general election.

§ 22. If a majority of all the votes cast both for and against the measure so enacted and submitted be for the measure, it shall then become a law of the State of South Dakota, and shall go into effect and be in force immediately after the result shall have been determined by the officers authorized by law to determine the same.

§ 23. Any laws which the legislature may have enacted, except laws which may be necessary for the immediate preservation of the public peace, health and safety, support to the state government and its existing institutions, shall, upon the filing of a petition as hereinafter provided, be submitted to a vote of the

[1] *Revised Codes of South Dakota*, 1903, pp. 5 f.

electors of the state at the next general election. Said petition shall be signed by not less than five per cent of the qualified electors of the state, and each elector shall add to his signature his place of residence, his business and post-office address, which petition shall be filed in the office of the secretary of state within ninety days after the adjournment of the legislature which passed such laws, and if a majority of all the votes cast both for and against the law be for the law, it shall then become a law of this state, and shall go into effect and be in force immediately after the result shall have been determined by the officers authorized by law to determine the same.

§ 24. Whenever a measure or law of the legislature is submitted to the electors, the said measure or law shall be printed upon a separate ballot from that upon which the names of the candidates for office are printed, but all measures and laws of the legislature to be voted upon at the same election shall be printed upon one ballot, and each measure and law shall be followed by the words: "Shall the above measure or law (as the case may be) become a law of this state?" Immediately to the left of which shall be printed the words "Yes" and "No," each preceded by a square in which the elector may place a cross within such square to indicate his vote. Each elector desiring to vote "Yes" may place a cross within the square before the word "Yes," and those desiring to vote "No" may place a cross within the square before the word "No," and the secretary of state shall prepare and certify to the county auditor of each county the measures and laws to be voted upon at such general election in the manner and at the same time he certifies to said auditor certificates of nominations for general elections, and it is hereby made the duty of the board of state canvassers to canvass the returns of votes cast for these measures and laws, and to declare the result, in the same manner and at the same time as other returns are canvassed, and the result declared by said board of state canvassers for state officers.

§ 25. The total number of votes cast at the last preceding gen-

The Initiative and Referendum 73

eral election shall be, for the purpose of this article, the basis upon which the five per cent of the electors shall be determined, and the vote upon which said basis shall be made shall be the vote cast for governor at such general election.

§ 26. Every petition to propose a measure must contain the substance of the initiative law desired, and must be signed in person by the petitioners; and every petition to submit a law to a vote of the electors of the state must be signed in person by the petitioners and must describe in said petition the law desired to be submitted by setting forth its title, together with the date of its passage and approval.

§ 27. Every person who is a qualified elector may sign a petition to propose a measure or submit a law, and any person signing any name other than his own to said petition, or any person signing such petition who is not a qualified elector of this state, shall, upon conviction therefor, be fined in any sum not to exceed five hundred dollars or may be imprisoned in the state penitentiary for a term not to exceed five years; and the court may, in its discretion, impose both such fine and imprisonment.

Elaborating Law — Local [1]

§ 1214. No law, ordinance or resolution, having the effect of law, for the government of any city or town passed by the legislative body or bodies thereof, except such as are for the immediate preservation of the public peace, or the public health, or safety, or expenditure of money in the ordinary course of the administration of the affairs of such public corporation, shall go into effect until twenty days after the passage of such law, ordinance, or resolution, and the words law, ordinance or resolution used in this article mean ordinances, resolves, orders, agreements, contracts, franchises, and any measure which it is in the power of the lawmakers or the electors of any municipality to enact.

§ 1215. The qualified electors residing in any city or town

[1] *Revised Codes of South Dakota*, 1903, pp. 205 ff.

may within the said twenty days file a petition with the auditor, or other proper officer or clerk thereof, requiring him to submit any such law, ordinance, or resolution, to a vote of the electors of the political subdivision affected thereby for its rejection or approval, at a special election to be held within thirty days immediately following the filing of said petition.

Provided, that in all cases where such petitions are filed at any time, not more than three months immediately prior to any election held for the purpose of electing the officers of said city or town, such law, ordinance or resolution shall be submitted at such election, provided such petitions are filed within sufficient time to give the notice above prescribed.

§ 1216. If the matter intended to be covered by said petition is the whole of said law, ordinance or resolution, said petition shall contain the title of the said law, ordinance or resolution to be voted on by the electors, and the date of the passage of said law, ordinance or resolution by the legislative body of said municipal corporation; but if a portion of said law, ordinance or resolution is only intended to be covered by the said petition, then the said petition shall contain the title of said law, ordinance or resolution, the date of its passage, following which that portion of said law, ordinance or resolution intended to be covered by said petition shall be set out at length, and said petition, to be mandatory, shall be signed by at least five per centum of the legal voters residing in such city, or town, the percentage to be based on the whole number of votes cast for the highest executive officer in said city or town, at the election immediately preceding the filing of said petition, which said petition shall conform substantially to the provisions of the preceding section, and each elector signing the same, shall after his name state his occupation, residence and post-office address.

§ 1217. An oath shall be made before a duly qualified officer by at least five voters signing said petition, or if more than one, each petition, to the effect that said petition is made in good faith, and that the affiant verily believes all the signatures to be genuine, and those of duly qualified voters, which said oath shall be substantially and in the following form: —

STATE OF SOUTH DAKOTA,
County of ...., ss.
.... being duly sworn, on their oaths, respectively, do say that the foregoing petition is made in good faith, and that they verily believe all the signatures thereto to be genuine, and those of duly qualified voters.

§ 1218. It shall be the duty of the auditor or clerk of the said city or town to cause the entire law, ordinance or resolution set forth in said petition to be advertised in one of the newspapers published in such municipal corporation at least five days prior to such election, which publication shall be daily until such election in one daily paper published within said municipal corporation, but if there is no daily newspaper published within such municipal corporation, one publication in a legal newspaper published in said municipal corporation not less than five nor more than twelve days prior to such election, shall be sufficient; *Provided*, if there is no newspaper published in such municipal corporation, then the auditor or clerk shall publish such law, ordinance or resolution, by posting or causing to be posted the entire law, ordinance or resolution at least five days prior to the date of said election at three public places within the limit of each voting precinct of said city or town. *Provided, further*, that the publication of said law, ordinance or resolution in the said newspaper, or by the said posting as above provided, shall contain a notification that on that day of election therein stated, the said law, ordinance or resolution will be submitted to the referendum, and if a portion of said law, ordinance or resolution only is covered by said petition, then a notification as to what particular portion of the said law, ordinance or resolution will be submitted to the said referendum.

§ 1219. It shall be the duty of said auditor or clerk to have the ballots printed for the vote upon said law, ordinance or resolution, and cause same to be distributed in the proper proportion in each voting precinct, in his city or town in the manner now provided for the distribution of ballots by the election laws of the state. Any or all questions shall be submitted on a separate ballot from those containing the names of the candidates for office, and shall be submitted to the people in such form as will enable the electors to vote understandingly upon each question presented, and shall conform as near as may be to the manner employed to vote upon constitutional amendments. *Provided,* that all questions to be voted upon at the same election may be submitted upon the same ballot.

§ 1220. The auditor or clerk of the said city or town shall preserve the original of all petitions filed in his office in voting the referendum for a period of at least two years from the date following said petition, during which time said petition shall be open to public inspection upon reasonable request made.

§ 1221. Such law, ordinance or resolution shall not go into effect unless approved by a majority of the votes cast for and against the same, and shall go into effect immediately after the canvassing and determination of the election returns, if approved by the electors.

§ 1222. The appointment of judges and clerks, holding of election, and time of election, the canvassing, counting, returning and announcing of a referendary vote on any law, ordinance or resolution, and payment of election expenses shall be done in the manner already prescribed by law in the case of the election of the officers of the municipal corporation to be affected by the law, ordinance or resolution in question.

§ 1223. The right to propose laws, ordinances or resolutions having the effect of law, for the government of any city or town shall rest with any five per centum of the electors of the political subdivision affected, the percentage in each instance to be based upon the number of votes cast at the last general election for the highest executive officer of such political subdivision held previously to the proposal of the law in question.

The Initiative and Referendum

§ 1224. A proposal for such law, ordinance or resolution shall be made by petition to the auditor or clerk of the municipal corporation. The petition shall be signed by five per centum of the legal voters of any political subdivision affected by such law, ordinance or resolution, each elector stating his occupation, residence and post-office address, and shall be filed with the auditor of said municipal corporation after the manner prescribed by the provisions of this article for the petition of the referendum, and said petition shall contain in proper form the proposed law, ordinance or resolution.

§ 1225. When such petition is filed with the auditor or clerk of such municipal corporation, he shall at the first ensuing session or special session called submit said proposal to the legislative body thereof; and if the proposal is not adopted, or cannot be adopted by reason of want of authority by such legislative body, it shall be referred to a vote of the electors of such municipal corporation within the time and manner prescribed by this article providing for the referendum.

§ 1226. Such law, ordinance or resolution shall go into effect if approved by a majority of the votes cast for and against the same.

§ 1227. The right of any person to vote at any election on any proposition submitted to the referendum or initiative may be challenged in the same manner and for the same cause as by law provided in the case of challenging electors.

§ 1228. Any person, or persons, violating any of the provisions of this article or wilfully failing to execute any of the provisions of this article shall be guilty of a misdemeanor, and on conviction be fined not less than one hundred dollars nor more than five hundred dollars, or by imprisonment not less than thirty days nor more than six months, in the county jail, or by both such fine and imprisonment, in the discretion of the court.

II. UTAH

[An initiative and referendum amendment was adopted by the voters of Utah at the general election held November 6, 1900. The vote was 19,219 for, to 7786 against. The total vote cast at the election was 92,980. The total vote on the amendment was 27,005, about 29 per cent of the entire vote. May 8, 1911, the Secretary of State, Mr. Charles S. Tingey, states, "The Legislature has failed to enact the necessary measures to put the initiative and referendum provisions of our constitution in force." The amendment follows.]

SEC. 1. [*Power vested in Senate, House and People.*] The legislative power of the State shall be vested:

1. In a Senate and House of Representatives, which shall be designated the Legislature of the State of Utah.

2. In the people of the State of Utah as hereinafter stated:

The legal voters or such fractional part thereof of the State of Utah, as may be provided by law, under such conditions and in such manner and within such time as may be provided by law, may initiate any desired legislation and cause the same to be submitted to a vote of the people for approval or rejection, or may require any law passed by the Legislature (except those laws passed by a two-thirds vote of the members elected to each house of the Legislature) to be submitted to the voters of the State before such law shall take effect.

The legal voters, or such fractional part thereof, as may be provided by law, of any legal subdivision of the State, under such conditions and in such manner and within such time as may be provided by law, may initiate any desired legislation and cause the same to be submitted to a vote of the people of said legal subdivision for approval or rejection, or may require any law or ordinance passed by the law-making body of said legal subdivision to be submitted to the voters thereof before such law or ordinance shall take effect.

SEC. 22. [*Enacting Clause. Passage and amendments of law.*] The enacting clause of every law shall be, "Be it enacted by the

The Initiative and Referendum

Legislature of the State of Utah." Except such laws as may be passed by the vote of the electors as provided in subdivision 2, section 1 of this article, and such laws shall begin as follows: "Be it enacted by the people of the State of Utah." No bill or joint resolution shall be passed, except with the assent of the majority of all the members elected to each house of the Legislature, and after it has been read three times. The vote upon the final passage of all bills shall be by yeas and nays; and no law shall be revised or amended by reference to its title only; but the act as revised, or section as amended, shall be reënacted and published at length.[1]

III. OREGON

[The section (§ 1) below is an amendment to the original constitution. It was passed by the Twentieth Legislative Assembly (1899); re-passed by the Twenty-first Legislative Assembly (1901); and adopted by the voters on June 2, 1902, by a vote of 62,024 for, to 5668 against. The total vote at the election was 90,692, so that 74.6 per cent voted on the amendment.

Section 1a was proposed by initiative petition, filed in the office of the Secretary of State February 3, 1906, and adopted by vote of the people, 47,678 for, to 16,735 against, June 4, 1906. This was 64.7 per cent of the total vote. It went into effect by proclamation of the Governor issued June 25, 1906.

As directed in Section 1, the legislature enacted elaborating legislation, February 24, 1903. However, this act was repealed February 25, 1907, and the Legislative Assembly enacted a substitute law, declaring it an emergency measure. The two constitutional amendments and the elaborating act of 1907 follow.]

Constitutional Amendments [2]

§ 1. LEGISLATIVE AUTHORITY — STYLE OF BILL — INITIATIVE AND REFERENDUM (1902)

The legislative authority of the State shall be vested in a Legislative Assembly, consisting of a Senate and House of Representa-

---

[1] Thorpe, *American Charters, Constitutions, and Organic Laws*, Vol. VI, p. 3734.   [2] Constitution of Oregon, 1910 (official).

tives, but the people reserve to themselves power to propose laws and amendments to the Constitution and to enact or reject the same at the polls, independent of the Legislative Assembly, and also reserve power at their own option to approve or reject at the polls any act of the Legislative Assembly. The first power reserved by the people is the initiative, and not more than eight per cent of the legal voters shall be required to propose any measure by such petition, and every such petition shall include the full text of the measure so proposed. Initiative petitions shall be filed with the Secretary of State not less than four months before the election at which they are to be voted upon. The second power is the referendum, and it may be ordered (except as to laws necessary for the immediate preservation of the public peace, health, or safety), either by the petition signed by five per cent of the legal voters, or by the Legislative Assembly, as other bills are enacted. Referendum petitions shall be filed with the Secretary of State not more than ninety days after the final adjournment of the session of the Legislative Assembly which passed the bill on which the referendum is demanded. The veto power of the Governor shall not extend to measures referred to the people. All elections on measures referred to the people of the State shall be had at the biennial regular general elections, except when the Legislative Assembly shall order a special election. Any measure referred to the people shall take effect and become the law when it is approved by a majority of the votes cast thereon, and not otherwise. The style of all bills shall be: "Be it enacted by the people of the State of Oregon." This section shall not be construed to deprive any member of the Legislative Assembly of the right to introduce any measure. The whole number of votes cast for Justice of the Supreme Court at the regular election last preceding the filing of any petition for the initiative or for the referendum shall be the basis on which the number of legal voters necessary to sign such petition shall be counted. Petitions and orders for the initiative and for the referendum shall be filed with the Secretary of State, and in submitting the same to the people he, and all other officers, shall be guided by the general laws and the act submitting this amendment, until legislation shall be especially provided therefor.

§ 1*a*. INITIATIVE AND REFERENDUM ON LOCAL, SPECIAL, AND MUNICIPAL LAWS AND PARTS OF LAWS (1906)

The referendum may be demanded by the people against one or more items, sections, or parts of any act of the Legislative Assembly in the same manner in which such power may be exercised against a complete act. The filing of a referendum petition against one or more items, sections, or parts of an act shall not delay the remainder of that act from becoming operative. The initiative and referendum powers reserved to the people by this Constitution are hereby further reserved to the legal voters of every municipality and district, as to all local, special and municipal legislation, of every character, in or for their respective municipalities and districts. The manner of exercising said powers shall be prescribed by general laws, except that cities and towns may provide for the manner of exercising the initiative and referendum powers as to their municipal legislation. Not more than ten per cent of the legal voters may be required to order the referendum nor more than fifteen per cent to propose any measure, by the initiative, in any city or town.

Elaborating Law (1907)

Be it enacted by the People of the State of Oregon:

Section 1. The following shall be substantially the form of petition for the referendum to the people on any act passed by the Legislative Assembly of the State of Oregon, or by a city council:

WARNING

It is a felony for any one to sign any initiative or referendum petition with any name other than his own, or to knowingly sign his name more than once for the same measure, or to sign such petition when he is not a legal voter.

PETITION FOR REFERENDUM

To the Honorable ...., Secretary of State for the State of Oregon (or to the Honorable ...., Clerk, auditor, or recorder, as the case may be, of the city of ....):

We, the undersigned citizens and legal voters of the State of Oregon (and the district of ...., county of ...., or city of ...., as the case may be), respectfully order that the Senate (or House) Bill No. ...., entitled (title of act, and if the petition is against less than the whole act then set forth here the part or parts on which the referendum is sought) passed by the .... Legislative Assembly of the State of Oregon, at the regular (special) session of said Legislative Assembly, shall be referred to the people of the State (district of ...., county of ...., or city of ...., as the case may be), for their approval or rejection, at the regular (special) election to be held on the ...... day of ......, A.D., 19.., and each for himself says: I have personally signed this petition; I am a legal voter of the State of Oregon (and district of ...., county of ...., city of ...., as the case may be); my residence and post office are correctly written after my name.

Name ...., Residence ...., Post Office ....
   (If in a city, street and number)

(Here follow twenty numbered lines for signatures.)

Section 2. The following shall be substantially the form of petition for any law, amendment to the constitution of the State of Oregon, city ordinance or amendment to a city charter, proposed by the initiative: —

WARNING

It is a felony for any one to sign any initiative or referendum petition with any name other than his own, or to knowingly sign his name more than once for the measure, or to sign such petition when he is not a legal voter.

INITIATIVE PETITION

To the Honorable ...., Secretary of State for the State of Oregon (or to the Honorable ...., Clerk, auditor, or recorder, as the case may be, for the city of ....):

We, the undersigned citizens and legal voters of the State of Oregon (and of the district of ...., county of ...., or city of ...., as the case may be), respectfully demand that the following proposed law (or amendment to the constitution, ordinance, or amendment to the city charter, as the case may be) shall be submitted to the legal voters of the State of Oregon (district of ...., county of ...., or city of ...., as the case may be), for their approval or rejection at the regular general election (or regular or special city election) to be held on the ...... day of ......, A.D. 19.., and each for himself says: I have personally signed this petition; I am a legal voter of the State of Oregon (and of the district of ...., county of ...., city of ...., as the case may be); my residence and post office are correctly written after my name.

Name ...., Residence ...., Post Office ....
    (If in a city, street and number)
(Here follow twenty numbered lines for signatures.)

Every such sheet for petitioners' signatures shall be attached to a full and correct copy of the title and text of the measure so proposed by the initiative petition; but such petition may be filed with the Secretary of State in numbered sections for convenience in handling, and referendum petitions shall be attached to a full and correct copy of the measure on which the referendum is demanded and may be filed in numbered sections in like manner. Not more than twenty signatures on one sheet shall be counted. When any such initiative or referendum petition shall be offered for filing, the Secretary of State, in the presence of the Governor and the person offering the same for filing, shall detach the sheets containing the signatures and affidavits and cause them all to be attached to one or more printed copies of the measure so proposed by initiative or referendum petitions; *provided*, all petitions for the initiative and for the referendum and sheets **for** signatures shall be printed on pages seven inches in width by ten inches in length, with a margin of one and three-fourths inches at the top for binding; if the aforesaid sheets shall be too bulky for convenient binding in one volume, they may be bound in two or more volumes, those in each volume to be attached to a single printed copy of such measure; the detached copies of such measure shall be delivered to the person offering the same for filing. If any such measure shall, at the ensuing election, be approved by the people, then the copies thereof so preserved, with the sheets and signatures and affidavits, and a certified copy of the Governor's proclamation declaring the same to have been approved by the people, shall be bound together in such form that they may be conveniently identified and preserved. The Secretary of State shall cause every such measure so approved by the people to be printed with the general laws enacted by the next ensuing session of the Legislative Assembly, with the date of the Governor's proclamation declaring the same to have been approved by the people. This act shall not apply to the general laws governing the method of determining whether stock of any kind shall be permitted to run at large in any county or portion thereof, nor to the provisions of the local option liquor laws providing methods of determining whether the sale of intoxicating liquors shall be prohibited in any county, city, precinct, ward, or district.

Section 3. Each and every sheet of every such petition containing signatures shall be verified on the back thereof, in substantially the following form, by the person who circulated said sheet of said petition, by his or her affidavit hereon and as a part thereof: —

STATE OF OREGON,
County of .... ss.

I, ..., being first duly sworn, say: (Here shall be legibly written or typewritten the names of the signers of the sheet), signed this sheet of the foregoing petition, and each of them signed his name thereto in my presence; I believe that each has stated his name, post office address and residence correctly, and that each signer is a legal voter of the State of Oregon and county of ...., (or of the city of ...., as the case may be).

(Signature and post office address of affiant.)

Subscribed and sworn to before me this ...... day of ......, A.D., 19...

(Signature and title of officer before whom oath is made, and his post office address.)

The forms herein given are not mandatory, and if substantially followed in any petition it shall be sufficient — disregarding clerical and merely technical errors.

Section 4. If the Secretary of State shall refuse to accept and file any petition for the initiative or for the referendum, any citizen may apply, within ten days after such refusal, to the circuit court for a writ of mandamus to compel him to do so. If it shall be decided by the court that such petition is legally sufficient, the Secretary of State shall then file it, with a certified copy of the judgment attached thereto, as of the date on which it was originally offered for filing in his office. On a showing that any petition filed is not legally sufficient, the court may enjoin the Secretary of State and all other officers from certifying or printing on the official ballot for the ensuing election the ballot title and numbers of such measure. All such suits shall be advanced on the court docket and heard and decided by the court as quickly as possible. Either party may appeal to the supreme court within ten days after a decision is rendered. The circuit court of Marion County shall have jurisdiction in all cases of measures to be submitted to the electors of the State at large; in cases of local and special measures, the circuit court of the county, or one of the counties in which such measures are to be voted upon, shall have jurisdiction; in cases of municipal legislation, the circuit court of the county in which the city concerned is situated shall have jurisdiction.

Section 5. When any measure shall be filed with the Secretary of State to be referred to the people of the State, or of any county or district composed of one or more counties, either by the Legislative Assembly or by the referendum petition, and when any measure shall be proposed by initiative petition, the Secretary of State shall forthwith transmit to the Attorney-General of the State a copy thereof, and within ten days thereafter the Attorney-General shall provide and return to the Secretary of State a ballot title for said measure. The ballot title may be distinct from the legislative title of the measure, and shall express, in not exceeding one hundred words, the purpose of the measure. The ballot title shall be printed with the numbers of the measure, on the official ballot. In making such ballot title the Attorney-General shall, to the best of his ability, give a true and impartial statement of the purpose of the measure, and in such language that the ballot title shall not be intentionally an argument, or likely to create prejudice, either for or against the measure. Any person who is dissatisfied with the ballot title provided by the Attorney-General for any measure may appeal from his decision to the circuit court, as provided by section 4 of this act, by petition, praying for a different title and setting forth the reasons why the title prepared by the Attorney-General is insufficient or unfair. No appeal shall be allowed from the decision of the Attorney-General on a ballot title, unless the same is taken within ten days after said decision is filed. A copy of every such decision shall be served by the Secretary of State or the clerk of the court, upon the person offering or filing such initiative or referendum petition or appeal. Service of such decision may be by mail or telegraph, and shall be made forthwith. Said circuit court shall thereupon examine said measure, hear arguments, and in its decision thereon certify to the Secretary of State a ballot title for the measure in accord with the intent of this section. The decision of the circuit court shall be final. The Secretary of State shall print on the official ballot the title thus certified to him.

Section 6. The Secretary of State, at the time he furnishes to the county clerks of the several counties certified copies of the names of the candidates for state and district offices, shall furnish to each of said county clerks his certified copy of the ballot titles and numbers of the several measures to be voted upon at the ensuing general election, and he shall use for each measure the ballot title designated in the manner herein provided. Such ballot title shall in no case exceed one hundred words, and shall not resemble, so far as to probably create confusion, any such title previously filed for any measure to be submitted at that election; he shall number such measures and such ballot titles shall be printed on the official ballot in the order in which the acts referred by the Legislative Assembly and petitions by the people shall be filed in his office. The affirmative of the first measure shall be numbered 300 and the negative 301 in numerals, and the succeeding measures shall be numbered consecutively 302, 303, 304, 305, and so on, at each election. It shall be the duty of the several county clerks to print said ballot titles and numbers upon the official ballot in the order presented to them by the Secretary of State and the relative position required by law. Measures referred by the Legislative Assembly shall be designated by the heading "Referred to the People by the Legislative Assembly"; measures referred by petition shall be designated "Referendum ordered by Petition of the People"; measures proposed by initiative petition shall be designated and distinguished on the ballot by the heading "Proposed by Initiative Petition."

Section 7. The manner of voting upon measures submitted to the people shall be the same as is now or may be required and provided by law; no measure shall be adopted unless it shall receive an affirmative majority of the total number of respective votes cast on such measure and entitled to be counted under the provisions of this act; that is to say, supposing seventy thousand ballots to be properly marked on any measure, it shall not be adopted unless it shall receive more than thirty-five thousand affirmative votes. If two or more conflicting laws shall be approved by the people at the same election, the law receiving the greatest number of affirmative votes shall be paramount in all particulars as to which there is a conflict, even though such law may not have received the greatest majority of affirmative votes. If two or more conflicting amendments to the constitution shall be approved by the people at the same election, the amendment which receives the greatest number of affirmative votes shall be paramount in all particulars as to which there is conflict, even though such amendment may not have received the greatest majority of affirmative votes.

Section 8. Not later than the first Monday, of the third month next before any regular general election, nor later than thirty days before any special election, at which any proposed law, part of an act, or amendment to the constitution is to be submitted to the people, the Secretary of State shall cause to be printed in pamphlet form a true copy of the title and text of each measure to be submitted, with the number and form in which the ballot title thereof will be printed on the official ballot. The person, committee, or duly authorized officers of any organization filing any petition for the initiative, but no other person or organization, shall have the right to file with the Secretary of State for printing and distribution any argument advocating such measure; said argument shall be filed not later than the first Monday of the fourth month before the regular election at which the measure is to be voted upon. Any person, committee, or organization may file with the Secretary of State, for printing and distribution, any arguments they may desire, opposing any measure, not later than the fourth Monday of the fourth month immediately preceding such election. Arguments advocating or opposing any measures referred to the people by the Legislative Assembly, or by referendum petition, at a regular general election, shall be governed by the same rules as to time, but may be filed with the Secretary of State by any person, committee, or organization; in the case of measures submitted at a special election, all arguments in support of such measure at least sixty days before such election. But in every case the person or persons offering such arguments for printing and distribution shall pay to the Secretary of State sufficient money to pay all the expenses for paper and printing to supply one copy with every copy of the measure to be printed by the State; and he shall forthwith notify the persons offering the same of the amount of money necessary. The Secretary of State shall cause one copy of each of said arguments to be bound in the pamphlet copy of the measures to be submitted as herein provided, and all such measures and arguments to be submitted at one election shall be bound together in a single pamphlet. All the printing shall be done by the State, and the pages of said pamphlet shall be numbered consecutively from one to the end. The pages of said pamphlet shall be six by nine inches in size, and the printed matter thereon shall be set in eight point Roman-faced type, single leaded, and twenty-five ems in width, with appropriate heads and printed on sized and super-calendered paper twenty-five by thirty-eight inches, weighing fifty pounds to the ream. The title page of every measure bound in said pamphlet shall show its ballot title and ballot numbers. The title page of each argument shall show the measure or measures it favors or opposes and by what persons or organization it is issued. When such arguments are printed he shall pay the State Printer therefor from the money deposited with him and refund the surplus, if any, to the parties who paid it to him. The cost of printing, binding, and distributing the measures proposed and of binding and distributing the arguments, shall be paid by the State as a part of the state printing, it being intended that only the cost of paper and printing the arguments shall be paid by the parties presenting the same, and they shall not be charged any higher rate for such work than is paid by the State for similar work and paper. Not later than the fifty-fifth day before the regular general election at which such measures are to be voted upon, the Secretary of State shall transmit by mail, with postage fully prepaid, to every voter in the State whose address he may have, one copy of such pamphlet; *provided*, that if the Secretary shall, at or about the same time be mailing any other pamphlet to every voter, he may, if practicable, bind the matter herein provided for in the first part of said pamphlet, numbering the pages of the entire pamphlet consecutively from one to the end, or he may enclose the pamphlets under one cover. In the case of a special election he shall mail said pamphlet to every voter not less than twenty days before said special election.

Section 9. The votes on measures and questions shall be counted, canvassed, and returned by the regular boards of judges, clerks and officers, as votes for candidates are counted, canvassed and returned, and the abstract made by the several county clerks of votes on measures shall be returned to the Secretary of State on separate abstract sheets, in the manner provided by section 2833 of Bellinger and Cotton's Annotated Codes and Statutes of Oregon, for abstracts of votes for state and county officers. It shall be the duty of the Secretary of State, in the presence of the Governor, to proceed within thirty days after the election, and sooner if the returns be all received, to canvass the votes given for each measure; and the Governor shall forthwith issue his proclamation, giving the whole number of votes cast in the State for and against each measure and question, and declaring such measures as are approved by majority of those voting thereon to be in full force and effect as the law of the State of Oregon from the date of said proclamation; *provided*, that if two or more measures shall be approved at said election which are known to conflict with each other or to contain conflicting provisions he shall also proclaim which is paramount in accordance with the provisions of section 7 of this act.

Section 10. In all cities and towns which have not or may not provide by ordinance or charter for the manner of exercising the initiative and referendum powers reserved by the constitution to the people thereof, as to their municipal legislation, the duties required of the Secretary of State by this act, as to state legislation, shall be performed as to such municipal legislation by the city auditor, clerk or recorder, as the case may be; the duties required of the Governor shall be performed by the mayor as to such municipal legislation, and the duties required by this act of the Attorney-General shall be performed by the city attorney as to such municipal legislation. The provisions of this act shall apply in every city and town in all matters concerning the operation of the initiative and referendum in its municipal legislation on which such city or town has not made or does not make conflicting provisions. The printing and binding of measures and arguments in municipal legislation shall be paid for by the city in like manner as payment is provided for by the State as to State legislation by section 8 of this act, and said printing shall be done in the same manner that other municipal printing is done; distribution of said pamphlets shall be made to every voter in the city, so far as possible, by the city clerk, auditor or recorder, as the case may be, either by mail or carrier, not less than eight days before the election at which the measures are to be voted upon. Arguments supporting municipal measures shall be filed with the city clerk, auditor or recorder, not less than thirty days before the election at which they are to be voted upon; opposing arguments shall be filed not less than twenty days before said election. It is intended to make procedure in municipal legislation as nearly as practicable the same as the initiative and referendum procedure for measures relating to the people of the State at large.

Section 11. Referendum petitions against any ordinance, franchise, or resolution passed by a city council shall be signed by not less than ten per cent of the voters of said city, and said signatures shall be verified in the manner herein provided; the petition shall be filed with the city clerk, auditor, or recorder, as the case may be, within thirty days after the passage of such ordinance, resolutions or franchise. No city ordinance, resolution or franchise shall take effect and become operative until thirty days after its passage by the council and approval by the mayor, unless the same shall be passed over his veto, and in that case it shall not take effect and become operative until thirty days after such final passage, except measures necessary for the immediate preservation of the peace, health or safety of the city; and no such emergency measure shall become immediately operative unless it shall state in a separate section the reasons why it is necessary that it should become immediately operative, and shall be approved by the affirmative vote of three-fourths of all the members elected to the city council, taken by ayes and noes, and also approved by the mayor.

Section 12. If any ordinance, charter or amendment to the charter of any city shall be proposed by initiative petition, said petition shall be filed with the city clerk, auditor or recorder, as the case may be, and he shall transmit it to the next session of the city council. The council shall either ordain or reject the same, as proposed, within thirty days thereafter, and if the council shall reject said proposed ordinance or amendment, or shall take no action thereon, then the city clerk, auditor or recorder, as the case may be, shall submit the same to the voters of the city or town at the next ensuing election held therein not less than ninety days after the same was first presented to the city council. The council may ordain said ordinance or amendment and refer it to the people, or it may ordain such ordinance without referring it to the people, and in that case it shall be subject to referendum petition in like manner as other ordinances; if the council shall reject said ordinance or amendment, or take no action thereon, it may ordain a competing ordinance or amendment, which shall be submitted by the city clerk, auditor or recorder, as the case may be, to the people of the said city or town, at the same election at which said initiative proposal is submitted. Such competing ordinance or amendment, if any, shall be prepared by the council and ordained within thirty days allowed for its action on the measure proposed by initiative petition. The mayor shall not have power to veto either of such measures. If conflicting ordinances or charter amendments shall be submitted to the people at the same election, and two or more of such conflicting measures shall be approved by the people, then the measure which shall have received the greatest number of affirmative votes shall be paramount in all particulars

The Initiative and Referendum

as to which there is conflict, even though such measure may not have received the greatest majority. Amendments to any city charter may be proposed and submitted to the people by the city council, with or without an initiative petition, but the same shall be filed with the city clerk for submission not less than sixty days before the election at which they are to be voted upon, and no amendment of a city charter shall be effective until it is approved by a majority of the votes cast thereon by the people of the city or town to which it applies. The city council may by ordinance order special elections to vote on municipal measures.

Section 13. Every person who is a qualified elector of the State of Oregon may sign a petition for the referendum or for the initiative for any measure which he is legally entitled to vote upon. Any person signing any name other than his own to any petition, or knowingly signing his name more than once for the same measure at one election, or who is not at the time of signing the same a legal voter of this State, or any officer or person wilfully violating any provision of this statute, shall, upon conviction thereof, be punished by a fine not exceeding $500, or by imprisonment in the penitentiary not exceeding two years, or by both such fine and imprisonment, in the discretion of the court before which such conviction shall be had.

Section 14. That an act entitled "An act making effective the initiative and referendum provisions of Section 1 of Article IV of the constitution of the State of Oregon, and regulating elections thereunder, and providing penalties for violations of the provisions of this act," approved February 24, 1903, Laws of Oregon, regular session, page 244, be and the same is hereby repealed.

Section 15. Whereas, there is no law to carry into effect the provisions of Section 1, Article IV of the constitution of Oregon, as to local, special, and municipal legislation, and of Section 2 of Article XI of the constitution, and because question has been raised as to the power of cities to amend their charters without an enabling act, and because the act herein repealed is not effective, therefore it is the judgment of this Legislative Assembly that an emergency exists, and that it is necessary for the public safety that this law shall become operative upon its approval by the Governor; therefore, this act shall take effect and be in force immediately upon its approval by the Governor.

Filed in the office of the Secretary of State February 25, 1907.[1]

Pages from a Publicity Pamphlet

[In accordance with the above act, the Secretary of State issued a "Publicity Pamphlet" in 1908 and 1910. Each voter received a copy of this voter's text-book fifty-five days before the election. The following bill extending the direct primary to presidential nominations was adopted Nov. 8, 1910, by a vote of 43,353 for, to 41,624 against. The bill and the arguments on it and on other referenda are given in full in order to illustrate how the law-makers are prepared for election day.]

A BILL

TO BE SUBMITTED TO THE LEGAL ELECTORS OF THE STATE OF OREGON FOR THEIR APPROVAL OR REJECTION
AT THE
REGULAR GENERAL ELECTION
TO BE HELD
ON THE EIGHTH DAY OF NOVEMBER, 1910

To propose by initiative petition a law to amend Section 2 of the Direct Primary Nominating Elections Law which was proposed by initiative petition and approved by the people of Oregon at the general election in June, 1904, and printed in the volume of the General Laws of Oregon for the year 1905, at pages 7 to 50 thereof; etc.

By initiative petition filed in the office of the Secretary of State July 7, 1910, in accordance with the provisions of Chapter 226, General Laws of Oregon, 1907

Printed in pursuance of Section 8 of Chapter 226, Laws of 1907.
Secretary of State.

---

[1] *Statutes of the State of Oregon Relating to Elections*, pp. 112 ff.

The Initiative and Referendum

The following is the form and number in which the question will be printed on the official ballot: —

PROPOSED BY INITIATIVE PETITION

A bill for a law to amend the direct primary law by extending its provisions to presidential nominations, allowing voters to designate their choice for their party candidate for President and Vice-President; for direct nomination of party candidates for presidential electors; for election by party voters of delegates to their party national nominating conventions, each voter voting for one delegate; for payment of delegates' actual traveling expenses, not exceeding two hundred dollars for each delegate, and extending the publicity rights of candidates in the State nominating and general election campaign books. Vote YES or NO.

356. Yes.

357. No.

[On Official Ballot, Nos. 356 and 357.]

A BILL

For a law to amend Section 2 of the Direct Primary Nominating Elections Law which was proposed by initiative petition and approved by the people of Oregon at the general election in June, 1904, and printed in the volume of the General Laws of Oregon for the year 1905, at pages 7 to 50 thereof; to provide for the expression, by the qualified voters of the several political parties subject to the said direct primary law, of their choice for nomination by their party for President and Vice-President of the United States; to provide for and regulate direct primary nominating elections for the election of said political parties' delegates to their respective national conventions, and for the payment of such delegates' necessary expenses, not exceeding two hundred dollars for any delegate; for the nomination of party candidates for the office of presidential elector; for space in the party and State campaign books to set forth the merits of aspirants for election and for nomination, and of candidates for the offices of President and Vice-President of the United States, of candidates for offices to be voted for in the State at large, and of candidates for United States Senators and Representatives in Congress.

Be it enacted by the People of the State of Oregon:

Section 1. That Section 2 of the Direct Primary Nominating Elections Law, which was proposed by initiative petition and enacted by the people of Oregon at the general election in June, 1904, as the same is printed in the volume of the General Laws of Oregon for the year 1905, at pages 7 to 50 thereof, be and the same is hereby amended to read as follows:

Section 2. On the forty-fifth day preceding any election (except special elections to fill vacancies, presidential elections, municipal elections in towns or cities having a population of less than two thousand, and school elections) at which public officers in this State and in any district or county, and in any city having a population of two thousand or more at which public officers *(sic)* are to be elected, except as provided in Section 6 of this law as to time in certain cities and towns, a primary nominating election shall be held in accordance with this law in the several election precincts comprised within the territory for which such officers are to be elected at the ensuing election, which shall be known as the primary nominating election, for the purpose of choosing candidates by the political parties, subject to the provisions of this law, for Senator in Congress and all other elective State, district, county, precinct, city, ward and all other officers, and delegates to any constitutional convention or conventions that may hereafter be called, who are to be chosen at the ensuing election wholly by electors within this State or any subdivision of this State, and also for choosing and electing the county central committee-men by the several parties subject to the provisions of this law. Provided:

(*a*) In the years when a President and Vice-President of the United States are to be elected, said primary nominating election shall be held on the forty-fifth day before the first Monday in June of said year; and all laws pertaining to the nomination of candidates, registration of voters and all other things incident and pertaining to the holding of the regular biennial nominating election, shall be enforced and effected the same number of days before the first Monday in June that they were under the said nominating election law immediately before the change in the date of the regular election from the first Monday in June to the first Tuesday after the first Monday in November.

(*b*) When candidates for the offices of President and Vice-President of the United States are to be nominated, every qualified elector of a political party subject to this law shall have opportunity to vote his preference, on his party nominating ballot, for his choice for one person to be the candidate of his political party for President, and one person to be the candidate of his political party for Vice-President of the United States, either by writing the names of such persons in blank spaces to be left on said ballot for that purpose, or by marking with a cross before the printed names of the persons of his choice, as in the case of other nominations. The names of any persons shall be so printed on said ballots solely on the petition of their political supporters in Oregon, without such persons themselves signing any petition, signature or acceptance. The names of persons in such political party who shall be presented by petition of their supporters for nomination to be party candidates for the office of President or

Vice-President of the United States, shall be printed on the nominating official ballot, and the ballots shall be marked, and the votes shall be counted, canvassed and returned in like manner and under the same conditions as to names, petitions and other matters, as far as the same are applicable, as the names and petitions of aspirants for the party nominations for the office of Governor and for United States Senator in Congress are or may be by law required to be marked, filed, counted, canvassed and returned.

(c) The members of the political parties subject to this law shall elect their party delegates to their national conventions for the nomination of their party candidates for President and Vice-President of the United States, and shall nominate candidates for their party presidential electors at such nominating election. The Governor shall grant a certificate of election to each of the delegates so elected, which certificates shall show the number of votes received in the State by each person of such delegate's political party for nomination as its candidate for President and Vice-President. Nominating petitions for the office of delegate to the respective party national conventions, to be chosen and elected at said nominating election, shall be sufficient if they contain a number of signatures of the members of the party equal to one per cent of the party vote in the State at the last preceding election for Representative in Congress; provided that not more than five hundred signatures shall be required on any such petition. Every qualified voter shall have the right at such nominating election to vote for the election of one person and no more to the office of national delegate for his party, and to vote for the nomination of one aspirant and no more for the office of presidential elector as the candidate of his party. A number of such candidates equal to the number of delegates to be elected by each party which is subject to the provisions of this law, receiving, respectively, each for himself, the highest number of votes for such office, shall be thereby elected. Every political party subject to the provisions of this law shall be entitled to nominate, at said nominating election, as many candidates for the office of presidential elector as there are such officers to be elected; that number of aspirants in every such party who shall receive, respectively, each for himself, the highest number of votes of his party for that nomination, shall be thereby nominated as a candidate of his political party for the office of presidential elector.

(*d*) Every delegate to a national convention of a political party recognized as such organization by the laws of Oregon, shall receive from the State treasury the amount of his travelling expenses necessarily spent in actual attendance upon said convention, as his account may be audited and allowed by the Secretary of State, but in no case to exceed two hundred dollars for each delegate; provided, that such expenses shall never be paid to any greater number of delegates of any political party than would be allowed such party under the plan by which the number of delegates to the Republican National Convention was fixed for the Republican party of Oregon in the year 1908. The election of such national delegates for political parties not subject to the Direct Primary Nominating Elections Law shall be certified in like manner as nominations of candidates of such political parties for elective public offices. Every such delegate to a national convention to nominate candidates for President and Vice-President, shall subscribe an oath of office that he will uphold the Constitution and laws of the United States and of the State of Oregon, and that he will, as such officer and delegate, to the best of his judgment and ability, faithfully carry out the wishes of his political party as expressed by its voters at the time of his election.

(*e*) The committee or organization which shall file a petition to place the name of any person on the nominating ballot of their political party to be voted for by its members for expression of their choice for nomination as the candidate of such party for President or Vice-Presedent of the United States, shall have the right, upon payment therefor, to four pages of printed space in the campaign books of such political party provided for by Sections 4 and 5 of the law proposed by initiative petition and enacted by the people of Oregon at the general election in June, 1908, entitled, "A bill to propose by initiative petition a law to limit candidates' election expenses; to define, prevent and punish corrupt and illegal practices in nominations and elections; to secure and protect the purity of the ballot; to amend Section 2775 of Bellinger and Cotton's Annotated Codes and Statutes of Oregon; to provide for furnishing information to the electors and to provide the manner of conducting contests for nominations and elections in certain cases," as printed on pages 15 to 38 of the General Laws of Oregon for the year 1909. In this space said committee shall set forth their statement of the reasons why such person should be voted for and chosen by the members of their party in Oregon and in the Nation as its candidate. Any qualified elector of any such political party who favors or opposes the nomination of any person by his own political party as its candidate for President or Vice-President of the United States, may have not exceeding four pages of space in his aforesaid party nominating campaign book, at a cost of one hundred dollars per printed page, to set forth his reasons therefor.

(f) Every person regularly nominated by a political party, recognized as such by the laws of Oregon, for President or Vice-President of the United States, or for any office to be voted for by the electors of the State at large, or for Senator or Representative in Congress, shall be entitled to use four pages of printed space in the State campaign book provided for by Sections 6 and 7 of the above entitled "Law to limit candidates' election expenses; to define, prevent and punish corrupt and illegal practices in nominations and elections; to secure and protect the purity of the ballot; to amend Section 2775 of Bellinger and Cotton's Annotated Codes and Statutes of Oregon; to provide for furnishing information to the electors and to provide the manner of conducting contests for nominations and elections in certain cases," as printed on pages 15 to 38 of the volume of the General Laws of Oregon for 1909. In this space, the candidate, or his supporters with his written permission filed with the Secretary of State, may set forth the reasons why he should be elected. No charge shall be made against candidates for President and Vice-President of the United States for this printed space. The other candidates above named shall pay at the rate of one hundred dollars per printed page for said space, and said payment shall not be counted as a part of the ten per cent of one year's salary that each candidate is allowed to spend for campaign purposes. If this bill shall be approved by the people the title of the bill shall stand as the title of the law.

ARGUMENT
(affirmative)
SUBMITTED BY
THE PEOPLE'S POWER LEAGUE OF OREGON
in favor of the measure designated on the official ballot as follows:

PROPOSED BY INITIATIVE PETITION

A bill for a law to amend the direct primary law by extending its provisions to presidential nominations, allowing voters to designate their choice for their party candidates for President and Vice-President; for direct nomination of party candidates for presidential electors; for election by party voters of delegates to their party national nominating conventions, each voter voting for one delegate; for payment of delegates' actual travelling expenses, not exceeding two hundred dollars for each delegate, and extending the publicity rights of candidates in the State nominating and general election campaign books.   Vote YES or NO.

356.	Yes.
357.	No.

THE PEOPLE'S POWER LEAGUE OF OREGON

offers this argument to explain and advocate the approval by the people of the following measures [1] proposed by the League by initiative petitions: —

Official Ballot No. 356. — A bill for a law to extend the Direct Primary Nominating Elections Law to presidential campaigns and nominations, to delegates to national conventions and to presidential electors by amending Section 2.

Official Ballot No. 360. — A constitutional amendment to provide a plan for the election of members of the Legislative Assembly by proportional representation; increase the people's initiative, referendum and recall powers; prevent log-rolling, hasty legislation and abuse of the emergency clause, and generally to provide for such organization of the Legislative Assembly as will fairly represent the people of Oregon and obtain performance of legislative duties.

Official Ballot No. 358. — A bill for a law to provide for impartial inspection and reports on State and local public offices, and publication of such reports, and of general news of progress in government, in the Oregon Official Gazette magazine to be mailed free to every registered voter.

Official Ballot No. 362. — A constitutional amendment to allow three-fourths of a jury to render a verdict in civil cases, and to generally simplify court procedure, especially appeals to the Supreme Court.

The following list gives the names of the officers, executive committee, and members of the People's Power League: —

OFFICERS

Ben Selling, of Portland . . . . *President*
George M. Orton, of Portland . . *Vice-President*
B. Lee Paget, of Portland . . . *Treasurer*
W. S. U'Ren, of Oregon City . . *Secretary*

[1] See above, p. 46 for the vote on these measures.

The Initiative and Referendum

EXECUTIVE COMMITTEE

| Henry Hahn | Will Daly | C. H. Gram |

[and eleven others]

MEMBERS

| Henry E. McGinn | J. P. Rasmussen | V. R. Hyde |

[and eighty others]

This league is largely composed of the same group of men who proposed the initiative and referendum amendment in 1902, the direct primary law in 1904, and home rule for cities and other measures of the People's Power League of 1906, and the recall and other People's Power measures in 1908. Its object is to perfect the direct power of the voters of Oregon over their State and local government in all its branches and officers. Many of our members were with Mr. Ed. Bingham in 1890 in his agitation for the Australian ballot law and the registration law in 1899.

We believe the approval of the above four measures by the people will greatly strengthen and improve the necessary practical methods by which the voters of Oregon will be able to quickly, directly and effectively use their supreme power over the officers as well as the laws of our State and local government, and at the same time to have accurate and full knowledge of the subjects on which they act.

DIRECT PRIMARY LAW AMENDMENT

The purpose of the bill extending the Direct Primary Nominations Law to presidential campaigns and nominations is to increase the people's power in four ways: —

1. Giving voters the right to express upon the official ballots, in the primaries, their choice for their party candidates for President and Vice-President (Section 2b).

2. Allowing all members of the political parties that are subject to the direct primary law to elect their party delegates to their national conventions (Section 2c).

3. Giving party voters the power to nominate their party candidates for presidential electors (Section 2c).

4. Extending the publicity rights of candidates in the party and State campaign books provided for by the corrupt practices law and including the above named classes of candidates for party nominations (Section 2e).

The people of Oregon have learned, and those in other states are learning, that the power to nominate is more important than the power to elect. When members of a party give the power of nomination to a few delegates in a convention, they open the door for selfish interests, combinations and fraud to control the convention. To delegate the power of nomination is to encourage carelessness among the voters. The system of convention nominations often causes the candidate to feel under greater obligation to the delegates and bosses than he does to the people. The candidate who is responsible to all the voters will give better service to the people than one who is under obligations to a party boss, a political machine or a few delegates.

Under the convention system, as is well known, a very few men make up the "slate" in the primaries, and delegates to state and national conventions are often chosen long before the nominating conventions are held. It is well known, too, that men who oppose a political machine are very seldom selected as delegates to a state or national convention.

The people of Oregon and of some other states have found that direct nominations of candidates for city, county and state officers are of benefit to the people. The extension of the direct primary system to candidates for President and Vice-President would be of much greater advantage to the people because of the great power of these officers.

In Mexico to-day we see the result of a great federal political machine controlled by the President. Under the convention system of appointing delegates to the national conventions it is possible for the same result to be brought about by the power of our President to control office-holders and build a huge political machine, with which he may dictate the nomination of his successor. This will be impossible if the people elect and instruct their own delegates and pay the necessary travelling expenses. The total expense to the State could not exceed eight thousand dollars at the 1912 election. It should be worth more than that to the earners of three dollars a day or less to make it possible that they should be represented by men of their own class in the national conventions that nominate the party candidates for President and Vice-President. It should be worth more than that to the man whose income is more than three dollars a day to know that the State and his political party are not deprived of the services of any citizen because he cannot afford to pay his travelling expenses to the convention, and also to know that every class of citizens within the party had an equal chance to be fairly represented among the delegates from Oregon who help to nominate the party candidates for President and Vice-President.

In the interest of American liberty and progress, the taking over by the people of the United States of this direct power to nominate the candidates for President and Vice-President, is of the utmost importance. No other power has so great influence on the daily lives and prosperity of the citizens as the President. He is as much more important than any State officers as the Governor is more important than the county judge. Oregon has already developed the steps necessary for the application of the principle of direct nominations, and now it remains only to extend and apply these principles to the nomination of President and Vice-President and the election of delegates to the respective national conventions. When this shall be done by the Nation, the people of the United States may directly exert and control all the influence and power nationally that the people of Oregon now have in the nomination and election of local candidates for office. The other States will very quickly follow the example of any State that succeeds in the practical application of these principles in its election laws.

PEOPLE'S POWER LEGISLATIVE AMENDMENT

The proposed amendment of Article IV of the Constitution, if approved by the voters, will increase the people's power; further restrict the powers of the legislature and of city councils; give legislators a salary equal to fair wages for their time, so that any qualified farmer, clerk, teacher or wage-worker can afford to serve in the legislature; secure election of legislators by equal proportions of the votes cast instead of by mere pluralities or actual minorities; prevent log-rolling, hasty legislation, abuse of the emergency clause and wasteful increase of appropriations.

Increase of People's Power. — The initiative and referendum are extended to every form of legislative act, ordinance and resolution. Power to alter, amend or repeal any law is expressly reserved by the people. The recall power of the people is increased (in Section 3) by giving them the right to recall the whole Legislative Assembly, or the Senate, or the House of Representatives, or any Senators or Representatives. The amendment increases the local initiative and referendum powers of the people.

Abuse of the Emergency. — Section 1c provides that no emergency law or ordinance can be made by the legislature or a city council unless three-fourths of all the members elected vote for the emergency on a separate roll call, and provides for referendum petitions against emergency measures; also, that an emergency shall not be declared on any measure creating or abolishing any office or to change the salary, term or duties of any officer. Section 1c prohibits the legislature or city council from amending or repealing any law or ordinance enacted by the people unless three-fourths of the members of the legislature, or a city council, vote for the repeal or amendment of the law or ordinance, as the case may be.

By Section 1d every attempt to grant a franchise or use of roads, streets or any other public property is subject to referendum by petition. No partly private corporation, like a railroad company, will be able to condemn property in towns or cities, and a purely private corporation cannot be allowed to condemn any property.

Term and Salary of Legislators. — Section 2 provides that Senators and Representatives shall be elected for a term of six years, and abolishes the "hold-over" system for Senators. Section 28 provides that each Senator and each Representative shall receive an annual salary of $350 and the amount of his necessary fares in going to and returning from the State Capital.

Is $350 a year too much to pay a legislator? This amendment will be approved or rejected by the voters who get $3 a day or less. Four out of five wage-workers, teachers, and farmers of Oregon do not make more than $3 a day. These men can be elected by the proportional system of elections, but they cannot serve in the legislature for $60 a year. A campaign generally takes about thirty days of a candidate's time, and if he is elected the session takes about forty more. As a rule, his campaign will cost him not less than $100; expenses at Salem, $100; loss of seventy days at $3 a day means a loss of $210; total cost of serving the people for one session, $410, and the State pays him now $120 for two years; so the net average loss to the member is $290. Every additional day the legislator gives to the State's business is that much more loss to himself.

Can the people afford to deprive themselves of the services of a qualified citizen because he is too poor to make the sacrifice now necessary to serve them? Four out of five of the voters of Oregon cannot afford to be candidates for the legislature. Are the teachers, farmers, and wage-workers who get $3 a day less intelligent or patriotic than the men who get $10 or $15 a day? Is it strange that most members of the legislature are lawyers, bankers, merchants and doctors, or professional politicians? The salary makes no difference to them. They would be glad to take the office without any salary. Surely $350 a year is not more salary than is necessary to make it possible for all classes of bread-winners to be represented in the legislature of Oregon.

The reason for the six-year term is that a member of the legislature is far more useful in his second than in his first session; and one who has served several sessions is more useful than a new member. If this amendment is adopted, every member will serve six years unless he is so much of a failure that his people at home recall him. State Senators are now elected for four years, and the Senate is generally believed to be a more efficient body than the House, but it is because of the Senators' longer experience and not because of greater natural ability.

The British House of Commons is one of the most efficient legislative bodies in the world. Its members are elected for seven years, but they cannot be recalled as the Oregon legislature can be if the voters approve this amendment. With the extensive recall power reserved by the people in this amendment, there can be no harm from the six-year term, and the people will have all the advantages of the efficiency that comes from long experience in legislative work. Annual sessions of the legislature are provided because if appropriations are made for only one year at a time, the legislators can estimate closely the State's actual needs and expenses, but where the appropriation is for two years, a good margin must be left for unforeseen expenses, and this is a temptation to extravagance. The difference will more than pay for the yearly session.

Proportional Representation. — The amendment provides (Section 4) that any candidate for State Representative shall be elected if he is voted for by one-sixtieth of the voters of the State, and that any candidate for State Senator shall be elected if he is voted for by one-thirtieth of the voters of the State. Section 4a provides for the nomination of candidates for the Senate and House. Every voter will have the right to vote for one candidate for State Representative and no more, and for one candidate for State Senator and no more (Section 4a). No change whatever is made in the present form of the ballot, or the manner of voting, nor in the counting of the ballots by the precinct judges and county clerks. Section 4b tells how the votes are to be canvassed by the

The Initiative and Referendum

Secretary of State for all the candidates for the legislature, and the work in his office is very simple.

Let us take, for example, the general election of 1908 and suppose that the whole number of votes cast in the State by the different parties for Representatives in the Legislative Assembly is the same as at that election for Representatives in Congress. The abstract in the Secretary of State's office of votes for Representatives in the Legislative Assembly would show a total of 110,252 votes; he would divide that number by 60, being the number of Representatives to be elected, and the quotient would be the number of votes necessary to insure the election of one Representative; it is called the "quota," and in this case would be 1837 votes. The Secretary of State would then use the quota to divide the total number of votes received by all the candidates of the Republican party in the State; that is, he would divide 67,468 votes by the quota 1837; the result shows that the Republican party would have 36 full quotas of votes and be thereby entitled to 36 seats for Representatives by full quotas, and would have a remainder of 1336 votes. Thirty-six Republicans would thus be elected by full quotas, beginning with that Republican candidate who had the highest number of votes for himself and going downward to the one who had the thirty-sixth highest number of votes for himself. In this particular example the Republican party would also be entitled to one seat for its remainder of 1336 votes, and this would be given to the candidate of that party having the next highest number of votes for himself, so that the 37 Republican candidates, the lowest of whom received a higher number of votes than any of the remaining 23 Republican candidates, would thereby be elected. The 23 Republican candidates having the lowest number of votes would be defeated.

The Secretary of State would treat the votes and candidates of the other parties in exactly the same manner. The Democrats have 28,706 votes, which divided by the quota of 1837 would show that party entitled to 15 seats by full quotas and there would be a remainder of 1151 votes.

This would be the second highest remainder and the Democrats would take one seat for that. The 16 Democrats who had personally, each for himself, the highest number of Democratic votes, would be thereby elected, and the remaining 44 Democratic candidates would be defeated. The Socialists have 8204 votes, which would entitle that party to four seats by full quotas and leave a remainder of 836 votes. The Prohibitionists have 5874 votes, which would entitle that party to three seats by full quotas and would leave a remainder of 363 votes. In this example 58 Representatives would be elected by full quotas of votes in four different parties and two seats must be filled by remainders; these two seats are distributed as above stated to the different parties having the highest remainders, beginning with that one whose remainder is nearest to the full quota of 1837 votes.

The work would be no more difficult in the Secretary of State's office if the vote were split up among a dozen different parties, but the system forces the existing parties to put forth as candidates their very best men; for that reason and because every new opinion in any party is able by this system at every election to elect its own just proportion of the party members, proportional representation satisfies in very great degree the demands that under the plurality system cause the continual effort to create new political parties. But the system proposed by this amendment insures the election of any independent or new party candidate for Representative who receives one-sixtieth of the whole vote of the State.

The process is exactly the same for the election of State Senators (Section 4e), except that the whole number of votes is to be divided by thirty instead of by sixty, because only thirty Senators are to be elected.

The theory under the plurality system is that the member when elected becomes the Representative of those who opposed as well as those who elected him. It is impractical and wrong; and legislators refuse to take any stock in it. Where the plurality that elects a legislator wants one thing, and the divided majority that failed to defeat him does not want that thing, it is impossible for that member to represent both sides; nevertheless, the divided majority composed of many minorities has a right to representation; and under this simple plan of proportional representation these minorities will be fairly represented by members of their own choice.

There is nothing in the amendment to prevent each party from nominating in the State a full list of sixty candidates for the office of Representative, but the smaller parties are not likely to do so because there will be no advantage in the sacrifice. For example, Clackamas County is a typical nominating district and the Representative section of the ballot at the general election would look something like this: —

FOR REPRESENTATIVE	VOTE FOR ONE
64 Brown, C. H.	
65 Smith, D. C.	Republican
66 Young, D. C.	
67 Lyte, R. A.	
68 Allen, A. C.	Democrat
69 White, R. M.	
70 Linn, E. C.	
71 Green, F. T.	Socialist
72 Arnold, G. R.	
73 Daly, T. C.	
74 Little, O. A.	Prohibitionist
75 Taylor, R. C.	

The following is an example of the Secretary of State's official canvass, except that he would give the names of the successful candidates of each party: —

	CANDIDATES IN THE STATE	WHOLE NO. OF VOTES FOR ALL CANDIDATES	QUOTAS, OR NUMBER OF 60THS OF THE WHOLE VOTE	REMAINDER OF VOTES FOR EACH PARTY
Republican	60	67,468	36	1336
Democrat	60	28,706	15	1151
Socialist	60	8,204	4	856
Prohibitionist	60	5,874	3	363
	240	110,252	58	3,686

Each organization is entitled to as many seats as it has full quotas of votes; and in the above example the four different organizations get fifty-eight seats by full quotas, two get seats by the highest remainders, and thus the sixty seats are filled.

Section 10 provides that the Speaker of the House must be chosen by the members but he shall not be a member. He shall not appoint standing committees and shall have no vote. The purpose is to obtain a Speaker who shall be a non-partisan presiding officer and nothing more than that. He is to have no more power than the presiding officer of the German Reichstag or the British House of Commons. The President of the Senate is to be chosen by the Senators in the same way and to have the same power and no more authority in the Senate. These officers will thus have no important committee places to trade for their own election, and therefore will be chosen by the members solely for their qualifications and fairness.

Hasty Legislation. — The six-year term leaves no excuse for hasty legislation. When a bill is introduced it is placed on the calendar and may be passed at any session during the six-year term of that legislature, so that there will be plenty of time for study of the bill. If a bill is introduced after the twentieth day of a session it shall not be passed at that session unless it is an emergency measure. (See Section 31.)

Log-rolling. — Section 30 revises the oath to be taken by a legislator, and is designed to prevent log-rolling and legislation by caucus. The experience of the people of Oregon with Statement No. 1 gives reason to believe that most of the legislators will keep that oath.

Section 33, relating to clerks for the Senate and House committees, will probably save $10,000 a year to the people of Oregon, as compared with the present practice.

OFFICIAL GAZETTE BILL

The purpose of this bill is to establish a publicly-owned magazine, or official gazette, to tell the people of Oregon about their State and local government, and to create a board of three People's Inspectors of Government, who shall edit the gazette and perform the duties defined in Sections 2, 3 and 4 of the bill. Sections 3 and 4 tell what is to be published in the gazette. Section 7 tells how the (3) People's Inspectors of Government are to be elected in 1912 and thereafter, and Section 6 how they are to be appointed this year if the voters approve this bill. Section 8 provides for the expenses and salaries of the inspectors. The gazette is to be mailed free to every registered voter; expense of publishing the gazette is limited to $1 a year for each registered voter, and will probably not exceed 60 cents per voter.

How can all the voters get all the important news of government? Congress publishes the Congressional Record, which tells what is said in Congress but does not give the much more important information as to what is done; the Department of Agriculture prints thousands of valuable reports for free distribution; the Treasury Department prints statistical abstracts and other important news, and the Interstate Commerce Commission publishes valuable reports; and from all of these the daily and weekly newspapers get important information that they publish as news for their readers. The Governor and all other public officers make reports, which are printed once in two years and distributed free; but long, detailed tables of statistics make up the greater part of these reports. The census bulletins are distributed free, and the newspapers publish as news many columns from the census reports.

The city of Denver, Colorado, publishes "Denver Municipal Facts" every week, and distributes the paper to the voters free. San Francisco publishes a paper called the "Municipal Report," which is distributed free. The purpose of all these reports is to give information to the voters concerning their government, but most of these publications are in some degree partisan. All of them together give only a little of the important news of government and to only a very few of the voters.

Oregon publishes a pamphlet of measures to be voted on, with arguments in favor of and against the measures, and mails it free to every registered voter. The proposed Oregon Official Gazette is an extension of the State pamphlet idea in that it is to be printed every two months, and differs from the other experiments in providing for absolutely non-partisan reports and all the news of government for all the voters, by officers who have no other duties than those defined in the proposed bill, who will get their offices, their authority and their appropriations directly from the people, and are responsible directly to the people and to no one else.

Need for Inspectors. — The people of Oregon pay $11,888,639.89 (almost twelve million dollars) every year of direct public taxes on property; they pay also at least another million dollars for poll and occupation taxes and licenses. These sums do not include any of the indirect taxes the people of Oregon pay to support the national government. Many business men say that if the State, county, city and district governments of Oregon were managed under an efficient business system, the people could get better public service for eight million dollars than they now get for thirteen million dollars.

A number of different plans have been published showing how an efficient business organization of State, city and county governments could be made to save the taxpayers at least five million dollars a year. The gazette, going every two months to every voter, will give the people ample opportunity to consider and discuss such proposals.

By such comparison of ideas and criticism of measures as will be possible in the gazette, the people will make a system for applying business principles to government business. The savings by such a system in one year would pay the cost of the gazette for fifty years at the estimated rate of expense.

Need for the Official Gazette. — To show the necessity for an official gazette, which would be owned and controlled by the people of Oregon, we quote the following from the *New York Evening Post* of June 9, 1910: —

As a protest against the daily journalism with which Boston is now favored or afflicted, one hundred and thirty-nine citizens have supplied the capital for a new weekly entitled the Boston Common, six issues of which have now appeared. No person is permitted to subscribe for less than $100 or more than $1000 worth of stock, and the names of the stockholders can be had on application at the office. The purpose of this weekly is thus stated: —

"The motive of the organization is to publish for Boston and New England a weekly journal of politics, industry, letters and criticism, the primary purpose of which is public service rather than private profit, and to secure for this publication absolute freedom from partisanship, sectarianism, prejudice and the control and muzzling of influence."

It is undubitably a serious state of affairs when 139 citizens, with no desire to enter journalism as a business venture, find it necessary to indict not only the ability of the press but its trustworthiness. It is evident that not one of Boston's many newspapers has convinced this group of men of its freedom from party or personal bias and from a malign counting-room influence.

In this connection we respectfully commend to all the voters of Oregon the following "General Report of the Committee on Legislation" which was unanimously approved and adopted by the Oregon State Grange, May 17, 1910: —

We do most earnestly urge the members of our order and the voters of Oregon, under all circumstances and at all times, to advocate and vote for every measure which will increase the power of the people of Oregon to control every department of their government, especially in applying just methods of taxation and the prudent spending of public money. *The voters can never get too much or too direct power of self-government, nor become too perfect in its practice.*

That "knowledge is power" is as true in the science and business of government by the people for the people as it is in any other science or business. Through the proposed gazette magazine, every citizen can get knowledge of government that no citizen can possibly get without it, and can get reliable information every two months about every department of our State and local government. The people cannot get this information now from any source, and they cannot get it in the future unless they pay for it themselves as a public undertaking.

This bill for the People's Inspectors of Government and Editors of the Gazette, to be mailed to every registered voter, was most bitterly condemned by the Lawyers' State Bar Association at Portland in May, 1910. About thirty-five out of more than 500 members were present. The light that such a magazine would give all the citizens about the ways that are dark and the tricks that are profitable to street railroads and other public service corporations is reason enough for the fierce opposition to this bill by all the corporation lawyers, and especially those at the head of the State Bar Association.

JUDICIARY AMENDMENTS

ARTICLE VII

The purpose of this amendment is to remove restrictions on the power of the people to make a law for any kind of court they want; to allow the people and the legislature to transfer to the circuit court the law and probate business of the county judge in counties where that can be done to good advantage; to simplify

The Initiative and Referendum 117

procedure on appeals to the Supreme Court and remove the pretext for new trials in those cases in which substantial justice is done by the verdict and judgment, but in which the trial court may have made a technical mistake; or if the verdict is just and the judgment is not, to make it the duty of the Supreme Court to enter the proper judgment, if that can be done, instead of sending the case back for a new trial; to allow the Supreme Court to take original jurisdiction in important cases of habeas corpus, mandamus and quo warranto, the latter being used principally to try the title to offices; to prevent mistrials and hung juries, by allowing three-fourths of a jury to render a verdict in civil cases. The amendment also removes the constitutional restrictions on the power of the people and the legislature over the offices of the county clerk, the sheriff, the county judge, and the district attorney.

Many states now allow a majority of the jury in civil cases to render a verdict. Usually three-fourths of the jury is required to render a verdict. No state has gone back to the old system of unanimous verdict in civil cases, after having experience with the majority verdict.

President Taft, speaking at St. Louis on the American Court Procedure, said: —

No, all I am appealing for is justice and a square deal — not especially for myself; indeed, I am in a position where I can get along better than some of the rest without it; but I am appealing for justice in dealing with all classes.

I said *all* classes. Of course, practically, it is pretty hard to give it. To our Socialistic friends, who are engaged in decrying our present institutions, I could furnish a good deal better ground for their complaints than they give themselves. I have talked about this before, and it is not a new theme with me. *I think if they were to object to our administration of justice and the delays in it arising from the traditional methods pursued in courts, by which the man with the longest purse has the advantage, because the litigation is drawn out, they would be getting, as the children say, "pretty warm" in reaching a subject that will bear full discussion, and upon which we shall have to have a very decided reform.*

Every voter knows of hung juries in civil cases, followed by new trials, appeals to the Supreme Court, reversals and another new trial, and perhaps yet another appeal to the Supreme Court. There have been such cases in the Oregon courts. One purpose of this amendment is to make that kind of injustice impossible in which the corporation or the rich man wins because of the longest purse.

Respectfully submitted to the electors of Oregon by the
PEOPLE'S POWER LEAGUE OF OREGON.

ARGUMENT

(negative)

SUBMITTED BY

E. W. McComas, L. Woldenberg, E. J. Sommerville, R. R. Corey, Geo. W. Hyatt, Frank E. Alley, W. H. Ragsdale, R. H. DeArmond, J. W. Donnelly, C. C. Wilson, C. N. McArthur, L. L. Mann, Timothy Mahoney, J. C. Smith and Ben Petigrow,

opposing the measure designated on the official ballot as follows:

PROPOSED BY INITIATIVE PETITION

A bill for a law to amend the direct primary law by extending its provisions to presidential nominations, allowing voters to designate their choice for their party candidate for President and Vice-President; for direct nomination of party candidates for presidential electors; for election by party voters of delegates to their party national nominating conventions, each voter voting for one delegate; for payment of delegates' actual travelling expenses, not exceeding two hun-

The Initiative and Referendum

dred dollars for each delegate, and extending the publicity rights of candidates in the State nominating and general election campaign books. Vote **YES** or **NO**.

356.	Yes.
357.	No.

THE PEOPLE ARE URGED TO VOTE "NO" ON THIS MEASURE FOR THE FOLLOWING REASONS:—

1. The delegates to political conventions are not public officials, but are representatives of their respective political parties, and *the taxpayers of the State should not be called upon* to pay railroad fare, hotel bills, etc. for these junketing trips. If this measure is approved, there will be an additional burden of several thousand dollars heaped upon the shoulders of the taxpayers every four years.

2. This bill is unfair in that it recognizes only the Republican and Democratic parties. *The Socialists, Prohibitionists, and members of other parties are not recognized.* If members of these last named parties go to conventions, they must do so at their own expense, while the Republicans and Democrats can ride in Pullman cars and stay at high-priced hotels at the expense of the taxpayers.

3. If this bill is approved, the time of the regular primary election will be changed from September to April, *during presidential election years,* but it will be held in September during other years. This would be an unbusinesslike arrangement, and would confuse and disarrange our entire code of election laws, resulting in great inconvenience to the Secretary of State, the county clerks and other officials; besides this, the proposed arrangement would, during presidential election years, keep the State in the throes of a political campaign from early spring until November. Ex-

perience has proved that campaigns should be as brief as possible and that business conditions are unsatisfactory when they are extended over a period of several months.

The people of Oregon, at the last State election, voted to change the primary election from April to September and the regular election from June to November. Now a group of men, who are constantly shouting about the "will of the people," wish to open up a question upon which the people have already expressed themselves.

4. There is no certainty that the national convention would seat delegates selected under the proposed arrangement. *The national committee of each party usually makes its own rules and regulations governing the selection of delegates.*

5. This measure is proposed by a group of men whose leaders are disgruntled because they were not sent as delegates to the Chicago convention in 1908. They assume to themselves all political virtue and purity, looking upon those who do not agree with their fads and schemes as undesirable citizens. They are now attempting to vent their spleen upon the taxpayers of Oregon.

The public good demands the rejection of this measure and you are respectfully urged to vote "NO" by the undersigned citizens and taxpayers.

E. W. McComas, Pendleton.
E. J. Sommerville, Pendleton.
Geo. W. Hyatt, Enterprise.
W. H. Ragsdale, Moro.
J. W. Donnelly, Condon.
C. N. McArthur, Portland.
Timothy Mahoney, Portland.
Ben Petigrew, Portland.

L. Woldenberg, Canyon City.
R. R. Corey, Baker City.
Frank E. Alley, Roseburg.
R. H. DeArmond, Ontario.
C. C. Wilson, Nyssa.
L. L. Mann, Pendleton.
J. C. Smith, Grants Pass.

IV. NEVADA

[Article XIX of the constitution of Nevada, establishing the referendum, was proposed and passed at the Twentieth Session of the Legislature, March 15, 1901 (*Statutes of* 1901, p. 139); agreed to and passed at the Twenty-first Session of the Legislature, March 3, 1903; and ratified by the voters at the general election of November 8, 1904. The total vote at this election was 12,050. The total vote on the amendment was 5185, of which 4393 were for, and 792 against. By an act approved March 24, 1909, the legislature elaborated the referendum amendment of 1904. In 1909 and 1911 the legislature elaborated the referendum provisions and also enacted initiative and recall amendments. These amendments will be submitted to the voters for ratification at the next general election.]

The Referendum (adopted 1904) [1]

SECTION 1. Whenever ten per centum or more of the voters of this State, as shown by the number of votes cast at the last preceding general election, shall express their wish that any law or resolution made by the Legislature be submitted to a vote of the people, the officers charged with the duty of announcing and proclaiming elections, and of certifying nominations, or questions to be voted on, shall submit the question of the approval or disapproval of said law or resolution to be voted on at the next ensuing election wherein a state or congressional officer is to be voted for, or wherein any question may be voted on by the electors of the entire State.

SEC. 2. When a majority of the electors voting at a state election shall by their votes signify approval of a law or resolution, such law or resolution shall stand as the law of the State and shall not be overruled, annulled, set aside, suspended, or in any way made inoperative except by the direct vote of the people. When such majority shall so signify disapproval the law or resolution so disapproved shall be void and of no effect.

[1] *Constitution of the State of Nevada* (Official), p. 59.

Referendum — Elaborating Law [1]

An Act to provide for submitting certain Acts of the Legislature for approval by the qualified electors of the State of Nevada in accordance with the referendum provisions of the Constitution.

SECTION 1. Whenever ten per centum or more of the voters of this State, as shown by the number of votes cast at the last preceding general election for Justice of the Supreme Court, shall express their wish that any law or resolution made by the Legislature be submitted to the vote of the people, they shall file with the Secretary of State, not less than four months before the time set for such general election, a petition, which petition shall contain the names and residences of at least ten per centum of the voters of this State, demanding that a referendum vote be had by the people of the State at the next general election upon the bill or resolution on which the referendum is demanded.

SEC. 2. The names of the electors so petitioning need not all be upon one petition, but may be contained in one or more petitions, but each petition must be verified by at least one of the voters who has signed such petition, and such voter making such verification must swear that the persons signing said petition are qualified voters of this State. Said petition may be verified upon information and belief.

SEC. 3. That upon receipt of said petition by the Secretary of State he shall file the same, and at the next general election shall submit the question of the approval or disapproval of said law or resolution to the people of the State to be voted upon at the next ensuing election wherein any State or Congressional officer is to be voted for, or wherein any question may be voted upon by the electors of the entire State. And the Secretary of State shall certify the said law to the several County Clerks in this State, and they shall publish the same in accordance with the provisions of law requiring the said County Clerks to publish

[1] *Election Laws* (1909), p. 89.

questions and constitutional amendments which are to be submitted for popular vote.

SEC. 4. That the title of the Act shall be set out on the ballot, and the question printed upon the ballot for the information of the voter shall be as follows: Shall the Act (setting out the title thereof) be approved? And the votes cast upon such questions shall be counted and canvassed as are the votes for State officers counted and canvassed.

SEC. 5. When a majority of the electors voting at a State election shall by their vote signify approval of a law or resolution, such law or resolution shall stand as the law of the State, and shall not be overruled, annulled, set aside, suspended or in any way made inoperative, except by a direct vote of the people. When a majority shall so signify disapproval, the law or resolution so disapproved shall be void and of no effect.

Initiative and New Referendum Amendment.
(Pending Adoption) [1]

SENATE SUBSTITUTE FOR ASSEMBLY JOINT AND CONCURRENT RESOLUTION NO. 7

Approved March 22, 1909. D. S. Dickerson, Lieutenant and Acting Governor.

Approved February 1, 1911. Tasker L. Oddie, Governor.

SENATE JOINT AND CONCURRENT RESOLUTION PROPOSING TO AMEND ARTICLE NINETEEN OF THE CONSTITUTION BY ADDING TO SAID ARTICLE SECTION THREE, RELATING TO THE INITIATIVE AND REFERENDUM, AND THE POWERS THEREBY CONFERRED UPON THE QUALIFIED ELECTORS.

Resolved by the Senate, the Assembly concurring, That section three be added to article nineteen of the constitution of the State of Nevada, said section so added to read as follows: —

---

[1] Official copy from Secretary of State. For the Recall Amendment see below page 272.

State-wide Initiative, Referendum, and Recall

SECTION 3. The people reserve to themselves the power to propose laws and the power to propose amendments to the constitution and to enact or reject the same at the polls, independent of the legislature, and also reserve the power at their option to approve or reject at the polls, in the manner herein provided, any act, item, section or part of any act or measure passed by the legislature, and section one of article four of the constitution shall hereafter be construed accordingly. The first power reserved by the people is the initiative, and not more than ten per cent (10 %) of the qualified electors shall be required to propose any measure by initiative petition, and every such petition shall include the full text of the measure so proposed. Initiative petitions, for all but municipal legislation, shall be filed with the secretary of state not less than thirty (30) days before any regular session of the legislature; the secretary of state shall transmit the same to the legislature as soon as it convenes and organizes. Such initiative measure shall take precedence over all measures of the legislature except appropriation bills, and shall be enacted or rejected by the legislature, without change or amendment, within forty (40) days. If any such initiative measure so proposed by petition as aforesaid, shall be enacted by the legislature and approved by the governor in the same manner as other laws are enacted, same shall become a law, but shall be subject to referendum petition as provided in section one and two of this article. If said initiative measure be rejected by the legislature, or if no action be taken thereon within said forty (40) days, the secretary of state shall submit same to the qualified electors for approval or rejection at the next ensuing general election; and if a majority of the qualified electors voting thereon shall approve of such measure it shall become a law and take effect from the date of the official declaration of the vote; an initiative measure so approved by the qualified electors shall not be annulled, set aside, or repealed by the legislature within three (3) years from the date said act takes effect. In case the legislature shall reject such initiative measure, said body may, with the approval of the governor, propose a different measure on the same subject, in which event both measures shall be submitted by the secretary of state to the qualified electors for approval or rejection at the next ensuing general election. The enacting clause of all bills proposed by the initiative shall be: "The People of the State of Nevada enact as follows." The whole number of votes cast for justice of the supreme court at the general election last preceding the filing of any initiative petition shall be the basis on which the number of qualified electors required to sign such petition shall be counted. The second power reserved by the people is the referendum, which shall be exercised in the manner provided in sections one and two of this article. The initiative and referendum powers in this article provided for are further reserved to the qualified electors of each county and municipality as to all local, special and municipal legislation of every character in or for said respective counties or municipalities. The legislature may provide by law for the manner of exercising the initiative and referendum powers as to county and municipal legislation, but shall not require a petition of more than ten per cent (10 %) of the qualified electors to order the referendum, and not more than fifteen per cent (15 %) to propose any municipal measure by initiative. If the conflicting measures submitted to the people at the next ensuing general election shall both be approved by a majority of the votes severally cast for and against each of said measures, the measure receiving the highest number of affirmative votes shall thereupon become a law as to all conflicting provisions. The provisions of this section shall be self-executing, but legislation may be especially enacted to facilitate its operation.

V: MONTANA

[The constitutional amendment providing for the initiative and referendum was approved by the Governor, March 2, 1905. It was ratified by the voters at the general election held in November, 1906. The vote was 36,374 for and 6616 against, or a total vote of 42,990. The total vote cast at the election was 56,041. The amendment and the elaborating act, approved by the Governor, March 2, 1907, follow.]

Constitutional Amendment (1906) [1]

An Act Entitled, "An Act for the submitting to the qualified electors of the State of Montana, an Amendment to Article V of the Constitution of the State of Montana, relating to the Legislative Department and providing for Direct Legislation and Reference of Laws."

Be it enacted by the Legislative Assembly of the State of Montana: —

SECTION 1.

There shall be submitted to the qualified electors of the State of Montana, at the next general election, the following amendment to Section I, Article V, of the constitution of the State of Montana: —

That Section I, Article V, of the constitution be, and the same is hereby amended so as to read as follows: —

SECTION I. The Legislative Authority of the State shall be vested in a Legislative Assembly, consisting of a Senate and House of Representatives; but the people reserve to themselves power to propose laws, and to enact or reject the same at the polls, except as to laws relating to appropriations of money, and except as to laws for the submission of constitutional amendments, and except as to local or special laws, as enumerated in Article V, Section 26, of this constitution, independent of the Legislative Assembly; and also reserve power at their own option, to approve or reject at the polls, any Act of the Legislative Assembly, except as to laws necessary for the immediate preservation of the public peace, health or safety, and except as to laws relating to appropriations of money, and except as to laws for the submission of constitutional amendments, and except as to local or special

[1] Official copy secured from the Secretary of State.

laws, as enumerated in Article V, Section 26, of this Constitution. The first power reserved by the people is the Initiative and eight per cent of the legal voters of the State shall be required to propose any measure by petition; provided, that two-fifths of the whole number of the Counties of the State must each furnish as signers of said petition eight per cent of the legal voters in such county, and every such petition shall include the full text of the measure so proposed. Initiative petitions shall be filed with the Secretary of State, not less than four months before the election at which they are to be voted upon.

The second power is the Referendum, and it may be ordered either by petition signed by five per cent of the legal voters of the State, provided that two-fifths of the whole number of the counties of the State must each furnish as signers of said petition five per cent of the legal voters in such County; or, by the Legislative Assembly as other Bills are enacted.

Referendum petitions shall be filed with the Secretary of State, not later than six months after the final adjournment of the Session of the Legislative Assembly which passed the Bill on which the Referendum is demanded. The veto power of the Governor shall not extend to measures referred to the people by the Legislative Assembly or by Initiative Referendum petitions.

All elections on measures referred to the people of the State shall be had at the biennial regular general election, except when the Legislative Assembly, by a majority vote, shall order a special election. Any measure referred to the people shall still be in full force and effect unless such petition be signed by fifteen per cent of the legal voters of a majority of the whole number of the counties of the State, in which case the law shall be inoperative until such time as it shall be passed upon at an election, and the result has been determined and declared as provided by law. The whole number of votes cast for Governor at the regular election last preceding the filing of any petition for the Initiative or Referendum, shall be the basis on which the number of the legal petitions and orders for the Initiative and for the Referendum shall

be filed with the Secretary of State; and in submitting the same to the people, he, and all other officers, shall be guided by the General Laws and the Act submitting this amendment, until Legislation shall be especially provided therefor. The enacting clause of every law originated by the Initiative shall be as follows:
"Be it enacted by the People of Montana:" —

This Section shall not be construed to deprive any member of the Legislative Assembly of the right to introduce any measure.

SECTION 2.

That separate Official Ballots be used at the general election, to be held in November, 1906, and shall have printed thereon the words: "For the Amendment to the Constitution providing for Direct Legislation and Reference of Laws," and the words, "Against the Amendment to the Constitution providing for Direct Legislation and Reference of Laws."

It shall be the duty of the Legislative Assembly to enact Legislation suitable for carrying this amendment into effect.

SECTION 3.

All Acts or parts of Acts in conflict with this Act are hereby repealed.

SECTION 4.

This Act shall take effect and be in full force from and after its passage and approval by the Governor.

Elaborating Act (1907)

INITIATIVE AND REFERENDUM [1]

Section 106. Form of petition for referendum.
Section 107. Form of petition for initiative.
Section 108. Clerk to verify signatures to petitions.
Section 109. Notice to governor and proclamation.

[1] *Election Laws of the State of Montana*, pp. 48 ff.

Section 110. Secretary of state to certify measures to be voted on. Printing ballots.
Section 111. Manner of voting.
Section 112. Printing and distribution of measures to be voted on.
Section 113. Canvass of votes.
Section 114. Who may petition. False signatures. Penalties.
Section 115. Referred bills not effective until approved.

106. Form of petition for referendum. — The following shall be substantially the form of petition for the referendum to the people on any act passed by the Legislative Assembly of the State of Montana.

WARNING

Any person signing any name other than his own to this petition or signing the same more than once for the same measure at one Election, or who is not, at the time of signing the same, a legal voter of this State, is punishable by a fine not exceeding Five Hundred Dollars ($500.00) or imprisonment in the penitentiary not exceeding two years or by both such fine and imprisonment.

PETITION FOR REFERENDUM

To the Honorable ...., Secretary of State for the State of Montana: —

We, the undersigned citizens and legal voters of the State of Montana, respectfully order that Senate (House) Bill Number ...... entitled (title of Act), passed by the .... Legislative Assembly of the State of Montana, at the regular (special) session of said Legislative Assembly, shall be referred to the people of the State for their approval or rejection, at the regular, general, or special election to be held on the ...... day of ......, 19.., and each for himself says: I have personally signed this petition; I am a legal voter of the State of Montana; and my residence, postoffice address and voting precinct are correctly written after my name.

Name...................... Residence................

Postoffice address ....

If in city, street and number................................

Voting Precinct..

(Here follow numbered lines for signatures.)

107. Form for petition for initiative. — The following shall be substantially the form of petition for any law of the State of Montana proposed by the initiative: —

WARNING

Any person signing any name other than his own to this petition or signing the same more than once for the same measure at one Election, or who is not, at the time of signing the same, a legal voter of this State, is punishable by a fine not exceeding Five Hundred Dollars ($500.00) or imprisonment in the penitentiary not exceeding two years or by both such fine and imprisonment.

PETITION FOR INITIATIVE

To the Honorable ...., Secretary of State of the State of Montana: —

We, the undersigned legal voters of the State of Montana, respectfully demand that the following proposed law shall be submitted to the legal electors of the State of Montana, for their approval or rejection, at the regular general or special election to be held on the ..... day of ......, 190.., and each for himself says: —

I have personally signed this petition, and my residence, postoffice address, and voting precinct are correctly written after my name.

Name...................... Residence............

Postoffice address...

If in city, street and number...............................

Voting Precinct ....

(Numbered lines for names on each sheet.)

The Initiative and Referendum

Every such sheet for petitioner's signature shall be attached to a full and correct copy of the title and text of the measure so proposed by initiative petition; but such petition may be filed with the Secretary of State in numbered sections, for convenience in handling, and referendum petitions may be filed in Sections in like manner.

108. Clerk to verify signatures to petitions. — The County Clerk of each county in which any such petition shall be signed shall compare the signatures of the electors signing the same with their signatures on the registration books and blanks on file in his office, for the preceding general election, and shall thereupon attach to the sheets of said petition containing such signatures, his certificate to the Secretary of State, substantially as follows:

State of Montana,} ss.
County of ....

To the Honorable ...., Secretary of State for Montana: —

I, ..., County Clerk of the County of .... hereby certify that I have compared the signatures on (number of sheets) of the referendum (initiative) petition, attached hereto, with the signatures of said electors as they appear on the registration books and blanks in my office; and I believe that the signatures of (names of signers) numbering (number of genuine signatures) are genuine. As to the remainder of the signatures thereon, I believe that they are not genuine, for the reason that .... and I further certify that .... the following names (............) do not appear on the registration books and blanks in my office.

Signed............

............County Clerk.

(Seal of Office)............ By........................
...............................Deputy ....

Every such certificate shall be prima facie evidence of the facts stated therein, and of the qualifications of the electors whose signatures are thus certified to be genuine, and the Secretary of State shall consider and count only such signatures on such petitions as shall be so certified by said county clerks to be genuine; Provided, that the Secretary of State may consider and count such of the remaining signatures as may be proved to be genuine, and that the parties so signing were legally qualified to sign such petitions, and the official certificate of a Notary Public of the County in which the signer resides shall be required as to the fact for each of such last named signatures; and the Secretary of State shall further compare and verify the official signatures and seals of all notaries so certifying with their signatures and seals filed in his office. Such notaries' certificates shall be substantially in the following form: —

State of Montana, } ss.
County of .... }

I, ..., a duly qualified and acting Notary Public in and for the above named county and state, do hereby certify: that I am personally acquainted with each of the following named electors whose signatures are affixed to the annexed petition, and I know of my own knowledge that they are legal voters of the State of Montana, and of the county and precincts written after their several names in the annexed petition, and that their residence and postoffice address is correctly stated therein, to-wit: (Names of such electors.)

In Testimony Whereof I have hereunto set my hand and Official Seal this ...... day of ...., 190...

....
Notary Public, in and for..........
............County, State of Montana.

The County Clerk shall not retain in his possession any such petition, or any part thereof, for a longer period than two days for the first two hundred signatures thereon, and one additional day for each two hundred additional signatures, or fraction thereof, on the sheets presented to him, and at the expiration of such time

The Initiative and Referendum

he shall forward the same to the Secretary of State, with his certificate attached thereto, as above provided. The forms herein given are not mandatory, and if substantially followed in any petition, it shall be sufficient, disregarding clerical and merely technical errors.

109. Notice to Governor and proclamation. — Immediately upon the filing of any such petition for the referendum or the initiative with the Secretary of State, signed by the number of voters and filed within the time required by the Constitution, he shall notify the Governor in writing of the filing of such petition, and the Governor shall forthwith issue his proclamation, announcing that such petition has been filed, with a brief statement of its tenor and effect. Said proclamation shall be published four times for four consecutive weeks in one daily or weekly paper in each county of the State of Montana.

110. Secretary of State to certify measures to be voted on. Printing ballots. — The Secretary of State, at the same time that he furnishes to the County Clerks of the several counties certified copies of the names of the candidates for state and county offices, shall furnish to said county clerks his certified copy of the titles and numbers of the various measures to be voted upon at the ensuing general or special election, and he shall use for each measure, a title designated for that purpose by the Legislative Assembly, Committee, or organization presenting and filing with him the act, or petition for the initiative or the referendum or in the petition or Act; provided, that such title shall in no case exceed 100 words, and shall not resemble any such title previously filed for any measure to be submitted at that election, which shall be descriptive of said measure, and he shall number such measures; and such title shall be printed on a separate official ballot in the order in which the Acts referred by the Legislative Assembly and petitions by the people shall be filed in his office. The affirmative of the first measure shall be numbered 300 and the negative 301, in numerals, and the succeeding measures shall be numbered consecutively 302, 303, 304, 305, and so on at each

election. It shall be the duty of the several county clerks to print said titles and numbers upon a separate official ballot, in the order presented to them by the Secretary of State, and the relative position required by law. Measures proposed by the initiative shall be designated and distinguished from measures proposed by the Legislative Assembly by the heading "Proposed Petition for Initiative."

111. Manner of voting. — The manner of voting measures submitted to the people shall be: By marking his ballot with a cross on diagram opposite and to the left of the proposition for which he desires to vote.

☐ For the Initiative Measure No..........

☐ Against Referendum Measure No......

☐ For Referendum Measure No..........

☐ Against Initiative Measure No..........

112. Printing and distribution of measures to be voted on. — The Secretary of State shall, not later than the first Monday of the third month next before any general or special election, at which any proposed law is to be submitted to the people, cause to be printed a true copy of the title and text of each measure to be submitted, with the number and form in which the question will be printed on a separate official ballot. The paper to be used for the covers of such pamphlets shall be twenty by twenty-five inches, and fifty pounds weight to the ream. The persons, committees, or duly authorized officers of any organization filing any petition for the initiative, but no other person or organization, shall have the right to place with the Secretary of State for distribution, any pamphlets advocating such measure, not later than the first Monday of the fifth month

The Initiative and Referendum 135

before the regular general or special election at which the measure is to be voted on; any person, committee or organization opposing any measure may place with the Secretary of State for distribution any pamphlets they may desire, not later than the first Monday of the fourth month immediately preceding such election; as to pamphlets advocating or opposing any measure referred to the people by the Legislative Assembly, they shall be governed by the same rules of time, but they may be placed with the Secretary of State by any person, committee or organization; Provided, that all such pamphlets shall be furnished to the Secretary of State in sheets of uniform size, as follows: Size of pamphlet page to be six inches wide by nine inches long; size of type page to be twenty-six ems pica wide, by forty ems pica long, set in long primer of ten-point type, and printed on sized and supercalendered paper, twenty-five by thirty-eight inches, weighing fifty pounds to the ream. All such pamphlets shall be furnished to the Secretary of State at the sole expense of the persons interested, and without cost to the State. In no case shall the Secretary of State be obliged to receive any such pamphlets unless a sufficient number is furnished to supply one to every legal voter in the State, but in such case, he shall forthwith notify the persons offering the same of the number required. The Secretary of State shall cause one copy of each of said pamphlets to be bound in with his copy of the measures to be submitted as herein provided. The title page of every such pamphlet shall show the official numbers for and against, and the ballot title of the measure to which it refers, and whether it is intended to favor or oppose such measure and by whom it is issued. The Secretary of State shall distribute to each County Clerk, before the second Monday in the third month next preceding such regular general election, a sufficient number of said bound pamphlets to furnish one copy to every voter in his county. And each county clerk shall be required to mail to each registered voter in each of the several counties in the State at least one copy of the same, within thirty days from the date of his receipt of the same from the Secretary of State. The mailing of said bound pamphlets shall be a part of the official duty of the County Clerk of each of the several counties and his official compensation shall be full compensation for this additional service. The Secretary of State shall not be obliged to receive or distribute any pamphlets advocating or opposing any measure unless the same shall be filed with him within the time herein provided.

113. Canvass of votes. — The votes on measures and questions shall be counted, canvassed, and returned by the regular boards of judges, clerks, and officers as votes for candidates are counted, canvassed, and returned, and the abstract made by the several county clerks of votes on measures shall be returned to the Secretary of State on separate abstract sheets in the manner provided by Sections 598 (1440) and 599 (1441), of the Political Code for abstracts of votes for State officers. It shall be the duty of the State Board of Canvassers to proceed within thirty days after the election, and sooner if the returns be all received, to canvass the votes given for each measure, and the Governor shall forthwith issue his proclamation, which shall be published in two daily newspapers printed at the capital, giving the whole number of votes cast in the State for and against each measure and question, and declaring such measures as are approved by a majority of those voting thereon to be in full force and effect as the law of the State of Montana, from the date of said proclamation designating such measures by their titles.

114. Who may petition. False signature. Penalties. — Every person who is a qualified elector of the State of Montana may sign a petition for the referendum or for the initiative. Any person signing any name other than his own to such petition or signing the same more than once for the same measure at one election, or who is not at the time of signing the same a legal voter of this state, or any officer or any person wilfully violating any provision of this statute, shall, upon conviction thereof, be punished by a fine not exceeding Five Hundred Dollars ($500.00) or by imprisonment in the penitentiary not exceeding two years,

or by both such fine and imprisonment in the discretion of the court before which such conviction shall be had.

115. *Referred bills not effective until approved.* — A Bill passed by the Legislative Assembly and referred to popular vote at the next general election, or at a special election, shall not be in effect until it is approved at such general or special election by a majority of those voting for and against it.

VI. OKLAHOMA

[The Oklahoma constitution was ratified September 17, 1907; the open vote was, 180,333 for; 73,059 against. By proclamation of President Roosevelt, Oklahoma was admitted to the Union, November 16, 1907.]

Constitutional Provisions Relative to the Initiative and Referendum.[1]

SECTION 1. The Legislative authority of the State shall be vested in a Legislature, consisting of a Senate and a House of Representatives; but the people reserve to themselves the power to propose laws and amendments to the Constitution and to enact or reject the same at the polls independent of the Legislature, and also reserve power at their own option to approve or reject at the polls any act of the Legislature.

SEC. 2. The first power reserved by the people is the initiative, and eight per centum of the legal voters shall have the right to propose any legislative measure, and fifteen per centum of the legal voters shall have the right to propose amendments to the Constitution by petition, and every such petition shall include the full text of the measure so proposed. The second power is the referendum, and it may be ordered (except as to laws necessary for the immediate preservation of the public peace, health, or safety), either by petition signed by five per centum of the legal voters or by the Legislature as other bills are enacted. The ratio

[1] Thorpe, *American Charters, Constitutions, and Organic Laws*, Vol. VII, pp. 4278 ff.

and per centum of legal voters hereinbefore stated shall be based upon the total number of votes cast at the last general election for the State office receiving the highest number of votes at such election.

SEC. 3. Referendum petitions shall be filed with the Secretary of State not more than ninety days after the final adjournment of the session of the Legislature which passed the bill on which the referendum is demanded. The veto power of the Governor shall not extend to measures voted on by the people. All elections on measures referred to the people of the State shall be had at the next election held throughout the State, except when the Legislature or the Governor shall order a special election for the express purpose of making such reference. Any measure referred to the people shall take effect and be in force when it shall have been approved by a majority of the votes cast thereon and not otherwise.

The style of all bills shall be: "Be it Enacted By the People of the State of Oklahoma."

Petitions and orders for the initiative and for the referendum shall be filed with the Secretary of State and addressed to the Governor of the State, who shall submit the same to the people. The Legislature shall make suitable provisions for carrying into effect the provisions of this article; and, if the Legislature shall fail to make such provisions, or shall make inadequate provisions, then the Governor of the State shall, by executive order, make such rules as may be necessary to carry these provisions into effect.

SEC. 4. The referendum may be demanded by the people against one or more items, sections, or parts of any act of the Legislature in the same manner in which such power may be exercised against a complete act. The filing of a referendum petition against one or more items, sections, or parts of an act shall not delay the remainder of such act from becoming operative.

SEC. 5. The powers of the initiative and referendum reserved to the people by this Constitution for the State at large, are hereby further reserved to the legal voters of every county and district therein, as to all local and special legislation and action in the administration of county and district government in and for their respective counties and districts.

The manner of exercising said powers shall be prescribed by general laws, except that Boards of County Commissioners may provide for the time of exercising the initiative and referendum powers as to local legislation in their respective counties and

NOTE.

Lines thirteen to sixteen on page 138 should read "*Any measure referred to the people by the initiative shall take effect and be in force when it shall have been approved by a majority of the votes cast in such election. Any measure referred to the people by the referendum shall take effect and be in force when it shall have been approved by a majority of the votes cast thereon and not otherwise.*"

of the United States.

SEC. 8. Laws shall be provided to prevent corruption in making, procuring, and submitting initiative and referendum petitions.

Elaborating Acts

[April 16, 1908 the legislature proceeded to enact the details of the system. The Supreme Court[1] decided that the initiative and referendum powers in the state constitution were not self-executing until such legislation was passed. The bill of 1908 extended the initiative and referendum to municipalities. Portions of it have been repealed by the legislatures of 1909, 1910, and

[1] *Ex parte* Wagner, 21 Okla. 33 : 95 Pac. 435, below, p. 330.

138 State-wide Initiative, Referendum, and Recall

and per centum of legal voters hereinbefore stated shall be based upon the total number of votes cast at the last general election for the State office receiving the highest number of votes at such election.

SEC. 3. Referendum petitions shall be filed with the Secretary of State not more than ninety days after the final adjournment of the session of the Legislature which passed the bill on which the referendum is demanded. The veto power of the Governor shall not extend to measures referred to the people. ... the provisions of this article; and, if the Legislature shall fail to make such provisions, or shall make inadequate provisions, then the Governor of the State shall, by executive order, make such rules as may be necessary to carry these provisions into effect.

SEC. 4. The referendum may be demanded by the people against one or more items, sections, or parts of any act of the Legislature in the same manner in which such power may be exercised against a complete act. The filing of a referendum petition against one or more items, sections, or parts of an act shall not delay the remainder of such act from becoming operative.

SEC. 5. The powers of the initiative and referendum reserved to the people by this Constitution for the State at large, are

The Initiative and Referendum

hereby further reserved to the legal voters of every county and district therein, as to all local and special legislation and action in the administration of county and district government in and for their respective counties and districts.

The manner of exercising said powers shall be prescribed by general laws, except that Boards of County Commissioners may provide for the time of exercising the initiative and referendum powers as to local legislation in their respective counties and districts.

The requisite number of petitioners for the invocation of the initiative and referendum in counties and districts shall bear twice, or double, the ratio to the whole number of legal voters in such county or district, as herein provided therefor in the State at large.

SEC. 6. Any measure rejected by the people, through the powers of the initiative and referendum, cannot be again proposed by the initiative within three years thereafter by less than twenty-five per centum of the legal voters.

SEC. 7. The reservation of the powers of the initiative and referendum in this article shall not deprive the Legislature of the right to propose or pass any measure, which may be consistent with the Constitution of the State and the Constitution of the United States.

SEC. 8. Laws shall be provided to prevent corruption in making, procuring, and submitting initiative and referendum petitions.

Elaborating Acts

[April 16, 1908 the legislature proceeded to enact the details of the system. The Supreme Court[1] decided that the initiative and referendum powers in the state constitution were not self-executing until such legislation was passed. The bill of 1908 extended the initiative and referendum to municipalities. Portions of it have been repealed by the legislatures of 1909, 1910, and

---

[1] *Ex parte* Wagner, 21 Okla. 33 : 95 Pac. 435, below, p. 330.

1911. The entire elaborating bill and the successive partial changes follow.]

Elaborating Act — 1908

AN ACT[1]

To Provide for Carrying into Effect the Initiative and Referendum Powers Reserved by the People in Articles Five and Eighteen of the Constitution of the State of Oklahoma; to Regulate Elections Thereunder and to Punish Violations of This Act.

Be it Enacted by the People of the State of Oklahoma:—

SECTION 1. (REFERENDUM PETITION)

The Referendum petition shall be substantially as follows:—

PETITION FOR REFERENDUM

To the Honorable ...., Governor of Oklahoma or (To the Honorable ...., Mayor, Chairman of County Commissioners, or other chief executive officer as the case may be, of the city, county or other municipal corporation, of ......):

We, the undersigned citizens and legal voters of the State of Oklahoma (or district of ...., county of .... or city of .... as the case may be) respectfully order that the Senate or (House) bill No............ entitled (title of act, and if the petition is against less than the whole act, then set forth here the part or parts on which the referendum is sought), passed by the .... legislature of the State of Oklahoma, at the regular or (special) session of said legislature, shall be referred to the people of the state (district of .... county of .... or city of .... as the case may be) for their approval or rejection, at the regular, or special election to be held on the .... day of ...., A.D. 19.., and each for himself says: I have personally signed this

[1] Oklahoma Session Laws 1907-1908, pp. 440 ff.

The Initiative and Referendum 141

petition; I am a legal voter of the State of Oklahoma (district of ...., county of ...., city of ...., as the case may be) my residence and postoffice are correctly written after my name.

Referendum petitions shall be filed with the Secretary of State not more than ninety days after the final adjournment of the session of the Legislature which passed the bill on which the referendum is demanded. (This for State referendum. For county, city or other municipality the length of time shall be three months.)

The question we herewith submit to our fellow voters is: Shall the following bill of the Legislature be vetoed?
Name............ Residence.......... Postoffice..........
If in city, street and number.
(Here follow twenty numbered lines for signatures.)

SECTION 2. (INITIATIVE PETITION)

The form of Initiative Petition shall be substantially as follows: —

INITIATIVE PETITION

To the Honorable ...., Governor of Oklahoma, or (To the Honorable .... Mayor, Chairman of County Commissioners, or other chief executive officer, as the case may be, for the city, county or other municipality): We the undersigned citizens and legal voters of the State of Oklahoma (and of the district of ...., county of ...., or city of ...., as the case may be), respectfully order that the following proposed law, or (amendment to the constitution, ordinance or amendment to the City Charter, as the case may be), shall be submitted to the legal voters of the State of Oklahoma, district of ...., county of ...., or city of ...., as the case may be), for their approval or rejection at the regular general election or (regular or special city election) to be held on the .... day of .... A.D. 19.., and each for himself says: I have personally signed this petition; I am a legal voter of the State of Oklahoma (and of the district of ...., county of ...., city of ......, as the case may be); my residence and postoffice are correctly written after my name. The time for filing this petition expires nine months from (insert date when petition is to be opened for signatures). (This for state Initiative. For county, city or other municipality, the length of time shall be three months.) The question we herewith submit to our fellow voters is: Shall the following bill (or proposed amendment to the constitution or resolution) be adopted.

(Insert here an exact copy of the title and text of the measure.)
Name............ Residence.......... Postoffice..........
If in city, street and number.
(Here follow twenty numbered lines for signatures.)

SECTION 3. (PAMPHLETS)

Each Initiative Petition and each Referendum Petition shall be duplicated for the securing of signatures, and each sheet for signatures shall be attached to a copy of the petition. Each copy of the petition and sheets for signatures is hereinafter termed a pamphlet. On the outer page of each pamphlet shall be printed the word "Warning," and underneath this in ten point type, the words: "It is a felony for any one to sign an initiative or referendum petition with any name other than his own, or knowingly to sign his name more than once for the measure, or to sign such petitions when he is not a legal voter." Not more than twenty signatures on one sheet shall be counted. When any such initiative or referendum petition shall be offered for filing, the Secretary of State in the presence of the Governor and the person offering the same for filing shall detach the sheets containing the signatures and affidavits and cause them all to be attached to one or more printed copies of the measure so proposed

The Initiative and Referendum 143

by initiative or referendum petition; provided, all petitions for the initiative and referendum and sheets for signatures shall be printed on pages seven inches in width, by ten inches in length, with a margin of one and three-fourths inches at the top for binding; if the aforesaid sheets shall be too bulky for convenient binding in one volume they may be bound in two or more volumes, those in each volume to be attached to a single printed copy of such measure; the detached copies of such measures shall be delivered to the person offering the same for filing. If any measure shall, at the ensuing election, be approved by the people, then the copies so preserved, with the sheets of signatures and affidavits, and a certified copy of the Governor's proclamation declaring the same to have been approved by the people, shall be bound together in such form that they may be conveniently identified and preserved. The Secretary of State shall cause every such measure approved by the people to be printed with the general laws enacted at the next ensuing session of the Legislature with the date of the Governor's proclamation declaring the same to have been approved by the people.

SECTION 4. (VERIFICATION OF SIGNATURES)

Each and every sheet of every such petition containing signatures shall be verified on the back thereof, in substantially the following form, by the person who circulated said sheet of said petition, by his or her affidavit thereon and as a part thereof:—

State of Oklahoma, } ss.
County of ...., }

I, ..., being first duly sworn, say: (Here shall be legibly written or typewritten the names of the signers of the sheet) signed this sheet of the foregoing petition and each of them signed his name in my presence; I believe that each has stated his name, postoffice address and residence correctly, and that each signer is a legal voter of the State of Oklahoma, and County of ...., or of the city of ...., (as the case may be) Signature and postoffice address of affiant. Subscribed and sworn to before me this .... day of .... A.D. 19.. (Signature and title of the officer before whom the oath is made, and his postoffice address.)

SECTION 5. (FILING AND NUMBERING PETITIONS)

Each order for a direct ballot by the voters that is filed with the Secretary of State by initiative petition, referendum petition and by the Legislature, shall be numbered consecutively, each in a series by itself, beginning with one, to be continued year after year, without duplication of numbers.

SECTION 6. (SUFFICIENCY OF PETITION. RIGHT OF APPEAL. SPEEDY TRIAL ASSURED)

Whenever an initiative petition or referendum petition shall be filed with the Secretary of State, he shall at once proceed to examine into its sufficiency. If any one desires to appear for or against it he shall receive testimony and arguments. Whenever such petition applies to a measure upon which the initiative or the referendum is invoked for the State at large, his decision may be appealed from to the Supreme Court of the State, and the case shall have precedence over all others. If the court is adjourned it shall be immediately convened. In all other cases said appeal shall be to the District Court of any county in which a petition was circulated, and said District Court may hear and determine same in term time or vacation. The appellants shall serve upon the Secretary of State written notice of appeal, and said Secretary shall thereupon transmit to the clerk of the court such of the original papers and documents in the case as may be specified, by the appellant or appellee. In case the court shall decide the petition is insufficient, it shall state in what respect it is insufficient and return the petition to the committee of petitioners for correction, which corrections may be made, and the petition returned to the Secretary of State, within five days, and when so corrected and returned the petition shall be considered filed as of the date that the original petition was presented for filing. No objection to the sufficiency of any petition shall be considered unless the same shall have been made in writing, and filed within five days after the filing of the petition.[1]

SECTION 7. (TITLE OF MEASURE)

When any measure shall be filed with the Secretary of State to be referred to the people of the State,. or of any county or district composed of one or more counties, either by the Legislature or by the referendum petition, and when any measure shall be proposed by initiative petition, the Secretary of State shall forthwith transmit to the Attorney General of the State a copy thereof, and within ten days thereafter the Attorney General shall provide and return to the Secretary of State a ballot title for said measure. The ballot title may be distinct from the legislative title of the measure and shall express in not exceeding one hundred words, the purpose of the measure. The ballot title shall be printed with the number of the measure, on the official ballot. In making such ballot title the Attorney General shall to the best of his ability, give a true and impartial statement of the purpose of the measure, and in such language that the ballot title shall not be intentionally an argument, or likely to create prejudice, either for or against the measure. Any person who is dissatisfied with the ballot title provided by the Attorney General for any measure may appeal from his decision to the Supreme or other court as provided by Section Six of this Act, by petition, praying for a different title and setting forth the reason why the title prepared by the Attorney General is insufficient or unfair. No appeal shall be allowed from the decision of the Attorney General on a ballot title, unless the same be taken within five days after said decision is filed. A copy of every such decision shall be served by the Secretary of State or the Clerk of the Court upon the

---

[1] Amended in 1910 and 1911. See below, p. 154 and p. 161.

person offering or filing such initiative or referendum petition or appeal. Service of such decision may be by mail or telegraph, and shall be made forthwith. The court shall thereupon examine said measure, hear arguments and in its decision thereon certify to the Secretary of State a ballot title for such measure in accord with the intent of this section. The decision of the court shall be final. The Secretary of State shall print on the official ballot the title thus certified to him.[1]

SECTION 8. (PROCLAMATION BY GOVERNOR)

Whenever a petition is accepted and its title has been decided upon the Secretary of State shall, in writing, notify the Governor, who forthwith shall issue a proclamation setting forth the substance of the measure and the date of the referendum vote.

SECTION 9. (PUBLICATION OF TEXT OF MEASURE. COPIES FOR DISTRIBUTION)

The Secretary of State shall submit to the State, or public printer, a copy of the title and text of each measure presented by initiative petition, referendum petition, and by the Legislature. Printed copies shall be supplied the document rooms, from time to time, and the chief of each shall supply copies to applicants and in such quantities as demanded, provided reasonable assurance is given that they will be placed singly in the hands of the people.

SECTION 10. (PUBLICATION OF OFFICIAL BALLOT. DISTRIBUTION OF COPIES)

At as early a day as is practicable the Secretary of State shall transmit to the State, or public printer, copy for the official referendum ballot, indicating the styles of type. The sample ballot shall be of colored paper, and there shall be placed at the

---

[1] For Amendment of 1910, see below, p. 154.

The Initiative and Referendum 147

head in bold type the words "State Question" (or Questions) and the following: "Official Referendum Ballot to be used (date) issued by order of the Legislature." The questions shall be printed in the order they were filed with the Secretary of State except that each competing measure which the Legislature may desire to submit shall immediately follow the one it aims to supplant. Measures proposed by initiative petition shall be designated "Proposed by Initiative Petition Number........;" measures proposed by referendum petition shall be designated "Proposed by Referendum Petition Number............;" (and each competing measure proposed by the Legislature in place of an initiative petition shall be headed "Proposed by the Legislature in place of Initiative Petition Number..........") Where the Legislature submits a competing question a brief catch-line shall be placed over both and below both shall be placed the words "I Vote for Initiative Petition Number......;" "I vote for the measure proposed by the Legislature in place of Initiative Petition Number............;" "I vote against both...." Second choice as to measure may be made.

Where a question is submitted without a competing one there shall be placed over it a brief catch-line, and at the close of the question there shall be added, "Shall it be adopted?"

Yes. ☐   No. ☐

Or shall it be repealed.

Yes. ☐   No. ☐

The voters shall be directed to express their will by placing a cross (X) in the square and to the right of the word expressing their choice. There shall be a provision for second choice.

SECTION 11. (PREPARATION OF ARGUMENTS)

Arguments shall be prepared for and against each measure to be submitted to a direct vote of the people of the state, the length of the arguments not to exceed two thousand words for each side, and which one-fourth may be in answer to opponents' arguments. For one side the arguments shall be prepared by a joint committee of the House and Senate, and for the other by a committee representing the petitioners. Where the Legislature submits a competing bill the argument against it shall be prepared by the committee that prepared the affirmative of the opposing bill. Where the Legislature submits any other question the argument for the negative shall be prepared by a committee representing the members in the Legislature who voted against the substance of the measure.

SECTION 12. (TIME FOR PREPARING ARGUMENTS)

The first part of each argument shall be completed not later than two weeks after the Governor's announcement of the submission of the measure. Twenty-five copies shall be filed with the Secretary of State, who shall at once deliver twenty-three copies to the chairman of the opposing committee. Each committee shall file its answer within two weeks. Provided, however, that in no case shall the time be so great as to bring the completion of the arguments nearer than one hundred days before any regular election nor later than forty days before any special election at which the measure is to be voted upon. Where the time for preparing the arguments is less than four weeks the time shall be divided equally between the two parts.

SECTION 13. (PRINTING AND DISTRIBUTION OF TEXT OF MEASURES, SAMPLE OF BALLOTS AND ARGUMENTS)

Before the mandatory primary election held prior to each general election held throughout the State, at which any proposed law, part of an act, or amendment to the Constitution is to be submitted to the people, the Secretary of State shall forward or cause to be forwarded, to the County Clerk of each county in this State, a sufficient number of the pamphlets hereinafter described, with which to supply each and every voter of his county and an additional number equal to ten per centum of such number of votes; and, at the time of furnishing the primary election supplies, said county clerk shall furnish each election inspector his quota for each precinct wherein a primary election is to be held, a sufficient number of copies of the text of each measure to be submitted to popular vote; also a copy of the arguments for and against such measures, and a copy of the official ballot, bound together in a single pamphlet with a table of contents. The pages shall be numbered consecutively, the title page of every measure bound in the pamphlet shall show its ballot title and ballot number. The title page of each argument shall indicate the measure it favors or opposes, the names of the committee, and whom they represent; and it shall be the duty of said inspector to furnish to each and every voter on said primary election day a copy of the same. All copies of said pamphlets remaining after said primary election, shall be preserved by said inspector and be by him distributed to electors, unsupplied with such pamphlets. Provided, however, when the Legislature or the Governor shall order a special election for the express purpose of making such reference, the Secretary of State shall, not later than forty days before any such special election, forward such pamphlets to the county clerk of each county, who shall in like manner immediately distribute them to the election inspectors for the election precincts of his county, and said inspector shall, within five days, convoke, hold or cause to be held, a public meeting of the electors of his district and distribute, or cause to be distributed, such pamphlets to the assembled voters; and use all other diligent means of distributing them to all the voters of such election precinct.

SECTION 14. (PUBLICATION OF BALLOTS BY COUNTY CLERKS)

The Secretary of State at the time he furnishes to the county clerks of the several counties certified copies of the names of the candidates for State and district offices, shall furnish to each of said county clerks a certified copy of the referendum ballot. It shall be the duty of the several county clerks to print said ballot titles and numbers upon the official ballot in the order presented to them by the Secretary of State and in the relative position required by law.

SECTION 15. (RESUBMISSION-CONFLICTING PROGRAMS)

Where there are competing measures and neither receive a majority of the votes cast for and against, the one receiving the greatest number of votes shall, if it has received more than one-third of the votes cast for and against both bills, be submitted by itself at the next general election. If two or more conflicting laws shall be approved by the people at the same election, the law receiving the greatest number of affirmative votes shall be paramount in all particulars as to which there is a conflict, even though such law may not have received the greatest majority of affirmative votes. If two or more conflicting amendments to the Constitution shall be approved by the people at the same election, the amendment which receives the greatest number of affirmative votes shall be paramount in all particulars as to which there is a conflict, even though such amendment may not have received the greatest majority of affirmative votes.

SECTION 16. (CANVASS AND RETURN OF VOTES)

The votes on measures and questions shall be counted, canvassed and returned by the regular board of judges, clerks and officers, as votes for candidates are counted, canvassed and returned, and the abstract made by the several county clerks of votes on measures shall be returned to the Secretary of State on separate abstract sheets, in the manner provided for abstract of votes for State and county officers. It shall be the duty of the Secretary of State, in the presence of the Governor to proceed within thirty days after the election, and sooner if the returns be all received, to canvass the votes given for each measure; and the Governor shall forthwith issue his proclamation giving the whole number of votes cast in the State for and against each measure and question, and declaring such measures as are approved such majority of those voting thereon as required by the Constitution to be in full force and effect as the law of the State of Oklahoma from the date of said proclamation, provided, that if two or more measures shall be approved at said election which are known to conflict with each other, or to contain conflicting provisions he shall also proclaim that which is paramount in accordance with the provisions of Section Fifteen of this Act.[1]

SECTION 17. (PROCEDURE IN MUNICIPALITIES)

In all cities, counties and other municipalities which do not provide by ordinance or charter for the manner of exercising the initiative and referendum powers reserved by the Constitution to the whole people thereof, as to their municipal legislation, the duties required by the Governor and Secretary of State, by this Act, as to state legislation, shall be performed as to such municipal legislation by the chief executive and the chief clerk; and the duties required by this Act of the Attorney-General shall be performed by the attorney for the county, district, or other municipality. The provisions of this act including those relating to preparation of arguments shall apply to every city and town in all matters concerning the operation of the initiative and referendum in its municipal legislation, on which such city or town has not made or does not make conflicting provisions. The printing and binding of measures and their distribution shall be paid for by the city in like manner as payment is provided for by the state as to state legislation by this Act, except that de-

[1] Be it Enacted by the People of the State of Oklahoma: Section I, Whenever any measure shall be initiated by the people in the manner provided by law, or whenever the referendum shall be demanded against any measure passed by the Legislature, the Governor shall have the power, in his discretion, to call a special election to vote upon such question. Approved March 11, 1909. *Session Laws of Oklahoma*, 1909, p. 270.

livery shall not be less than eight days before the election at which the measures are to be voted upon. The arguments shall be completed not less than twelve days before the election at which they are to be voted upon. It is intended to make the procedure in municipal legislation as nearly as practicable, the same as the initiative and referendum procedure for measures relating to people of the state at large.

SECTION 18. (MUNICIPALITIES TO FOLLOW PROCEDURE FOR STATE)

The signatures to each referendum petition against any ordinance, or resolution, passed by a municipal legislative body shall be verified in the manner provided in section four of this Act. The petition shall be filed with the chief executive officer within thirty days after the passage of such ordinance or resolution. No ordinance or resolution of a municipal legislature shall become operative until thirty days after its passage and approval by the executive officer, unless the same shall be passed over his veto and in that case it shall not take effect and become operative until thirty days after such final passage except such measures necessary for the immediate preservation of peace, health, or safety; and no such emergency measure shall become immediately operative, unless it shall state, in a separate section, the reasons why it is necessary that it shall become immediately operative, and the question of emergency shall be ruled upon separately and be approved by the affirmative vote of three-fourths of all the members elected to the city council taken by ayes and noes, and the whole measure be approved by the executive officer.

SECTION 19. (MUNICIPAL LEGISLATIVE BODY MAY SUBMIT COMPETING MEASURE)

Each measure proposed within a municipality by initiative petition and referendum petition shall be filed with the chief clerk of the municipality. Along with each initiative measure the municipal legislature may submit a competing bill or resolution.

The Initiative and Referendum

If conflicting ordinances or charter amendments shall be submitted to the people at the same election, and two or more of such conflicting measures shall be approved by the people, then the measure which shall have received the greatest number of affirmative votes shall be paramount in all particulars as to which there is conflict, even though such measure may not have received the greatest majority. Amendments to any municipal charter may be proposed and submitted to the people by the municipal legislature, with or without any initiative petition but the same shall be filed with the chief clerk for submission not less than sixty days before the election at which they are to be voted upon, and no amendment of a municipal charter shall be effective until it is approved by a majority of the votes cast thereon by the people of the city or town to which it applies. The municipal legislature may order a special election to vote on a municipal measure.

SECTION 20. (WHO MAY FILE PETITIONS AND VOTE. PENALTIES)

Every person who is a qualified elector of the State of Oklahoma may sign a petition for the referendum or for the initiative for any measure for which he is legally entitled to vote upon. Any person signing any name other than his own to any petition, or knowingly signing his name more than once for the same measure at one election, or who is not at the time of signing the same a legal voter of this state, or whoever falsely makes or wilfully destroys a petition or any part thereof, or who signs or files any certificate or petition, knowing the same or any part thereof to be falsely made, or suppresses any certificate or petition or any part thereof which has been duly filed or who shall violate any provision of this statute, or who shall aid or abet any other person in doing any of said acts; or any officer or any person violating any provision of this statute, shall upon conviction thereof be punished by a fine of not exceeding five hundred dollars or by imprisonment in the penitentiary not exceeding two years, **or** by both such fine and imprisonment in the discretion of the court before which such conviction shall be had.

SECTION 21. (SUFFICIENCY OF PROCEDURE)

The procedure herein prescribed is not mandatory, but if substantially followed will be sufficient. If the end aimed at can be attained and procedure shall be sustained, clerical and mere technical errors shall be disregarded.

That this Act take effect from and after its passage and approval.

Approved April 16th, 1908.

Partial Change of Procedure, 1910[1]

A BILL ENTITLED

An Act carrying into effect Provisions relating to the Initiative and Referendum; prescribing the Method of Procedure for Submitting and Voting for Proposed Amendments to the Constitution and other Propositions, and prescribing the Method of Appeals from Petitions Filed or from the Ballot Title; repealing Sections 6, 7 and 16, Article One, Chapter Forty-four of the Session Laws of Oklahoma, 1907–1908.

Be it Enacted by the People of the State of Oklahoma: —

Section 1. Sections 6 and 7 of article I, chapter 44, Session Laws of 1907–1908, are hereby expressly repealed.

Sec. 2. When a citizen or citizens desire to circulate a petition initiating a proposition of any nature, whether to become a statute law or an amendment to the constitution, or for the purpose of invoking a referendum upon legislative enactments, such citizen or citizens shall, when such petition is prepared, and before the same is circulated or signed by electors, file a true and exact copy of same in the office of the Secretary of State, and within sixty days after the date of such filing the original petition shall be filed in the office of the Secretary of State, and no petition not

[1] See above, p. 146.

The Initiative and Referendum

filed in accordance with this provision shall be considered. When such original petition is filed in said office it shall be the duty of the Secretary of State to forthwith cause to be published in at least one newspaper of general circulation within the State, a notice setting forth the date of such filing. Any citizen of the State may, within ten days, by written notice to the Secretary of State and to the party or parties who filed such petition, protest against the same, whereupon the Secretary of State shall fix a day, not sooner than five days thereafter, at which he will hear testimony and arguments for and against the sufficiency of such petition. A protest filed by any one hereunder may, if abandoned by the party filing same, be revived within five days by any other citizen. After such hearing the Secretary of State shall decide whether such petition be in form as required by the statutes, and his decision shall be subject to appeal to the Supreme Court of the State, and such court shall give such cause precedence over all others. *Provided,* Such appeal must be taken within ten days after the decision of the Secretary of State has been made. If the court be at the time adjourned, the Chief Justice shall immediately convene the same for such hearing. It shall be the duty of the appellants to serve notice upon the Secretary of State, in writing, of such appeal. Whereupon said Secretary of State shall immediately transmit all papers and documents on file in his office relating to such petition to such court. If the court shall adjudge such petition insufficient the parties responsible for same shall have the right to correct or amend their petition to conform to the opinion of the court, provided said amendment or change is made within five days. No objection to the sufficiency of a petition shall be considered unless the same shall have been made and filed as herein provided.

Sec. 3. When a measure is proposed as a constitutional amendment by the Legislature, when the referendum is ordered against any measure passed by the Legislature, or when any measure is proposed by initiative petition, whether as an amendment to the constitution or as a statute law, it shall be the duty of the parties submitting such proposition to prepare and file one copy of same with the Secretary of State and one copy with the Attorney-General of the State, such copies to contain a ballot title of not exceeding one hundred words, which shall be a gist of the proposition without containing any argument or prejudicial statement either for or against such measure. Within three days after the filing of such copy and ballot title with the Attorney-General, such official shall, in writing, notify the Secretary of State as to whether or not such proposed title is in legal form and in harmony with the law. Should such title not be in proper form, in the opinion of the Attorney-General, it shall be the duty of that official to, within said three days, prepare and file a title which does conform to the law. Within five days after the receipt of the notice of approval by the Attorney-General, or of a revised or amended title from such official, the Secretary of State shall transmit to the Secretary of the State Election Board an attested copy of the pending proposition, including such approved title; *Provided*, however, that should an appeal be prosecuted within the time specified by this act, from such ballot title, then the Secretary of State shall certify to said Secretary of the State Election Board the title which is finally approved by the court. If the measure is such as to require its being printed upon the ballots of a district or of the entire State, the State Election Board shall have supervision of such printing. If the measure is such as must appear upon ballots printed in the several counties of the State, or any portion of same, it shall be the duty of the State Election Board to transmit, within ten days, true copies of such ballot title to the chairman or secretary of all the county election boards of the counties in which such measure is to be voted upon, and such county boards shall supervise such printing.

Sec. 4. Any person who is dissatisfied with the wording of the ballot title prepared, as hereinbefore provided, may, within ten days after the same is filed as aforesaid, appeal to the Supreme Court by petition in which shall be offered a substitute title for the one appealed from. Upon the hearing of such appeal the court may correct or amend the title before the court, or may draft a new one which will conform to this act.

Sec. 5. Notice of the appeal provided for in the foregoing section shall be served upon the Attorney-General and upon the party who filed such title, or on any of such parties, at least five days before such appeal is heard by the court. The Attorney-General shall, and any citizen interested may, defend the title appealed from. Other procedure upon such appeals shall be the same as is prescribed for appeals from petitions filed as set forth in section 2 hereof.

Sec. 6. Whenever any measure or proposition is submitted to a vote by the initiative or referendum, it shall be the duty of the official counters of the precinct to make and transmit to the county election board the returns thereof in the same manner that they make their returns in the case of an election of public officers, transmitting to such county election board a certificate of the total number of electors voting in such election; and the county election board shall keep a record showing such total number of votes cast in each of such precincts as shown by such returns. Should the proposition be one covering the State at large, or any district therein, or be of such other nature as to require it, the county election board shall certify the result of such election to the State Election Board in the same manner as it certifies the result of election for public officers, and such county election board shall transmit to the State Election Board a certificate showing the total number of votes cast at such election. It shall be the duty of the State Election Board to keep a record of all such election returns made to it under the provisions of this section.

Sec. 7. Section 1, article 16, chapter 44, Session Laws of 1907-1908, is hereby expressly repealed.

ARTICLE II

Section 1. If the Legislature should desire to ascertain the sentiment of the people upon any proposed amendment to the constitution, it may, by concurrent resolution, suggest to the citizens of the State such proposition as an amendment to the constitution. Such resolution shall set forth the proposed amendment in full and should the citizens of the State proceed to initiate such proposition within one year thereafter, then it shall be the duty of the Secretary of State, when the required petitions have been filed in his office, to cause an attested copy thereof to be filed with the chairman of the State Election Board, together with a certificate of the fact that the proposition was originated by concurrent resolution of the Legislature, setting forth such resolution.

Sec. 2. All propositions first suggested to the people by the Legislature, as provided by section 1 of this article, shall be printed by such election board, and they shall have the supervision of the printing of the ballots, for such proposed amendment, and such proposition shall be printed either on a separate and independent ballot or upon the ballot upon which the names of candidates appear, should such election occur upon the day when candidates are being voted for. *Provided, however*, that the State Election Board shall not be empowered to change the form of any ballot as prescribed by the Legislature, should such title be printed upon ballots containing the names of candidates. If separate ballots are used at such election for county candidates, only local propositions can be printed thereon. All state-wide or district propositions shall be printed only upon the State ballots. Such election board shall cause the said title of each proposition to be printed, followed by the words "for the amendment," which words shall be in a separate paragraph and at least one-fourth of an inch below such title. Said words shall have no distinguishing marks about them.

Sec. 3. Any person having ballots, or sample ballots, outside the election inclosure either at the time of or before the election, in which is printed the said ballot title, and which were not printed by order of the State Election Board and furnished him by the inspector of elections, shall be deemed guilty of a misdemeanor and upon conviction shall be fined not less than twenty-five

The Initiative and Referendum 159

dollars ($25.00), nor more than five hundred dollars ($500.00), and imprisonment in the county jail not less than thirty days nor more than ninety days. Any person printing or distributing sample or extra ballots not authorized by the State Election Board, and which contain such ballot title, shall be deemed guilty of a misdemeanor and upon conviction shall be fined not less than fifty dollars ($50.00) nor more than five hundred dollars ($500.00), and imprisonment in the county jail not less than ninety days nor more than twelve months; *Provided*, That nothing herein shall prevent newspapers from publishing in their papers educational ballots, provided the same shall not be of the same size as are the official ballots.

Sec. 4. Electors shall vote upon all propositions submitted under the provisions of this act, and which were first suggested by concurrent resolution of the Legislature, in the following manner:

Should the elector desire to vote for the proposed amendment he shall leave the words, "for the amendment," intact without erasing same. But should he desire to vote against such proposition he shall strike out the words, "for the amendment," with a pencil mark. When such words are so erased after any proposition, the ballot shall be recorded as having been cast against the same, and whenever they are not so erased, such ballot shall be recorded as having been voted for such proposition.

Sec. 5. On all other questions, propositions or proposed amendments, whether presented by initiative or referendum petition, the same shall be voted for as is provided by the general act of the State Legislature of 1907-1908, known as "An act for the carrying into effect initiative and referendum powers reserved by the people in articles 5 and 18 of the constitution of the State of Oklahoma, to regulate elections thereunder, and to punish violations of this act," the same being section 3682 of the Compiled Laws of Oklahoma, 1909, by Snyder.

Sec. 6. It shall be the duty of the election officers to make out separate abstract sheets upon which the returns relating to proposed amendments shall be certified, each proposition appearing in an abstract to itself. It shall be the duty of the State Election Board to certify to the Governor, immediately upon the receipt of all the returns upon any such proposition, the result thereof, and upon the receipt of such certificate, from said board, it shall be the duty of the Governor to issue his proclamation giving the whole number of votes cast in the State or any district and declaring the results of the vote upon any proposition.

Sec. 7. The duties of any nature whatsoever, which, by the Session Law of Oklahoma, 1907–1908, entitled, "An act to provide for carrying into effect the initiative and referendum powers reserved by the people in articles 5 and 18 of the constitution of the State of Oklahoma, to regulate elections thereunder, and to punish violators of this act," imposed upon the Secretary of State, shall be hereafter performed by the State Election Board, provided such board is continued in existence. Should such board be discontinued, the duties herein imposed upon the same shall be performed by the Secretary of State. All duties imposed by said act of 1907–1908 upon county clerks shall hereafter be performed by the county election board, provided such board is continued in existence, otherwise, the duties herein imposed upon the county election boards shall be performed by the county clerks. The duties imposed upon precinct election officers by said act shall be performed by precinct election boards and the official counters, respectively, provided such election board and official counters are retained as precinct election boards. Should they be discontinued, the duties imposed upon them by this act shall be performed by the regularly chosen precinct election officers.

Passed by the Senate March 10, 1910.

J. C. GRAHAM,
President Pro Tempore of the Senate.

Passed by the House of Representatives March 17, 1910.

BEN F. WILSON,
Speaker of the House of Representatives.

Approved March 17, 1910.

C. N. HASKELL, *Governor.*

The Initiative and Referendum

Partial Change of Procedure—1911[1]

A BILL

Entitled an act amending Section 2 of Article 1, Chapter 66 of the Session Laws of 1910, the same being a bill entitled "An Act carrying into effect provisions relating to the Initiative and Referendum, prescribing the Method of Procedure for submitting and voting proposed amendments to the Constitution, and other Propositions, and Prescribing the Method of Appeal from Petitions filed or from the Ballot," etc.

Be it Enacted by the People of the State of Oklahoma: —

Section 1. That Section 2 of Article 1, Chapter 66 of the Session Laws of 1910 be, and the same is, hereby amended to read as follows: —

Section 2. When a citizen, or citizens, desire to circulate a petition initiating a proposition of any nature, whether to become a statute law or an amendment to the constitution, or for the purpose of invoking a referendum upon legislative enactments, such citizen or citizens shall, when such petition is prepared, and before the same is circulated or signed by electors, file a true and exact copy of the same in the office of the Secretary of State, and within ninety days after the date of such filing, the original petition shall be filed in the office of the Secretary of State, and no petition not filed in accordance with this provision shall be considered. When such original petition is filed in said office it it shall be the duty of the Secretary of State to forthwith cause to be published in at least one newspaper of general circulation within the state, a notice setting forth the date of such filing. Any citizen of the State may, within ten days, by written notice to the Secretary of State and to the party or parties, who filed such petition, protest against the same at which time he will hear testimony and argument for and against the sufficiency of such petition. A protest filed by any one hereunder may, if abandoned

[1] See above, pp. 146 and 154.

by the party filing same, be revived within five days by any other citizen. After such hearing the Secretary of State shall decide whether such petition be in form as required by the statutes, and his decision shall be subject to appeal to the Supreme Court of the State, and such court shall give such cause precedence over all others, provided, such appeal must be taken within ten days after the decision of the Secretary of State has been made. If the court be at the time adjourned, the Chief Justice shall immediately convene the same for such hearing. It shall be the duty of the appellants to serve notice upon the Secretary of the State, in writing of such an appeal. Whereupon said Secretary of State shall immediately transmit all papers and documents on file in his office relating to such petition to such court. If the court shall adjudge such petition insufficient the parties responsible for same shall have the right to correct or amend their petition to conform to the opinion of the court, provided said amendment or change is made within five days. No objection to the sufficiency shall be considered unless the same shall have been made and filed as herein provided.

VII. MAINE

[The amendment introducing the initiative and referendum in Maine was approved March 20, 1907. It was ratified by the voters at the general election held September 14, 1908. As yet, the initiative has not been used. However the referendum was invoked on three acts of the Legislature in 1910, and in each case the action taken by the Legislature was not sustained.]

Constitutional Amendment

Resolves proposing an amendment to article four of the constitution of the state of Maine, establishing a people's veto through the optional referendum, and a direct initiative by petition and at general or special elections.

Resolved, That the following amendment to the constitution of this state be proposed for the action of the legal voters of this state in the manner provided by the constitution, to wit: —

STATE OF MAINE.

Measures referred to the people to be voted on in the Town of Alfred,
September 12, 1910.

Penalty for wilfully defacing, tearing down, removing or destroying a list of candidates or specimen ballot, five to one hundred dollars fine.

A. I. BROWN, Secretary of State

If you are in favor of the first measure, mark a cross (X) in the square under the word "yes." If you are opposed to the measure, mark a cross (X) in the square under the word "no."

If you are in favor of the second measure, mark a cross (X) in the square under the word "yes." If you are opposed to the measure, mark a cross (X) in the square under the word "no."

If you are in favor of the third measure, mark a cross (X) in the square under the word "yes." If you are opposed to the measure, mark a cross (X) in the square under the word "no,"

SPECIMEN BALLOT

Measures Referred to the People

Under the Constitutional Provisions for Referendum.

Shall the following measures, or any one of them

Part first of article four is hereby amended as follows, namely:

By striking out all of section one after the word 'Maine' in the third line thereof, and inserting in lieu thereof the following words 'But the people reserve to themselves power to propose laws and to enact or reject the same at the polls independent of the legislature, and also reserve power at their own option to approve or reject at the polls any act, bill, resolve or resolution passed by the joint action of both branches of the legislature, and the style of their laws and acts shall be " Be it enacted by the people of the state of Maine,"' so that said section as amended shall read as follows, namely:—

'The legislative power shall be vested in two distinct branches, a house of representatives and a senate, each to have a negative on the other, and both to be styled the legislature of Maine, but the people reserve to themselves power to propose laws and to enact or reject the same at the polls independent of the legislature, and also reserve power at their own option to approve or reject at the polls any act, bill, resolve or resolution passed by the joint action of both branches of the legislature, and the style of their laws and acts shall be, 'Be it enacted by the people of the state of Maine.'

Part third of article four is hereby amended as follows, namely:

By inserting in section one, after the words "biennially and" in the second line thereof, the words 'with the exceptions hereinafter stated,' so that said section shall read as amended:—

'The legislature shall convene on the first Wednesday of January, biennially, and, with the exceptions hereinafter stated, shall have full power to make and establish all reasonable laws and regulations for the defence and benefit of the people of this state, not repugnant to this constitution nor to that of the United States.'

Part third of article four is further amended by adding to said article the following sections to be numbered from sixteen to twenty-two inclusive, namely:

'Sec. 16. No act or joint resolution of the legislature, except such orders or resolutions as pertain solely to facilitating the performance of the business of the legislature, of either branch, or of any committee or officer thereof, or appropriate money therefor or for the payment of salaries fixed by law, shall take effect until ninety days after the recess of the legislature passing it, unless in case of emergency (which with the facts constituting the emergency shall be expressed in the preamble of the act), the legislature shall, by a vote of two-thirds of all the members elected to each house, otherwise direct. An emergency bill shall include only such measures as are immediately necessary for the preservation of the public peace, health or safety; and shall not include (1) an infringement of the right of home rule for municipalities, (2) a franchise or a license to a corporation or an individual to extend longer than one year, or (3) provision for the sale or purchase or renting for more than five years of real estate.'

'Sec. 17. Upon written petition of not less than ten thousand electors, addressed to the governor and filed in the office of the secretary of state within ninety days after the recess of the legislature, requesting that one or more acts, bills, resolves or resolutions, or part or parts thereof, passed by the legislature, but not then in effect by reason of the provisions of the preceding section, be referred to the people, such acts, bills, resolves, or resolutions or part or parts thereof as are specified in such petition shall not take effect until thirty days after the governor shall have announced by public proclamation that the same have been ratified by a majority of the electors voting thereon at a general or special election. As soon as it appears that the effect of any act, bill, resolve, or resolution or part or parts thereof has been suspended by petition in manner aforesaid, the governor by public proclamation shall give notice thereof and of the time when such measure is to be voted on by the people, which shall be at the next general election not less than sixty days after such proclamation, or in case of no general election within six months thereafter the governor may, and if so requested in said written petition therefor, shall order such measure submitted to the people at a special

The Initiative and Referendum

election not less than four nor more than six months after his proclamation thereof.

'Sec. 18. The electors may propose to the legislature for its consideration any bill, resolve or resolution, including bills to amend or repeal emergency legislation but not an amendment of the state constitution, by written petition addressed to the legislature or to either branch thereof and filed in the office of the secretary of state or presented to either branch of the legislature at least thirty days before the close of its session. Any measure thus proposed by not less than twelve thousand electors, unless enacted without change by the legislature at the session at which it is presented, shall be submitted to the electors together with any amended form, substitute, or recommendation of the legislature, and in such manner that the people can choose between the competing measures or reject both. When there are competing bills and neither receives a majority of the votes given for or against both, the one receiving the most votes shall at the next general election to be held not less than sixty days after the first vote thereon be submitted by itself if it receives more than one-third of the votes given for and against both. If the measure initiated is enacted by the legislature without change, it shall not go to a referendum vote unless in pursuance of a demand made in accordance with the preceding section. The legislature may order a special election on any measure that is subject to a vote of the people. The governor may, and if so requested in the written petitions addressed to the legislature, shall, by proclamation, order any measure proposed to the legislature by at least twelve thousand electors as herein provided, and not enacted by the legislature without change, referred to the people at a special election to be held not less than four or more than six months after such proclamation, otherwise said measure shall be voted upon at the next general election held not less than sixty days after the recess of the legislature, to which such measure was proposed.'

'Sec. 19. Any measure referred to the people and approved by a majority of the votes given thereon shall, unless a later date is specified in said measure, take effect and become a law in thirty days after the governor has made public proclamation of the result of the vote on said measure, which he shall do within ten days after the vote thereon has been canvassed and determined. The veto power of the governor shall not extend to any measure approved by vote of the people, and any measure initiated by the people and passed by the legislature without change, if vetoed by the governor and if his veto is sustained by the legislature shall be referred to the people to be voted on at the next general election. The legislature may enact measures expressly conditioned upon the people's ratification by a referendum vote.'

'Sec. 20. As used in either of the three preceding sections the words "electors" and "people" mean the electors of the state qualified to vote for governor; "recess of the legislature" means the adjournment without day of a session of the legislature; "general election" means the November election for choice of presidential electors or the September election for choice of governor and other state and county officers; "measure" means an act, bill, resolve or resolution proposed by the people, or two or more such, or part or parts of such, as the case may be; "written petition" means one or more petitions written or printed, or partly written and partly printed, with the original signatures of the petitioners attached, verified as to the authenticity of the signatures by the oath of one of the petitioners certified thereon, and accompanied by the certificate of the clerk of the city, town or plantation in which the petitioners reside that their names appear on the voting list of his city, town or plantation as qualified to vote for governor. The petitions shall set forth the full text of the measure requested or proposed. The full text of a measure submitted to a vote of the people under the provisions of the constitution need not be printed on the official ballots, but, until otherwise provided by the legislature, the secretary of state shall prepare the ballots in such form as to present the question or questions concisely and intelligibly.'

'Sec. 21. The city council of any city may establish the

The Initiative and Referendum 167

initiative and referendum for the electors of such city in regard to its municipal affairs, provided that the ordinance establishing and providing the method of exercising such initiative and referendum shall not take effect until ratified by vote of a majority of the electors of said city, voting thereon at a municipal election. Provided, however, that the legislature may at any time provide a uniform method for the exercise of the initiative and referendum in municipal affairs.'

'Sec. 22. Until the legislature shall enact further regulations not inconsistent with the constitution for applying the people's veto and direct initiative, the election officers and other officials shall be governed by the provisions of this constitution and of the general law, supplemented by such reasonable action as may be necessary to render the preceding sections self-executing.'

Resolved, That all the foregoing is proposed to be voted upon as one amendment, and not as two or more several amendments.

Resolved, That the aldermen of cities, the selectmen of towns and the assessors of the several plantations in this state are hereby empowered and directed to notify the inhabitants of their respective cities, towns, and plantations in the manner prescribed by law to vote at the meeting in September in the year one thousand nine hundred and eight upon the amendment proposed in the foregoing resolutions, and the question shall be

"Shall the constitution be amended as proposed by a resolution of the legislature providing for the establishment of a people's veto through the optional referendum and a direct initiative by petition and at general or special elections?" and the inhabitants of said cities, towns and plantations shall vote by ballot on said question, those favoring the amendment voting "yes" and those opposing voting "no" upon their ballots, and the ballots shall be received, sorted, counted, and declared in open ward, town and plantation meetings and lists of the votes so received shall be made and returned to the office of the secretary of state, in the same manner as votes for governor and members of the legislature, and the governor and council shall count the same and make return to the next legislature, and if it shall appear that a majority of the votes are in favor of the amendment, the constitution shall be amended accordingly.

Resolved, That the secretary of state shall prepare and furnish to the several cities, towns and plantations, ballots and blank returns in conformity to the foregoing resolves accompanied by a copy thereof.

VIII. MISSOURI

[Mr. Roach, Secretary of State, writes as follows (May, 1911): "The Initiative and Referendum Amendment to the constitution of Missouri was adopted, by a popular vote of 177,615 for, to 147,290 against, at the general election held November 3, 1908. The enabling act followed at the session of the General Assembly that convened in January, 1909. In the general election of 1910, two proposed constitutional amendments were submitted under the said act; the one prohibiting sale and manufacture of intoxicating liquor in the state being lost by a vote of 207,281 for, to 425,406 against; the other providing for a 3-cent tax on $100 for support of the University being lost by a vote of 181,659 for, to 344,274 against. Constitutional amendments have always been submitted to popular vote under the constitution of this State, the only distinction attaching to the above mentioned being that they were initiated by popular petition instead of by resolution of the General Assembly.

"No statute law has yet been proposed under the act, nor has one passed by the Legislature been referred. No pamphlet publication is issued by the State. Experience on which to base criticism is yet too limited. There is no public agitation for repeal of the law."]

The Constitutional Amendment [1]

The legislative authority of the State shall be vested in a legislative assembly, consisting of a senate and house of representatives, but the people reserve to themselves power to propose laws and amendments to the Constitution, and to enact or reject the same at the polls, independent of the legislative assembly, and also reserve power at their own option to approve or reject at the

---

[1] *Constitution of the State of Missouri* (Official, 1909), pp. 38 f.

polls any act of the legislative assembly. The first power reserved by the people is the initiative, and not more than eight per cent of the legal voters in each of at least two-thirds of the congressional districts in the State shall be required to propose any measure by such petition, and every such petition shall include the full text of the measure so proposed. Initiative petitions shall be filed with the Secretary of State not less than four months before the election at which they are to be voted upon. The second power is the referendum, and it may be ordered (except as to laws necessary for the immediate preservation of the public peace, health or safety and laws making appropriations for the current expenses of the State government, for the maintenance of the state institutions and for the support of public schools) either by the petitions signed by five per cent of the legal voters in each of at least two-thirds of the congressional districts in the State, or by the Legislative Assembly, as other bills are enacted. Referendum petitions shall be filed with the Secretary of State not more than ninety days after the final adjournment of the session of the legislative assembly which passed the bill on which the referendum is demanded. The veto power of the governor shall not extend to measures referred to the people. All elections on measures referred to the people of the State shall be had at the biennial regular general elections, except when the legislative assembly shall order a special election. Any measure referred to the people shall take effect and become the law when it is approved by a majority of the votes cast thereon, and not otherwise. The style of all bills shall be: "Be it enacted by the people of the State of Missouri." This section shall not be construed to deprive any member of the legislative assembly of the right to introduce any measure. The whole number of votes cast for Justice of the Supreme Court at the regular election last preceding the filing of any petition for the initiative, or for the referendum, shall be the basis on which the number of legal voters necessary to sign such petition shall be counted. Petitions and orders for the initiative and for the referendum shall be filed with the Secretary of State, and in submitting the same to the people he, and all other officers, shall be guided by the general laws and the act submitting this amendment, until legislation shall be especially provided therefor.

The Elaborating Law

[In 1909, the Legislature passed the following act providing the procedure for the initiative and referendum.]

INITIATIVE AND REFERENDUM: FORM OF PROCEDURE GOVERNING THE ADOPTION OF SAME [1]

An Act to provide the forms of petition for the referendum and initiative, with warning order; for verification of signatures, affidavit to petitions and minimum number of signatures to be filed with secretary of state, to provide for filing of petitions and for judicial proceedings thereon; to provide for certifying ballot titles to county clerks and for printing the same; to provide for manner of voting on measures, and what measure may be paramount in case of conflict; to provide for canvass and returns of votes on measures and for proclamation on paramount measures; to provide penalty for violation of this act; to define term "county clerks" as used herein; and to repeal conflicting acts.

SECTION

1. Form of petition to refer.
2. Form of petition to initiate an act.
3. Verification of petition sheets.
4. Secretary of state to file petitions, when — may be mandamused, when.
5. Duties of secretary of state and attorney-general relating to petitions.
6. Secretary to certify to county clerks, how.
7. Voting on initiative and referendum subjects — how done.
8. Votes, how counted and canvassed.
9. Who may sign petitions.
10. Term county clerks to include city election boards.
11. Inconsistent acts repealed.

[1] Laws, Missouri, 1909, Initiative and Referendum, pp. 554 ff.

The Initiative and Referendum

Be it enacted by the General Assembly of the State of Missouri, as follows: —

Section 1. Form of petition to refer. — The following shall be substantially the form of petition for the referendum to the people on any act passed by the general assembly of the State of Missouri.

WARNING

It is a felony for any one to sign any initiative or referendum petition with any name other than his own, or to knowingly sign his name more than once for the same measure, or to sign such petition when he is not a legal voter.

PETITION FOR REFERENDUM

To the Honorable ...., secretary of state for the state of Missouri: We, the undersigned, citizens and legal voters of the state of Missouri (and the county of ....), respectfully order that the senate (or house) bill No. ...., entitled (title of act) passed by the .... general assembly of the state of Missouri, at the regular (special) session of said general assembly, shall be referred to the people of the state, for their approval or rejection, at the regular (special) election to be held on the ...... day of ...... A.D. 19..., and each for himself says: I have personally signed this petition; I am a legal voter of the state of Missouri and county of ....; my residence and postoffice are correctly written after my name.
Name ...., Residence ...., Postoffice ....
(If in a city, street and number.)
(Here follow numbered lines for signatures.)

Sec. 2. Form of petition to initiate an act. — The following shall be substantially the form of petition for any law or amendment to the Constitution of the State of Missouri, proposed by the initiative.

WARNING

It is a felony for any one to sign any initiative or referendum petition with any name other than his own, or to knowingly sign his name more than once for the measure, or to sign such petition when he is not a legal voter.

INITIATIVE PETITION

To the Honorable ...., secretary of state for the state of Missouri: —

We, the undersigned, citizens and legal voters for the state of Missouri, and of the county of ...., respectfully demand that the following proposed law (or amendment to the Constitution, as the case may be), shall be submitted to the legal voters of the state of Missouri, for their approval or rejection, at the regular general (special) election to be held on the ..... day of ...... A.D. 19.., and each for himself says: I have personally signed this petition; I am a legal voter of the state of Missouri and of the county of ....; my residence and postoffice are correctly written after my name.

Name ...., Residence ...., Postoffice ....
(If in a city, street and number.)
(Here follow numbered lines for signatures.)

Every such sheet for petitioners' signatures shall be attached to a full and correct copy of the title and text of the measure so proposed by the initiative petition; but such petition may be filed with the secretary of state in numbered sections, for convenience in handling, and referendum petitions shall be attached to a full and correct copy of the measure on which the referendum is demanded, and may be filed in numbered sections in like manner: Provided, that the minimum number of petitioners to either an initiative or referendum petition, when filed with the secretary of state, shall be five per cent of the legal voters in each of at least two-thirds of the congressional districts in the state. When any such initiative or referendum petition shall be offered for filing, the secretary of state, in the presence of the governor and the person offering the same for filing, shall detach the sheet containing the signatures and affidavits and cause them all to be attached to one or more printed copies of the measure so proposed by initiative or referendum petition; the detached copies of such measure shall be delivered to the person offering the same for filing. If any such measure shall, at the ensuing election, be approved by the people, then the copies thereof so preserved, with the sheets and signatures and affidavits, and a certified copy of the governor's proclamation, declaring the same to have been approved by the people, shall be bound together in such form that they may be conveniently identified and preserved. The secretary of state shall cause every such measure so approved by the people to be printed with the general laws enacted by the next ensuing session of the general assembly, with the date of the governor's proclamation declaring the same to have been approved by the people.

Sec. 3. Verification of petition sheets. — Each and every sheet of every such petition containing signatures shall be verified in substantially the following form by the person who circulated said sheet of said petition, by his or her affidavit thereon and as part thereof: —

State of Missouri, } ss.
County of .... }

I, ..., being duly sworn, say (here shall be legibly written or typewritten the name of the signers of the sheet), signed this sheet of the foregoing petition, and each of them signed his name thereto in my presence; I believe that each has stated his name, postoffice address and residence correctly, and that each signer is a legal voter of the state of Missouri and county of.............

(Signatures and postoffice address of affiant.)

Subscribed and sworn to before me this ...... day of ...... A.D. 19...

(Signature and title of officer before whom oath is made and his postoffice address.)

The forms herein given are not mandatory, and if substantially followed in any petition it shall be sufficient, disregarding clerical and merely technical errors.

Sec. 4. Secretary of state to file petitions, when — may be mandamused, when. — If the secretary of state shall refuse to accept and file any petitions for the initiative or for the referendum, any citizen may apply, within ten days after such refusal, to the circuit court for a writ of mandamus to compel him to do so. If it shall be decided by the court that such petition is legally sufficient, the secretary of state shall then file it, with a certified copy of the judgment attached thereto, as of the date on which it was originally offered for filing in his office. On showing that any petition filed is not legally sufficient, the court may enjoin the secretary of state and all other officers from certifying or printing on the official ballot for the ensuing election the ballot title and numbers of such measure. All such suits shall be advanced on the court docket and heard and decided by the court as quickly as possible. Either party may appeal to the supreme court within ten days after a decision is rendered. The circuit court of Cole county shall have jurisdiction in all such cases.

Sec. 5. Duties of secretary of state and attorney-general relating to petitions. — When any measure shall be filed with the secretary of state, to be referred to the people thereof by the referendum petition, and when any measure shall be proposed by the initiative petition, the secretary of state shall forthwith transmit to the attorney-general of the state a copy thereof, and within ten days thereafter the attorney-general shall provide and return to the secretary of state a ballot title for said measure. The ballot title may be distinct from the legislative title of the measure, and shall express, in not exceeding one hundred words, the purpose of the measure. The ballot title shall be printed with the number of the measure on the official ballot. In making such ballot title the attorney-general shall, to the best of his ability, give a true and impartial statement of the purpose of the measure, and in such language that the ballot title shall not be

The Initiative and Referendum 175

intentionally an argument likely to create prejudice either for or against the measure. Any person who is dissatisfied with the ballot title provided by the attorney-general for any measure may appeal from his decision to the circuit court, as provided by section 4 of this act, by petition, praying for a different title, and setting forth the reasons why the title prepared by the attorney-general is insufficient or unfair. No appeal shall be allowed from the decision of the attorney-general on a ballot title unless the same is taken within ten days after said decision is filed. A copy of every such decision shall be served by the secretary of state or the clerk of the court, upon the person offering or filing such initiative or referendum petition or appeal. Service of such decision may be by mail or telegram, and shall be made forthwith. Said circuit court shall thereupon examine said measure, hear arguments, and in its decision thereon certify to the secretary of state a ballot title for the measure in accord with the intent of this section. The decision of the circuit court shall be final. The secretary of state shall print on the official ballot the title thus certified to him.

Sec. 6. Secretary to certify to county clerks, how. — The secretary of state, at the time he furnishes to the county clerks of the several counties certified copies of the names of the candidates of state and county offices, shall furnish to each of said county clerks his certified copy of the ballot title and numbers of the several measures to be voted upon at the coming general election, and he shall use for each measure the ballot title designated in the manner herein provided. Such ballot title shall in no case exceed one hundred words, and shall not resemble, so far as probably to create confusion, any such title previously filed for any measure to be submitted at that election; he shall number such measures, and such ballot titles shall be printed on the official ballot in the order in which the acts referred by the general assembly and petitions by the people shall be filed in his office. It shall be the duty of the several county clerks to print said ballot title and numbers upon the official ballot in the order presented to them by the secretary of state and the relative position required by law. Measures referred by petition shall be designated "Referendum ordered by the petition of the people"; measures proposed by initiative petitions shall be designated and distinguished on the ballot by the heading "Proposed by initiative petition."

Sec. 7. Voting on initiative and referendum subjects, how done.—The manner of voting upon the measures submitted to the people shall be the same as is now or may be required and provided by law; no measure shall be adopted unless it shall receive an affirmative majority of the total number of respective votes cast on such measures and entitled to be counted under the provisions of this act. If two or more conflicting laws shall be approved by the people at the same election, the law receiving the greatest number of affirmative votes shall be paramount in all particulars as to which there is a conflict, even though such law may not have received the greatest majority of affirmative votes. If two or more conflicting amendments to the Constitution shall be approved by the people at the same election, the amendment which receives the greatest number of affirmative votes shall be paramount in all particulars as to which there is a conflict, even though such amendment may not have received the greatest majority of affirmative votes.

Sec. 8. Votes, how counted and canvassed. — The votes on measures and questions shall be counted, canvassed and returned by the regular boards of judges, clerks and officers as votes for candidates are counted, canvassed and returned, and the abstract made by the several county clerks of votes on measures, shall be returned to the secretary of state on separate abstract sheets, in the manner provided for abstract of votes for state and county officers. It shall be the duty of the secretary of state, in the presence of the governor, to proceed within thirty days after the election, and sooner if the returns be all received, to canvass the votes given for each measure; and the governor shall forthwith issue his proclamation, giving the whole number of votes cast in the state for and against each measure and question, and declaring such measures as are approved by majority of those voting thereon to be in full force and effect as the law of the state of Missouri from the date of said proclamation: Provided, that if two or more measures shall be approved at said election which are known to conflict with each other or to contain conflicting provisions, he shall also proclaim which is paramount in accordance with the provisions of section 7 of this act.

Sec. 9. Who may sign petitions. — Every person who is a qualified elector of the state of Missouri may sign a petition for the referendum or for the initiative of any measure on which he is legally entitled to vote upon. Any person signing any name other than his own to any petition, or knowingly signing his name more than once for the same measure at one election, or who is not at the time of signing the same a legal voter of this state, or any officer or person wilfully violating any provision of this statute shall, upon conviction thereof, be punished by a fine not exceeding five hundred dollars ($500) or by imprisonment in the penitentiary not exceeding two years or by both such fine and imprisonment.

Sec. 10. Term county clerks to include city election boards. — That the term "county clerks" in this act shall be construed to include the board of election commissioners for the city of Saint Louis and the board or similar officer or officers in any other city in this state, so far as the same relates to any act or duty required to be performed in said city like to that required of or with such county clerks in this act in the respective counties of the state.

Sec. 11. Inconsistent acts repealed. — All acts or parts of acts in conflict with the provisions of this act are hereby repealed.

Approved, June 12, 1909.

IX. MICHIGAN [1]

[The constitution adopted in 1908 provided that the Legislature might refer bills to the voters, and that the initiative might be used for constitutional amendments. These provisions follow.]

Art V, Sec. 38. Any bill passed by the legislature and approved by the governor, except appropriation bills, may be referred by the legislature to the qualified electors; and no bill so referred shall become law unless approved by a majority of the electors voting thereon.

Art. XVII, Sec. 2. Amendments may also be proposed to this constitution by petition of the qualified electors of this state but no proposed amendment shall be submitted to the electors unless the number of petitioners therefor shall exceed twenty per cent of the total number of electors voting for secretary of state at the preceding election of such officer. All petitions shall contain the full text of any proposed amendment, together with any existing provisions of the constitution which would be altered or abrogated thereby. Such petitions shall be signed at the regular registration or election places at a regular registration or election under the supervision of the officials thereof, who shall verify the genuineness of the signatures and certify the fact that the signers are registered electors of the respective townships and cities in which they reside, and shall forthwith forward the petitions to the secretary of state. All petitions for amendments filed with the secretary of state shall be certified by that officer to the legislature at the opening of its next regular session; and, when such petitions for any one proposed amendment shall be signed by not less than the required number of petitioners, he shall also submit the proposed amendment to the electors at the first regular election thereafter, unless the legislature in joint convention shall disapprove of the proposed amendment by a majority of the members elected. The legislature may, by a like

---

[1] *Legislative Manual*, 1909, pp. 566 ff.

vote, submit an alternative or a substitute proposal on the same subject. The action of the legislature shall be entered on the journal of each house, with the yeas and nays taken thereon. But no amendment to this section may be proposed in the manner prescribed.

If a majority of the electors qualified to vote for members of the legislature voting thereon shall ratify and approve any such amendment or amendments, the same shall become a part of the constitution: *Provided*, That for any amendment proposed under this section, the affirmative vote shall be not less than one-third of the highest number of votes cast at the said election for any office. In case alternatives proposed on the same subject are submitted at the same election, the vote shall be for one of such alternatives or against such proposed amendments as a whole. If the affirmative vote for one proposed amendment is the required majority of all the votes cast for and against such proposed amendments, it shall become a part of the constitution. If the total affirmative vote for such alternative proposed amendments is the required majority of all the votes for and against them, but no one proposed amendment receives such majority, then the proposed amendment which receives the largest number of affirmative votes shall be submitted at the next regular election, and if it then receives the required majority of all the votes cast thereon it shall become a part of the constitution. The legislature shall enact appropriate laws to carry out the provisions of this section.

Sec. 3. All proposed amendments to the constitution submitted to the electors shall be published in full, with any existing provisions of the constitution which would be altered or abrogated thereby, and a copy thereof shall be posted at each registration and election place. Proposed amendments shall also be printed in full on a ballot or ballots separate from the ballot containing the names of nominees for public office.

X. ARKANSAS [1]

[The Legislature of Arkansas adopted an initiative and referendum amendment on February 19, 1909. It was ratified by the voters at the general election held September 12, 1910, and is as follows.]

The legislative powers of this state shall be vested in a General Assembly, which shall consist of a Senate and a House of Representatives, but the people of each municipality, each county, and of the state reserve to themselves power to propose laws and amendments to the Constitution and to enact or reject the same at the polls as independent of the legislative assembly, and also reserve power at their own option to approve or reject at the polls any act of the legislative assembly.

The first power reserved by the people is the Initiative, and not more than 8 per cent of the legal voters shall be required to propose any measure by such petition, and every such petition shall include the full text of the measure so proposed. Initiative petitions shall be filed with the Secretary of State not less than four months before the election at which they are to be voted upon.

The second power is the Referendum, and it may be ordered (except as to laws necessary for the immediate preservation of the public peace, health or safety) either by the petition signed by 5 per cent of the legal voters or by the legislative assembly as other bills are enacted. Referendum petitions shall be filed with the Secretary of State not more than ninety days after the final adjournment of the session of the legislative assembly which passed the bill on which the referendum is demanded. The veto power of the Governor shall not extend to measures referred to the people. All elections on measures referred to the people of the State shall be had at the biennial regular general elections, except when the legislative assembly shall order a special

[1] *Acts of Arkansas*, 1909, pp. 1238 ff.

The Initiative and Referendum 181

election. Any measure referred to the people shall take effect and become a law when it is approved by a majority of the votes cast thereon and not otherwise.

The style of all bills shall be, "Be it enacted by the State of Arkansas." This section shall not be construed to deprive any member of the legislative assembly of the right to introduce any measure. The whole number of votes cast for Governor at the regular election last preceding the filing of any petition for the Initiative or the Referendum shall be the basis on which the number of legal votes necessary to sign such petition shall be counted. Petitions and orders for the Referendum and Initiative shall be filed with the Secretary of State, and in submitting the same to the people he and all other officers shall be guided by the general election laws and the acts submitting this amendment until legislation shall be specially provided therefor.

XI. COLORADO

[At an extraordinary session and as an emergency measure, the Colorado Legislature passed an initiative and referendum amendment on September 2, 1910. It was adopted November 8, 1910, by a vote of 89,141 for, to 28,698 against, or a majority of 60,443.]

The Constitutional Amendment[1]

An Act to submit to the qualified voters of the state of Colorado an amendment to Section 1 of Article V of the constitution of the state of Colorado, providing for the initiative and referendum.

Be it Enacted by the General Assembly of the State of Colorado: —

Section 1. There shall be submitted to the qualified electors of the State of Colorado, at the next general election for members of the General Assembly for their approval or rejection, the following constitutional amendment, which, when ratified by a majority of those voting thereon, shall be valid as part of the Constitution.

[1] *Session Laws of Colorado*, 1910, pp. 11 ff.

Section 2. That Section 1 of Article V of the Constitution of the State of Colorado be so amended as to read as follows: —

Section 1. The legislative power of the State shall be vested in the General Assembly consisting of a Senate and House of Representatives, both to be elected by the people, but the people reserve to themselves the power to propose laws and amendments to the Constitution and to enact or reject the same at the polls independent of the General Assembly, and also reserve power at their own option to approve or reject at the polls any act, item, section or part of any act of the General Assembly.

The first power hereby reserved by the people is the INITIATIVE, and at least eight per cent of the legal voters shall be required to propose any measure by petition, and every such petition shall include the full text of the measure so proposed. Initiative petitions for State legislation and amendments to the Constitution shall be addressed to and filed with the Secretary of State at least four months before the election at which they are to be voted upon.

The second power hereby reserved is the REFERENDUM, and it may be ordered, except as to laws necessary for the immediate preservation of the public peace, health, or safety, and appropriations for the support and maintenance of the department of state and state institutions, against any act, section or part of any act of the General Assembly, either by a petition signed by five per cent of the legal voters or by the General Assembly. Referendum petitions shall be addressed to and filed with the Secretary of State not more than ninety days after the final adjournment of the session of the General Assembly, that passed the bill on which the referendum is demanded. The filing of a referendum petition against any item, section or part of any act shall not delay the remainder of the act from becoming operative. The veto power of the Governor shall not extend to measures initiated by or referred to the people. All elections on measures referred to the people of the State shall be held at the biennial regular general election, and all such measures shall become the law or a part of the Constitution, when approved by a majority of the votes cast thereon, and not otherwise, and shall take effect from and after the date of the official declaration of the vote thereon by proclamation of the Governor, but not later than thirty days after the vote has been canvassed. This section shall not be construed to deprive the General Assembly of the right to enact any measure. The whole number of votes cast for Secretary of State at the regular general election last preceding the filing of any petition for the initiative or referendum shall be the basis on which the number of legal voters necessary to sign such petition shall be counted.

The Secretary of State shall submit all measures initiated by or referred to the people for adoption or rejection at the polls, in compliance herewith. The petition shall consist of sheets having such general form printed or written at the top thereof as shall be designated or prescribed by the Secretary of State; such petition shall be signed by qualified electors in their own proper persons only, to which shall be attached the residence address of such person and the date of signing the same. To each of such petitions, which may consist of one or more sheets, shall be attached an affidavit of some qualified elector, that each signature thereon is the signature of the person whose name it purports to be, and that to the best of the knowledge and belief of the affiant, each of the persons signing said petition was at the time of signing a qualified elector. Such petition so verified shall be prima facie evidence that the signatures thereon are genuine and true and that the persons signing the same are qualified electors. The text of all measures to be submitted shall be published as constitutional amendments are published, and in submitting the same and in all matters pertaining to the form of all petitions the Secretary of State and all other officers shall be guided by the general laws, and the act submitting this amendment, until legislation shall be especially provided therefor.

The style of all laws adopted by the people through the Initiative shall be, "Be it Enacted by the People of the State of Colorado."

The initiative and referendum powers reserved to the people by this section are hereby further reserved to the legal voters of every city, town and municipality as to all local, special and municipal legislation of every character in or for their respective municipalities. The manner of exercising said powers shall be prescribed by general laws, except that cities, towns and municipalities may provide for the manner of exercising the initiative and referendum powers as to their municipal legislation. Not more than ten per cent of the legal voters may be required to order the referendum, nor more than fifteen per cent to propose any measure by the initiative in any city, town or municipality.

This section of the Constitution shall be in all respects self-executing.

Section 3. Each elector voting at said election and desirous of voting for or against this amendment shall deposit in the ballot box a ticket whereon shall be printed or written the words, "For the amendment to Section one of Article V of the Constitution providing for the initiative and referendum," and "Against the amendment to Section one of Article V of the Constitution providing for the initiative and referendum," and shall indicate his or her approval or rejection of the proposition by placing a cross (X) after one of such sentences. The vote cast for the adoption or rejection of said amendment shall be canvassed and the result determined in the manner provided by the laws of the State of Colorado for the canvass of votes for Representative in Congress.

Section 4. In the opinion of the General Assembly an emergency exists, therefore this act shall take effect on and after its passage.

XII. CALIFORNIA

[The Legislature of California passed initiative, referendum and recall amendments on February 20, 1911, and they were adopted by an overwhelming vote on October 10, 1911. The initiative and referendum amendment follows. For the recall see below, p. 264.]

The Constitutional Amendment [1]

Senate Constitutional Amendment No. 22. A resolution to propose to the people of the State of California an amendment to the constitution of said state, by amending section 1 of article 4 thereof, relating to legislative powers, and reserving to the people of the State of California the power to propose laws, statutes and amendments to the constitution and to enact the same at the polls, independent of the legislature and also reserving to the people of the State of California the power to approve or reject at the polls any act or section or part of any act of the legislature.

The legislature of the State of California, at its regular session commencing on the 2d day of January, 1911, two-thirds of all the members elected to each of the two houses of said legislature voting in favor thereof, hereby propose that section 1 of article 4 of the constitution of the State of California, be amended so as to read as follows: —

Section 1. The legislative power of this state shall be vested in a senate and assembly which shall be designated "The legislature of the State of California," but the people reserve to themselves the power to propose laws and amendments to the constitution, and to adopt or reject the same, at the polls independent of the legislature, and also reserve the power, at their own option, to so adopt or reject any act, or section or part of any act, passed by the legislature.

The enacting clause of every law shall be "The people of the State of California do enact as follows:" —

The first power reserved to the people shall be known as the initiative. Upon the presentation to the secretary of state of a petition certified as herein provided to have been signed by qualified electors, equal in number to eight per cent of all the votes cast for all candidates for governor at the last preceding general election, at which a governor was elected, proposing a law or amendment to the constitution, set forth in full in said petition,

---

[1] Official copy from the office of the Secretary of State. See below, p. 264, for recall amendment.

the secretary of state shall submit the said proposed law or amendment to the constitution to the electors at the next succeeding general election occurring subsequent to ninety days after the presentation aforesaid of said petition, or at any special election called by the governor in his discretion prior to such general election. All such initiative petitions shall have printed across the top thereof in twelve point black-face type the following: "Initiative measure to be submitted directly to the electors."

Upon the presentation to the secretary of state, at any time not less than ten days before the commencement of any regular session of the legislature, of a petition certified as herein provided to have been signed by qualified electors of the state equal in number to five per cent of all the votes cast for all candidates for governor at the last preceding general election, at which a governor was elected, proposing a law set forth in full in said petition, the secretary of state shall transmit the same to the legislature as soon as it convenes and organizes. The law proposed by such petition shall be either enacted or rejected without change or amendment by the legislature, within forty days from the time it is received by the legislature. If any law proposed by such petition shall be enacted by the legislature it shall be subject to referendum, as hereinafter provided. If any law so petitioned for be rejected, or if no action is taken upon it by the legislature within said forty days, the secretary of state shall submit it to the people for approval or rejection at the next ensuing general election. The legislature may reject any measure so proposed by initiative petition and propose a different one on the same subject by a yea and nay vote upon separate roll call, and in such event both measures shall be submitted by the secretary of state to the electors for approval or rejection at the next ensuing general election or at a prior special election called by the governor, in his discretion, for such purpose. All said initiative petitions last above described shall have printed in twelve point black-face type the following: "Initiative measure to be presented to the legislature."

The Initiative and Referendum 187

The second power reserved to the people shall be known as the referendum. No act passed by the legislature shall go into effect until ninety days after the final adjournment of the session of the legislature which passed such act, except acts calling elections, acts providing for tax levies or appropriations for the usual current expenses of the state, and urgency measures necessary for the immediate preservation of the public peace, health or safety, passed by a two-thirds vote of all the members elected to each house. Whenever it is deemed necessary for the immediate preservation of the public peace, health or safety that a law shall go into immediate effect, a statement of the facts constituting such necessity shall be set forth in one section of the act, which section shall be passed only upon a yea and nay vote, upon a separate roll call thereon; provided, however, that no measure creating or abolishing any office or changing the salary, term or duties of any officer, or granting any franchise or special privilege, or creating any vested right or interest, shall be construed to be an urgency measure. Any law so passed by the legislature and declared to be an urgency measure shall go into immediate effect.

Upon the presentation to the secretary of state within ninety days after the final adjournment of the legislature of a petition certified as herein provided, to have been signed by qualified electors equal in number to five per cent of all the votes cast for all candidates for governor at the last preceding general election at which a governor was elected, asking that any act or section or part of any act of the legislature, be submitted to the electors for their approval or rejection, the secretary of state shall submit to the electors for their approval or rejection, such act, or section or part of such act, at the next succeeding general election occurring at any time subsequent to thirty days after the filing of said petition or at any special election which may be called by the governor, in his discretion, prior to such regular election, and no such act or section or part of such act shall go into effect until and unless approved by a majority of the qualified electors voting thereon; but if a referendum petition is filed against any section or part of any act the remainder of such act shall not be delayed from going into effect.

Any act, law or amendment to the constitution submitted to the people by either initiative or referendum petition and approved by a majority of the votes cast thereon, at any election, shall take effect five days after the date of the official declaration of the vote by the secretary of state. No act, law or amendment to the constitution, initiated or adopted by the people, shall be subject to the veto power of the governor, and no act, law or amendment to the constitution, adopted by the people at the polls under the initiative provisions of this section, shall be amended or repealed except by a vote of the electors, unless otherwise provided in said initiative measure; but acts and laws adopted by the people under the referendum provisions of this section may be amended by the legislature at any subsequent session thereof. If any provision or provisions of two or more measures, approved by the electors at the same election, conflict, the provision or provisions of the measure receiving the highest affirmative vote shall prevail. Until otherwise provided by law, all measures submitted to a vote of the electors, under the provisions of this section, shall be printed, and together with arguments for and against each such measure by the proponents and opponents thereof, shall be mailed to each elector in the same manner as now provided by law as to amendments to the constitution, proposed by the legislature; and the persons to prepare and present such arguments shall, until otherwise provided by law, be selected by the presiding officer of the senate.

If for any reason any initiative or referendum measure, proposed by petition as herein provided, be not submitted at the election specified in this section, such failure shall not prevent its submission at a succeeding general election, and no law or amendment to the constitution, proposed by the legislature, shall be submitted at any election unless at the same election there shall be submitted all measures proposed by petition of the electors, if any be so proposed, as herein provided.

The Initiative and Referendum 189

Any initiative or referendum petition may be presented in sections, but each section shall contain a full and correct copy of the title and text of the proposed measure. Each signer shall add to his signature his place of residence, giving the street and number if such exist. His election precinct shall also appear on the paper after his name. The number of signatures attached to each section shall be at the pleasure of the person soliciting signatures to the same. Any qualified elector of the state shall be competent to solicit said signatures within the county or city and county of which he is an elector. Each section of the petition shall bear the name of the county or city and county in which it is circulated, and only qualified electors of such county or city and county shall be competent to sign such section. Each section shall have attached thereto the affidavit of the person soliciting signatures to the same, stating his own qualifications and that all the signatures to the attached section were made in his presence and that to the best of his knowledge and belief each signature to the section is the genuine signature of the person whose name it purports to be, and no other affidavit thereto shall be required. The affidavit of any person soliciting signatures hereunder shall be verified free of charge by any officer authorized to administer oaths. Such petitions so verified shall be prima facie evidence that the signatures thereon are genuine and that the persons signing the same are qualified electors. Unless and until it be otherwise proven upon official investigation, it shall be presumed that the petition presented contains the signatures of the requisite number of qualified electors.

Each section of the petition shall be filed with the clerk or registrar of voters of the county or city and county in which it was circulated, but all said sections circulated in any county or city and county shall be filed at the same time. Within twenty days after the filing of such petition in his office the said clerk, or registrar of voters, shall determine from the records of registration what number of qualified electors have signed the same, and if necessary the board of supervisors shall allow said clerk or registrar additional assistants for the purpose of examining such petition and provide for their compensation. The said clerk or registrar, upon the completion of such examination, shall forthwith attach to said petition, except the signatures thereto appended, his certificate, properly dated, showing the result of said examination and shall forthwith transmit said petition, together with his said certificate, to the secretary of state and also file a copy of said certificate in his office. Within forty days from the transmission of the said petition and certificate by the clerk or registrar to the secretary of state, a supplemental petition identical with the original as to the body of the petition, but containing supplemental names, may be filed with the clerk or registrar of voters, as aforesaid. The clerk or registrar of voters shall within ten days after the filing of such supplemental petition make like examination thereof, as of the original petition, and upon the completion of such examination shall forthwith attach to said petition his certificate, properly dated, showing the result of said examination, and shall forthwith transmit a copy of said supplemental petition, except the signatures thereto appended, together with his certificate, to the secretary of state.

When the secretary of state shall have received from one or more county clerks or registrars of voters a petition certified as herein provided to have been signed by the requisite number of qualified electors, he shall forthwith transmit to the county clerk or registrar of voters of every county or city and county in the state his certificate showing such fact. A petition shall be deemed to be filed with the secretary of state upon the date of the receipt by him of a certificate or certificates showing said petition to be signed by the requisite number of electors of the state. Any county clerk or registrar of voters shall, upon receipt of such copy, file the same for record in his office.

The duties herein imposed upon the clerk or registrar of voters shall be performed by such registrar of voters in all cases where the office of registrar of voters exists.

The initiative and referendum powers of the people are hereby further reserved to the electors of each county, city and county, city and town of the state, to be exercised under such procedure as may be provided by law. Until otherwise provided by law, the legislative body of any such county, city and county, city or town may provide for the manner of exercising the initiative and referendum powers herein reserved to such counties, cities and counties, cities and town, but shall not require more than fifteen per cent of the electors thereof to propose any initiative measure nor more than ten per cent of the electors thereof to order the referendum. Nothing contained in this section shall be construed as affecting or limiting the present or future powers of cities or cities and counties having charters adopted under the provisions of section eight of article eleven of this constitution.

In the submission to the electors of any measure under this section, all officers shall be guided by the general laws of this state, except as is herein otherwise provided.

This section is self-executing, but legislation may be enacted to facilitate its operation, but in no way limiting or restricting either the provisions of this section or the powers herein reserved.

XIII. WASHINGTON [PROPOSED]

[An initiative and referendum amendment to the Constitution of Washington was passed by the House February 14, 1911, and by the Senate March 1, 1911. It was approved by the Governor March 10, 1911, and will be submitted to the voters for ratification at the general election to be held in November, 1912.]

Proposed Constitutional Amendment [1]

An Act to amend section 1 of article 11 of the Constitution of the State of Washington, relating to legislative powers, providing for the initiative and referendum, and striking section 31 of said article 11, relating to the time when laws take effect.

Be it enacted by the Legislature of the State of Washington: —

SECTION 1. That at the general election to be held in this state on the Tuesday next succeeding the first Monday in No-

[1] *Session Laws*, 1911, chapter 42.

vember, 1912, there shall be submitted to the qualified electors of the state for adoption and approval of [or] rejection an amendment to article II of the Constitution of the State of Washington, relating to legislative powers, by striking from article II all of sections 1 and 31, and inserting in lieu thereof as section 1 the following, so that the same shall read as follows: —

Article II, section 1. The legislative authority of the State of Washington shall be vested in the legislature, consisting of a senate and house of representatives, which shall be called the legislature of the State of Washington, but the people reserve to themselves the power to propose bills, laws, and to enact or reject the same at the polls, independent of the legislature, and also reserve power, at their own option, to approve or reject at the polls any act, item, section or part of any bill, act or law passed by the legislature.

(*a*) Initiative: The first power reserved by the people is the initiative. Ten per centum, but in no case more than fifty thousand, of the legal voters shall be required to propose any measure by such petition, and every such petition shall include the full text of the measure so proposed. Initiative petitions shall be filed with the secretary of state not less than four months before the election at which they are to be voted upon, or not less than ten days before any regular session of the legislature. If filed at least four months before the election at which they are to be voted upon, he shall submit the same to the vote of the people at the said election. If such petitions are filed not less than ten days before any regular session of the legislature, he shall transmit the same to the legislature as soon as it convenes and organizes. Such initiative measure shall take precedence over all other measures in the legislature except appropriation bills and shall be either enacted or rejected without change or amendment by the legislature before the end of such regular session. If any such initiative measure shall be enacted by the legislature it shall be subject to the referendum petition, or it may be enacted and referred by the legislature to the people for

The Initiative and Referendum 193

approval or rejection at the next regular election. If it is rejected or if no action is taken upon it by the legislature before the end of such regular session, the secretary of state shall submit it to the people for approval or rejection at the next ensuing regular general election. The legislature may reject any measure so proposed by initiative petition and propose a different one dealing with the same subject, and in such event both measures shall be submitted by the secretary of state to the people for approval or rejection at the next ensuing regular general election. When conflicting measures are submitted to the people the ballots shall be so printed that a voter can express separately by making one cross (X) for each, two preferences, first, as between either measure and neither, and secondly, as between one and the other. If the majority of those voting on the first issue is for neither, both fail, but in that case the votes on the second issue shall nevertheless be carefully counted and made public. If a majority voting on the first issue is for either, then the measure receiving a majority of the votes on the second issue shall be law.

(b) Referendum. The second power reserved by the people is the referendum, and it may be ordered on any act, bill, law, or any part thereof passed by the legislature, except such laws as may be necessary for the immediate preservation of the public peace, health or safety, support of the state government and its existing public institutions, either by petition signed by the required percentage of the legal voters, or by the legislature as other bills are enacted. Six per centum, but in no case more than thirty thousand, of the legal voters shall be required to sign and make a valid referendum petition.

(c) No act, law, or bill subject to referendum shall take effect until ninety days after the adjournment of the session at which it was enacted. No act, law, or bill approved by a majority of the electors voting thereon shall be amended or repealed by the legislature within a period of two years following such enactment. But such enactment may be amended or repealed at any general regular or special election by direct vote of the people thereon.

(*d*) The filing of a referendum petition against one or more items, sections or parts of any act, law or bill shall not delay the remainder of the measure from becoming operative. Referendum petitions against measures passed by the legislature shall be filed with the secretary of state not later than ninety days after the final adjournment of the session of the legislature which passed the measure on which the referendum is demanded. The veto power of the governor shall not extend to measures initiated by or referred to the people. All elections on measures referred to the people of the state shall be had at the biennial regular elections, except when the legislature shall order a special election. Any measure initiated by the people or referred to the people as herein provided shall take effect and become the law if it is approved by a majority of the votes cast thereon: *Provided*, That the vote cast upon such question or measure shall equal one-third of the total votes cast at such election and not otherwise. Such measure shall be in operation on and after the thirtieth day after the election at which it is approved. The style of all bills proposed by initiative petition shall be: "Be it enacted by the people of the State of Washington." This section shall not be construed to deprive any member of the legislature of the right to introduce any measure. The whole number of electors who voted for governor at the regular gubernatorial election last preceding the filing of any petition for the initiative or for the referendum shall be the basis on which the number of legal voters necessary to sign such petition shall be counted. All such petitions shall be filed with the secretary of state, who shall be guided by the general laws in submitting the same to the people until additional legislation shall especially provide therefor. This section is self-executing, but legislation may be enacted especially to facilitate its operation.

The legislature shall provide methods of publicity of all laws or parts of laws, and amendments to the constitution referred to the people with arguments for and against the laws and amendments so referred, so that each voter of the state shall receive the

The Initiative and Referendum

publication at least fifty days before the election at which they are to be voted upon.

SEC. 2. The secretary of state shall cause the amendment proposed in section 1 of this act to be published for three months next preceding the said election therein described in some weekly newspaper in every county where such newspaper is published throughout the state.

SEC. 3. There shall be printed on all ballots provided for the said election, the words: —

"For the proposed amendment of section 1 of article II of the constitution of the State of Washington, relating to legislative powers and providing for the initiative and referendum."

"Against the proposed amendment of section 1 of article II of the constitution of the State of Washington, relating to legislative powers, and providing for the initiative and referendum."

"For the proposed amendment of article II of the constitution of the State of Washington, by striking section 31 therefrom, which relates to the time when laws take effect."

"Against the proposed amendment of article II of the constitution of the State of Washington, by striking section 31 therefrom, which relates to the time when laws take effect."

SEC. 4. If it shall appear from the ballots cast at the said election that a majority of the qualified electors voting upon the question of the adoption of the said amendment have voted in favor of the same, the governor shall make proclamation of the same in the manner provided by law, and the said amendment shall be held to have been adopted and to have been a part of the constitution from the date of such proclamation.

XIV. NEBRASKA (PROPOSED)

[The Legislature of Nebraska passed a joint resolution on March 17, 1911, providing for the submission of an initiative and referendum amendment to the state constitution. The resolution was approved by the Governor, March 24, 1911. The electors will vote on the proposition at the regular election in November, 1912. The amendment is to be self-executing, on proclamation by the Governor, if it receives a majority of the votes cast at the election. The copy here is certified under the seal of the secretary of state of Nebraska, April 24, 1911.]

An Act for a joint resolution proposing amendment to Section 1 and Section 10, Article 3 of the Constitution of the State of Nebraska, and supplementing Article entitled "Amendments."

Be it Resolved and Enacted by the Legislature of the State of Nebraska: —

Section 1. That at the general election for state and legislative officers to be held on the Tuesday succeeding the first Monday in November, 1912, the following provisions be proposed and submitted as amendment to Section 1 and Section 10 of Article 3 of the Constitution of the State of Nebraska: —

Section 2. That Section 1 of Article 3 of the Constitution of the State of Nebraska is hereby amended to read as follows: —

Section 1. The legislative authority of the state shall be vested in a legislature consisting of a senate and house of representatives, but the people reserve to themselves power to propose laws, and amendments to the constitution, and to enact or reject the same at the polls independent of the legislature, and also reserve power at their own option to approve or reject at the polls any act, item, section or part of any act passed by the legislature.

Section 1 *A*. The first power reserved by the people is the initiative. Ten per cent of the legal voters of the state, so distributed as to include five per cent of the legal voters in each of two-fifths of the counties of the state, may propose any measure by petition, which shall contain the full text of the measure so proposed. Provided, that proposed Constitutional Amendments shall require a petition of fifteen per cent of the legal voters of the State distributed as above provided. Initiative petitions (except for municipal and wholly local legislation) shall be filed with the Secretary of State and be by him submitted to the voters at the first regular state election held not less than four months after such filing. The same measure, either in form or in essential substance, shall not be submitted to the people by initiative petition (either affirmatively or negatively) oftener than once in three years. If conflicting measures submitted to the people at the same election shall be approved, the one receiving the highest number of affirmative votes shall thereby become law as to all conflicting provisions. The Constitutional limitations as to scope and subject matter of statutes enacted by the legislature shall apply to those enacted by the initiative.

Section 1 *B*. The second power reserved is the referendum. It may be ordered by a petition of ten per cent of the legal voters of the state, distributed as required for initiative petitions. Referendum petitions against measures passed by the legislature shall be filed with the Secretary of State within ninety days after the legislature enacting the same adjourns sine die or for a period longer than ninety days: and elections thereon shall be had at the first regular state election held not less than thirty days after such filing.

Section 1 *C*. The referendum may be ordered upon any act, except acts making appropriations for the expenses of the state government, and state institutions existing at the time such act is passed. When the referendum is ordered upon an act or any part thereof it shall suspend its operation until the same is approved by the voters; provided, that emergency acts, or acts for the immediate preservation of the public peace, health, or safety shall continue in effect until rejected by the voters or repealed by the legislature. Filing of a referendum petition against one or more items, sections, or parts of an act shall not delay the remainder of the measure from becoming operative.

Section 1 *D*. Nothing in this section shall be construed to deprive any member of the legislature of the right to introduce any measure. The whole number of votes cast for governor at the regular election last preceding the filing of any initiative or referendum petition shall be the basis on which the number of legal voters required to sign such petition shall be computed. The veto power of the governor shall not extend to measures initiated by or referred to the people. All such measures shall become the law or a part of the constitution when approved by a majority of the votes cast thereon, provided, the votes cast in favor of said initiative measure or part of said Constitution shall constitute thirty-five per cent (35 %) of the total vote cast at said election, and not otherwise, and shall take effect upon proclamation by the governor, which shall be made within ten days of the completion of the official canvass. The vote upon initiative and referendum measures shall be returned and canvassed in the same manner as is prescribed in the case of presidential electors. The method of submitting and adopting amendments to the constitution provided by this section shall be supplementary to the method prescribed in the article of this constitution, entitled "Amendments" and the latter shall in no case be construed to conflict herewith. This amendment shall be self-executing, but legislation may be enacted especially to facilitate its operation. In submitting petitions and orders for the initiative and the referendum, the Secretary of State and all other officers shall be guided by this amendment and the general laws until additional legislation shall be especially provided therefor; all propositions submitted in pursuance hereof shall be submitted in a nonpartisan manner and without any indication or suggestion on the ballot that they have been approved or endorsed by any political party or organization, and provided further that only the title of measures shall be printed on the ballot and when two or more measures have the same title they shall be numbered consecutively in the order of filing with the Secretary of State and including the name of the first petitioner.

Section 3. That Section 10, of Article 3, of the Constitution of the state of Nebraska be amended to read as follows: —

Section 10. The style of all bills shall be "Be it enacted by the people of the State of Nebraska," and no law shall be enacted except by bill. No bill shall be passed by the legislature unless by assent of a majority of all the members elected to each house of the legislature and the question upon final passage shall be taken immediately upon its last reading and the yeas and nays shall be entered upon the journal.

Section 4. That at said election on the Tuesday succeeding the first Monday in November, 1912, on the ballot of each elector voting thereat there shall be printed or written the words: "For proposed amendment to the constitution reserving to the people the right of direct legislation through the initiative and referendum," and "Against proposed amendment to the constitution reserving to the people the right of direct legislation through the initiative and referendum." And if a majority of all voters at said election shall be in favor of such amendment the same shall be deemed to be adopted. The returns of said election upon the adoption of this amendment shall be made to the state canvassing board and said board shall canvass the vote upon the amendment herein in the same manner as is prescribed in the case of presidential electors. If a majority of the votes cast at the election be in favor of the proposed amendment the governor, within ten days after the result is ascertained, shall make proclamation declaring the amendment to be part of the constitution of the state, and when so declared the amendment herein proposed shall be in force and self-executing.

M. R. HOPEWELL,
President of the Senate.

Attest:

WM. H. SMITH,
Secretary of the Senate.

JOHN KUHL,
Speaker of the House of Representatives.

Attest:

HENRY C. RICHMOND,
Chief Clerk of the House of Representatives.

Approved March 24, 1911.

CHESTER H. ALDRICH,
Governor.

XV. Idaho (Proposed)

[The 1911 session of the Idaho Legislature passed initiative, referendum and recall (not including the judiciary) amendments to the state constitution. (See below, p. 271, for the recall amendment.) The electors will vote on these measures at the next general election in the state — November, 1912.]

Referendum Amendment [1]

Be it Resolved By the Legislature of the State of Idaho: —

Section 1. That Section 1 of Article 3 of the Constitution of the State of Idaho be amended by adding thereto the following: The people reserve to themselves the power to approve or reject at the polls any act or measure passed by the Legislature. This power is known as the Referendum, and legal voters may, under such conditions and in such manner as may be provided by Acts of the Legislature, demand a referendum vote on any act or measure passed by the Legislature and cause the same to be submitted to a vote of the people for their approval or rejection.

Section 2. The question to be submitted to the electors of the State shall be in form as follows, to-wit: "Shall Section 1 of Article 3 of the Constitution of the State of Idaho be so amended as to give the people the power (under conditions to be hereafter prescribed by act of the Legislature) to propose a referendum vote on any act or measure passed by the State Legislature and to approve or reject the same at the polls, independent of the Legislature?"

Section 3. The Secretary of State is hereby authorized to make publication of this constitutional amendment in each county for at least six consecutive weeks prior to the next general election in not less than one newspaper of general circulation published in each county.

Passed Senate, February 17, 1911.
Passed House, February 24, 1911.

[1] Official copy.

Initiative Amendment

Be it Resolved by the Legislature of the State of Idaho: —

Section 1. That Section 1 of Article 3 of the Constitution of the State of Idaho be amended by adding thereto the following: The people reserve to themselves the power to propose laws, and enact the same at the polls independent of the Legislature. This power is known as the initiative, and legal voters may, under such conditions and in such manner as may be provided by Acts of the Legislature, initiate any desired legislation and cause the same to be submitted to the vote of the people at a general election for their approval or rejection, provided that legislation thus submitted shall require the approval of a number of voters equal to a majority of the aggregate vote cast for the office of Governor at such general election, to be adopted.

Sec. 2. The question to be submitted to the electors of the state shall be in form as follows: "Shall Section 1 of Article 3 of the Constitution of the State of Idaho be so amended as to give the people power (under conditions to be hereafter prescribed by acts of the Legislature) to propose laws of their own initiative and enact the same at the polls independent of the Legislature?"

Section 3. The Secretary of State is hereby authorized to make publication of this constitutional amendment in each county for at least six consecutive weeks prior to the next general election in not less than one newspaper of general circulation published in each county.

Passed Senate, February 17, 1911.
Passed House, February 24, 1911.

XVI. WYOMING (PROPOSED) [1]

[The following act providing for the submission of a constitutional amendment relative to the initiative and referendum in Wyoming was approved on February 18, 1911. It will be submitted to the voters at the election in November, 1912.]

[1] *Session Laws*, 1911, pp. 71 ff.

State-wide Initiative, Referendum, and Recall

An Act to submit to the qualified voters of the State of Wyoming an amendment to Section 1 of Article 3 of the Constitution of the State of Wyoming, providing for the initiative and referendum, and for the manner of submitting to the voters laws and amendments to the Constitution.

Be It Enacted by the Legislature of the State of Wyoming: —
Shall be Submitted.

Section 1. The following constitutional amendment shall be submitted to the qualified electors of the State of Wyoming at the next general election [November, 1912] for their approval or rejection, and when ratified by a majority of the electors voting at said election the same shall be valid as a part of the Constitution.

People May Approve or Reject.

Sec. 2. That Section 1 of Article 3 of the Constitution of the State of Wyoming be so amended as to read as follows: —

"Section 1. The legislative power of the state shall be vested in a Senate and House of Representatives, which shall be designated 'The Legislature of the State of Wyoming,' but the people reserve to themselves the power to propose laws and amendments to the Constitution and to enact or reject the same at the polls, and also reserve power at their option to approve or reject at the polls any act of the Legislature.

Initiative — Twenty-five Per Cent Required.

"The first power hereby reserved by the people is the initiative, and at least twenty-five per cent of the legal voters shall be required to propose any measure by petition, and every such petition shall include the full text of the measure so proposed. Initiative petitions for state legislation and amendments to the Constitution shall be addressed to and filed with the Secretary of State at least four months before the election at which they are to be voted upon.

Referendum — Provisions of Same.

"The second power hereby reserved is the referendum, and it may be ordered, except as to appropriations, against any act of the Legislature after it has become a law either by the approval of the Governor or his failure to veto, either by petition signed by not less than twenty-five per cent of the legal voters or by the Legislature. Referendum petitions shall be addressed to and filed with the Secretary of State not more than ninety days after the final adjournment of the session of the Legislature that passed the bill on which the referendum is demanded. The filing of a referendum petition against any act shall not affect the validity of the act until disapproved by the people as hereinafter provided. The veto power of the Governor shall not extend to measures initiated and passed by the people, but laws passed by initiative shall be subject to amendment and repeal as other statutes. All elections on measures referred to the people of the state shall be held at the biennial general election. Each measure submitted to the people by the initiative as a law shall become a law when approved by a majority of the votes cast thereon, and not otherwise, save that no measure shall become a law unless it shall receive in its favor the votes of not less than one-third of the electors voting at such election.

Shall Become Part of Constitution — When.

"Each measure submitted to the people by initiative as a part of the Constitution shall become a part of the Constitution when approved by a majority of the electors voting at such election, and not otherwise, and such laws and parts of the Constitution when approved as above stated shall take effect from and after the date of the official declaration of the vote thereon by proclamation of the Governor, but not later than thirty days after the vote has been canvassed.

One-third of Electors Must Vote.

"Each statute submitted to the electors on referendum shall remain in full force as if not so submitted, unless a majority of the votes cast thereon shall be against such statute, but no law submitted by referendum shall be declared defeated unless at least one-third of the electors voting at such election shall cast their votes against the same.

On Regular Ballot — Constitutional Amendments on Separate Ballot.

"Every measure submitted to the people, whether by the legislature or by initiative or by referendum, to become a law, shall be submitted on a regular ballot which contains the names of candidates for office; constitutional amendment shall be submitted to the people upon a separate ballot.

Basis Determined.

"This section shall not be construed to deprive the Legislature of the right to enact any measure. The whole number of votes cast for Secretary of State at the regular general election last preceding the filing of any petition for the initiative or referendum shall be the basis on which the number of legal voters necessary to sign such petition shall be determined.

Secretary of State Shall Submit — Signatures Must Be Verified.

"The Secretary of State shall submit all measures initiated by, or referred to the people for adoption or rejection at the polls, in compliance herewith. The petition shall consist of sheets having such general form written or printed at the top thereof, as shall be designated or prescribed by the Secretary of State; such petition shall be signed by qualified electors, in their own proper persons only, to which shall be attached the residence address of such person and the date of signing the same. To each of such petitions, which may consist of one or more sheets, shall be attached affidavits by three separate qualified electors, that each signature thereon is the signature of the person whose name it purports to be, and that to the best of the knowledge and belief of the affiant each of the persons signing said petition so verified was, at the time of signing, a qualified elector. Such petition so verified shall be prima facie evidence that the signatures thereon are genuine and true, and that the persons signing the same are qualified electors. The text of all measures to be submitted shall be published as constitutional amendments are published, and in submitting the same and all matters pertaining

The Initiative and Referendum

to the form of all petitions, the Secretary of State and all other officers shall be guided by the Constitution and general laws, and the act submitting this amendment, until legislation in harmony herewith shall be especially provided therefor.

Each Measure Voted for Separately.

"Each separate measure, whether a law or a constitutional amendment, shall be voted upon separately, and no general mark either at the head or elsewhere on any official ballot shall be counted as voting separately on any measure.

Must Contain Enacting Clause.

"The style of all laws adopted by the people through the initiative shall be, 'Be It Enacted by the People of the State of Wyoming.'

"This section of the Constitution shall be, in all respects, self-executing."

Ballot Must Contain — How Voted.

Sec. 3. The general ballot upon which are the names of the candidates for offices at the next general election shall have printed or written thereon the words, "For the amendment to Section 1 of Article 3 of the Constitution, providing for the initiative and referendum, and for the manner of submitting to the voters laws and amendments to the Constitution," and "Against the amendment to Section 1 of Article 3 of the Constitution, providing for the initiative and referendum, and for the manner of submitting to the voters laws and amendments to the Constitution." Each elector voting at said election who desires to indicate his or her approval or rejection of the proposition for said constitutional amendment shall indicate the same by a cross (X) after one of such sentences so as to indicate his or her approval or rejection. The vote cast for the adoption or rejection of said amendment shall be canvassed and the result determined in the manner provided by the laws of the State of Wyoming for the canvass of votes for Representative in Congress, save and except that said amendment shall be declared carried only when approved by a majority of the electors, and not otherwise.

Sec. 4. This act shall take effect and be in force from and after its passage.

Approved February 18th, 1911.

XVII. WISCONSIN (PROPOSED)

[The following amendment to the constitution of Wisconsin was passed by the legislature at the 1911 session. It must be repassed by the next legislature before being submitted to popular vote.] [1]

[Jt. Res. No. 36, A.]

Joint Resolution to amend section 1, of article IV of the constitution, to give to the people the power to propose laws and to enact or reject the same at the polls, and to approve or reject at the polls any act of the legislature; and to create section 3, of article XII of the constitution, providing for the submission of amendments to the constitution upon the petition of the people.

Resolved by the Assembly, the Senate concurring, That section 1, of article IV of the constitution, be amended to read: —

SECTION 1. *1.* The legislative power shall be vested in a senate and assembly, *but the people reserve to themselves power, as herein provided, to propose laws and to enact or reject the same at the polls, independent of the legislature, and to approve or reject at the polls any law or any part of any law enacted by the legislature. The limitations expressed in the constitution on the power of the legislature to enact laws, shall be deemed limitations on the power of the people to enact laws.*

2. a. Any senator or member of the assembly may introduce, by presenting to the chief clerk in the house of which he is a member, in open session, at any time during any session of the legislature, any bill or any amendment to any such bill; provided, that the time for so introducing a bill may be limited by rule to not less than thirty legislative days.

b. The chief clerk shall make a record of such bill and every amendment offered thereto and have the same printed.

---

[1] Official copy furnished by Mr. Gale Lowrie, in the Legislative Reference Library of Wisconsin.

3. *A proposed law shall be recited in full in the petition, and shall consist of a bill which has been introduced in the legislature during the first thirty legislative days of the session, as so introduced; or, at the option of the petitioners, there may be incorporated in said bill any amendment or amendments introduced in the legislature. Such bill and amendments shall be referred to by number in the petition. Upon petition filed not later than four months before the next general election, such proposed laws shall be submitted to a vote of the people, and shall become a law if it is approved by a majority of the electors voting thereon, and shall take effect and be in force from and after thirty days after the election at which it is approved.*

4. a. No law enacted by the legislature, except an emergency law, shall take effect before ninety days after its passage and publication. If within said ninety days there shall have been filed a petition to submit to a vote of the people such law or any part thereof, such law or such part thereof shall not take effect until thirty days after its approval by a majority of the qualified electors voting thereon.

b. An emergency law shall remain in force, notwithstanding such petition, but shall stand repealed thirty days after being rejected by a majority of the qualified electors voting thereon.

c. An emergency law shall be any law declared by the legislature to be necessary for any immediate purpose by a two-thirds vote of the members of each house voting thereon, entered on their journals by the yeas and nays. No law making any appropriation for maintaining the state government or maintaining or aiding any public institution, not exceeding the next previous appropriation for the same purpose, shall be subject to rejection or repeal under this section. The increase in any such appropriation shall only take effect as in case of other laws, and such increase, or any part thereof, specified in the petition may be referred to a vote of the people upon petition.

5. If measures which conflict with each other in any of their essential provisions are submitted at the same election, only the measure receiving the highest number of votes shall stand as the enactment of the people.

6. *The petition shall be filed with the secretary of state and shall be sufficient to require the submission by him of a measure to the people when signed by eight per cent of the qualified electors calculated upon the whole number of votes cast for governor at the last preceding election, of whom not more than one-half shall be residents of any one county.*

7. *The vote upon measures referred to the people shall be taken at the next election occurring not less than four months after the filing of the petition, and held generally throughout the state pursuant to law or specially called by the governor.*

8. *The legislature shall provide for furnishing electors the text of all measures to be voted upon by the people.*

9. *Except that measures specifically affecting a subdivision of the state may be submitted to the people of that subdivision, the legislature shall submit measures to the people only as required by the constitution.*

Be it further resolved by the assembly, the senate concurring, That article XII of the constitution be amended by creating a new section to read: —

Section 3. 1. *a.* Any senator or member of the assembly may introduce, by presenting to the chief clerk in the house in which he is a member, in open session, at any time during any session of the legislature, any proposed amendment to the constitution or any amendment to any such proposed amendment to the constitution; provided, that the time for so introducing a proposed amendment to the constitution may be limited by rule to not less than thirty legislative days.

b. The chief clerk shall make a record of such proposed amendments to the constitution and any amendment thereto and have the same printed.

2. Any proposed amendment to the constitution shall be recited in full in the petition and shall consist of an amendment which has been introduced in the legislature during the first thirty legislative days, as so introduced, or, at the option of the petitioners, there may be incorporated therein any amendment

The Initiative and Referendum

or amendments thereto introduced in the legislature. Such amendment to the constitution and amendments thereto shall be referred to by number in the petition. Upon petition filed not later than four months before the next general election, such proposed amendment shall be submitted to the people.

3. The petition shall be filed with the secretary of state and shall be sufficient to require the submission by him of a proposed amendment to the constitution to the people when signed by ten per cent of the qualified electors, calculated upon the whole number of votes cast for governor at the last preceding election of whom not more than one-half shall be residents of any one county.

4. Any proposed amendment or amendments to this constitution, agreed to by a majority of the members elected to each of the two houses of the legislature, shall be entered on their journals with the yeas and nays taken thereon, and be submitted to the people by the secretary of state upon petition filed with him signed by five per cent of the qualified electors, calculated upon the whole number of votes cast for governor at the last preceding election of whom not more than one-half shall be residents of any one county.

5. The legislature shall provide for furnishing the electors the text of all amendments to the constitution to be voted upon by the people.

6. If the people shall approve and ratify such amendment or amendments by a majority of the electors voting thereon, such amendment or amendments shall become a part of the constitution, from and after the election at which approved; provided, that if more than one amendment be submitted they shall be submitted in such manner that the people may vote for or against such amendments separately.

7. If proposed amendments to the constitution which conflict with each other in any of their essential provisions are submitted at the same election, only the proposed amendment receiving the highest number of votes shall become a part of the constitution.

XVIII. NORTH DAKOTA

[In 1907 the legislature of North Dakota passed a constitutional amendment providing for the initiative and referendum, but it was not adopted by the 1909 session, in accordance with the requirements of the Constitution of the State, and hence it was not submitted for popular ratification. In the 1910 primary campaign the Progressive Republicans adopted the initiative and referendum as a plank in their platform and the party ratified it in the campaign following. At the last session of the legislature the five following resolutions were passed and referred to the 1913 session for adoption or rejection. Any one of these resolutions so adopted will then be referred to the voters in the 1914 election. The texts here are from *The Session Laws of 1911.*]

CHAPTER 85
(S. B. No. 281 — Bessesen)

Concurrent Resolution (The Recall)

Concurrent Resolution for an Amendment to the Constitution of the State of North Dakota, Providing for the Recall of Public Officers by the People.

Be it Resolved by the Senate of the State of North Dakota, the House of Representatives Concurring: —

That the following Proposed Amendment to the Constitution of the State of North Dakota is Agreed to and Referred to the Legislative Assembly to be Chosen at the Next General Election in said State for the Approval, to be by Said Last Mentioned Legislative Assembly Submitted to the Qualified Electors of the State for Approval or Rejection, in Accordance with the Provisions of Section 202 of the Constitution of the State of North Dakota.

AMENDMENT. The constitution of the state of North Dakota is amended by the addition of the following article: —

Article. — Every public officer in North Dakota is subject as herein provided, to recall by the legal voters of the state or of the electoral district from which he is elected. There shall be required twenty-five (25) per cent, but no more, of the number of electors who voted in his district at the preceding election for justice of the supreme court to file their petition demanding his recall by the people. They shall set forth in said petition the reasons for said demand. If he shall offer his resignation it shall be accepted and take effect on the day it is offered, and the vacancy shall be filled as may be provided by law. If he shall not resign within five days after the petition is filed, a special election shall be ordered to be held within twenty days in his said electoral district to determine whether the people will recall said officer. On the sample ballot at said election shall be printed in not more than two hundred words the reason for demanding the recall of said officer as set forth in the recall petition, and in not more than two hundred words the officer's justification of his course in office. He shall continue to perform the duties of his office until the result of said special election shall be officially declared. Other candidates for the office may be nominated to be voted for at said special election, the candidate who shall receive the highest number of votes shall be deemed elected for the remainder of the term, whether it be the person against whom the recall petition was filed or another. The recall petition shall be filed with the officer with whom a petition for nomination to such office should be filed, and the same officer shall order the special election when it is required. No such petition shall be circulated against any officer until he has actually held his office six months, save and except that it may be filed against a senator or representative in the legislative assembly at any time after fifteen days from the beginning of the first session after his election. After one such petition and special election, no further recall petition shall be filed against the same officer during the term for which he was elected unless such further petitioners shall first pay into the public treasury which has paid such special election expenses, the whole amount of its expenses for the preceding special election. Such additional legislation as may aid the operation of this section shall be provided by the legislative assembly, including provision for payment by the public treasury of the reasonable special election campaign expenses of such officer. But the words "the legislative assembly shall provide," or any similar or equivalent words in this constitution or any amendment thereto shall not be construed to grant to the legislative assembly any exclusive power of lawmaking nor in any way to limit the initiative and referendum powers reserved by the people.

CHAPTER 86

(S. B. No. 84 — Plain)

Providing Direct Legislation

A Concurrent Resolution Amending the Constitution of the State of North Dakota, Relating to the Legislative Department and Providing for Direct Legislation; the Proposing of Constitutional Amendments, and Reference of Laws.

Be It Resolved by the Senate of the State of North Dakota, the House of Representatives Concurring: —

That the following amendment to the constitution of the state of North Dakota be referred to by Legislative Assembly to be chosen at the next general election in said state, and, if approved by the last named legislative assembly, the same be submitted to the qualified electors of the state for approval or rejection, in accordance with the provisions of Section 202 of the Constitution of the State of North Dakota.

AMENDMENT TO THE CONSTITUTION. That Section 25 of Article 2 of the constitution of the state of North Dakota is hereby amended to read as follows: —

25. The legislative authority of the state of North Dakota shall be vested in a legislative assembly consisting of a senate and a house of representatives, but the people reserve to themselves the power to propose laws and amendments to the state constitution and to enact and approve or reject the same at the

The Initiative and Referendum 213

polls, except as to local or special laws, as enumerated in Section 70 of Article 2 of this constitution, independently of the legislative assembly; and also reserve the power, at their own option, to approve or reject and annul at the polls any act, item, section or part of any act or measure passed by the legislative assembly except as to laws relating to appropriation of money, and except as to local or special laws, as enumerated in Section 70 of Article 2 of this constitution. The first power reserved by the people is the initiative. Any measure or constitutional amendment may be proposed by the people by initiative petition, signed by not less than ten per cent, or if an amendment to the constitution not less than fifteen per cent of the legal voters in each county of at least one-half of the counties of the state. Any such petition shall contain the full text of the proposed measure. Such petitions shall be filed with the secretary of state not less than four months prior to the election at which they are to be voted on, or not less than twenty days after the opening session of the legislative assembly to which such petitions are to be presented. The secretary of state shall transmit the same to the house of representatives of such legislative assembly on the first day of the session thereof, or not later than ten days after the same are filed. Measures or amendments to the constitution so proposed shall take precedence over all other measures in the legislative assembly, except appropriation bills, and shall be either enacted or rejected by the legislative assembly without amendment, at that session. Any such measure or amendment, if enacted or agreed to by the legislative assembly, shall be subject to referendum upon a petition as hereinafter provided, or it may be referred to the people by the legislative assembly for approval or rejection. In the event that it is rejected, or if no action is taken upon it by the legislative assembly at that session, the secretary of state shall submit it to the people for approval or rejection at the next general election. The legislative assembly may propose a different measure or constitutional amendment to accomplish the same purpose, whereupon both measures, or both amendments, shall be submitted by the secretary of state to the people for approval or rejection at the next ensuing general election. If conflicting measures or amendments are submitted to the people at a general election and each receives a majority of the votes cast for and against the same respectively, then the one receiving the highest number of affirmative votes shall be thereby deemed enacted and approved and all others rejected. When any measure so approved at the polls, as provided herein, is a constitutional amendment, it shall be referred to the next legislative assembly, and should such amendment be approved by a majority of the members elected to each house thereof, such amendment shall become a part of the constitution of the state. If such amendment be rejected by the next legislative assembly, it shall again be submitted to the people at the next general election for approval or rejection, and if the said amendment the second time receives a majority of all the votes cast thereon at such election, it shall become a part of the constitution of the state. The second power reserved is the referendum, or the power to order any act, item, or part of any act of the legislative assembly to be referred to the people for their approval or rejection at the polls. A referendum may be ordered as to any measure or any part, item or section of any measure passed by the legislative assembly upon a majority vote of the members elect thereof, or by a petition signed by at least ten per cent of the legal voters in each county of at least one-half of the counties of the state, whereupon such act, measure, part or parts thereof so ordered shall be suspended until the referendum vote shall determine whether or not the law is sustained or defeated, provided, that when it is necessary for immediate preservation of the public health, peace or safety that a law become effective without delay, such necessity and the facts creating the same, shall be stated in one section of the bill, and if upon aye and nay vote in each house of the legislative assembly, two thirds of all the members-elect thereto shall vote on a separate roll call in favor of such law going into instant operation on account of the necessity for the same, such law shall become operative upon approval by the governor, and shall not be subject to a referendum. The reference to the people of one or more items, sections or parts of any duly enacted act or emergency law shall not delay the remainder of that act or law from becoming operative. All referendum petitions shall be filed with the secretary of state within ninety days after the final adjournment of the session of the legislative assembly which passed the measure upon which the referendum is demanded. The veto power of the governor shall not extend to measures initiated by, or referred to and approved by the people. All elections on measures referred to the people shall be had at biennial regular general elections, unless provisions be made by law for a special election on such measures. Any measure thus referred to the people shall become a law when it is approved by a majority of the votes cast thereon, and not otherwise, and shall be in force from the date of the official declaration of the vote by the state board of canvassers. The enacting clause of all measures initiated by the people shall be; "Be it enacted by the people of North Dakota." The basis for the computation of the number of signatures required for any initiative or referendum petition shall be the total vote cast for governor at the last general election in the counties where such petitions are signed.

The section shall not be construed to deprive any member of the legislative assembly of the right to introduce any measure.

The secretary of state and all other officers shall be guided by the general laws and this act in filing and submitting initiative and referendum petitions until legislation shall be enacted therefor.

This amendment shall be self-executing, but laws may be enacted for the purpose of facilitating its operation.

CHAPTER 89

(S. B. No. 153 — Gibbens)

Concurrent Resolution

A Concurrent Resolution Amending the Constitution of the State of North Dakota, Providing for the Future Amendment Thereof.

Be It Resolved by the Senate of the State of North Dakota, the House of Representatives Concurring: —

§ 1. That the following proposed amendment to section 202 of article 15 of the constitution of the state of North Dakota, be referred to the legislative assembly to be chosen at the next general election in the state of North Dakota to be, if approved by said last mentioned legislative assembly, submitted to the qualified electors of the state for approval or rejection in accordance with the provisions of section 202 of the constitution of the state of North Dakota.

AMENDMENT. Article 15, section 202 of the constitution of the state of North Dakota is amended so as to read as follows:

§ 202. This constitution may be amended as follows: —

First. Any amendment or amendments to this constitution may be proposed in either house of the legislative assembly; and if the same shall be agreed to by a majority of the members elected to each of the two houses, such proposed amendment shall be entered on the journal of the house with the yeas and nays taken thereon, and referred to the legislative assembly to be chosen at the next general election, and shall be published, as provided by law, for three months previous to the time of making such choice, and if in the legislative assembly so next chosen as aforesaid such proposed amendment or amendments shall be agreed to by a majority of all members elected to each house, then it shall be the duty of the legislative assembly to submit such proposed amendment or amendments to the people in such

The Initiative and Referendum 217

manner and at such times as the legislative assembly shall provide; and if the people shall approve and ratify such amendment or amendments by a majority of the electors qualified to vote for members of the legislative assembly voting thereon, such amendment or amendments shall become a part of the constitution of this state. If two or more amendments shall be submitted at the same time they shall be submitted in such manner that the electors shall vote for or against each of such amendments separately.

Second. Any amendment or amendments to this constitution may also be proposed by the people by the filing with the secretary of state, at least six months previous to a general election, of an initiative petition containing the signatures of at least twenty-five per cent of the legal voters in each of not less than one-half of the counties of the state. When such petition has been properly filed the proposed amendment or amendments shall be published as the legislature may provide for three months previous to the general election, and shall be placed upon the ballot to be voted upon by the people at the next general election. Should any such amendment or amendments proposed by initiative petition and submitted to the people receive a majority of all the legal votes cast at such general election, such amendment or amendments shall be referred to the next legislative assembly and should such proposed amendment or amendments be agreed upon by a majority of all the members elected to each house, such amendment or amendments shall become a part of the constitution of this state. Should any amendment or amendments proposed by initiative petition and receiving a majority of all the votes cast at the general election as herein provided, but failing to receive approval by the following legislative assembly to which it has been referred, such amendment or amendments shall again be submitted to the people at the next general election for their approval or rejection as at the previous general election. Should such amendment or amendments receive a majority of all the legal votes cast at such succeeding general election, such amendment or amendments at once become a part of the constitution of this state. Any amendment or amendments proposed by initiative petition and failing of adoption as herein provided, shall not be again considered until the expiration of six years.

CHAPTER 93

(S. B. No. 5 — Bessesen)

Concurrent Resolution

A Concurrent Resolution for an Amendment to the Constitution Providing for the Initiative and Referendum.

Be It Resolved by the Senate of the State of North Dakota, the House of Representatives Concurring: —

That the following amendment to the constitution of the state of North Dakota, providing for the initiative and referendum, shall be referred to the next legislative assembly to be chosen at the next general election in said state, and with the approval of said legislative assembly be submitted to the qualified electors for adoption or rejection, in accordance with the provisions of section 202 of the constitution of the state of North Dakota.

AMENDMENT. Section 25 of Article 2 of the constitution of the state of North Dakota is hereby amended to read as follows:

§ 25. The legislative authority of the state of North Dakota shall be vested in a legislative assembly consisting of a senate and house of representatives, but the people reserve to themselves power to propose laws and to enact or reject the same at the polls, independent of the legislative assembly, and also reserve power, at their own option, to approve or reject at the polls any act, item, section or part of any act or measure passed by the legislative assembly. The first power reserved by the people is the initiative, or the power to propose measures for enactment into laws, and at least ten per cent of the legal voters to be secured in a majority of the counties of this state shall be required to propose any measure by initiative petition, and every such

The Initiative and Referendum

petition shall include the full text of the measure so proposed. Initiative petitions shall be filed with the secretary of state not less than thirty days before any regular session of the legislative assembly; he shall transmit the same to the legislative assembly as soon as it convenes. Such initiative measure shall take precedence over all other measures in the legislative assembly except appropriation bills, and shall be either enacted or rejected without change or amendment by the legislative assembly within forty days. If any such initiative measure shall be enacted by the legislative assembly it shall be subject to referendum petition or it may be referred by the legislative assembly to the people for approval or rejection. If it is rejected or no action is taken upon it by the legislative assembly within said forty days, the secretary of state shall submit it to the people for approval or rejection at the next ensuing regular general election. The legislative assembly may reject any measure so proposed by initiative petition and propose a different one to accomplish the same purpose, and in any such event both measures shall be submitted by the secretary of state to the people for approval or rejection at the next ensuing regular election. If conflicting measures submitted to the people at the next ensuing election shall be approved by a majority of the votes cast for and against the same, the one receiving the highest number of affirmative votes shall thereby become valid and the other shall thereby be rejected. The second power is the referendum, or the power to order any act, item, or part of any act to be referred to the people for their approval or rejection at the polls, and it may be ordered (except as to laws necessary for the immediate preservation of the public peace, health or safety), as to any measure or any parts, items or sections of any measure passed by the legislative assembly either by a petition signed by ten per cent of the legal voters of the state from a majority of the counties or by the legislative assembly, if a majority of the members elect vote therefor. When it is necessary for the immediate preservation of the public peace, health or safety that a law shall become effective without delay, such necessity and the facts creating the same shall be stated in one section of the bill, and if upon aye and no vote in each house two-thirds of all the members elected to each house shall vote on a separate roll call in favor of the said law going into instant operation for the immediate preservation of the public peace, health or safety, such law shall become operative upon approval by the governor.

The filing of a referendum petition against one or more items, sections or parts of an act shall not delay the remainder of that act from becoming operative. Referendum petitions against measures passed by the legislative assembly shall be filed with the secretary of state not more than ninety days after the final adjournment of the session of the legislative assembly which passed the measure on which the referendum is demanded. The veto power of the governor shall not extend to measures referred to the people. All elections on measures referred to the people of the state shall be had at biennial regular elections, except as provision may be made by law for a special election or elections. Any measure referred to the people shall take effect when it is approved by a majority of the votes cast thereon and not otherwise and shall be in force from the date of the official declaration of the vote.

The enacting clause of all the initiative bills shall be "Be it enacted by the people of the state of North Dakota." This section shall not be construed to deprive any member of the legislative assembly of the right to introduce any measure. The whole number of votes cast for secretary of state at the regular election last preceding the filing of any petition for the initiative or for the referendum shall be the basis on which the number of legal votes necessary to sign such petition shall be counted.

Petitions and orders for the initiative and for the referendum shall be filed with the secretary of state, and in submitting the same to the people he and all other officers shall be guided by the general laws and the act submitting this amendment until legislation shall be specially provided therefor.

This amendment shall be self-executing, but legislation may be enacted to facilitate its operation.

CHAPTER 94

(H. B. No. 237 — Doyle of Foster and Ployhar)

Concurrent Resolution

A Concurrent Resolution for Amendment of the Constitution Providing for the Initiative and Referendum, and the Provisions Thereof, the Recall of Public Officers and Future Amendments to the Constitution.

Be It Resolved by the House of Representatives of the State of North Dakota, and the Senate Therein Concurring: —

That the following amendments to the constitution of the state of North Dakota be referred to the legislative assembly to be chosen at the next general election, be published, and upon agreement to by the legislative assembly so next chosen as aforesaid, be submitted to the people at the general election in the year 1914 for approval or rejection, in accordance with the provisions of section 202 of the constitution of the state of North Dakota.

AMENDMENTS. Section twenty-five (25), fifty-seven (57), fifty-eight (58), fifty-nine (59), and sixty-five (65) of article two (2) and section 201 of article fourteen (14), and section 202 of article fifteen (15) of the constitution of the state of North Dakota shall be and are hereby amended to read as follows: —

§ 25. The legislative authority of the state shall be vested in a legislative assembly, consisting of a senate and house of representatives, but the people reserve to themselves the power: First to propose laws, legislative measures, resolutions and amendments to the constitution and to enact and approve or reject the same at the polls independent of the legislative assembly or the governor (except that amendments to the constitution shall be once referred to the legislative assembly) and

Second, at their own option, to order submitted to them, and to enact, approve and confirm or reject and annul at the polls any act, measure or resolution, or item, section, part or parts of any such as submitted to, proposed, enacted or rejected by the legislative assembly, or vetoed by the governor.

The power first above reserved by the people is the Initiative and the second is the Referendum. Every initiative petition shall include the full text of the measure proposed, and not more than eight per cent, nor in any case more than twenty thousand (20,000) legal electors, shall be required to petition for and propose any measure to compel it to be submitted to the people at the polls, independent and regardless of, or notwithstanding non-enactment thereof by, the legislative assembly, or veto by the governor; providing that the initiative petition proposing an amendment or amendments to the constitution shall be signed by not more than 15 per cent of the legal electors in at least one-half of the counties of the state. Not more than five per cent, nor in any case more than ten thousand (10,000) legal electors, shall be required to petition and propose any measure or resolution for enactment or agreement by the legislative assembly, or to order and employ the referendum power as to initiative measure or resolution so submitted, or as to any other act, measure or resolution, or part thereof, as herein provided under the second power reserved by the people. All initiative petitions for measures, except for municipal and wholly local legislation, shall be filed in the office of the secretary of state not less than four months prior to the election at which they are to be voted on, or, within twenty days after the opening session of the legislative assembly; and whenever so filed and not submitted to vote at the election last preceding, shall be transmitted to the house of representatives at the opening session thereof (except proposed constitutional amendments approved at the preceding election shall be transmitted to the state senate together with any not voted on), or within ten days after filing; provided, none shall be so transmitted after the thirtieth day of the term. Initiative measures shall take precedence over all others in such legislative assembly except appropriation bills and constitutional amendments referred by the people or a preceding legislative assembly, and shall be enacted, referred or rejected, without amendment, by the legislative assembly at that term. If enacted, such measures shall be subject to referendum. If not enacted and not entitled hereby to be submitted to vote, then the legislative assembly, as it enacts other bills, may refer such proposed measures to the electors either alone or together with any to the same purpose and end, proposed and preferred by the legislative assembly. Whenever it shall be necessary for the immediate preservation of the public peace, health or safety that a law shall become effective, without delay, such necessity shall be stated in a separate section, and if, by a vote of yeas and nays, three-fourths of all members elected to each house, city council or commission, as the case may be, shall vote on a separate roll call, in favor of the measure going into instant operation because necessary for the immediate preservation of the public peace, health or safety, such law shall become operative upon approval by the governor or mayor, as the case may be; provided, that an emergency shall not be so declared in any measure creating or abolishing any office, or to change the salary, term or duty of any officer, or in disposing of any lands and natural resources belonging to the state.

Referendum petitions or orders shall be filed in the office of the secretary of state not less than ninety days after the final adjournment of the legislative assembly which passed or to which was referred the measure on which referendum is demanded. A referendum petition ordering submitted an emergency law shall not affect the same until said law is rejected and annulled at the polls, whereupon such law, item, section or part thereof so submitted shall be repealed. The filing of a referendum petition ordering submitted one or more items, sections or parts of any duly enacted act, legislative measure, resolution or ordinance shall not delay the remainder, not so ordered, from becoming operative.

Whenever the purpose and object sought, stated and contained in conflicting or competing measures or resolutions submitted to the people, shall be affirmatively approved by a majority of the votes cast for and against such measures or resolutions, then the measure or resolution, embodying the purpose or object so approved, which received the largest number of affirmative votes, shall thereby become the law or constitutional amendment and all others shall thereby be rejected and repealed.

The veto power of the governor or mayor shall not extend to measures initiated by or referred to or enacted by the people.

All elections on general, local and special measures referred to the people of the state or of any locality shall be had at the biennial regular general elections, except when otherwise provided by law, but counties, cities and towns may provide for special elections on their municipal and wholly local legislation.

In case of laws, chiefly of local interest, whether submitted by initiative or referendum petition or by the legislative assembly, as for example, the division or creation of counties or creation of new or additional offices or officers, the same shall be submitted to, voted on and approved or rejected only by the people of the counties chiefly interested.

Any measure submitted to the people at the polls, shall become enacted, be and become the law when it is approved by a majority of the votes cast thereon (except as herein provided conflicting or competing measures are submitted) and shall be in force and effect and become operative upon date of the certified statement of such vote by the state board of canvassers.

Proposed amendments to the constitution shall in all cases be submitted to the people for approval or rejection.

No statute, ordinance or resolution approved and enacted by vote of the electors shall be amended, repealed or in any particular nullified by any subsequent legislation by the legislative assembly, city council or commission, except by a three-fourths vote of all members elected thereto, taken by yeas and nays.

The enacting clause of all initiative bills shall be "Be it enacted by the people of the state of North Dakota." And of all ordinances "Be it ordained by the people of (name of municipality). This section shall not be construed to deprive any member of the legislative assembly, city council or commission, of the right to introduce any measure, nor shall this amendment be construed to limit in any degree the inherent right of petition to any person or persons.

The whole number of votes cast for the office of secretary of state at the regular election last preceding the filing of any initiative or referendum petition shall be the basis on which the number of legal electors necessary to sign such petition shall be computed.

It shall be the duty of the secretary of state to submit to the electors at the polls all measures proposed and ordered by petitions or referred by the legislative assembly, so entitled and filed in his office, and to transmit all others to the legislative assembly in accordance herewith, and he and all other officers shall be guided by the general laws, the act submitting this amendment and the terms hereof until legislation shall be especially provided.

It shall be the duty of the legislative assembly to which this amendment is referred to make provision by law for its execution in accordance herewith, in anticipation of its ratification by the people.

All original initiative petitions shall be returned to or filed in the office of the secretary of state by the secretary of the senate not later than ten days after the final adjournment of that branch of the legislative assembly, with endorsement thereon, or, securely attached thereto, showing full and complete record of the action taken relative thereto in either and both houses of the legislative assembly and its final disposition thereof.

The initiative and referendum powers are hereby further reserved to the electors of each municipality and district, as to all local, special and municipal legislation of every character, in and for their respective municipalities and districts. The provisions of this section shall apply as far as may be made applicable to city councils, and commission forms of city government.

Every extension, enlargement, grant or conveyance of a franchise or of any right, property, easement, lease or occupation of, or in any road, street, alley or park, or any part thereof, or in any real property owned by a municipal corporation, whether the same be made by statute, ordinance, resolution or otherwise, shall be subject to referendum by petition.

Until general laws shall prescribe the manner of exercising the initiative and referendum powers as to their municipal legislation, cities and towns may provide by ordinance therefor. But not more than ten per cent of the legal electors may be required to order the referendum, not more than fifteen per cent to propose any measure by initiative in any city or town, and petitions for such measures ordering any submitted shall be filed with such officers within the county, city or district as is by law provided for the filing of petitions for nomination of candidates for public office.

This amendment shall be self-executing, but legislation may be enacted especially to facilitate its operation.

§ 57. Any bill may originate in either house of the legislative assembly, and a bill so originating, passed by one house may be amended by the other.

§ 58. No law shall be passed by the legislative assembly except by a bill adopted by both houses, and no bill shall be so altered and amended on its passage through either house as to change its original purpose.

§ 59. The enacting clause of every law originating in the legislative assembly shall be as follows: "Be it enacted by the Legislative Assembly of the State of North Dakota."

§ 65. No bill (other than that approved and enacted by the people at the polls) shall become a law except by a vote of a majority of all the members elect in each house, nor unless, on its final passage in the legislative assembly, the vote be taken by yeas and nays, and the names of those voting be entered on the journal.

The words "Legislative Assembly shall pass," "Legislative

Assembly shall provide," "approve," etc., or words similar or equivalent in this constitution or any amendments thereto, wherever occurring, shall not be construed to grant to the legislative assembly any exclusive power of legislating, nor in any way to limit the initiative and referendum reserved by the people.

ARTICLE XIV

§ 201. No person shall be liable to impeachment twice for the same offence.

§ 201 A. Every public officer in North Dakota is subject as herein provided, to recall by the legal voters of the state or of the electoral district from which he is elected. There may be required thirty per cent, but not more, of the number of electors who voted in his district at the preceding election for the office of secretary of state to file their petition demanding his recall by the people. They shall set forth in said petition the reasons for said demand. If he shall file an offer of his resignation, it shall be accepted and take effect on the day it is filed, and the vacancy shall be filled as may be provided by law. If he shall not resign within five days after the petition is filed, a special election shall be ordered to be held within twenty days in his said electoral district to determine whether the people will recall said officer.

On the sample ballot at said election shall be printed in not more than two hundred words, the reason for demanding the recall of said officer as set forth in the recall petition, and in not more than two hundred words, the officer's justification of his course in office. He shall continue to perform the duties of his office until the result of said special election shall be officially declared. Other candidates for the office, previously nominated, may be voted for at said special election. The candidate who shall receive the highest number of votes shall be deemed elected for the remainder of the term, whether it be the person against whom the recall petition was filed, or another. The recall petition shall be filed with the officer with whom a petition for nomination to such office should be filed, and the recalled officer's resignation, should he resign, shall be filed with the same officer, and the same officer shall order a special election when it is required. No such petition shall be circulated against any officer until he has actually held his office six months, save and except that it may be filed against a senator or representative in the legislative assembly or a member of the city council, or commission or mayor at any time after five days from the beginning of his term of office.

After one such petition and special election, no further recall petition shall be filed against same officer during the term for which he was elected unless such further petitioners shall first pay into the public treasury which has paid such special election expenses, the whole of its expenses for the preceding special election. Such additional legislation as may aid the operation of this section shall be provided by law, including provision for payment by the public treasury of the reasonable special election campaign expenses of such officer.

ARTICLE XV

FUTURE AMENDMENTS

§ 202. Any amendment or amendments to this constitution may be proposed in either house of the legislative assembly, or by the people by initiative petition. Every initiative petition shall include the full text of the amendment or amendments proposed and shall be filed in the office of the secretary of the state not less than four months prior to the election at which such proposed amendment or amendments shall be voted on.

When any measure, act or resolution, or item, section or part or parts of any such (irrespective of source) proposed as an amendment or amendments to this constitution, and published as provided by law, for three months previous to any general state election, and at such election, shall be approved by a majority of the electors voting thereon, and, without amendment, such proposed and approved amendment or amendments shall be agreed to and confirmed by a majority of the members elected to each of the two houses of the next legislative assembly, the same shall be entered in the journals of the two houses with the yea and nay vote and names of the members voting thereon; then and thereby such amendment or amendments shall become a part of the constitution of this state.

If not agreed to and confirmed by the legislative assembly at that term, without amendment, then such proposed and approved amendment or amendments shall be submitted, by the secretary of state, a second time to the electors at the ensuing regular general election, or special election, provided by law. And, if the same shall be the second time approved and ratified by a majority of the electors voting thereon, then and thereby such amendment or amendments, shall become a part of the constitution of this state. Or, if the legislative assembly shall agree to any amendment or amendments, (excepting any approved at the last preceding election, above provided for) the same shall be entered in both journals with the yea and nay vote as aforesaid, and it shall be the duty of the legislative assembly to refer the same to the people for approval or rejection at the ensuing general election, or at a special state election, provided by law; and such proposed amendment or amendments shall be published as aforesaid and be submitted to the electors at the polls; and if approved and confirmed by a majority of the electors voting thereon, then and thereby such amendment or amendments shall become a part of the constitution of this state.

All amendments submitted to the voters and approved as herein shall be effective and operative as a part of the constitution on the date of the certified statement of such vote by the state board of canvassers. If two or more amendments shall be submitted at the same election they shall be submitted in such manner that the electors shall vote for or against such amendment separately; but may be presented, designated and identified on the ballot as provided by law.

No convention shall be called to amend or propose amendments to this constitution, or to propose a new constitution, unless the law providing for such convention shall first be approved by the people on a referendum vote at a regular general election.

XIX. ARIZONA (PROPOSED)

[The convention which framed the Arizona constitution met at Phœnix from October 10 to December 9, 1910. The constitution was ratified February 27, 1911 by a vote of 12,187 for, to 3822 against. On August 8–10, Congress adopted a joint resolution admitting Arizona on condition that an amendment excepting judicial officers from the operation of the recall provision should be submitted to the voters at the time of electing the state officers. This resolution was vetoed by President Taft on August 15, 1911. See below, pp. 245, 256.]

The Initiative and Referendum Provisions [1]

SECTION 1. (1) The legislative authority of the State shall be vested in a legislature, consisting of a senate and a house of representatives, but the people reserve the power to propose laws and amendments to the constitution and to enact or reject such laws and amendments at the polls independently of the legislature; and they also reserve, for use at their own option, the power to approve or reject at the polls any act, or item, section, or part of any act, of the legislature.

(2) The first of these reserved powers is the initiative. Under this power 10 per cent of the qualified electors shall have the right to propose any measure, and 15 per cent shall have the right to propose any amendment to the constitution.

(3) The second of these reserved powers is the referendum. Under this power the legislature, or 5 per cent of the qualified electors, may order the submission to the people at the polls of any measure, or item, section, or part of any measure, enacted

---

[1] Constitution of Arizona, *Senate Document*, 61st Congress, 3d Session, No. 798, pp. 5 ff. For the recall provision see below, pp. 244, 263.

by the legislature, except laws immediately necessary for the preservation of the public peace, health, or safety, or for the support and maintenance of the departments of the State government and State institutions; but to allow opportunity for referendum petitions no act passed by the legislature shall be operative for 90 days after the close of the session of the legislature enacting such measure, except such as require earlier operation to preserve the public peace, health, or safety, or to provide appropriations for the support and maintenance of the departments of the State and of State institutions: *Provided*, That no such emergency measure shall be considered passed by the legislature unless it shall state in a separate section why it is necessary that it shall become immediately operative and shall be approved by the affirmative votes of two-thirds of the members elected to each house of the legislature, taken by roll call of ayes and nays, and also approved by the governor; and should such measure be vetoed by the governor it shall not become a law unless it shall be approved by the votes of three-fourths of the members elected to each house of the legislature, taken by roll call of ayes and nays.

(4) All petitions submitted under the power of the initiative shall be known as initiative petitions, and shall be filed with the secretary of state not less than four months preceding the date of the election at which the measures so proposed are to be voted upon. All petitions submitted under the power of the referendum shall be known as referendum petitions, and shall be filed with the secretary of state not more than 90 days after the final adjournment of the session of the legislature which shall have passed the measure to which the referendum is applied. The filing of a referendum petition against any item, section, or part of any measure shall not prevent the remainder of such measure from becoming operative.

(5) Any measure or amendment to the constitution proposed under the initiative, and any measure to which the referendum is applied, shall be referred to a vote of the qualified electors, and

shall become law when approved by a majority of the votes cast thereon and upon proclamation of the governor, and not otherwise.

(6) The veto power of the governor shall not extend to initiative or referendum measures approved by a majority of the qualified electors.

(7) The whole number of votes cast for all candidates for governor at the general election last preceding the filing of any initiative or referendum petition on a State or county measure shall be the basis on which the number of qualified electors required to sign such petition shall be computed.

(8) The powers of the initiative and the referendum are hereby further reserved to the qualified electors of every incorporated city, town, and county as to all local, city, town, or county matters on which such incorporated cities, towns, and counties are, or shall be empowered by general laws to legislate. Such incorporated cities, towns, and counties may prescribe the manner of exercising said powers within the restrictions of general laws. Under the power of the initiative 15 per cent of the qualified electors may propose measures on such local, city, town, or county matters, and 10 per cent of the electors may propose the referendum on legislation enacted within and by such city, town, or county. Until provided by general law, said cities and towns may prescribe the basis on which said percentages shall be computed.

(9) Every initiative or referendum petition shall be addressed to the secretary of state in the case of petitions for or on State measures, and to the clerk of the board of supervisors, city clerk, or corresponding officer in the case of petitions for or on county, city, or town measures; and shall contain the declaration of each petitioner, for himself, that he is a qualified elector of the State (and in the case of petitions for or on city, town, or county measures, of the city, town, or county affected), his post-office address, the street and number, if any, of his residence, and the date on which he signed such petition. Each sheet containing

The Initiative and Referendum

petitioners' signatures shall be attached to a full and correct copy of the title and text of the measure so proposed to be initiated or referred to the people, and every sheet of every such petition containing signatures shall be verified by the affidavit of the person who circulated said sheet or petition, setting forth that each of the names on said sheet was signed in the presence of the affiant and that in the belief of the affiant each signer was a qualified elector of the State, or in the case of a city, town, or county measure, of the city, town, or county affected by the measure so proposed, to be initiated or referred to the people.

(10) When any initiative or referendum petition or any measure referred to the people by the legislature shall be filed, in accordance with this section, with the secretary of state, he shall cause to be printed on the official ballot of the next regular general election the title and number of said measure, together with the words "Yes" and "No" in such manner that the electors may express at the polls their approval or disapproval of the measure.

(11) The text of all measures to be submitted shall be published as proposed amendments to the constitution are published, and in submitting such measures and proposed amendments the secretary of state and all other officers shall be guided by the general law until legislation shall be especially provided therefor.

(12) If two or more conflicting measures or amendments to the constitution shall be approved by the people at the same election, the measure or amendment receiving the greatest number of affirmative votes shall prevail in all particulars as to which there is conflict.

(13) It shall be the duty of the secretary of state, in the presence of the governor and the chief justice of the supreme court, to canvass the votes for and against each such measure or proposed amendment to the constitution within thirty days after the election, and upon the completion of the canvass the governor shall forthwith issue a proclamation, giving the whole number of votes cast for and against each measure or proposed amendment,

and declaring such measures or amendments as are approved by a majority of those voting thereon to be law.

(14) This section shall not be construed to deprive the legislature of the right to enact any measure.

(15) This section of the constitution shall be, in all respects, self-executing.

SEC. 2. The legislature shall provide a penalty for any wilful violation of any of the provisions of the preceding section.

XX. NEW MEXICO (PROPOSED)

[Following the act of Congress approved June 20, 1910, to enable the people of New Mexico to form a constitution and state government, a constitutional convention met at Sante Fé, from October 3 to November 21, 1910. The constitution was ratified by the people of New Mexico January 21, 1911 by a vote of 31,742 for, to 13,399 against. The provisions of the constitution relating to the Referendum and method of amendment follow. On August 8–10, Congress passed a joint resolution admitting New Mexico on condition that an amendment relative to the Amendment Clause of the new Constitution be submitted to the voters. See below, pp. 245 ff.]

ARTICLE 4. — *Legislative Department*[1]

SECTION 1. The legislative power shall be vested in a senate and house of representatives which shall be designated the Legislature of the State of New Mexico, and shall hold its sessions at the seat of government.

The people reserve the power to disapprove, suspend, and annul any law enacted by the legislature, except general appropriation laws; laws providing for the preservation of the public peace, health, or safety; for the payment of the public debt or interest thereon, or the creation or funding of the same, except as in this constitution otherwise provided; for the maintenance of the public schools or State institutions, and local or special laws.

---

[1] The Constitution of New Mexico, House of Representatives Document, 61st Cong., 3d Sess., No. 1369, pp. 11 ff.

Petitions disapproving any law, other than those above expected, enacted at the last preceding session of the legislature, shall be filed with the secretary of state not less than four months prior to the next general election. Such petitions shall be signed by not less than ten per centum of the qualified electors of each of three-fourths of the counties and in the aggregate by not less than ten per centum of the qualified electors of the state, as shown by the total number of votes cast at the last preceding general election. The question of the approval or rejection of such law shall be submitted by the secretary of state to the electorate at the next general election; and if a majority of the legal votes cast thereon, and not less than forty per centum of the total number of legal votes cast at such general election, be cast for the rejection of such law, it shall be annulled and thereby repealed with the same effect as if the legislature had then repealed it, and such repeal shall revive any law repealed by the act so annulled; otherwise, it shall remain in force unless subsequently repealed by the legislature. If such petition or petitions be signed by not less than twenty-five per centum of the qualified electors under each of the foregoing conditions, and be filed with the secretary of state within ninety days after the adjournment of the session of the legislature at which such law was enacted, the operation thereof shall be thereupon suspended and the question of its approval or rejection shall be likewise submitted to a vote at the next ensuing general election. If a majority of the votes cast thereon and not less than forty per centum of the total number of votes cast at such general election be cast for its rejection, it shall be thereby annulled; otherwise, it shall go into effect upon publication of the certificate of the secretary of state declaring the result of the vote thereon. It shall be a felony for any person to sign any such petition with any name other than his own, or to sign his name more than once for the same measure, or to sign such petition when he is not a qualified elector in the county specified in such petition; provided, that nothing herein shall be construed to prohibit the writing thereon of the name of any person who can not write, and who signs the same with his mark. The legislature shall enact laws necessary for the effective exercise of the power hereby reserved.

ARTICLE 19. — *Amendments*

SECTION 1. Any amendment or amendments to this constitution may be proposed in either house of the legislature at any regular session thereof, and if two-thirds of all members elected to each of the two houses voting separately, shall vote in favor thereof, such proposed amendment or amendments shall be entered on their respective journals with the yeas and nays thereon; or any amendment or amendments to this constitution may be proposed at the first regular session of the legislature held after the expiration of two years from the time this constitution goes into effect, or at the regular session of the legislature convening each eighth year thereafter, and if a majority of all the members elected to each of the two houses voting separately at said sessions shall vote in favor thereof, such proposed amendment or amendments shall be entered on their respective journals with the yeas and nays thereon. The secretary of state shall cause any such amendment or amendments to be published in at least one newspaper in every county of the State where a newspaper is published, once each week, for four consecutive weeks, the last publication to be not less than two weeks prior to the next general election, at which time the said amendment or amendments shall be submitted to the electors of the State for their approval or rejection.

If the same be ratified by a majority of the electors voting thereon and by an affirmative vote equal to at least forty per centum of all the votes cast at said election in the State and in at least one-half of the counties thereof, then, and not otherwise, such amendment or amendments shall become part of this constitution. Not more than three amendments shall be submitted at one election and if two or more amendments are proposed, they shall be so submitted as to enable the electors to vote on each of

The Initiative and Referendum

them separately; provided, that no amendment shall apply to or affect the provisions of sections one and three of article seven hereof on elective franchise and sections eight and ten of article twelve hereof on education unless it be proposed by vote of three-fourths of the members elected to each house.

SEC. 2. Whenever, during the first twenty-five years after the adoption of this constitution the legislature by a three-fourths vote of the members elected to each house, or after the expiration of said period of said twenty-five years by a two-thirds vote of the members elected to each house, shall deem it necessary to call a convention to revise or amend this constitution, they shall submit the question of calling such convention to the electors at the next general election, and if a majority of all the electors voting at said election in the State and in at least one-half of the counties thereof shall vote in favor of calling a convention, the legislature shall at the next session provide by law for calling the same. Such convention shall consist of at least as many delegates as there are members of the house of representatives.

The constitution adopted by such convention shall have no validity until it has been submitted to and ratified by the people.

SEC. 3. If this constitution be in any way so amended as to allow laws to be enacted by direct vote of the electors, the laws which may be so enacted shall be only such as might be enacted by the legislature under the provisions of this constitution.

SEC. 4. When the United States shall consent thereto, the legislature, by a majority vote of the members in each house, may submit to the people the question of amending any provision of article 21 of this constitution on compact with the United States to the extent allowed by the act of Congress permitting the same, and if a majority of the qualified electors who vote upon any such amendment shall vote in favor thereof, the said article shall be thereby amended accordingly.

SEC. 5. The provisions of section one of this article shall not be changed, altered, or abrogated in any manner except through a general convention called to revise this constitution as herein provided.

XXI. ILLINOIS

[The following act[1] providing for securing an expression of public opinion on measures was passed by the Illinois legislature in 1901.]

1. PETITION — DUTY OF ELECTION OFFICERS.] [§ 428, Ch. 46, R. S.] That on a written petition signed by 25 per cent of the registered voters of any incorporated town, village, city, township, county or school district; or 10 per cent of the registered votes [voters] of the State, it shall be the duty of the proper election officers in each case to submit any question of public policy so petitioned for, to the electors of the incorporated town, village, city, township, county, school district or State, as the case may be, at any general or special election named in the petition: *Provided*, such petition is filed with the proper election officers, in each case not less than sixty (60) days before the date of the election at which the question or questions petitioned for are to be submitted. Not more than three propositions shall be submitted at the same election, and such propositions shall be submitted in the order of its [their] filing.

2. FORM OF BALLOT.] [§ 429, Ch. 46, R. S.] Every question submitted to electors shall be printed in plain, prominent type, upon a separate ballot, in form required by law, the same as a constitutional amendment or other public measure proposed to be voted upon by the people.

Voting under the Public Opinion Law

[This statement is taken from *Senate Document*, No. 603, 61st Cong., 2d Sess.]

The petitions that have been circulated and filed, and the questions that have been voted upon under the Illinois Public Opinion law include the following: —

---

[1] *Illinois Election Laws* (1910), p. 80.

FIRST PETITION (109,418 SIGNATURES)
[Vote of Chicago, April 1, 1902]

	For	Against
Municipal ownership of gas and electric light . . .	139,999	21,364
Municipal ownership of street railways	142,826	27,998
Direct nomination of candidates	140,086	17,654

SECOND PETITION (146,134 SIGNATURES)
[Vote of State, November 4, 1902]

Initiative and referendum on state laws amendment to state laws	428,469	87,654
Initiative and referendum for counties, cities, towns, etc.	390,972	83,377
Direct election of United States Senators	451,319	76,975

THIRD PETITION (131, 417 SIGNATURES)
[Vote of Chicago, April 5, 1904]

Immediate municipal ownership of street railways .	121,957	50,807
Police power licenses and good service instead of franchises	120,863	48,200
Direct election, Chicago school board	116,617	57,729

FOURTH PETITION (137, 842 SIGNATURES)
[Vote of State, November 8, 1904]

Direct primaries	590,976	78,446
People's veto or referendum (local)	535,501	95,420
Home rule in taxation	476,780	140,896

FIFTH PETITION, FOR CHICAGO

Proposed franchise to Chicago City Railway . . .	64,391	150,785
Any franchise to Chicago City Railway	60,020	151,974
Any franchise to any company	59,013	152,135

Since the foregoing was compiled Chicago has had another election, at which four questions were submitted to the people. The manner in which the people of Chicago improved this opportunity elicited this comment from the *Record-Herald:* —

The referendum vote on the four propositions that were submitted to the electorate of the entire city shows conclusively that the people of Chicago can make an intelligent and discriminating use of this instrument of good government. It answers effectively the sneers of those who habitually assert that the voters, like a flock of sheep, will approve anything.

The extent of popular interest may be shown in the fact that out of about 180,000 voters who went to the polls in the city precincts, from 115,000 to 145,000 voted on each of the propositions. That is a proportion of the total vote that is very satisfactory.

On the proposition to revise the charter the vote stood 101,000 to 45,000. On the "gas rate" proposition it was 124,000 to 20,000, and on the forest preserve proposition (city precincts only), it was 82,000 to 55,000.

XXII. THE TEXAS PARTY INITIATIVE [1]

[By an act passed in 1908, the legislature of Texas made the following provision for taking a party vote on measures.]

Whenever delegates are to be selected by any political party to any State or county convention by primary election or primary convention or candidates are instructed for or nominated, it shall be the duty of the chairman of the county or precinct executive committee of said political party upon the application of ten per cent of the members of said party (who are legally qualified voters in said county or precinct) to submit at the time and place of selecting said delegates any proposition, desired to be voted upon by said voters, and the delegates selected at that time shall be considered instructed for whichever proposition for which a majority of the votes are cast; provided, that the number of voters belonging to said political party shall be de-

[1] *The Terrell Election Law* (1908), p. 29, sec. 140.

termined by the votes cast for the party nominee for Governor at the preceding election; and provided further, that said application is filed with the county or precinct chairman at least five days before the tickets are to be printed, and the chairman may require a sworn statement that the names of said applicants are genuine.

II. THE STATE-WIDE RECALL

XXIII. Oregon

[Oregon was the first state to adopt the recall of all state officers including the judiciary. The following constitutional amendment was proposed by initiative petition and adopted by the voters at the general election held June 1, 1908. The vote on this measure was 58,381 for, to 31,002 against.]

The Constitutional Amendment[1]

Article II of the Constitution of the State of Oregon shall be, and hereby is, amended by adding thereto at the end of said article a new section, which shall be numbered Section 18 of said Article II and shall be as follows: —

SECTION 18. Every public officer in Oregon is subject, as herein provided, to recall by the legal voters of the State or of the electoral district from which he is elected. There may be required twenty-five per cent, but not more, of the number of electors who voted in his district at the preceding election for justice of the Supreme Court to file their petition demanding his recall by the people. They shall set forth in said petition the reasons for said demand. If he shall offer his resignation, it shall be accepted and take effect on the day it is offered, and the vacancy shall be filled as may be provided by law. If he shall not resign within five days after the petition is filed, a special election shall be ordered to be held within twenty days in his said electoral district to determine whether the people will recall said officer. On the sample ballot at said election shall be printed in not more than two hundred words, the reasons for demanding the recall of said officer as set forth in the recall petition, and in not more than two hundred

[1] Official copy from the Secretary of State.

words, the officer's justification of his course in office. He shall continue to perform the duties of his office until the result of said special election shall be officially declared. Other candidates for the office may be nominated to be voted for at said special election. The candidate who shall receive the highest number of votes shall be deemed elected for the remainder of the term, whether it be the person against whom the recall petition was filed, or another. The recall petition shall be filed with the officer with whom a petition for nomination to such office should be filed, and the same officer shall order the special election when it is required. No such petition shall be circulated against any officer until he has actually held his office six months, save and except that it may be filed against a senator or representative in the legislative assembly at any time after five days from the beginning of the first session after his election. After one such petition and special election, no further recall petition shall be filed against the same officer during the term for which he was elected unless such further petitioners shall first pay into the public treasury which has paid such special election expenses, the whole amount of its expenses for the preceding special election. Such additional legislation as may aid the operation of this section shall be provided by the Legislative Assembly, including provision for payment by the public treasury of the reasonable special election campaign expenses of such officer. But the words "the Legislative Assembly shall provide" or any similar or equivalent words in this Constitution or any amendment thereto, shall not be construed to grant to the Legislative Assembly any exclusive power of law-making nor in any way to limit the initiative and referendum powers reserved by the people.

XXIV. Arizona (Proposed)

[The recall provisions of the Arizona Constitution follow.]

Article VIII. — Removal from Office[1]

1. RECALL OF PUBLIC OFFICERS

SECTION 1. Every public officer in the State of Arizona, holding an elective office, either by election or appointment, is subject to recall from such office by the qualified electors of the electoral district from which candidates are elected to such office. Such electoral district may include the whole State. Such number of said electors as shall equal 25 per cent of the number of votes cast at the last preceding general election for all of the candidates for the office held by such officer may by petition, which shall be known as a recall petition, demand his recall.

SEC. 2. Every recall petition must contain a general statement, in not more than 200 words, of the grounds of such demand, and must be filed in the office in which petitions for nominations to the office held by the incumbent are required to be filed. The signatures to such recall petition need not all be on one sheet of paper, but each signer must add to his signature the date of his signing said petition, and his place of residence, giving his street and number, if any, should he reside in a town or city. One of the signers of each sheet of such petition, or the person circulating such sheet, must make and subscribe an oath on said sheet that the signatures thereon are genuine.

SEC. 3. If said officer shall offer his resignation, it shall be accepted, and the vacancy shall be filled as may be provided by law. If he shall not resign within five days after a recall petition is filed, a special election shall be ordered to be held not less than 20 nor more than 30 days after such order to determine whether such officer shall be recalled. On the ballots at said election shall be printed the reasons as set forth in the petition for de-

---

[1] *Senate Document*, No. 798, 61st Cong., 3d Session, pp. 18 f.

manding his recall, and, in not more than 200 words, the officer's justification of his course in office. He shall continue to perform the duties of his office until the result of said election shall have been officially declared.

SEC. 4. Unless he otherwise request, in writing, his name shall be placed as a candidate on the official ballot without nomination. Other candidates for the office may be nominated to be voted for at said election. The candidate who shall receive the highest number of votes shall be declared elected for the remainder of the term. Unless the incumbent receive the highest number of votes he shall be deemed to be removed from office upon qualification of his successor. In the event that his successor shall not qualify within five days after the result of said election shall have been declared, the said office shall be vacant and may be filled as provided by law.

SEC. 5. No recall petition shall be circulated against any officer until he shall have held his office for a period of six months, except that it may be filed against a member of the legislature at any time after five days from the beginning of the first session after his election. After one recall petition and election no further recall petition shall be filed against the same officer during the term for which he was elected unless petitioners signing such petition shall first pay into the public treasury which has paid such election expenses, all expenses of the preceding election.

SEC. 6. The general election laws shall apply to recall elections in so far as applicable. Laws necessary to facilitate the operation of the provisions of this article shall be enacted, including provision for payment by the public treasury of the reasonable special-election campaign expenses of such officer.

President Taft's Veto on the Recall [1]

[After lengthy debates, Congress on August 8-10 passed a resolution admitting Arizona and New Mexico to the Union on condition that an amendment to the provision in the Arizona

[1] Congressional Record, August 15, 1911.

constitution relating to recall and an amendment to sections of the New Mexico constitution relating to future amendments be specially submitted to the voters of the respective territories for ratification or rejection. On August 15, 1911, President Taft vetoed this resolution and sent to Congress the following message.]

To the House of Representatives: —

I return herewith, without my approval, House joint resolution No. 14, "To admit the Territories of New Mexico and Arizona as States into the Union on an equal footing with the original States."

Congress, by an enabling act approved June 20, 1910, provided for the calling of a constitutional convention in each of these Territories, the submission of the Constitution proposed by the convention to the electors of the Territory, the approval of the Constitution by the President and Congress, the proclamation of the fact by the President, and the election of State officers. Both in Arizona and New Mexico conventions have been held, Constitutions adopted and ratified by the people, and submitted to the President and Congress. I have approved the Constitution of New Mexico, and so did the House of Representatives of the Sixty-first Congress. The Senate, however, failed to take action upon it. I have not approved the Arizona constitution, nor have the two houses of Congress, except as they have done so by the joint resolution under consideration. The resolution admits both Territories to Statehood with their constitutions, on condition that at the time of the election of State officers New Mexico shall submit to its electors an amendment to its new constitution altering and modifying its provision for future amendments, and on the further condition that Arizona shall submit to its electors, at the time of the election of its State officers, a proposed amendment to its constitution by which judicial officers shall be excepted from the section permitting a recall of all elective officers.

If I sign this joint resolution, I do not see how I can escape responsibility for the judicial recall of the Arizona Constitution. The joint resolution admits Arizona with the judicial recall, but requires the submission of the question of its wisdom to the voters. In other words, the resolution approves the admission of Arizona with the judicial recall, unless the voters themselves repudiate it. Under the Arizona Constitution all elective officers, and this includes county and State judges, six months after their election, are subject to the recall. It is initiated by a petition signed by electors equal to 25 per cent of the total number of votes cast for all the candidates for the office at the previous general election. Within five days after the petition is filed the officer may resign. Whether he does or not, an election ensues in which his name, if he does not resign, is placed on the ballot with that of all other candidates. The petitioners may print on the official ballot 200 words showing their reasons for recalling the officer, and he is permitted to make defence in the same place in 200 words. If the incumbent receives the highest number of the votes, he continues in his office; if not, he is removed from office and is succeeded by the candidate who does receive the highest number.

This provision of the Arizona Constitution, in its application to county and State judges, seems to me so pernicious in its effect, so destructive of independence in the judiciary, so likely to subject the rights of the individual to the possible tyranny of a popular majority, and therefore to be so injurious to the cause of free government, that I must disapprove a Constitution containing it. I am not now engaged in performing the office given me in the enabling act already referred to, approved June 20, 1910, which was that of approving the Constitutions ratified by the peoples of the Territories. It may be argued from the text of that act that in giving or withholding the approval under the act, my only duty is to examine the proposed Constitution, and if I find nothing in it inconsistent with the federal Constitution, the principles of the Declaration of Independence, or the enabling act, to register my approval. But now I am discharging my Constitutional function in respect to the enactment of laws, and my discretion is equal to that of the houses of Congress. I must therefore withhold my approval from this resolution if in fact I do not approve it as a matter of governmental policy. Of course, a mere difference of opinion as to the wisdom of details in a State Constitution ought not to lead me to set up my opinion against that of the people of the Territory. It is to be their government, and, while the power of Congress to withhold or grant Statehood is absolute, the people about to constitute a State should generally know better the kind of government and Constitution suited to their needs than Congress or the Executive. But when such a Constitution contains something so destructive of free government as the judicial recall, it should be disapproved.

A government is for the benefit of all the people. We believe that this benefit is best accomplished by popular government, because in the long run each class of individuals is apt to secure better provision for themselves through their own voice in government than through the altruistic interest of others, however intelligent or philanthropic. The wisdom of ages has taught that no government can exist except in accordance with laws and unless the people under it either obey the laws voluntarily or are made to obey them. In a popular government the laws are made by the people — not by all the people — but by those supposed and declared to be competent for the purpose, as males over twenty-one years of age, and not by all of these — but by a majority of them only. Now, as the government is for all the people, and is not solely for a majority of them, the majority in exercising control either directly or through its agents is bound to exercise the power for the benefit of the minority as well as the majority.

But all have recognized that the majority of a people, unrestrained by law, when aroused and without the sobering effect of deliberation and discussion, may do injustice to the minority or to the individual when the selfish interest of the majority prompts. Hence arises the necessity for a Constitution by which the will of the majority shall be permitted to guide the course of the government only under controlling checks that experience has shown to be necessary to secure for the minority its share of the benefit to the whole people that a popular government is established to bestow. A popular government is not a government of a majority, by a majority, for a majority of the people. It is a government of the whole people, by a majority of the whole people under such rules and checks as will secure a wise, just, and beneficent government for all the people.

It is said you can always trust the people to do justice. If that means all the people and they all agree, you can. But ordinarily they do not all agree, and the maxim is interpreted to mean that you can always trust a majority of the people. This is not invariably true; and every limitation imposed by the people upon the power of the majority in their Constitutions is an admission that it is not always true. No honest, clearheaded man, however great a lover of popular government, can deny that the unbridled expression of the majority of a community converted hastily into law or action would sometimes make a government tyrannical and cruel. Constitutions are checks upon the hasty action of the majority. They are the self-imposed restraints of a whole people upon a majority of them to secure sober action and a respect for the rights of the minority, and of the individual in his relation to other individuals, and in his relation to the whole people in their character as a State or government.

The Constitution distributes the functions of government into three branches — the legislative, to make the laws; the executive, to execute them; and the judicial, to decide in cases arising before it the rights of the individual as between him and others and as between him and the government. This division of government into three separate branches has always been regarded as a great security for the maintenance of free institutions, and the security is only firm and assured when the judicial branch is independent and impartial. The executive and legislative branches are representative of the majority of the people which elected them in guiding the course of the government within the limits of the Constitution. They must act for the whole people, of course; but they may properly follow, and usually ought to follow, the views of the majority which elected them in respect to the governmental policy best adapted to secure the welfare of the whole people.

But the judicial branch of the government is not representative of a majority of the people in any such sense, even if the mode of selecting judges is by popular election. In a proper sense, judges are servants of the people; that is, they are doing work which must be done for the government, and in the interest of all the people, but it is not work in the doing of which they are to follow the will of the majority, except as that is embodied in statutes lawfully enacted according to constitutional limitations. They are not popular representatives. On the contrary, to fill their office properly, they must be independent. They must decide every question which comes before them according to law and justice. If this question is between individuals, they will follow the statute, or the unwritten law, if no statute applies, and they take the unwritten law growing out of tradition and custom from previous judicial decisions. If a statute or ordinance affecting a cause before them is not lawfully enacted, because it violates the Constitution adopted by the people, then they must ignore the statute and decide the question as if the statute had never been passed.

This power is a judicial power, imposed by the people on the judges by the written constitution. In early days, some argued that the obligations of the constitution operated directly on the conscience of the Legislature and only in that manner, and that it was to be conclusively presumed that whatever was done by the Legislature was constitutional. But such a view did not obtain with our hardheaded, courageous, and far-sighted statesmen and judges, and it was soon settled that it was the duty of judges in cases properly arising before them to apply the law and so to declare what was the law, and that if what purported to be statutory law was at variance with the fundamental law, *i.e.*, the constitution, the seeming statute was not law at all, was not binding on the courts, the individuals, or any branch of the government, and that it was the duty of the judges so to decide. This power conferred on the judiciary in our form of government is unique in the history of governments and its operation has attracted and deserved the admiration and commendation of the world. It gives to our judiciary a position higher, stronger, and more responsible than that of the judiciary of any other country, and more effectively secures adherence to the fundamental will of the people.

What I have said has been to little purpose if it has not shown that judges to fulfill their functions properly in our popular government must be more independent than in any other form of government, and that need of independence is greatest where the individual is one litigant, and the State, guided by the successful and governing majority, is the other. In order to maintain the rights of the minority and the individual and to preserve our constitutional balance we must have judges with courage to decide against the majority when justice and law require.

By the recall in the Arizona Constitution, it is proposed to give to the majority power to remove arbitrarily and without delay any judge who may have the courage to render an unpopular decision. By the recall it is proposed to enable a minority of 25 per cent of the voters of the district or State, for no prescribed cause, after the judge has been in office six months, to submit the question of his retention in office to the electorate. The petitioning minority must say on the ballot what they can against him in 200 words, and he must defend as best he can in the same space. Other candidates are permitted to present themselves and have their names printed on the ballot, so that the recall is not based solely on the record or the acts of the judge, but also on the question whether some other and more popular candidate has been found to unseat him. Could there be a system more ingeniously devised to subject judges to momentary gusts of popular passion than this?

We cannot be blind to the fact that often an intelligent and respectable electorate may be so roused upon an issue that it will visit with condemnation the decision of a just judge, though exactly in accord with the law governing the case, merely because it affects unfavorably their contest. Controversies over elections, labor troubles, racial or religious issues, issues as to the construction or constitutionality of liquor laws, criminal trials of popular or unpopular defendants, the removal of county seats, suits by individuals to maintain their constitutional rights in obstruction of some popular improvement — these and many other cases could be cited in which a majority of a district electorate would be tempted by hasty anger to recall a conscientious judge if the opportunity were open all the time.

No period of delay is interposed for the abatement of popular feeling. The recall is devised to encourage quick action, and to lead the people to strike while the iron is hot. The judge is treated as the instrument and servant of a majority of the people and subject to their momentary will, not after a long term in which his qualities as a judge and his character as a man have been subjected to a test of all the varieties of judicial work and duty so as to furnish a proper means of measuring his fitness for continuance in another term. On the instant of an unpopular ruling, while the spirit of protest has not had time to cool and even while an appeal may be pending from his ruling in which he may be sustained, he is to be haled before the electorate as a tribunal, with no judicial hearing, evidence, or defence, and thrown out of office and disgraced for life because he has failed, in a single decision, it may be, to satisfy the popular demand.

Think of the opportunity such a system would give to unscrupulous political bosses in control as they have been in control not only of conventions but elections! Think of the enormous power for evil given to the sensational, muckraking portion of the press in rousing prejudice against a just judge by false charges and insinuations the effect of which in the short period of an election by recall it would be impossible for him to meet and offset! Supporters of such a system seem to think that it will work only in the interest of the poor, the humble, the weak, and the oppressed: that it will strike down only the judge who is supposed to favor corporations and be affected by the corrupting influence of the rich. Nothing could be further from the ultimate result.

The motive it would offer to unscrupulous combinations to seek to control politics in order to control the judges is clear. Those would profit by the recall who have the best opportunity of arousing the majority of the people to action on a sudden impulse. Are they likely to be the wisest or the best people in a community? Do they not include those who have money enough to employ the firebrands and slanderers in a community and the stirrers-up of social hate? Would not self-respecting men well hesitate to accept judicial office with such a sword of Damocles hanging over them? What kind of judgments might those on the unpopular side expect from courts whose judges must make their decisions under such legalized terrorism? The character of the judges would deteriorate to that of trimmers and time-servers, and independent judicial action would be a thing of the past. As the possibilities of such a system pass in review, is it too much to characterize it as one which will destroy the judiciary, its standing, and its usefulness?

The argument has been made to justify the judicial recall that it is only carrying out the principle of the election of the judges by the people. The appointment by the Executive is by the representative of the majority, and so far as future bias is concerned there is no great difference between the appointment and the election of judges. The independence of the judiciary is secured rather by a fixed term and fixed and irreducible salary. It is true that when the term of judges is for a limited number of years and reëlection is necessary, it has been thought and charged sometimes that shortly before election in cases in which popular interest is excited, judges have leaned in their decisions toward the popular side.

As already pointed out, however, in the election of judges for a long and fixed term of years, the fear of popular prejudice as a motive for unjust decisions is minimized by the tenure on the one hand, while the opportunity which the people have, calmly to consider the work of a judge for a full term of years in deciding as to his reëlection, generally insured from them a fair and reasonable consideration of his qualities as a judge. While, therefore, there have been elected judges who have bowed before unjust popular prejudice, or who have yielded to the power of political bosses in their decisions, I am convinced that these are exceptional, and that, on the whole, elected judges have made a great American judiciary. But the success of an elective judiciary certainly furnishes no reason for so changing the system as to take away the very safeguards which have made it successful.

Attempt is made to defend the principle of judicial recall by reference to States in which judges are said to have shown themselves to be under corrupt corporate influence, and in which it is claimed that nothing but a desperate remedy will suffice. If the political control in such States is sufficiently wrested from corrupting corporations to permit the enactment of a radical Constitutional amendment, like that of judicial recall, it would seem possible to make provision, in its stead, for an effective remedy by impeachment in which the cumbrous features of the present remedy might be avoided, but the opportunity for judicial hearing and defence before an impartial tribunal might be retained. Real reforms are not to be effected by patent short-cuts, or by abolishing those requirements which the experience of ages has shown to be essential in dealing justly with every one. Such innovations are certain in the long run to plague the inventor or first user, and will come readily to the hand of the enemies and corrupters of society after the passing of the just popular indignation that prompted their adoption.

Again, judicial recall is advocated on the ground that it will bring the judges more into sympathy with the popular will and the progress of ideas among the people. It is said that now judges are out of touch with the movement toward a wider democracy and a greater control of governmental agencies in the interest and for the benefit of the people. The righteous and just course for a judge to pursue is ordinarily fixed by statute or clear principles of law, and the cases in which his judgment may be affected by his political, economic, or social views are infrequent. But even in such cases, judges are not removed from the people's influence. Surround the judiciary with all the safeguards possible, create judges by appointment, make their tenure for life, forbid diminution of salary during their term, and still it is impossible to prevent the influence of popular opinion from coloring judgments in the long run. Judges are men, intelligent, sympathetic men, patriotic men, and in those fields of the law in which the personal equation unavoidably plays a part, there will be found a response to sober popular opinion as it changes to meet the exigency of social, political, and economic changes.

Indeed, this should be so. Individual instances of a hide-bound and retrograde conservatism on the part of courts in decisions which turn on the individual economic or sociological views of the judges may be pointed out; but they are not many, and do not call for radical action. In treating of courts we are dealing with a human machine, liable like all the inventions of man to err, but we are dealing with a human institution that likens itself to a divine institution, because it seeks and preserves justice. It has been the cornerstone of our gloriously free government in which the rights of the individual and of the minority have been preserved, while governmental action of the majority has lost nothing of beneficent progress, efficacy, and directness. This balance was planned in the Constitution by its framers, and has been maintained by our independent judiciary.

Precedents are cited from State Constitutions said to be equivalent to a popular recall. In some, judges are removable by a vote of both houses of the Legislature. This is a mere adoption of the English address of Parliament to the Crown for the removal of judges. It is similar to impeachment in that a form of hearing is always granted. Such a provision forms no precedent for a popular recall without adequate hearing and defence, and with new candidates to contest the election.

It is said the recall will be rarely used. If so, it will be rarely needed. Then why adopt a system so full of danger? But it is a mistake to suppose that such a powerful lever for influencing judicial decisions and such an opportunity for vengeance because of adverse ones, will be allowed to remain unused.

But it is said that the people of Arizona are to be become an independent State when created, and even if we strike out judicial recall now, they can reincorporate it in their constitution after Statehood. To this I would answer that in dealing with the courts, which are the cornerstone of good government, and in which not only the voters, but the non-voters and non-residents, have a deep interest as a security for their rights of life, liberty, and property, no matter what the future action of the State may be, it is necessary for the authority which is primarily responsible for its creation to assert in no doubtful tones the necessity for an independent and untrammeled judiciary.

WILLIAM H. TAFT.

The White House, August 15, 1911.

Joint Resolution for the Admission of Arizona and New Mexico

[Congress at once took up President Taft's veto measure, and passed the following substitute resolution, which was approved August 21, 1911.]

Resolved by the Senate and House of Representatives of the United States of America in Congress assembled, That the Territories of New Mexico and Arizona are hereby admitted into the Union upon an equal footing with the original States, in accordance with the terms of an Act entitled "An Act to enable the people of New Mexico to form a constitution and State government and be admitted into the Union on an equal footing with the original States; and to enable the people of Arizona to form a constitution and State government and be admitted into the Union on an equal footing with the original States" commonly called the enabling Act approved June twentieth, nineteen hundred and ten, and upon the terms and conditions hereinafter set forth. The admission herein provided for shall take effect upon the proclamation of the President of the United States, when the conditions explicitly set forth in this joint resolution shall have been complied with, which proclamation shall issue at the earliest practicable time after the results of the election herein provided for shall have been certified to the President, and also after evidence shall have been submitted to him of the compliance with the terms and conditions of this resolution.

The President is authorized and directed to certify the adoption of this resolution to the governor of each Territory as soon as practicable after the adoption hereof, and each of said governors shall issue his proclamation for the holding of the first general election as provided for in the constitution of New Mexico heretofore adopted and the election ordinance numbered two adopted by the constitutional convention of Arizona, respectively, and for the submission to a vote of the electors of said Territories of the amendments of the constitutions of said proposed States, respectively, herein set forth in accordance with the terms and conditions of this joint resolution. The results of said elections shall be certified to the President by the governor of each of said Territories; and if the terms and conditions of this joint resolution shall have been complied with, the proclamation shall immediately issue by the President announcing the result of said elections so ascertained, and upon the issuance of said proclamation the proposed State or States so complying shall be deemed admitted by Congress into the Union upon an equal footing with the other States.

SEC. 2. That the admission of New Mexico shall be subject to the terms and conditions of a joint resolution approved February sixteenth, nineteen hundred and eleven, and entitled "Joint resolution reaffirming the boundary line between Texas and the Territory of New Mexico."

SEC. 3. That before the proclamation of the President shall issue announcing the result of said election in New Mexico, and at the same time that the State election aforesaid is held, the electors of New Mexico shall vote upon the following proposed amendment of their State constitution as a condition precedent to the admission of said State, to wit:—

"Article XIX of the constitution, as adopted by the electors of New Mexico at an election held on the twenty-first day of January, anno Domini nineteen hundred and eleven, be, and the same is hereby, amended so as to read as follows:—

"'ARTICLE XIX.

"'AMENDMENT.

"'SECTION 1. Any amendment or amendments to this constitution may be proposed in either house of the legislature at any regular session thereof; and if a majority of all members elected to each of the two houses voting separately shall vote in favor thereof, such proposed amendment or amendments shall be entered on their respective journals with the yeas and nays thereon.

"'The secretary of state shall cause any such amendment or amendments to be published in at least one newspaper in every county of the State, where a newspaper is published once each week, for four consecutive weeks, in English and Spanish when newspapers in both of said languages are published in such counties, the last publication to be not more than two weeks prior to the election at which time said amendment or amendments shall be submitted to the electors of the State for their approval or rejection; and the said amendment or amendments shall be voted upon at the next regular election held in said State after the adjournment of the legislature proposing such amendment or amendments, or at such special election to be held not less than six months after the adjournment of said legislature, at such time as said legislature may by law provide. If the same be ratified by a majority of the electors voting thereon such amendment or amendments shall become part of this constitution. If two or more amendments are proposed, they shall be so submitted as to enable the electors to vote on each of them separately: *Provided*, That no amendment shall apply to or affect the provisions of sections one and three of Article VII hereof, on elective franchise, and sections eight and ten of Article XII hereof, on education, unless it be proposed by vote of three-fourths of the members elected to each house and be ratified by a vote of the people of this State in an election at which at least three-fourths of the electors voting in the whole State and at least two-thirds of those voting in each county in the State shall vote for such amendment.

"'SEC. 2. Whenever, during the first twenty-five years after the adoption of this constitution, the legislature, by a three-fourths vote of the members elected to each house, or, after the expiration of said period of twenty-five years, by a two-thirds vote of the members elected to each house, shall deem it necessary to call a convention to revise or amend this constitution, they shall submit the question of calling such convention to the electors at the next general election, and if a majority of all the electors voting on such question at said election in the State shall vote in favor of calling a convention the legislature shall, at the next session, provide by law for calling the same. Such convention shall consist of at least as many delegates as there are members of the house of representatives. The constitution adopted by such convention shall have no validity until it has been submitted to and ratified by the people.

"'SEC. 3. If this constitution be in any way so amended as to allow laws to be enacted by direct vote of the electors the laws which may be so enacted shall be only such as might be enacted by the legislature under the provisions of this constitution.

"'SEC. 4. When the United States shall consent thereto, the legislature, by a majority vote of the members in each house, may submit to the people the question of amending any provision of Article XXI of this constitution on compact with the United States to the extent allowed by the Act of Congress permitting the same, and if a majority of the qualified electors who vote upon any such amendment shall vote in favor thereof the said article shall be thereby amended accordingly.

"'SEC. 5. The provisions of section one of this article shall not be changed, altered, or abrogated in any manner except through a general convention called to revise this constitution as herein provided.'"

SEC. 4. That the probate clerks of the several counties of New Mexico shall provide separate ballots for the use of the electors at said first State election for the purpose of voting upon said amendment. Said separate ballots shall be printed on paper of a blue tint, so that they may be readily distinguished from the white ballots provided for the election of county and State officers. Said separate ballots shall be delivered only to the election officers authorized by law to receive and have the custody of the ballot boxes for use at said election and shall be delivered by them only to the individual voter and only one ballot to each elector at the time he offers to vote at the said general election, and shall have the initials of two election officers of opposite political parties written by them upon the back thereof. Said separate ballot shall not be marked either for or against the said amendment at the time it is handed to the elector by the election officer, and if the elector desires to vote upon said amendment, the ballot must be marked by the voter, unless he shall request one of the election officers to mark the same for him, in which case such election officer so called upon shall mark said ballot as such voter shall request.

Any elector receiving such ballot shall return the same before leaving the polls to one of the election judges, who shall immediately deposit the same in the ballot box whether such ballot be marked or not. No ballots on said amendment except those so handed to said electors and so initialled shall be deposited in the ballot box or counted or canvassed. Said separate ballots shall have printed thereon the proposed amendment in both the English and the Spanish language. There shall be placed on said ballots two blank squares with dimensions of one-half an inch and opposite one of said squares shall be printed in both the English and the Spanish language the words "For constitutional amendment," and opposite the other blank square shall be printed in both the English and Spanish language the words "Against constitutional amendment."

Any elector desiring to vote for said amendment shall mark his ballot with a cross in the blank square opposite the words "For constitutional amendment," or cause the same to be so marked by an election officer as aforesaid, and any elector desiring to vote against said amendment shall mark his ballot with a cross in the blank square opposite the words "Against constitutional amendment," or cause the same to be so marked by an election officer as aforesaid.

SEC. 5. That said ballots shall be counted and canvassed by said election officers, and the returns of said election upon said amendment shall be made by said election officers direct to the secretary of the Territory of New Mexico at Santa Fe, who, with the governor and chief justice of said Territory, shall constitute a canvassing board; and they, or any two of them, shall meet at said city of Santa Fe on the third Monday after said election and shall canvass the same. If a majority of the legal votes cast at said election upon said amendment shall be in favor thereof, the said canvassing board shall forthwith certify said result to the governor of the Territory, together with the statement of votes cast upon the question of the ratification or rejection of said amendment; whereupon the governor of said

Territory shall by proclamation declare the said amendment a part of the constitution of the proposed State of New Mexico, and thereupon the same shall become and be a part of said constitution; but if the same shall fail of such majority, then Article XIX of the constitution of New Mexico as adopted on January twenty-first, nineteen hundred and eleven, shall remain a part of said constitution.

Except as herein otherwise provided, said election upon this amendment shall be in all respects subject to the election laws of New Mexico now in force.

SEC. 6. That the fifth clause of section two of "An Act to enable the people of New Mexico to form a constitution and State government and be admitted into the Union on an equal footing with the original States; and to enable the people of Arizona to form a constitution and be admitted into the Union on an equal footing with the original States," approved June twentieth, anno Domini nineteen hundred and ten, be, and the same is hereby, amended so as to read as follows: —

"Fifth. That said State shall never enact any law restricting or abridging the right of suffrage on account of race, color, or previous condition of servitude."

SEC. 7. That before the proclamation of the President shall issue, announcing the result of said election in Arizona, and at the same time that the State election is held, as aforesaid, the electors of Arizona shall vote upon and ratify and adopt the following proposed amendment to their State constitution as a condition precedent to the admission of said State, to wit: —

"Section one of Article VIII of the constitution of the State of Arizona, adopted by the electors of said State at an election held on the ninth day of February, anno Domini nineteen hundred and eleven, be, and the same is hereby, amended so as to read as follows: —

"'ARTICLE VIII. — REMOVAL FROM OFFICE.

"'1. RECALL OF PUBLIC OFFICERS.

"'SECTION 1. Every public officer in the State of Arizona, except members of the judiciary, holding an elective office, either by election or appointment, is subject to recall from such office by the qualified electors of the electoral district from which candidates are elected to such office. Such electoral district may include the whole State. Such number of said electors as shall equal twenty-five per centum of the number of votes cast at the last preceding general election for all of the candidates for the office held by such officer may by petition, which shall be known as a recall petition, demand his recall.'"

The ballots to be provided for said first State election shall have printed thereon this proposed amendment and there shall be placed on said ballots two blank squares with dimensions of one-half an inch and opposite one of said squares shall be printed the words "For constitutional amendment" and opposite the other blank square shall be printed the words "Against constitutional amendment."

Any elector desiring to vote for said amendment shall place a cross in the blank square opposite the words "For constitutional amendment," and those desiring to vote against such amendment shall place a cross in the blank square opposite the words "Against constitutional amendment," and said ballots shall be counted and canvassed by the election officers of said State authorized by law to count and canvass the ballots cast at the election for State officers; and the returns of said election upon said amendment shall be made by said election officers direct to the secretary of the Territory of Arizona at Phoenix, who, with the governor and chief justice of said Territory, shall constitute a canvassing board, and they, or any two of them, shall meet at said city of Phoenix on the third Monday after said election and shall canvass the same. If a majority of the legal votes cast at said election upon said amendment shall be in favor thereof, the said canvassing board shall forthwith certify said result to the governor of the Territory, together with the statement of votes cast upon the question of the ratification or rejection of said amendment; whereupon the governor of said Territory shall, by proclamation, declare the said amendment a part of the constitution of the proposed State of Arizona and thereupon the same shall become and be a part of said constitution; and if the said proposed amendment to section one of Article VIII of the constitution of Arizona is not adopted and ratified as aforesaid then, and in that case, the Territory of Arizona shall not be admitted into the Union as a State, under the provisions of this Act.

Except as herein otherwise provided said election upon this amendment shall be in all respects except as to the educational qualifications of electors subject to the election laws of Arizona now in force.

Approved, August 21, 1911.

XXV. CALIFORNIA

[The Legislature of California at the session, beginning January 2, 1911, passed an amendment providing for the recall of all elective public officers. The amendment passed the Senate on February 24, 1911, and the Assembly on March 7, 1911. This amendment together with an initiative and referendum amendment was adopted by an overwhelming majority at a special election held October 10, 1911. The initiative, referendum and recall have already been extended to municipal corporations by an act passed by the 1911 Legislature. The provisions of the state-wide recall amendment follow.]

Senate Constitutional Amendment No. 23. A resolution to propose to the people of the State of California an amendment to the constitution of the state by adding a new article thereto to be numbered Article XXIII, providing for the recall by the electors, of public officials.

The legislature of the State of California, at its regular session commencing on the second day of January, 1911, two-thirds of all the members elected to each of the two houses of said legislature voting in favor thereof, hereby proposes that a new article be added to the constitution of the State of California to be numbered Article XXIII thereof, to read as follows: —

ARTICLE XXIII

SECTION 1. Every elective public officer of the State of California may be removed from office at any time by the electors entitled to vote for a successor of such incumbent, through the procedure and in the manner herein provided for, which procedure shall be known as the recall, and is in addition to any other method of removal provided by law.

The procedure hereunder to effect the removal of an incumbent of an elective public office shall be as follows: A petition signed by electors entitled to vote for a successor of the incumbent sought to be removed, equal in number to at least twelve per cent of the entire vote cast at the last preceding election for all candidates for the office which the incumbent sought to be removed occupies; *provided*, that if the officer sought to be removed is a state officer who is elected in any political subdivision of the state, said petition shall be signed by electors entitled to vote for a successor to the incumbent sought to be removed, equal in number to at least twenty per cent of the entire vote cast at the last preceding election for all candidates for the office which the incumbent sought to be removed occupies, demanding an election of a successor to the officer named in said petition, shall be addressed to the secretary of state and filed with the clerk, or registrar of voters, of the county or city and county in which the petition was circulated; *provided*, that if the officer sought to be removed was elected in the state at large such petition shall be circulated in not less than five counties of the state, and shall be signed in each of such counties by electors equal in number to not less than one per cent of the entire vote cast, in each of said counties, at said election, as above estimated. Such petition shall contain a general statement of the ground on which the removal is sought, which statement is intended solely for the information of the electors, and the sufficiency of which shall not be open to review.

When such petition is certified as is herein provided to the secretary of state, he shall forthwith submit the said petition, together with a certificate of its sufficiency, to the governor, who shall thereupon order and fix a date for holding the election, not less than sixty days nor more than eighty days from the date of such certificate of the secretary of state.

The governor shall make or cause to be made publication of notice for the holding of such election, and officers charged by law with duties concerning elections shall make all arrangements for such election and the same shall be conducted, returned, and the result thereof declared, in all respects as are other state elections. On the official ballot at such election shall be printed, in not more than two hundred words, the reasons set forth in the petition for demanding his recall. And in not more than three hundred words there shall also be printed, if desired by him, the officer's justification of his course in office. Proceedings for the recall of any officer shall be deemed to be pending from the date of the filing with any county, or city and county clerk, or registrar of voters, of any recall petition against such officer; and if such officer shall resign at any time subsequent to the filing thereof, the recall election shall be held notwithstanding such resignation, and the vacancy caused by such resignation, or from any other cause, shall be filled as provided by law, but the person appointed to fill such vacancy shall hold his office only until the person elected at the said recall election shall qualify.

Any person may be nominated for the office which is to be filled at any recall election by a petition signed by electors, qualified to vote at such recall election, equal in number to at least one per cent of the total number of votes cast at the last preceding election for all candidates for the office which the incumbent sought to be removed occupies. Each such nominating petition shall be filed with the secretary of state not less than twenty-five days before such recall election.

There shall be printed on the recall ballot, as to every officer whose recall is to be voted on thereat, the following question: "Shall (name of person against whom the recall petition is filed) be recalled from the office of (title of the office)?" following which question shall be the words "yes" and "no" on separate lines, with a blank space at the right of each, in which the voter shall indicate, by stamping a cross (X), his vote for or against such recall. On such ballots, under each such question, there shall also be printed the names of those persons who have been nominated as candidates to succeed the person recalled, in case he shall be removed from office by said recall election; but no vote cast shall be counted for any candidate for said office unless the voter also voted on said question of the recall of the person sought to be recalled from said office. The name of the person against whom the petition is filed shall not appear on the ballot as a candidate for the office. If a majority of those voting on said question of the recall of any incumbent from office shall vote "No," said incumbent shall continue in said office. If a majority shall vote "Yes," said incumbent shall thereupon be deemed removed from such office, upon the qualification of his successor. The canvassers shall canvass all votes for candidates for said office and declare the result in like manner as in a regular election. If the vote at any such recall election shall recall the officer, then the candidate who has received the highest number of votes for the office shall be thereby declared elected, for the remainder of the term. In case the person who received the highest number of votes shall fail to qualify within ten days after receiving the certificate of election, the office shall be deemed vacant and shall be filled according to law.

Any recall petition may be presented in sections, but each section shall contain a full and accurate copy of the title and text of the petition. Each signer shall add to his signature his place of residence, giving the street and number, if such exist.

His election precinct shall also appear on the paper after his name. The number of signatures appended to each section shall be at the pleasure of the person soliciting signatures to the same. Any qualified elector of the state shall be competent to solicit such signatures within the county, or city and county, of which he is an elector. Each section of the petition shall bear the name of the county, or city and county in which it is circulated, and only qualified electors of such county or city and county shall be competent to sign such section. Each section shall have attached thereto the affidavit of the person soliciting signatures to the same stating his qualifications and that all the signatures to the attached section were made in his presence and that to the best of his knowledge and belief each signature to the section is the genuine signature of the person whose name it purports to be; and no other affidavit thereto shall be required. The affidavit of any person soliciting signatures hereunder shall be verified free of charge by any officer authorized to administer an oath. Such petition so verified shall be prima facie evidence that the signatures thereto appended are genuine and that the persons signing the same are qualified electors. Unless and until it is otherwise proven upon official investigation, it shall be presumed that the petition presented contains the signatures of the requisite number of electors. Each section of the petition shall be filed with the clerk, or registrar of voters, of the county or city and county in which it was circulated; but all such sections circulated in any county or city and county shall be filed at the same time. Within twenty days after the date of filing such petition, the clerk, or registrar of voters, shall finally determine from the records of registration what number of qualified electors have signed the same; and, if necessary, the board of supervisors shall allow such clerk or registrar additional assistants for the purpose of examining such petition and provide for their compensation. The said clerk or registrar, upon the completion of such examination, shall forthwith attach to such petition his certificate, properly dated, showing the result of such examination, and submit

The State-wide Recall

said petition, except as to the signatures appended thereto, to the secretary of state and file a copy of said certificate in his office. Within forty days from the transmission of the said petition and certificate by the clerk or registrar of voters to the secretary of state, a supplemental petition, identical with the original as to the body of the petition but containing supplemental names, may be filed with the clerk or registrar of voters, as aforesaid. The clerk or registrar of voters shall within ten days after the filing of such supplemental petition make like examination thereof as of the original petition, and upon the conclusion of such examination shall forthwith attach to such petition his certificate, properly dated, showing the result of such examination, and shall forthwith transmit such supplemental petition, except as to the signatures thereon, together with his said certificate, to the secretary of state.

When the secretary of state shall have received from one or more county clerks, or registrars of voters, a petition certified as herein provided to have been signed by the requisite number of qualified electors, he shall forthwith transmit to the county clerk or registrar of voters of every county or city and county in the state a certificate showing such fact; and such clerk or registrar of voters shall thereupon file said certificate for record in his office.

A petition shall be deemed to be filed with the secretary of state upon the date of the receipt by him of a certificate or certificates showing the said petition to be signed by the requisite number of electors of the state.

No recall petition shall be circulated or filed against any officer until he has actually held his office for at least six months; save and except it may be filed against any member of the state legislature at any time after five days from the convening and organizing of the legislature after his election.

If at any recall election the incumbent whose removal is sought is not recalled, he shall be repaid from the state treasury any amount legally expended by him as expenses of such election, and the legislature shall provide appropriation for such purpose, and no proceedings for another recall election of said incumbent shall be initiated within six months after such election.

If the governor is sought to be removed under the provisions of this article, the duties herein imposed upon him shall be performed by the lieutenant governor; and if the secretary of state is sought to be removed, the duties herein imposed upon him shall be performed by the state controller; and the duties herein imposed upon the clerk or registrar of voters, shall be performed by such registrar of voters in all cases where the office of registrar of voters exists.

The recall shall also be exercised by the electors of each county, city and county, city and town of the state, with reference to the elective officers thereof, under such procedure as shall be provided by law.

Until otherwise provided by law, the legislative body of any such county, city and county, city or town may provide for the manner of exercising such recall powers in such counties, cities and counties, cities and towns, but shall not require any such recall petition to be signed by electors more in number than twenty-five per cent of the entire vote cast at the last preceding election for all candidates for the office which the incumbent sought to be removed occupies. Nothing herein contained shall be construed as affecting or limiting the present or future powers of cities or counties or cities and counties having charters adopted under the authority given by the constitution.

In the submission to the electors of any petition proposed under this article all officers shall be guided by the general laws of the state, except as otherwise herein provided.

This article is self-executing, but legislation may be enacted to facilitate its operation, but in no way limiting or restricting the provisions of this article or the powers herein reserved.

XXVI. IDAHO (PROPOSED) [1]

[The following recall provision was passed on March 1, 1911, and will be submitted to the voters at the general election in November, 1912.]

Be It Resolved by the Legislature of the State of Idaho: —

Section 1. That Article 6 of the Constitution of the State of Idaho be amended by adding thereto Section 6, which shall read as follows: —

Section 6. Every public officer in the State of Idaho, excepting the Judicial officers, is subject to recall by the legal voters of the State or of the Electoral District from which he is elected. The Legislature shall pass the necessary laws to carry this provision into effect.

Section 2. The question to be submitted to the electors of the State at the next general election shall be in form as follows: "Shall Article 6 of the Constitution of the State of Idaho be amended by adding thereto Section 6 so as to reserve to the people of the State, or any Electoral District therein, the right to recall any public officer except Judicial officers in the State or said Electoral District?"

Section 3. The Secretary of State is hereby authorized to make publication of this Constitutional Amendment in each county for at least six (6) consecutive weeks prior to the next general election in at least one (1) newspaper of general circulation published in each county.

Passed House, February 24, 1911.
Passed Senate, March 1, 1911.

[1] Official copy.

XXVII. Nevada (Proposed)[1]

[The following recall provision has been duly passed by the Nevada legislature and will be submitted to the voters in November, 1912. See above, p. 121.]

No. 4 — *Senate Substitute for Assembly Joint and Concurrent Resolution No. 8, proposing that section nine be added to article two of the constitution of the State of Nevada.*

[Approved March 22, 1909]
[Approved February 2, 1911]

Resolved by the Senate, the Assembly concurring, That section nine be added to article two of the constitution of the State of Nevada, to read as follows: —

Section 9. Every public officer in the State of Nevada is subject, as herein provided, to recall from office by the qualified electors of the state, or of the county, district, or municipality, from which he was elected. For this purpose not less than twenty-five per cent (25 %) of the qualified electors who vote in the state or in the county, district, or municipality electing said officer, at the preceding election, for justice of the supreme court, shall file their petition, in the manner herein provided, demanding his recall by the people; they shall set forth in said petition, in not exceeding two hundred (200) words, the reasons why said recall is demanded. If he shall offer his resignation, it shall be accepted and take effect on the day it is offered, and the vacancy thereby caused shall be filled in the manner provided by law. If he shall not resign within five (5) days after the petition is filed, a special election shall be ordered to be held within twenty days (20) after the issuance of the call therefor, in the state, or county, district, or municipality electing said officer, to determine whether the people will recall said officer. On the ballot at said election shall be printed verbatim as set forth in the recall petition, the reasons for demanding the recall of said officer, and in

[1] Official copy.

not more than two hundred (200) words, the officer's justification of his course in office. He shall continue to perform the duties of his office until the result of said election shall be finally declared. Other candidates for the office may be nominated to be voted for at said special election. The candidate who shall receive the highest number of votes at said special election shall be deemed elected for the remainder of the term, whether it be the person against whom the recall petition was filed, or another. The recall petition shall be filed with the officer with whom the petition for nomination to such office shall be filed, and the same officer shall order the special election when it is required. No such petition shall be circulated or filed against any officer until he has actually held his office six (6) months, save and except that it may be filed against a senator or assemblyman in the legislature at any time after ten (10) days from the beginning of the first session after his election. After one such petition and special election, no further recall petition shall be filed against the same officer during the term for which he was elected, unless such further petitioners shall pay into the public treasury from which the expenses of said special election have been paid, the whole amount paid out of said public treasury as expenses for the preceding special election. Such additional legislation as may aid the operation of this section shall be provided by law.[1]

[1] For the North Dakota recall provision (proposed), see above, pp. 210, 221.

III. INITIATIVE AND REFERENDUM IN MUNICIPAL GOVERNMENT

XXVIII. Ohio [1]

[The initiative and referendum are extended to cities in most of the states having the state-wide system. In a few states, they are also extended to counties. However, in a number of states not having the state-wide initiative and referendum or the commission form of city government this plan has been added to the regular city government. A satisfactory example is the law in force in Ohio. Governor Harmon succeeded in forcing the legislature of 1911 to adopt the following bill approved June 14, 1911.]

A BILL

To provide for the initiative and referendum in municipal corporations

Be it enacted by the General Assembly of the State of Ohio: —

SECTION 1. Ordinances providing for and declaratory of any and all powers of government which the general assembly has delegated or may hereafter delegate to any municipal corporation, in accordance with the provisions of the constitution, and also ordinances repealing other ordinances, may be proposed to the council of any municipal corporation for passage by initiative petition signed as hereafter provided by *thirty* per cent of the qualified voters of such municipality, which petition is to be filed with the clerk of such municipal corporation within 120 days after the date of the first signature thereon. Any proposed ordinances so petitioned for, shall be submitted by said clerk to the council for its action thereon at its next meeting. If within sixty days

[1] *Laws of Ohio* (1911), pp. 521 ff.

after its first submission to the council, said ordinance is not passed by the council without change or amendment, it shall be the duty of the clerk within ten days after the expiration of said sixty days to certify said proposed ordinance to the officers having control of the elections in such municipal corporation, who shall cause the question of the passage of such ordinance to be submitted to the vote of the electors of such municipal corporation at the next regular election; provided, however, that *same shall not become operative until it shall have been submitted and receive the majority of the vote cast at such election.*

The highest total vote cast for the office of mayor at the regular municipal election immediately preceding the filing of such petition shall be the basis upon which the number of signatures of qualified electors of such municipal corporation required upon the aforesaid petitions, shall be determined. If a majority of those voting on said ordinance are in favor of same, it shall become a valid ordinance of said municipal corporation from the date of the determination of the vote, and shall not be subject to the veto of the mayor; and said ordinance shall be recorded and published in the same manner as other ordinances of said municipality.

SECTION 2. Any ordinance, resolution or other measure of a municipal corporation, granting a franchise creating a right, involving the expenditure of money or exercising any other power delegated to such municipal corporation by the general assembly, shall be submitted to the qualified electors for their approval or rejection in the manner herein provided, if within thirty days after the passage or adoption of such ordinance, resolution or measure by the council, there be filed with the clerk of such municipal corporation, a petition or petitions *signed by fifteen per cent of the qualified electors of such municipal corporation as determined by the highest number of votes cast for the office of mayor at such municipal election immediately preceding*, ordering the submission of such ordinance, resolution or measure to the vote of the electors of such municipal corporation. Within ten days after the filing of such petition or petitions with the clerk as aforesaid, such clerk shall certify such ordinance, resolution or other measure to the officer or officers having control of elections in such municipal corporation who shall submit such ordinance, resolution or other measure to the vote of the electors of such municipal corporation at the next general election.

No resolution, ordinance, or measure of any municipal corporation, creating a right, involving the expenditure of money, granting a franchise, conferring, extending or renewing a right to use of the streets, or regulating the use of the streets for water, gas, electricity, telephone, telegraph, power or street railways, or other public or quasi-public utility shall become effective in less than sixty days after its passage, during which time, if petitions signed by fifteen per cent of the qualified electors of such municipal corporation as determined by the highest number of votes cast for the office of mayor of such municipal corporation at the municipal election immediately preceding, are filed with the clerk of such municipal corporation petitioning for the submission of any such ordinance or resolution to a vote of the people, such clerk shall certify the fact of the filing of such petition to the officers having control of the elections in such municipal corporation, who shall cause said resolution or ordinance to be voted on at the next regular election; Provided, however, that at least thirty days' notice of the election upon such ordinance, resolution or measure must be given, *when* such election is to be held.

SECTION 3. All other acts of city council not included among those specified in section 2 of this act, shall also remain inoperative for sixty days after passage and may be submitted to popular vote in the manner herein provided, except that any act, not included within those specified in section 2 of this act, as remaining inoperative for sixty days, and which is declared to be an emergency measure, and receiving a three-fourths majority in council of such municipal corporation may go into effect immediately and remain in effect until repealed by city council or by direct vote of the people as herein provided.

SECTION 4. The form of petition for the referendum to the people on any act of a city council shall be substantially as follows: —

NOTICE

It is a *misdemeanor* for any one to sign any initiative or referendum petition with any name other than his own or knowingly to sign his name more than once for the same measure, or to sign such petition when he is not a qualified elector.

To ...., clerk of .... :
We, the undersigned, electors of .... of ...., respectfully order that council ordinance No......., entitled .... shall be referred to the electors for their approval or rejection, at the regular election to be held on the ...... day of ...., A.D. 19.., and each for himself says: I know the contents of and have personally signed this petition and my residence is correctly stated opposite my name.
Name ...., Residence ...., Date of signature.

Here place as many lines as convenient for the placing of signatures, places of residence and date of signature, under the respective headings indicated.

The form of petition for any ordinance proposed by the initiative shall be substantially the same as for referendum petitions, except that in place of number and title of the ordinance passed by council, shall be inserted, the text of the proposed ordinance.

Petitions may be filed in numbered sections accompanied by the affidavit of the person or persons circulating same, which affidavit shall be in substantially the following form: —
State of Ohio, County of .... ss.: —

I, ... being first duly sworn, say: The signatures upon the petitions herewith attached were made in my presence; I believe that each signer is a qualified elector and has stated his name and address correctly.

Signature and address of affiant ....

Subscribed and sworn to before me by .... this
.... day of ...., A.D. ......

Signature and title of officer before whom oath is made together with such officer's seal, if the use of same be otherwise required by law.

The forms herein given are not mandatory, and if substantially followed in any petition it shall be sufficient, regardless of clerical and technical errors.

SECTION 5. Ordinances, resolutions or other measures referred by petition shall be designated, "Referendum ordered by petition of the *electors*," ordinances or other measures proposed by initiative petition shall be designated by the heading, "Proposed by initiative petition."

The manner of voting upon ordinances, resolutions or other measures submitted to the *electors*, and upon ordinances, resolutions or other measures proposed by initiative and submitted to the *electors*, shall be the same as is now or may hereafter be required and provided by law; no ordinance or other measure shall be adopted unless it shall receive an affirmative majority of the total number of the lawful and effective votes cast at such election and entitled to be counted under the provisions of this act; separate ballots shall be provided and so printed as to permit a vote for or against each ordinance or measure submitted in accordance with the order of the petition or petitions demanding such submission and for or against each ordinance or measure proposed by initiative petition; and all ordinances and measures passed by council or ordinances and measures proposed by initiative petition, so submitted, shall be indicated on the ballots by the title of such ordinance or measure passed by the council, or the title of the proposed ordinance or measure given in the petitions asking for the popular vote upon the same.

Every person who is a qualified elector of the state of Ohio, may lawfully sign any of the petitions mentioned in this act, for an initiative or referendum vote, in the municipality where he is entitled to vote. Any person signing any name other than his own to any petition, or knowingly signing his name more than once upon a petition or petitions for a referendum election upon the same ordinance or measure or upon a petition or petitions proposing the same ordinance or measure, at one election, or who is not at the time of signing his name a qualified elector of the city, or any officer or any person wilfully violating any provision of this statute, shall be punished by a fine not exceeding *one hundred dollars or* by imprisonment in the *county jail or workhouse* not exceeding *six months*, or both.

SECTION 6. If any section or portion of this act shall for any reason be declared to be unconstitutional, such invalidity shall not affect any other section or portion hereof.

All laws and parts of laws in conflict herewith are hereby repealed.

IV. INITIATIVE, REFERENDUM, AND RECALL IN COMMISSION GOVERNMENT

XXIX. Iowa

[The provisions of the Iowa law passed in 1907 (under which the Des Moines plan is organized), relative to the initiative, referendum, and recall, are as follows.][1]

SEC. 18. The holder of any elective office may be removed at any time by the electors qualified to vote for a successor of such incumbent. The procedure to effect the removal of an incumbent of an elective office shall be as follows: A petition signed by electors entitled to vote for a successor to the incumbent sought to be removed, equal in number to at least 25 per cent of the entire vote for all candidates for the office of mayor at the last preceding general municipal election, demanding an election of a successor of the person sought to be removed, shall be filed with the city clerk, which petition shall contain a general statement of the grounds for which the removal is sought. The signatures to the petition need not all be appended to one paper, but each signer shall add to his signature his place of residence, giving the street and number. One of the signers of each such paper shall make oath before an officer competent to administer oaths that the statements therein made are true as he believes, and that each signature to the paper appended is the genuine signature of the person whose name it purports to be. Within 10 days from the date of filing such petition the city clerk shall examine and from the voters' register ascertain whether or not said petition is signed by the requisite number of qualified electors, and, if necessary, the council shall allow him extra help for that pur-

---

[1] Beard, *Digest of Short Ballot Charters*, folio 51,206.

In Commission Government 281

pose; and he shall attach to said petition his certificate, showing the result of said examination. If by the clerk's certificate the petition is shown to be insufficient, it may be amended within 10 days from the date of said certificate. The clerk shall, within 10 days after such amendment make like examination of the amended petition, and if his certificate shall show the same to be insufficient, it shall be returned to the person filing the same; without prejudice, however, to the filing of a new petition to the same effect. If the petition shall be deemed to be sufficient, the clerk shall submit the same to the council without delay. If the petition shall be found to be sufficient, the council shall order and fix a date for holding the said election not less than 30 days or more than 40 days from the date of the clerk's certificate to the council that a sufficient petition is filed.

The council shall make, or cause to be made, publication of notice and all arrangements for holding such election, and the same shall be conducted, returned, and the result thereof declared, in all respects as are other city elections. The successor of any officer so removed shall hold office during the unexpired term of his predecessor. Any person sought to be removed may be a candidate to succeed himself, and unless he requests otherwise in writing, the clerk shall place his name on the official ballot without nomination. In any such removal election, the candidate receiving the highest number of votes shall be declared elected. At such election if some other person than the incumbent receives the highest number of votes the incumbent shall thereupon be deemed removed from the office upon qualification of his successor. In case the party who receives the highest number of votes should fail to qualify, within 10 days after receiving notification of election, the office shall be deemed vacant. If the incumbent receives the highest number of votes he shall continue in office. The same method of removal shall be cumulative and additional to the methods heretofore provided by law.

SEC. 19. Any proposed ordinance may be submitted to the council by petition signed by electors of the city equal in number to the percentage hereinafter required. The signatures, verification, authentication, inspection, certification, amendment, and submission of such petition shall be the same as provided for petitions under section 18 hereof.

If the petition accompanying the proposed ordinance be signed by electors equal in number to 25 per cent of the votes cast for all candidates for mayor at the last preceding general election, and contains a request that the said ordinance be submitted to a vote of the people if not passed by the council, such council shall either —

(*a*) Pass said ordinance without alteration within 20 days after attachment of the clerk's certificate to the accompanying petition, or

(*b*) Forthwith after the clerk shall attach to the petition accompanying such ordinance his certificate of sufficiency, the council shall call a special election, unless a general municipal election is fixed within 90 days thereafter, and at such special or general municipal election, if one is so fixed, such ordinance shall be submitted without alteration to the vote of the electors of said city.

But if the petition is signed by not less than 10 nor more than 25 per cent of the electors, as above defined, then the council shall, within 20 days, pass said ordinance without change, or submit the same at the next general city election occurring not more than 30 days after the clerk's certificate of sufficiency is attached to said petition.

The ballots used when voting upon said ordinance shall contain these words: "For the ordinance" (stating the nature of the proposed ordinance) and "Against the ordinance" (stating the nature of the proposed ordinance). If a majority of the qualified electors voting on the proposed ordinance shall vote in favor thereof, such ordinance shall thereupon become a valid and binding ordinance of the city; and any ordinance proposed by petition, or which shall be adopted by a vote of the people, cannot be repealed or amended except by a vote of the people.

In Commission Government

Any number of proposed ordinances may be voted upon at the same election, in accordance with the provisions of this section; but there shall not be more than one special election in any period of six months for such purpose.

The council may submit a proposition for the repeal of any such ordinance or for amendments thereto, to be voted upon at any succeeding general city election; and should such proposition so submitted receive a majority of the votes cast thereon at such election, such ordinance shall thereby be repealed or amended accordingly. Whenever any ordinance or proposition is required by this act to be submitted to the voters of the city at any election, the city clerk shall cause such ordinance or proposition to be published once in each of the daily newspapers published in said city, such publication to be not more than 20 nor less than 5 days before the submission of such proposition or ordinance to be voted on.

SEC. 20. No ordinance passed by the council, except when otherwise required by the general laws of the State or by the provisions of this act, except an ordinance for the immediate preservation of the public peace, health, or safety, which contains a statement of its urgency and is passed by a two-thirds vote of the council, shall go into effect before 10 days from the time of its final passage; and if during said 10 days a petition signed by electors of the city equal in number to at least 25 per cent of the entire vote cast for all candidates for mayor at the last preceding general municipal election at which a mayor was elected, protesting against the passage of such ordinance, be presented to the council, the same shall thereupon be suspended from going into operation, and it shall be the duty of the council to reconsider such ordinance; and if the same is not entirely repealed, the council shall submit the ordinance, as is provided by subsection (b) of section 19 of this act, to the vote of the electors of the city, either at the general election or at a special municipal election to be called for that purpose; and such ordinance shall not go into effect or become operative unless a majority of the qualified electors voting on the same shall vote in favor thereof. Said petition shall be in all respects in accordance with the provisions of said section 19, except as to the percentage of signers, and be examined and certified to by the clerk in all respects as is therein provided.

SEC. 21. Any city which shall have operated for more than six years under the provisions of this act may abandon such organization hereunder and accept the provisions of the general law of the State then applicable to cities of its population, or if now organized under special charter, may resume said special charter by proceeding as follows: —

Upon the petition of not less than 25 per cent of the electors of such city a special election shall be called, at which the following proposition only shall be submitted: "Shall the city of (name the city) abandon its organization under chapter — of the acts of the thirty-second general assembly and become a city under the general law governing cities of like population, or if now organized under special charter, shall resume said special charter?"

If a majority of the votes cast at such special election be in favor of such proposition, the officers elected at the next succeeding biennial election shall be those then prescribed by the general law of the State for cities of like population, and upon the qualification of such officers such city shall become a city under such general law of the State; but such change shall not in any manner or degree affect the property, right, or liabilities of any nature of such city, but shall merely extend to such change in its form of government.

The sufficiency of such petition shall be determined, the election ordered and conducted, and the results declared, generally as provided by section 18 of this act, in so far as the provisions thereof are applicable.

SEC. 22. Petitions provided for in this act shall be signed by none but legal voters of the city. Each petition shall contain, in addition to the names of the petitioners, the street and house number in which the petitioner resides, his age, and length of residence in the city. It shall also be accompanied by the affidavit of one or more legal voters of the city stating that the signers thereof were, at the time of signing, legal voters of said city, and the number of signers at the time the affidavit was made.

XXX. NEW JERSEY

[The 1911 Legislature of New Jersey, under the leadership of Governor Woodrow Wilson, adopted the commission form of government for cities, April 25, 1911. Each city can decide for itself whether or not it desires to avail itself of the plan. Elections are to be held if twenty per centum of the voters at the last election so petition. The plan must be favored by a majority of those voting at the election, and this majority must be equal to "at least thirty per centum of the votes cast for members of the General Assembly at the last general election." The initiative, referendum, and recall features of the New Jersey plan follow.]

RECALL

15. The holder of any elective office may be removed at any time by the electors qualified to vote for a successor of such incumbent. The procedure to effect the removal of an incumbent of an elective office shall be as follows: A petition signed by the electors entitled to vote for a successor to the incumbent sought to be removed, equal in number to at least twenty-five per cent of the entire vote at the last preceding general election demanding an election of a successor of the person sought to be removed, shall be filed with the city clerk, which petition shall contain a general statement of the grounds for which the removal is sought.

The signatures to the petition need not all be appended to one paper, but each signer shall add to his signature his place of residence, giving the street and number. One of the signers of each such paper shall make an oath before an officer competent to administer oaths that the statement therein made is true as he believes, and that each signature to the paper appended is the genuine signature of the person whose name it purports to be. Within ten days from the date of filing such petition the city clerk shall examine, ascertain whether or not said petition is signed by the requisite number of qualified electors, and he shall attach to said petition his certificate, showing the result of said examination. If, by the clerk's certificate, the petition is shown to be **insufficient**, it may be amended within ten days from the date of said certificate.

The clerk shall, within ten days after such amendment, make like examination of the amended petition, and if this certificate shall show the same to be insufficient, it shall be returned to the person filing the same, without prejudice to the filing of a new petition to the same effect. If the petition shall be deemed to be sufficient, the clerk shall submit the same to the board of commissioners without delay.

If the petition shall be found to be **sufficient** the board of commissioners shall, if the officer sought to be removed shall not resign within five days after the date on the clerk's certificate, order and fix a date for holding the said election, not less than thirty days or more than forty days from the date on the clerk's certificate to the board of commissioners that a sufficient petition is filed.

The board of commissioners shall make, or cause to be made, publication of notice and all arrangements for holding such election, and the same shall be conducted, returned and the result thereof declared in all respects as are other city elections. The successor of any officer so removed shall hold office during the unexpired term of his predecessor. Any person sought to be removed may be a candidate to succeed himself, and unless he requests otherwise in writing, the clerk shall place his name on the official ballot without nomination. In any such removal election, the candidate receiving the highest number of votes shall be declared elected. At such election, if some other person than the incumbent receives the highest number of votes the incumbent shall thereupon be deemed removed from the office upon qualification of his successor. In case the person who receives the highest number of votes should fail to qualify within ten days after receiving notification of election, the office shall be deemed vacant. If the incumbent receives the highest number of votes, he shall continue in office. The same method of removal shall be cumulative and additional to the methods heretofore provided by law. No person who has been recalled from an elective office, or who has resigned from such office while recall proceedings were pending against him, shall be appointed to any office within one year after such recall or resignation.

No recall petition shall be filed against any officer until he has actually held his office for at least twelve months, and but one recall petition shall be filed against the same officer during his term of office.

INITIATIVE

16. Any proposed ordinance may be submitted to the board of commissioners by petition signed by electors of the city equal in number to the percentage hereinafter required. The signatures, verification, authentication, inspection, certification, amendment and submission of such petition shall be the same as provided for petitions under the last section.

If the petition accompanying the proposed ordinance be signed by electors equal in number to fifteen per centum of the votes cast at the last preceding general election, and contains a request that the said ordinance be submitted to a vote of the people if not passed by the board of commissioners, such board of commissioners shall either —

(*a*) Pass said ordinance without alteration within twenty days after attachment of the clerk's certificate to the accompanying petition, or,

(*b*) Forthwith, after the clerk shall attach to the petition accompanying such ordinance his certificate of sufficiency, the board of commissioners shall call a special election, unless a general municipal election is fixed within ninety days thereafter, and at such special or general municipal election, if one is so fixed, such ordinance shall be submitted without alteration to the vote of the electors of the city.

But if the petition is signed by not less than ten nor more than fifteen per centum of the electors, as above defined, then the board of commissioners shall, within twenty days, pass said ordinance without change, or submit the same at the next general city election occurring not more than thirty days after the clerk's certificate of sufficiency is attached to said petition.

The ballots used when voting upon said ordinance shall contain these words: "For the ordinance" (stating the nature of the proposed ordinance) and "Against the ordinance" (stating the nature of the proposed ordinance). If a majority of the qualified electors voting on the proposed ordinance shall vote in favor thereof, such ordinance shall thereupon become a valid and binding ordinance of the city; and any ordinance proposed by petition, or which shall be adopted by a vote of the people, cannot be repealed or amended except by a vote of the people.

Any number of proposed ordinances may be voted upon at the same election in accordance with the provisions of this section; but there shall not be more than one special election in any period of six months for such purpose.

The board of commissioners may submit a proposition for the repeal of any such ordinance or for amendment thereto, to be voted upon at any succeeding general city election, and should such proposition so submitted receive a majority of the votes cast thereon at such election, such ordinance shall thereby be repealed or amended accordingly. Whenever any ordinance or proposition is required by this act to be submitted to the voters of the city at any election, the city clerk shall cause such ordinance or proposition to be published once in at least one of the newspapers published in said city; such publication to be not more than twenty nor less than five days before the submission of such proposition or ordinance to be voted on.

REFERENDUM

17. No ordinance passed by the board of commissioners, except when otherwise required by the general laws of the State or by the provisions of this act, except an ordinance for the immediate preservation of the public peace, health or safety, which contains a statement of its urgency and is passed by a two-thirds vote of the board of commissioners, shall go into effect before ten days from the time of its final passage; and if during said ten days a petition signed by electors of the city equal in number to at least fifteen per centum of the entire vote cast at the last preceding general municipal election, protesting against the passage of such ordinance, be presented to the board of commissioners, the same shall thereupon be suspended from going into operation, and it shall be the duty of the board of commissioners to reconsider such ordinance; and if the same is not entirely repealed, the board of commissioners shall submit the ordinance, as is provided by sub-section *b* of section sixteen of this act, to the vote of the electors of the city, either at the general election or at a special municipal election to be called for that purpose; and such ordinance shall not go into effect or become operative unless a majority of the qualified electors voting on the same shall vote in favor thereof. Said petition shall be in all respects in accordance with the provisions of said section sixteen, except as to the percentage of signers, and be examined and certified to by the clerk in all respects as therein provided. Any ordinance or measure that the board of commissioners or the qualified electors of the city shall have authority to enact, the board of commissioners may of its own motion submit to the electors for adoption or rejection at a general or special municipal election, in the same manner and with the same force and effect as is provided in this act for ordinances or measures submitted on petition. At any special election called under the provisions of this act, there shall be no bar to the submission of other questions to a vote of the electors in addition to the ordinances or measures herein provided

for, if said other questions are such as may legally be submitted to such election. If the provisions of two or more measures approved or adopted at the same election conflict, then the measure receiving the highest affirmative vote shall control.

V. JUDICIAL DECISIONS

XXXI. LUTHER v. BORDEN

(7 Howard, 1, 1848)

[The meaning of Art. IV, Sec. 4 of the federal Constitution relative to republican government came before the Court in the case of Luther v. Borden in 1848; and the Court held that it is for Congress to decide what government is established in a state and whether that government is republican.]

TANEY, C. J., delivered the opinion of the court.

This case has arisen out of the unfortunate political differences which agitated the people of Rhode Island in 1841 and 1842.

It is an action of trespass brought by Martin Luther, the plaintiff in error, against Luther M. Borden and others, the defendants, in the Circuit Court of the United States for the District of Rhode Island, for breaking and entering the plaintiff's house. The defendants justify upon the ground that large numbers of men were assembled in different parts of the State for the purpose of overthrowing the government by military force, and were actually levying war upon the State; that, in order to defend itself from this insurrection, the State was declared by competent authority to be under martial law; that the plaintiff was engaged in the insurrection; and that the defendants, being in the military service of the State, by command of their superior officer, broke and entered the house and searched the rooms for the plaintiff, who was supposed to be there concealed, in order to arrest him, doing as little damage as possible. The plaintiff replied, that the trespass was committed by the defendants of their own proper wrong, and without any such cause; and upon the issue joined on this replication, the parties proceeded to trial.

The evidence, offered by the plaintiff and the defendants, is stated at large in the record; and the questions decided by the Circuit Court, and brought up by the writ of error, are not such as commonly arise in an action of trespass. The existence and authority of the government, under which the defendants acted, was called in question; and the plaintiff insists, that, before the acts complained of were committed, that government had been displaced and annulled by the people of Rhode Island, and that the plaintiff was engaged in supporting the lawful authority of the State, and the defendants themselves were in arms against it.

This is a new question in this court, and certainly a very grave one; and at the time when the trespass is alleged to have been committed, it had produced a general and painful excitement in the State, and threatened to end in bloodshed and civil war.

The evidence shows that the defendants, in breaking into the plaintiff's house and endeavoring to arrest him, as stated in the pleadings, acted under the authority of the government which was established in Rhode Island at the time of the Declaration of Independence, and which is usually called the charter government. For when the separation from England took place, Rhode Island did not, like the other States, adopt a new constitution, but continued the form of government established by the charter of Charles II in 1663; making only such alterations, by acts of the legislature, as were necessary to adapt it to their condition and rights as an independent State. It was under this form of government that Rhode Island united with the other States in the Declaration of Independence, and afterwards ratified the Constitution of the United States and became a member of this Union; and it continued to be the established and unquestioned government of the State until the difficulties took place which have given rise to this action.

In this form of government, no mode of proceeding was pointed out by which amendments might be made. It authorized the legislature to prescribe the qualification of voters, and in the exercise of this power the right of suffrage was confined to freeholders, until the adoption of the constitution of 1843.

For some years previous to the disturbances of which we are now speaking, many of the citizens became dissatisfied with the charter government, and particularly with the restriction upon the right of suffrage. Memorials were addressed to the legislature upon this subject, urging the justice and necessity of a more liberal and extended rule. But they failed to produce the desired effect. And thereupon meetings were held and associations formed by those who were in favor of a more extended right of suffrage, which finally resulted in the election of a convention to form a new constitution to be submitted to the people for their adoption or rejection. This convention was not authorized by any law of the existing government. It was elected at voluntary meetings, and by those citizens only who favored this plan of reform; those who were opposed to it, or opposed to the manner in which it was proposed to be accomplished, taking no part in the proceedings. The persons chosen as above mentioned, came together and framed a constitution, by which the right of suffrage was extended to every male citizen of twenty-one years of age, who had resided in the State for one year, and in the town in which he offered to vote, for six months, next preceding the election. The convention also prescribed the manner in which this constitution should be submitted to the decision of the people; permitting every one to vote on that question who was an American citizen, twenty-one years old, and who had a permanent residence or home in the State, and directing the votes to be returned to the convention.

Upon the return of the votes, the convention declared that the constitution was adopted and ratified by a majority of the people of the State, and was the paramount law and constitution of Rhode Island. And it communicated this decision to the governor under the charter government, for the purpose of being laid before the legislature; and directed elections to be held for a governor, members of the legislature, and other officers under the new constitution. These elections accordingly took place, and the governor, lieutenant-governor, secretary of state, and senators and representatives thus appointed, assembled at the city of Providence on May 3, 1842, and immediately proceeded to organize the new government, by appointing the officers and passing the laws necessary for that purpose.

The charter government did not, however, admit the validity of these proceedings, nor acquiesce in them. On the contrary, in January, 1842, when this new constitution was communicated to the governor, and by him laid before the legislature, it passed resolutions declaring all acts done for the purpose of imposing that constitution upon the State to be an assumption of the powers of government, in violation of the rights of the existing government and of the people at large; and that it would maintain its authority and defend the legal and constitutional rights of the people.

In adopting this measure, as well as in all others taken by the charter government to assert its authority, it was supported by a large number of the citizens of the State, claiming to be a majority, who regarded the proceedings of the adverse party as unlawful and disorganizing, and maintained that, as the existing government had been established by the people of the State, no convention to frame a new constitution could be called without its sanction; and that the times and places of taking the votes, and the officers to receive them, and the qualification of the voters, must be previously regulated and appointed by law.

But notwithstanding the determination of the charter government, and of those who adhered to it, to maintain its authority, Thomas W. Dorr, who had been elected governor under the new constitution, prepared to assert the authority of that government by force, and many citizens assembled in arms to support him. The charter government thereupon passed an act declaring the State under martial law, and at the same time proceeded to call out the militia, to repel the threatened attack, and to subdue those who were engaged in it. In this state of the contest, the house of the plaintiff, who was engaged in supporting the authority of the new government, was broken and entered in order to arrest him. The defendants were, at the time, in the military service of the old government, and in arms to support its authority.

It appears, also, that the charter government, at its session of January, 1842, took measures to call a convention to revise the existing form of government; and after various proceedings, which it is not material to state, a new constitution was formed by a convention elected under the authority of the charter government, and afterwards adopted and ratified by the people; the times and places at which the votes were to be given, the persons who were to receive and return them, and the qualification of the voters, having all been previously authorized and provided for by law passed by the charter government. This new government went into operation in May, 1843, at which time the old government formally surrendered all its powers; and this constitution has continued ever since to be the admitted and established government of Rhode Island.

The difficulties with the government, of which Mr. Dorr was the head, were soon over. They had ceased before the constitution was framed by the convention elected by the authority of the charter government. For after an unsuccessful attempt made by Mr. Dorr, in May, 1842, at the head of a military force, to get possession of the State arsenal at Providence, in which he was repulsed, and an assemblage of some hundreds of armed men under his command at Chepatchet in the June following, which dispersed upon the approach of the troops of the old government, no further effort was made to establish it; and until the constitution of 1843 went into operation, the charter government continued to assert its authority and exercise its powers, and to enforce obedience, throughout the State, arresting and imprisoning, and punishing, in its judicial tribunals, those who had appeared in arms against it.

We do not understand, from the argument, that the constitution, under which the plaintiff acted, is supposed to have been in force after the constitution of May, 1843, went into operation. The contest is confined to the year preceding. The plaintiff contends that the charter government was displaced, and ceased to have any lawful power, after the organization, in May, 1842, of the government which he supported; and although that government never was able to exercise any authority in the State, nor to command obedience to its laws or to its officers, yet he insists that it was the lawful and established government, upon the ground that it was ratified by a large majority of the male people of the State of the age of twenty-one and upwards, and also by a majority of those who were entitled to vote for general officers under the then existing laws of the State. The fact that it was so ratified was not admitted; and at the trial in the Circuit Court he offered to prove it by the production of the original ballots, and the original registers of the persons voting, verified by the oaths of the several moderators and clerks of the meetings, and by the testimony of all the persons so voting, and by the said constitution; and also offered in evidence, for the same purpose, that part of the census of the United States for the year 1840 which applies to Rhode Island; and a certificate of the secretary of state of the charter government, showing the number of votes polled by the freemen of the State for the ten years then last past.

The Circuit Court rejected this evidence, and instructed the jury that the charter government and laws under which the defendants acted were, at the time the trespass is alleged to have been committed, in full force and effect as the form of government and paramount law of the State, and constituted a justification of the acts of the defendants as set forth in their pleas.

It is this opinion of the Circuit Court that we are now called upon to review. It is set forth more at large in the exception, but is in substance as above stated; and the question presented is certainly a very serious one. For, if this court is authorized to enter upon this inquiry as proposed by the plaintiff, and it should be decided that the charter government had no legal existence during the period of time above mentioned, if it had been annulled by the adoption of the opposing government, then the laws passed by its legislature during that time were nullities; its taxes wrongfully collected; its salaries and compensation to its officers illegally paid; its public accounts improperly settled; and the judgments and sentences of its courts in civil and criminal cases null and void, and the officers who carried their decisions into operation answerable as trespassers, if not in some cases as criminals.

When the decision of this court might lead to such results, it becomes its duty to examine very carefully its own powers before it undertakes to exercise jurisdiction.

Certainly, the question which the plaintiff proposed to raise by the testimony he offered has not heretofore been recognized as a judicial one in any of the State courts. In forming the constitutions of the different States, after the Declaration of Independence, and in the various changes and alterations which have since been made, the political department has always determined whether the proposed constitution or amendment was ratified or not by the people of the State, and the judicial power has followed its decision. In Rhode Island, the question has been directly decided. Prosecutions were there instituted against some of the persons who had been active in the forcible opposition to the old government. And in more than one of the cases evidence was offered on the part of the defence similar to the testimony offered in the Circuit Court, and for the same purpose; that is, for the purpose of showing that the proposed constitution had been adopted by the people of Rhode Island, and had, therefore, become the established government, and consequently that the parties accused were doing nothing more than their duty in endeavoring to support it.

But the courts uniformly held that the inquiry proposed to be made belonged to the political power and not to the judicial; that it rested with the political power to decide whether the charter government had been displaced or not; and when that decision was made, the judicial department would be bound to take notice of it as the paramount law of the State, without the aid of oral evidence or the examination of witnesses; that, according to the laws and institutions of Rhode Island, no such change had been recognized by the political power; and that the charter government was the lawful and established government of the State during the period in contest, and that those who were in arms against it were insurgents, and liable to punishment. This doctrine is clearly and forcibly stated in the opinion of the Supreme Court of the State in the trial of Thomas W. Dorr, who was the governor elected under the opposing constitution, and headed the armed force which endeavored to maintain its authority.

Indeed, we do not see how the question could be tried and judicially decided in a State court. Judicial power presupposes an established government capable of enacting laws and enforcing their execution, and of appointing judges to expound and administer them. The acceptance of the judicial office is a recognition of the authority of the government from which it is derived. And if the authority of that government is annulled and overthrown, the power of its courts and other officers is annulled with it. And if a State court should enter upon the inquiry proposed in this case, and should come to the conclusion that the government under which it acted had been put aside and displaced by an opposing government, it would cease to be a court, and be incapable of pronouncing a judicial decision upon the question it undertook to try. If it decides at all as a court, it necessarily affirms the existence and authority of the government under which it is exercising judicial power.

Upon what ground could the Circuit Court of the United States, which tried this case, have departed from this rule, and disregarded and overruled the decisions of the courts of Rhode Island? Undoubtedly the courts of the United States have certain powers under the Constitution and laws of the United States which do not belong to the State courts. But the power of determining that a State government has been lawfully established, which the courts of the State disown and repudiate, is not one of them. Upon such a question the courts of the United States are bound to follow the decisions of the State tribunals, and must therefore regard the charter government as the lawful and established government during the time of this contest.

Besides, if the Circuit Court had entered upon this inquiry, by what rule could it have determined the qualification of voters upon the adoption or rejection of the proposed constitution, unless there was some previous law of the State to guide it? It is the province of a court to expound the law, not to make it. And certainly it is no part of the judicial functions of any court of the United States to prescribe the qualification of voters in a State, giving the right to those to whom it is denied by the written and established constitution and laws of the State, or taking it away from those to whom it is given; nor has it the right to determine what political privileges the citizens of a State are entitled to, unless there is an established constitution or law to govern its decision.

And if the then existing law of Rhode Island, which confined the right of suffrage to freeholders, is to govern, and this question is to be tried by that rule, how could the majority have been ascertained by legal evidence, such as a court of justice might lawfully receive? The written returns of the moderators and clerks of mere voluntary meetings, verified by affidavit, certainly would not be admissible; nor their opinions or judgments as to the freehold qualification of the persons who voted. The law requires actual knowledge in the witness of the fact to which he testifies in a court of justice. How, then, could the majority of freeholders have been determined in a judicial proceeding?

Moreover, the Constitution of the United States, as far as it has provided for an emergency of this kind, and authorized the general government to interfere in the domestic concerns of a State, has treated the subject as political in its nature, and placed the power in the hands of that department.

The fourth section of the fourth article of the Constitution of the United States provides that the United States shall guarantee to every State in the Union a republican form of government, and shall protect each of them against invasion; and on the application of the legislature or of the executive (when the legislature cannot be convened) against domestic violence.

Under this article of the Constitution it rests with Congress to decide what government is the established one in a State. For as the United States guarantee to each State a republican government, Congress must necessarily decide what government is established in the State before it can determine whether it is republican or not. And when the senators and representatives of a State are admitted into the councils of the Union, the authority of the government under which they are appointed, as well as its republican character, is recognized by the proper constitutional authority. And its decision is binding on every other department of the government, and could not be questioned in a judicial tribunal. It is true that the contest in this case did not last long enough to bring the matter to this issue; and as no senators or representatives were elected under the authority of the government of which Mr. Dorr was the head, Congress was not called upon to decide the controversy. Yet the right to decide was placed there, and not in the courts.

So, too, as relates to the clause in the above-mentioned article of the Constitution, providing for cases of domestic violence. It rested with Congress, too, to determine upon the means proper to be adopted to fulfil this guarantee. They might, if they had deemed it most advisable to do so, have placed it in the power of a court to decide when the contingency had happened which required the federal government to interfere. But Congress thought otherwise, and no doubt wisely; and by the act of February 28, 1795, provided, that, "in case of an insurrection in any State against the government thereof, it shall be lawful for the President of the United States, on application of the legislature of such State or of the executive, when the legislature cannot be convened, to call forth such number of the militia of any other State or States, as may be applied for, as he may judge sufficient to suppress such insurrection."

By this act, the power of deciding whether the exigency had arisen upon which the government of the United States is bound to interfere, is given to the President. He is to act upon the application of the legislature, or of the executive, and consequently he must determine what body of men constitute the legislature, and who is the governor, before he can act. The fact that both parties claim the right to the government cannot alter the case, for both cannot be entitled to it. If there is an armed conflict, like the one of which we are speaking, it is a case of domestic violence, and one of the parties must be in insurrection against the lawful government. And the President must, of necessity, decide which is the government, and which party is unlawfully arrayed against it, before he can perform the duty imposed upon him by the act of Congress.

After the President has acted and called out the militia, is a Circuit Court of the United States authorized to inquire whether his decision was right? Could the court, while the parties were actually contending in arms for the possession of the government, call witnesses before it, and inquire which party represented a majority of the people? If it could, then it would become the duty of the court (provided it came to the conclusion that the President had decided incorrectly) to discharge those who were arrested or detained by the troops in the service of the United States, or the government which the President was endeavoring to maintain. If the judicial power extends so far, the guarantee contained in the Constitution of the United States is a guarantee of anarchy, and not of order. Yet if this right does not reside in the courts, when the conflict is raging — if the judicial power is, at that time, bound to follow the decision of the political, it must be equally bound when the contest is over. It cannot, when peace is restored, punish as offences and crimes the acts which it before recognized, and was bound to recognize, as lawful.

It is true that in this case the militia were not called out by the President. But upon the application of the governor under the charter government, the President recognized him as the executive power of the State, and took measures to call out the militia to support his authority, if it should be found necessary for the general government to interfere; and it is admitted in the argument that it was the knowledge of this decision that put an end to the armed opposition to the charter government, and prevented any further efforts to establish by force the proposed constitution. The interference of the President, therefore, by announcing his determination, was as effectual as if the militia had been assembled under his orders. And it should be equally authoritative. For certainly no court of the United States, with a knowledge of this decision, would have been justified in recognizing the opposing party as the lawful government, or in treating as wrongdoers or insurgents the officers of the government which the President had recognized, and was prepared to support by an armed force. In the case of foreign nations, the government acknowledged by the President is always recognized in the courts of justice. And this principle has been applied by the act of Congress to the sovereign States of the Union.

It is said that this power in the President is dangerous to liberty, and may be abused. All power may be abused if placed in unworthy hands. But it would be difficult, we think, to point out any other hands in which this power would be more safe, and at the same time equally effectual. When citizens of the same State are in arms against each other, and the constituted authorities unable to execute the laws, the interposition of the United States must be prompt, or it is of little value. The ordinary course of proceedings in courts of justice would be utterly unfit for the crisis. And the elevated office of the President, chosen as he is by the people of the United States, and the high responsibility he could not fail to feel when acting in a case of so much moment, appear to furnish as strong safeguards against a wilful abuse of power as human prudence and foresight could well provide. At all events, it is conferred upon him by the Constitution and laws of the United States, and must, therefore, be respected and enforced in its judicial tribunals.

Much of the argument on the part of the plaintiff turned upon political rights and political questions, upon which the court has been urged to express an opinion. We decline doing so. The high power has been conferred on this court, of passing judgment upon the acts of the State sovereignties, and of the legislative and executive branches of the federal government, and of determining whether they are beyond the limits of power marked out for them respectively by the Constitution of the United States. This tribunal, therefore, should be the last to overstep the boundaries which limit its own jurisdiction. And while it should always be ready to meet any question confided to it by the Constitution, it is equally its duty not to pass beyond its appropriate sphere of action, and to take care not to involve itself in discussions which properly belong to other forums. No one, we believe, has ever doubted the proposition that, according to the institutions of this country, the sovereignty in every State resides in the people of the State, and that they may alter and change their form of government at their own pleasure. But whether they have changed it or not, by abolishing an old government, and establishing a new one in its place, is a question to be settled by the political power. And when that power has decided, the courts are bound to take notice of its decision, and to follow it.

The judgment of the Circuit Court must, therefore, be affirmed.

XXXII. KADDERLY et al. v. CITY OF PORTLAND et al.

(Supreme Court of Oregon, December 21, 1903, 74 Pacific Reporter, 710, 719)

[The decision in this case was rendered by Justice Bean. All of the opinion dealing directly with the initiative and referendum is printed here. The other points in the case decided by the court dealt with the questions as to whether the constitutional amendment establishing the initiative and referendum in Oregon had been legally adopted, and whether certain portions of the charter of Portland were invalid under the provisions of the Oregon constitution.]

Nor do we think the amendment void because in conflict with section 4, art. 4, of the Constitution of the United States, guaranteeing to every state a republican form of government. The purpose of this provision of the Constitution is to protect the people of the several states against aristocratic and monarchical invasions, and against insurrections and domestic violence, and to prevent them from abolishing a republican form of government. Cooley, Const. Lim. (7th Ed.) 54; 2 Story, Const. (5th Ed.) § 1815. But it does not forbid them from amending or changing their Constitution in any way they may see fit, so long as none of these results is accomplished. No particular style of government is designated in the Constitution as republican, nor is its exact form in any way prescribed. A republican form of government is a government administered by representatives chosen or appointed by the people or by their authority. Mr. Madison says it is "a government which derives all its powers directly or indirectly from the great body of the people, and is administered by persons holding their offices during pleasure, for a limited period, or during good behavior." *The Federalist*, 302. And in discussing the section of the Constitution of the United States now under consideration, he says: "But the authority extends no further than to a guaranty of a republican form of government, which supposes a preëxisting government of the form which is to be guaranteed. As long, therefore, as the existing republican forms are continued by the states, they are guaranteed by the federal Constitution. Whenever the states may choose to substitute other republican forms, they have a right to do so, and to claim the federal guaranty for the latter. The only restriction imposed on them is that they shall not exchange republican for anti-republican constitutions." Id. 342. Now, the initiative and referendum amendment does not abolish or destroy the republican form of government, or substitute another in its place. The representative character of the government still remains. The people have simply reserved to themselves a larger share of legislative power, but they have not overthrown the republican form of the government, or substituted another in its place. The government is still divided into the legislative, executive, and judicial departments, the duties of which are discharged by representatives selected by the people. Under this amendment, it is true, the people may exercise a legislative power, and may, in effect, veto or defeat bills passed and approved by the Legislature and the Governor; but the legislative and executive departments are not destroyed, nor are their powers or authority materially curtailed. Laws proposed and enacted by the people under the initiative clause of the amendment are subject to the same constitutional limitations as other statutes, and may be amended or repealed by the Legislature at will. The veto power of the Governor is not abridged in any way, except as to such laws as the Legislature may refer to the people. The provision of the amendment that "the veto power of the governor shall not extend to measures referred to the people" must necessarily be confined to the measures which the Legislature may refer, and cannot apply to acts upon which the referendum may be invoked by petition. The Governor is required, under the Constitution, to exercise his veto power, if at all, within five days after the act shall have been presented to him, unless the general adjournment of the Legislature shall prevent its return within that time, in which case he shall exercise his right within five days after

x

the adjournment. He must necessarily act, therefore, before the time expires within which a referendum by petition on any act of the Legislature may be invoked, and before it can be known whether it will be invoked or not. Unless, therefore, he has a right to veto any act submitted to him, except such as the Legislature may specially refer to the people, one of the safeguards against hasty or ill-advised legislation which is everywhere regarded as essential is removed — a result manifestly not contemplated by the amendment.

This brings us to the question as to whether the legislative declaration that the Portland charter was necessary for the preservation of the public peace, health, and safety is conclusive on the courts. Under the initiative and referendum amendment, laws "necessary for the immediate preservation of the public peace, health, or safety" are excepted from its operation. As to them, the action of the legislative and executive departments is conclusive and final, so far as their enactment is concerned. No power is reserved to the people to approve or disapprove them. They are not subject to the referendum amendment, and as to them the powers of the other departments of the government derived from the Constitution are unaffected. The legislative assembly may, in its discretion, put them into operation through an emergency clause, as provided in section 28, art. 4, of the Constitution, or it may allow them to become laws without an emergency clause; the necessity or expediency of either course being a matter for its exclusive determination. As to all other laws the amendment applies, and they cannot be made to go into operation for 90 days after the adjournment of the session at which they were adopted, or until after approval by the people if the referendum is invoked. Section 28, art. 4, of the Constitution, giving the legislative assembly power to put any law into force upon approval by declaring an emergency, has been modified by the amendment of 1902, so as to exclude from the power to declare an emergency all laws except those necessary for the immediate preservation of the public peace, health, or safety. So far, all are agreed. But the vital question is, what tribunal is to determine whether a law does or does not fall under this classification? Are the judgment and findings of the legislative assembly conclusive, or are they subject to review by the courts? The inquiry is much simplified by bearing in mind that the exception in the constitutional amendment is not confined to such laws as the legislative assembly may legally enact by virtue of the police powers of the state, or to those alone that may affect the public peace, health or safety. The police power is limited to the imposition of restraints and burdens on persons and property, in order to secure the general comfort, health, and prosperity of the state. Tiedeman, Lim. Pol. Power, § 1. But the language of the constitutional amendment is broader, and includes all laws, of whatsoever kind, necessary for the immediate preservation of the public peace, health or safety, whether they impose restraints on persons and property, or come strictly within the police powers, or not. The laws excepted from the operation of the amendment do not depend alone upon their character, but upon the necessity for their enactment in order to accomplish certain purposes. As to such laws, the amendment of 1902 does not in any way abridge or restrict the power of the Legislature, which, by the insertion of a proper emergency clause, may unquestionably cause them to go into effect upon approval by the Governor. As the Legislature may exercise this power when a measure is in fact necessary for the purposes stated, and as the amendment does not declare what shall be deemed laws of the character indicated, who is to decide whether a specific act may or may not be necessary for the purpose? Most unquestionably, those who make the laws are required, in the process of their enactment, to pass upon all questions of expediency and necessity connected therewith, and must therefore determine whether a given law is necessary for the preservation of the public peace, health, and safety. It has always been the rule, and is now everywhere understood, that the judgment of the legislative and executive departments as to the wisdom, expediency, or necessity of any given law is conclusive on the courts, and cannot be reviewed or called in question by them. It is the duty of the courts, after a law has been enacted, to determine in a proper proceeding whether it conflicts with the fundamental law, and to construe and interpret it so as to ascertain the rights of the parties litigant. The powers of the courts do not extend to the mere question of expediency or necessity, but, as said by Mr. Justice Brewer, "they are wrought out and fought out in the Legislature and before the people. Here the single question is one of power. We make no laws. We change no constitutions. We inaugurate no policy. When the Legislature enacts a law, the only question which we can decide is whether the limitations of the Constitution have been infringed upon." Prohibitory Am. Cas., 24 Kan. 700, 706. The amendment excepts such laws as may be necessary for a certain purpose. The existence of such necessity is therefore a question of fact, and the authority to determine such fact must rest somewhere. The Constitution does not confer it upon any tribunal. It must therefore necessarily reside with that department of the government which is called upon to exercise the power. It is a question of which the Legislature alone must be the judge, and, when it decides the fact to exist, its action is final. Biggs v. McBride, 17 Or. 640, 21 Pac. 878, 5 L. R. A. 115; Umatilla Irrigation Co. v. Barnhart, 22 Or. 389, 30 Pac. 37; Gentile v. State 29 Ind. 409; Wheeler v. Chubbuck, 16 Ill. 361; Sutherland, St. Const. 108. In this view we are supported by the Supreme Court of South Dakota. In 1898 an amendment to the Constitution of that state was adopted by the people; similar in many respects to the amendment now under consideration; and, so far as the laws exempted from its operation are concerned, the language of the two amendments is identical. In State ex rel. v. Bacon, 14 S. D. 394, 404, 85 N. W. 225, the court say in referring to this amendment: "It will be observed that the law of 1901 which we are considering not only declares that an emergency exists, but also that the 'provision is necessary for the immediate preservation and support of the existing public institutions of this state.' It seems to have been uniformly held under Constitutions containing an emergency clause, and providing that laws containing such a clause shall take effect as therein directed, that the action of the Legislature in inserting such a clause is conclusive upon the courts. (Citing authorities.) No reason occurs to us why the same rule should not apply to the act in question. The Legislature having declared that the provisions of that act are necessary for the immediate preservation and support of the existing public institutions of the state, that declaration is conclusive upon this court, and brings this class clearly within the exception contained in section 1 (as amended) of article 3 of the Constitution."

But, it is argued, what remedy will the people have if the Legislature, either intentionally or through mistake, declares falsely or erroneously that a given law is necessary for the purposes stated? The obvious answer is that the power has been vested in that body, and its decision can no more be questioned or reviewed than the decision of the highest court in a case over which it has jurisdiction. Nor should it be supposed that the Legislature will disregard its duty, or fail to observe the mandates of the Constitution. The courts have no more right to distrust the Legislature than it has to distrust the courts. The Constitution has wisely divided the government into three separate and distinct departments, and has provided that no person charged with official duties under one of these departments shall exercise any of the functions of another, except as in the Constitution expressly provided. Const. art. 3, § 1. It is true that power of any kind may be abused when in unworthy hands. That, however, would not be a sufficient reason for one coördinate branch of the government to assign for attempting to limit the power and authority of another department. If either of the departments, in the exercise of the powers vested in it, should exercise them erroneously or wrongfully, the remedy is with the people, and must be found, as said by Mr. Justice Strahan in Biggs *v.* McBride, *supra*, in the ballot box.

We are of the opinion, therefore, that the findings and declarations of the Legislature that the act of 1903 for the incorporation of the city of Portland was necessary for the immediate preservation of the public peace, health, and safety are conclusive on the courts, and consequently the charter was not subject to the referendum power, and was in force and effect from and after its approval.

This disposes of the most important questions in the case. The result is, first, that the initiative and referendum amendment was legally proposed and adopted; second, that it is not in conflict with the provisions of the Constitution of the United States guaranteeing to every state a republican form of government; and, third, that the question whether a law is necessary for the immediate preservation of the public peace, health, or safety, and consequently excepted from the operations of the amendment, is a legislative, and not a judicial question.

XXXIII. STATE v. PACIFIC STATES TELEPHONE & TELEGRAPH COMPANY

[This is the important case on the initiative and referendum now (October, 1911) pending before the Supreme Court of the United States.]

(99 Pacific Reporter, 427)

(Supreme Court of Oregon. Feb. 2, 1909.)

Appeal from Circuit Court, Multnomah County; John B. Cleland, Judge.

Action by the State against the Pacific States Telephone & Telegraph Company to recover a 2 per cent tax on the gross receipts of the defendant. From a judgment for plaintiff after sustaining a demurrer to the answer, defendant appeals. Affirmed.

This is an action by the state against the Pacific States Telephone & Telegraph Company to recover 2 per cent of the gross receipts of such company for the year 1906. The case is as follows: In 1903 the Legislature passed an act requiring all corporations domestic and foreign, doing business in the state, to pay an annual license fee of from $10 to $200, according to their capital stock. Laws 1903, p. 39. In 1906 there was proposed by an initiative petition, and adopted by the people in June of that year, pursuant to the provisions of the initiative and referendum amendment to the Constitution, and without reference to the Legislature, an act requiring telephone and telegraph companies to pay a license of 2 per cent per annum on the gross receipts of the company, and requiring such corporations to make annual statements to the state treasurer of the amount of such receipts as a basis for such tax. The defendant corporation is an Oregon concern and made the returns, required by the act, for the year 1906, but refused to pay the tax thereon, and hence this suit. It answered the complaint, denying liability on the grounds: (1) That the initiative act requiring it to pay such license or tax was never approved by the Governor, nor submitted to him for his approval; (2) that the defendant has paid the annual license fee required by the act of 1903, and also all state, county, and school taxes levied upon all of its property, "including its franchise to do business," and therefore the act of 1906 is unconstitutional and void because violative of section 32, art. 1, of the state Constitution, requiring that "all taxation shall be equal and uniform"; (3) that the initiative and referendum amendment to the Constitution, under which the act of 1906 was proposed and adopted, is unconstitutional and void, because repugnant to sections 2, 3, 4, and 8 of article 1, section 1 of article 2, sections 3 and 4 of article 4, article 5, article 6, and section 1 of the fourteenth amendment to the Constitution of the United States; and also to Act. Cong. Feb. 14, 1859, c. 33, 11 Stat. 383, admitting Oregon to the Union, and the act approved June 1, 1789 (chapter 1, § 3, 1 Stat. 23, Rev. St. U. S. § 1836 (U. S. Comp. St. 1901, p. 1256). Other grounds of objection are set forth in paragraphs 24, 25, 26, and 27 of the answer, but were stricken out on application of the defendant. The plaintiff demurred to the new matter pleaded in the answer, on the ground that it did not constitute a defence to the cause of action stated in the complaint. The demurrer was sustained, judgment rendered in favor of plaintiff, and defendant appeals.

Chas. H. Carey, for appellant. A. M. Crawford, Atty. Gen., and A. S. Bennett, for the State.

BEAN, J. (after stating the facts as above). The question whether an initiative measure is subject to the veto power of the Governor was decided in State v. Kline, 50 Or. 426, 93 Pac. 237, and that case is conclusive here. What is said on the subject in Kadderly v. Portland, 44 Or. 118, 146, 74 Pac. 710, 75 Pac. 222, was in answer to the point that the initiative and referendum amendment deprived the Governor of a veto power over acts of the Legislature and had no reference to measures proposed by the initiative. The annual license fee required by the act of 1903 to be paid by corporations is a business or excise tax on the right to be or exercise the powers of a corporation, and is in no sense a tax on property; nor is it a tax on the business or franchise which the corporation, when organized, may exercise. Am. S. & R. Co. v. People, 34 Colo. 240, 82 Pac. 531; Delaware R. R. Tax, 18 Wall. 206, 21 L. Ed. 888; Home Ins. v. New York, 134 U. S. 594, 10 Sup. Ct. 593, 33 L. Ed. 1025.

The right to be a corporation, or do business as such, rests entirely within the discretion of the state, and it may therefore require it to pay a specified sum each year, or at stated intervals, for the privilege. The payment of such fee or tax, however, does not exempt the corporation from other forms of taxation. It may be also required to pay a tax on its tangible property and a tax on its intangible property or franchise; the latter to be in proportion to its income or measured in any other way the law-making power may adopt. 27 Enc. Law, 932; 57 L. R. A. 98, note. "The State," says Mr. Justice Field, "may impose taxes upon the corporation as an entity existing under its laws, as well as upon the capital stock of the corporation, or its separate corporate property; and the manner in which its value shall be assessed and the rate of taxation, however arbitrary or capricious, are mere matters of legislative discretion. It is not for us to suggest in any case that a more equitable mode of assessment or rate of taxation might be adopted than the one prescribed by the Legislature of the state. Our only concern is with the validity of the tax. All else lies beyond the domain of our jurisdiction." 18 Wall. 231, 21 L. Ed. 888. See, also, Maine v. Grand Trunk Ry. Co., 142 U. S. 217, 12 Sup. Ct. 121, 35 L. Ed. 994. Among the elements of corporate taxable values are the franchise, capital stock in the hands of the corporation, the tangible corporate property, and shares of stock in the hands of individual holders; and all of the authorities agree that a tax upon the franchise, whether based on income or measured in some other manner, and a tax on the tangible corporate property, is not double taxation. Cooley on Taxation, 406; Commissioners v. Tobacco Co., 116 N. C. 441, 21 S. E. 423; Home Ins. Co. v. New York, 119 U. S. 129, 8 Sup. Ct. 1385, 30 L. Ed. 350; Commonwealth v. New England Slate & Tile Co. 13 Allen (Mass.), 391; Commonwealth v. Railroad Co., 150 Pa. 234, 24 Atl. 609; Wil. Col. & Augusta R. R. Co. v. Board of Commissioners of Brunswick Co., 72 N. C. 10; State Tax Ry. on Gross Receipts, 15 Wall. 284, 21 L. Ed. 164. Nor does the fact that plaintiff may have paid all taxes assessed and levied on its property "including the value of its franchise," render invalid the law levying a tax on its gross income. At the time the assessment and levy alluded to were made, there was no law specifically requiring the franchise of a corporation to be assessed, nor providing the manner of estimating the value thereof, and clearly a law on the subject regularly enacted could not be rendered nugatory or invalid by local assessors including in the value of corporate property their estimate of the value of the franchise.

Whether the initiative and referendum amendment to the Constitution is invalid, because repugnant to the provisions of the Constitution of the United States, was thoroughly argued to and considered by this court in Kadderly v. Portland, and the views of the court as then and now entertained are indicated in the opinion filed in that case, and it is needless to restate them at this time.

It follows from these views that the judgment of the court must be affirmed, and it is so ordered.

XXXIV. KIERNAN v. CITY OF PORTLAND et al.

(112 Pacific Reporter, p. 402)

Supreme Court of Oregon. Dec. 31, 1910.

1. MUNICIPAL CORPORATIONS (§ 64) — INITIATIVE AND REFERENDUM PROVISIONS.

Const. art. 11, § 2, as amended June 4, 1906, provides that corporations may be formed only under general laws, but shall not be created by the legislative assembly by special laws, and, further, that "the legislative assembly shall not enact, amend, or repeal any charter, or act of incorporation for any municipality, city or town," and that "the legal voters of every city and town are hereby granted power to enact and amend their municipal charter, subject to the Constitution and criminal laws of Oregon." *Held*, that the first sentence of section 2 places no restriction on the Legislature as to the enactment of general laws, except that no special laws creating or affecting municipalities shall be enacted by the Legislature, the exception reserving to the legislative department the right, whether by the people directly through the initiative, or indirectly through the Legislature, to enact general laws on the subject, indicating that the inhibition in the next sentence has reference only to special laws.

2. STATES (§ 4) — "REPUBLICAN FORM OF GOVERNMENT."

The term "republican," as used in the federal constitutional provision (article 4, § 4) guaranteeing to every state a republican form of government, means a government by the citizens en masse acting directly, though not personally, according to rules established by the majority.

3. STATUTES (§ 35½) — INITIATIVE AND REFERENDUM PROVISIONS — MUNICIPAL CORPORATIONS — REPUBLICAN FORM OF GOVERNMENT.

Const. art. 1, as amended June 4, 1906 (section 1 a), provides that initiative and referendum powers reserved in the people are also reserved to the legal voters of any municipality and district, as to all local, special, and municipal legislation. Section 2 provides that the legal voters of every city and town are granted power to enact and amend their municipal charter, subject to the Constitution and criminal laws of Oregon. *Held*, that such provisions did not deprive the state of a republican form of government, in violation of Const. U. S. art. 47, § 4, in that they were a deprivation of legislative power to enact, amend, or repeal a city charter, or act of incorporation, since the sovereign power to legislate residing in the people may be exercised either directly by the initiative, or referendum, or indirectly by the Legislature, without in any way endangering the republican form of government.

KING, J. The principal point suggested by the petition for rehearing is the contention that the people of Oregon have no power, by constitutional provision or otherwise, to deprive the Legislature of the sovereign power to enact, amend, or repeal any charter or act of incorporation for any city or town, and any attempt so to do is void. The constitutional provisions, amending article 11, adopted in June, 1906, known as the "Charter Amendments," are as follows: —

"Section 1 a. The referendum may be demanded by the people against one or more items, sections, or parts of any act of the legislative assembly in the same manner in which such power may be exercised against a complete act. The filing of a referendum petition against one or more items, sections, or parts of an act shall not delay the remainder of that act from becoming operative. The initiative and referendum powers reserved to the people by this Constitution are hereby further reserved to the legal voters of every municipality and district as to all local, special, and municipal legislation, of every character, in or for their respective municipalities and districts. The manner of exercising said powers shall be prescribed by general laws, except that cities and towns may provide for the manner of exercising the initiative and referendum powers as to their municipal legislation. Not more than ten per cent of the legal voters may be required to order the referendum, nor more than fifteen per cent to propose any measure, by the initiative, in any city or town.

"Sec. 2. Corporations may be formed under general laws, but shall not be created by the legislative assembly by special laws. The legislative assembly shall not enact, amend, or repeal any charter or act of incorporation for any municipality, city, or town. The legal voters of every city and town are hereby granted power to enact and amend their municipal charter, subject to the Constitution and criminal laws of Oregon."

It will be observed from the first sentence in section 2 that no restriction is placed upon the Legislature with respect to the enactment of general laws; the exception being that no special laws creating or affecting the municipalities shall be enacted by the Legislature. Under all the rules of construction, this exception reserves to the legislative department the right, whether by the people directly through the initiative, or indirectly through the Legislature, to enact general laws upon the subject, making it clear that the inhibition in the next sentence has reference to special laws.

In Farrell v. Port of Portland, 52 Or. 582, 586, 98 Pac. 145, it is held that the initiative amendments to the Constitution, bearing upon the creation and government of municipalities, including section 1 of article 11, must be construed together. In considering the effect of section 2, art. 11, it is there said: "But this section and the language used in it should not be construed alone. It is a part of the initiative and referendum scheme first inaugurated by the amendment of 1902, and subsequently enlarged and extended by the amendments of 1906. All these amendments, so far as they refer to the same subject-matter, should be read together, and be so interpreted as to carry out the purpose of the people in adopting them, regardless of the technical construction of some of the language used." Since the above is the rule regarding the various amendments taken as a whole, much stronger must be the reason for reading and construing together all the sentences in the one section, from which it is obvious that the only restriction placed upon the Legislature by section 2 pertains to the passage of special laws affecting municipalities. These agencies of the state are thereby enabled to enact such local measures, to revise existing local laws, and to exercise their powers affecting them, and thus carry out their general scope and purpose, so long as they are not inconsistent with the Constitution of the state, or of the United States, and are in harmony with all the special laws and general laws of the state constitutionally enacted. Straw v. Harris, 54 Or. 424, 443, 103 Pac. 777. The language following the above excerpt from page 587 of 52 Or., 98 Pac. 145, of the opinion of Farrell v. Port of Portland, concerning the limitations placed by the amendment upon the Legislature, must be interpreted in the light of the questions there under consideration, from which it is manifest reference was had only to special laws affecting municipalities. The so-termed "general initiative and referendum scheme," there alluded to, and whether it is in violation of this provision of the federal Constitution, is fully considered and determined adversely to petitioner's contention in Kadderly v. Portland, 44 Or. 118, 74 Pac. 710, 75 Pac. 222, and State v. Pacific States Tel. & Tel. Co., 52 Or. 163, 99 Pac. 427, and there held to be not in conflict or inconsistent therewith. Other cases impliedly if not expressly sustaining this position are: Farrell v. Port of Portland, 52 Or. 582, 98 Pac. 145; Straw v. Harris, 54 Or. 424, 103 Pac. 777; Haines v. City of Forest Grove, 54 Or. 443, 103 Pac. 775; State v. Langworthy, 104 Pac. 424.

The question, however, as to whether the people may, by constitutional amendment, reserve to themselves the right to enact any law to the exclusion of the Legislature, and, by such method, delegate to municipalities powers not subject to abridgment, change, limitation, or recall by special acts of the legislative assembly, was not directly involved in any of the cases above cited. It would seem, however, that the views and conclusions reached in the decisions named necessarily dispose of this feature, but since counsel for petitioner insists that such disposal has not been made, and presents his contention in good faith, we will, at the possible expense of repetition of views announced in the above cases, consider the points thus presented. To begin, article 4, § 4, Const. U. S., reads "The United States shall guarantee to every state in this Union a republican form of government, and shall protect each of them against invasion; and on application of the Legislature, or of the executive (when the Legislature cannot be convened), against domestic violence." In Luther v. Borden, 7 How. 1, 48, 12 L. Ed. 581, the court observes: "Moreover, the Constitution of the United States, as far as it has provided for an emergency of this kind, and authorized the general government to interfere in the domestic concerns of a state, has treated the subject as political in its nature, and placed the power in the hands of that department. The fourth section of the fourth article of the Constitution of the United States provides that the United States shall guarantee to every state in the Union a republican form of government, and shall protect each of them against invasion; and on the application of the Legislature or of the executive (when the Legislature cannot be convened) against domestic violence. Under this article of the Constitution, it rests with Congress to decide what government is the established one in a state. For as the United States guarantee to each state a republican government, Congress must necessarily decide what government is established in the state before it can determine whether it is republican or not. And when the senators and representatives of a state are admitted into the councils of the Union, the authority of the government under which they are appointed, as well as its republican character, is recognized by the proper constitutional authority. And its decision is binding on every other department of the government, and could not be questioned in a judicial tribunal." See, also, Cooley, Const. Lim. (6th Ed.), pp. 42, 45; Texas v. White, 7 Wall. 700, 730, 19 L. Ed. 227; Taylor v. Beckham, 178 U. S. 548, 20 Sup. Ct. 890, 1009, 44 L. Ed. 1187, and 6 Mich. Law Review, 304, where authorities sustaining the above view are collated. We have an illustration of the principles announced in Luther v. Borden in the admission of Oklahoma as a state. Before its statehood was recognized, Oklahoma had adopted, as a part of its Constitution, the initiative and referendum law-making system, patterned after the Oregon plan, regardless of which its senators and representatives were "admitted into the councils of the Union," and "the authority of the government under which they were appointed, as well as its republican character, is recognized by the proper constitutional authority," thus determining that state, with its comparatively new legislative system, to be republican in form. This recent historical precedent should in itself be adequate to set at rest the temporarily mooted question in hand.

This court, however, has heretofore taken jurisdiction of cases of this character (Kadderly v. Portland, 44 Or. 118, 74 Pac. 710, 75 Pac. 222; State v. Cochrane, 105 Pac. 884), and, owing to the importance of the points presented, we will proceed to a consideration thereof. To ascertain whether taking from the Legislature and delegating to the municipalities, or to the localities affected, local self-government, or a right to enact, maintain, and alter their charters as the Legislature formerly did, and whether the taking from the Legislature the right to make special laws upon the subject violates this provision of the national Constitution, makes it important that we first ascertain what is meant by a republican form of government. It is an expression which all assume to understand, yet, judging from the many unsuccessful attempts of eminent statesmen and writers to give it a clear meaning, it would seem the phrase is not susceptible to being given a precise definition. Expecially is this true when sought to be applied to the Constitution of different states, concerning which Mr. James Madison, a member of the Constitutional Convention, said: " . . . If we resort for a criterion to the different principles on which different forms of government are established, we may define a republic to be, or may at least bestow that name on, a government which derives all its powers directly or indirectly from the great body of the people, and is administered by persons holding their offices during pleasure for a limited period or during good behavior. It is essential to such government that it be derived from the great body of society, and not from any inconsiderable portion or a favored class of it. . . ." *The Federalist* (Hamilton, Ed.), paper 39, p. 301. Another and more pointed definition appears in Chisholm *v.* Georgia, 2 Dall. 419, 457, 1 L. Ed. 440, by Mr. Justice Wilson, a member of the Constitutional Convention, who, but a short time after the adoption of the federal Constitution, in adverting to what is meant by a republican form of government, remarked: "As a citizen, I know the government of that state (Georgia) to be republican, and my short definition of such a government — one constructed on this principle, that the supreme power resides in the body of the people." From which it follows that the converse must be true; that is to say, any government in which the supreme power resides with the people is republican in form. See, also, Mr. Justice Wilson's remarks to the same effect, reported in 5 Elliott's Debates, 160.

Measured in the light of the above, it is difficult to conceive of any system of law-making coming nearer to the great body of the people of the entire state, or by those comprising the various municipalities, than that now in use here, and, being so, we are at a loss to understand how the adoption and use of this system can be held a departure from a republican form of government. It was to escape the oppression resulting from governments controlled by the select few, so often ruling under the assumption that "might makes right," that gave birth to republics. Monarchial rulers refuse to recognize their accountability to the people governed by them. In a republic the converse is the rule. The tenure of office may be for a short or a long period, or even for life, yet those in office are at all times answerable, either directly or indirectly, to the people, and in proportion to their responsibility to those for whom they may be the public agents, and the nearer the power to enact laws and control public servants lies with the great body of the people, the more nearly does a government take unto itself the form of a republic — not in name alone, but in fact. From this it follows that each republic may differ in its political system or in the political machinery by which it moves, but, so long as the ultimate control of its officials and affairs of state remain in its citizens, it will in the eye of all republics, be recognized as a government of that class. Of this we have many examples in Central and South America. It becomes then a matter of degree, and the fear manifested by the briefs filed in this case would seem to indicate, not that we are drifting from the secure moorings of a republic, but that our state, by the direct system of legislation complained of, is becoming too democratic — advancing too rapidly towards a republic pure in form. This, it is true, counsel for petitioner does not concede, but under any interpretation of which the term is capable, or from any view thus far found expressed in the writings of the prominent statesmen who were members of the Constitutional Convention, or who figured in the early upbuilding of the nation, it follows that the system here assailed brings us nearer to a state republican in form than before its adoption. Mr. Thomas Jefferson, in 1816, when discussing the term republic, defined and illustrated his view thereof as follows: "Indeed, it must be acknowledged that the term 'republic' is of very vague application in every language. Witness the self-styled republics of Holland, Switzerland, Genoa, Venice, Poland. Were I to assign to this term a precise and definite idea, I would say, purely and simply, it means a government by its citizens in mass, acting directly and not personally, according to rules established by the majority, and that every other government is more or less repub-

Y

lican in proportion as it has in its composition more or less of this ingredient of the direct action of the citizens." Writings of Thomas Jefferson, vol. 15, p. 19. It is well known that at the time of the adoption of the federal Constitution there existed in some of the Atlantic states a system of local government, known as "New England towns," in which the people had the right to legislate upon various matters, the masses assembling at stated periods for that purpose, all of which was within the knowledge of those composing the Constitutional Convention. After observing that a true republic, under his definition, would necessarily be restrained to narrow limits, such as in a New England township, and that the next step in use at that time was through the representative system, Mr. Jefferson pointed out that the further the officials of state or nation are separated from the masses proportionately less does such state or government retain the elements of a republic, and on page 23 concludes: "On this view of the import of the term 'republic,' instead of saying, as has been said, that it may mean anything or nothing, we may say with truth and meaning that governments are more or less republican, as they have more or less of the element of popular election and control in their composition; and believing, as I do, that the mass of citizens is the safest depository of their own rights and especially, that the evils flowing from the duperies of the people, are less injurious than those from the egoism of their agents, I am a friend to that composition of government which has in it the most of this ingredient." The observations quoted are in full accord with the recorded views of all the writers and statesmen of that time, when the intention of the framers of our national Constitution was fully understood, in the light of which it seems inconceivable that a state, merely because it may evolve a system by which its citizens become a branch of its legislative department, co-ordinate with their representatives in the Legislature, loses caste as a republic. The extent to which a Legislature of any state may enact laws is, and always has been, one of degree, depending upon the limitations prescribed by its constitution; some constitutions having few and others many limitations. But in all states, whatever may be the restriction placed upon their representatives, the people, either by constitutional amendment or by convention called for that purpose, have had, and have, the power to directly legislate, and to change all or any laws so far as deemed proper — limited only by clear inhibitions of the national Constitution. Cooley, Const. Lim. (6th Ed.) 44.

An examination of our state Constitution, as first adopted, discloses many restrictions upon the law-making department, among which is a provision to the effect that no amendment thereto should be submitted to the people for ratification until after it passed two successive sessions of the Legislature. In course of time, an amendment under this provision was legally submitted and adopted by a majority vote of the people, by which the people reserved the right to change the Constitution or any part thereof without awaiting this legislative formality, the validity of which is not open to doubt. Is it not possible, indeed, is it not practicable, then, for the people further to restrict the power of their representatives to legislate upon matters of public interest, and in so doing are they not, and even under the old system were they not, directly legislating? This system of direct legislation has been in common use throughout the various state governments since their inception, but until the adoption of the initiative and referendum amendments no one was heard to assert that an amendment to the Constitution of a state merely because of depriving the Legislature of some law-making power or powers held by it at the adoption of the national Constitution was void on the grounds of being inconsistent with a republican form of government. The absurdity of such a contention, if made, would at once be obvious. But, viewed from any standpoint, such is the logical sequence of appellant's contention to the effect, that because the people have, by constitutional amendment, reserved the exclusive right to enact special laws concerning municipalities and by constitutional amendment have delegated to municipal corporations the right to exercise such powers as before were only within the province of their representatives, through the Legislature, to delegate, violates the provision of the federal Constitution, guaranteeing to our state a republican form of government. In other words, it is argued that the right of the city of Portland to legislate upon matters of municipal concern, to provide for the exercise of its right of eminent domain, to build bridges, etc., would be in harmony with the above provision of the federal Constitution, if delegated by the people through their representatives, but not so if done directly by them through the initiative. In brief, the effect of this argument is that the people may legally do indirectly by the mere enactment of a law what they cannot do directly by constitutional amendment. The statement of this contention should be sufficient for its answer.

We held in Straw v. Harris, 54 Or. 424, 103 Pac. 777, that a state could not by amendment of its fundamental laws or otherwise, except in the manner provided in section 3, art. 4, Const. U. S., delegate to any municipality or subdivision of the state prerogatives not subject to recall, that so to do would, in effect, be the creation of a state within a state, and that, so long as the Legislature is not precluded by the Constitution from enacting general laws affecting them, it may by that method amend, modify, or even abolish municipal corporations, and that even should this power be removed from the Legislature there must remain with the people a right to do so, if not by enacting a law to that effect, then by the former system of direct legislation, consisting in the adopting of amendments to the Constitution, known as the fundamental laws of the state, and that this right of state government to retain control of these agencies and department of state cannot be surrendered, but must always remain somewhere within the reach of that source of all power — the people. We held, and still hold, to this view, not on the ground that to hold otherwise would be destructive of a republican form of government, but because to do so would in effect permit a state within a state and accordingly violate section 3, art. 4, of the federal

Constitution, the first paragraph of which reads: "New states may be admitted by the Congress into this Union; but no new state shall be formed or erected within the jurisdiction of any other state; nor any state be formed by the junction of two or more states, or parts of states, without the consent of the Legislatures of the states concerned, as well as of the Congress." Suppose our law-making department should pass an ex post facto act, or a bill of attainder, such purported laws would be void, not because of being subversive of a republican form of government, but by reason of some express inhibition against legislation of that character contained in another section of the federal Constitution. If the national Constitution permitted or provided for the creation of a state within a state, could it be said that by reason thereof the state thus created would be unrepublican in form? Under section 3 of article 4, above quoted, states may be divided and new ones created, the limitation being that no states shall be created within a state, but the creation of new states under that section has never been considered an unrepublican step. Should our state attempt to surrender its powers to an executive for life, with the provision that upon his death his authority should pass by entailed inheritance to his son or other relative, and at the same time, by constitutional change or otherwise, further surrender any right to alter the system, except with the consent of such executive, it would lose its republican form, and in effect become a local monarchy within the Union, thereby furnishing an example of a violation of section 4, art. 4, of the federal Constitution. But, so long as the people retain the power within themselves to conduct and manage the affairs of state — either directly or indirectly — a republican form of government is maintained, and comes within the provision of the federal Constitution guaranteeing the same, being circumscribed in its powers only by the provisions of such Constitution. The effect of petitioner's contention is that any attempt on the part of the state to enact and enforce a law which may be in conflict with any provision of the national Constitution is not void because in conflict or inconsistent with the special provision violated, but because it deprives the state of its republican form of government, and this seems to be the character of reasoning adopted by the majority in People v. Johnson, 34 Colo. 143, to which we are cited as sustaining petitioner's view. In that case the question was whether the consolidation of the city and county of Denver, the boundaries of which were made coterminous, abolished the city government, as distinguished from county government, thereby giving to such organization home rule to the extent of permitting it to do as the constitutional amendment of 1902 provided might be done — enact all local laws, and elect such officers at such times as deemed advisable, concerning which it was held by the majority that the city and county governments, although covering the same territory, remained separate and distinct, requiring different officers to be selected for each, and in a different manner, as before the change. The reason for the conclusion appears to be on account of other provisions in the Constitution of Colorado, the majority not recognizing the rule invoked without exception in all other jurisdictions, including ours, that Constitutions with amendments must be construed as a whole, and that when two constructions are possible, one of which takes away the meaning of a section, and another giving effect to all the provisions, the latter must prevail. State v. Cochrane, 105 Pac. 884; Farrell, v. Port of Portland, 52 Or. 582, 98 Pac. 145. In an able and exhaustive dissenting opinion in that case by Mr. Justice Steele, concurred in by Mr. Justice Gunter, it is made clear that a federal question (such as here presented) was not involved; that the 1902 amendment of Colorado's Constitution was not inconsistent with section 4, art. 4, of the federal Constitution. After demonstrating that the conclusion announced by the majority "overlooks the fundamental rule in the construction of Constitutions and statutes that a special provision controls the general one and that both may stand . . ." (People ex rel. Atty. Gen. v. Johnson, 34 Colo. 189, 193, 86 Pac. 233, 249), at the close of his opinion (page 193) it is observed: "Wherever the question has been presented, the courts have given effect to the wishes of the people and sustained the power to establish the form of government here provided as not being in violation of the federal Constitution, and not in excess of the powers of the people to so provide in their organic law. And it is to be regretted that this court felt in duty bound to undo the work of the charter convention and to deny the people of this city and county the right to provide for a simple and economical plan of government as directed by the Constitution." Our holding is that the state may, by constitutional provisions, directly delegate to municipalities any powers which it, through the Legislature, could formerly have granted indirectly. All the prerogatives attempted to be exercised by Portland in the construction of the Broadway bridge formerly could have been granted by the Legislature, and the power to provide therefor, having been delegated to the city by amendment to our organic laws, is valid, and the right to exercise such powers will continue until such time as changed by general enactments of the law-making department of our state, provision for which may be made by the Legislature by general laws, applying alike to all municipalities of that class, or by the people through the initiative, by the enactment of either general or special laws on the subject. Cooley, Const. Lim. (6th Ed.) 41, 45; Hopkins v. Duluth, 81 Minn. 189, 83 N. W. 536; In re Pfahler, 150 Cal. 71, 88 Pac. 270, 11 L. R. A. (N. S.) 1092; Ex parte Wagner, 21 Okl. 33, 95 Pac. 435; State v. Field, 99 Mo. 352, 12 S. W. 802; Kansas v. Marsh, 140 Mo. 458, 41 S. W. 943; Kadderly v. Portland, 44 Or. 118, 74 Pac. 710, 75 Pac. 222; State v. Pacific States Tel. & Tel. Co., 53 Or. 163, 99 Pac. 427; Straw v. Harris, 54 Or. 424, 103 Pac. 777; City of McMinnville v. Hownestine, 109 Pac. 81.

In a public address prepared by Hon. Frederick V. Holman, attached to and filed as an appendix to petitioner's brief, it is argued that our previous holding in Hall v. Dunn, 52 Or. 475, 97 Pac. 811, 25 L. R. A. (N. S.) 193, and Straw v. Harris, 54 Or. 424, 103 Pac. 777, to the effect that we have but one law-making department, composed of two separate and distinct law-making bodies — (1) The people, acting directly through the initiative; and (2) the people acting indirectly through the Legislature — either of which in a manner provided by law may undo the work of the other, and necessarily must lead to disastrous results, etc., in that an act passed by the first may immediately on the convening of the Legislature be repealed, and one enacted by the legislative assembly may also be rescinded through either the initiative or the referendum. But that objection applies only to the question of expediency, with regard to which the lawmakers, and not the courts, are concerned. It might not be inappropriate, however, to observe that the same objection may with equal force apply to all legislative bodies. Our Legislature to convene next week can, if it so chooses, repeal all the laws (not included in constitutional amendments) enacted at the recent November election, and also undo the work of the last legislative assembly. Again, two years later or earlier a special session of the Legislature might be called, and enact many laws, and the day following its adjournment the newly elected Legislature could be convened and repeal all the laws going into effect the preceding day. The same may also be said of Congress, but this is seldom, if ever, urged as an argument against a representative system, or alluded to as indicating that our government is becoming unrepublican in form. In the appendix mentioned, it is observed that under our system, as interpreted by this court, we have four legislative bodies in place of two: (1) The Legislature; (2) the people of the whole state; (3) the people of a municipality; (4) the common council or commissioners. This suggestion, however, overlooks the fact that in the above-cited cases advertence was made only to legal departments of the state, and not to municipal or other minor and quasi legislative bodies. The fallacy of this illustration (like many others to which our attention is directed, and which will not be specifically discussed) is obvious. The observation to the effect that under the interpretation given by this court to the charter amendments cities may invade the domain of state legislation to the extent, if desired, of condemning state property (such as capitol buildings, etc.) has no justification, either in the language of the charter amendments, or in anything said in any opinion of this court in interpreting such amendments. Many of the statements in our former opinions bearing upon points here presented are adverted to as dictum, and like contention is also made respecting our holding in the case at hand, to the effect that it is unnecessary to obtain the consent of the Port of Portland before the bridge in question may be constructed. The points decided, determining the status of the Port of Portland in the matter, were all forcibly presented in the briefs and at the oral argument, and the effect of the conclusion reached by this court was that, taking either horn of the dilemma, appellant's position is untenable. It cannot, therefore, be said that our views upon either point are dicta, and the same may be remarked of much, if not all, of the numerous like references to previous adjudications by this court (as in Straw *v.* Harris and other cases) in which the views alluded to as dicta hold adversely to the wishes and contention of the writers of petitioner's brief, and the appendix thereto. On what is dicta and the effect thereof see Kirby *v.* Boyette, 118 N. C. 244, 254, 24 S. E. 18; Buchner *v.* C. M. & N. W. Ry. Co., 60 Wis. 264, 19 N. W. 56; Kane *v.* McCown, 55 Mo. 181; Ocean Beach Ass'n *v.* Brinley, 34 N. J. Eq. 438; 26 Am. & Eng. Ency. L., 165, 171; Florida Cent. Ry. Co. *v.* Schutte, 103 U. S. 118, 143, 26 L. Ed. 327. The terms "Obiter dicta," "dictum," etc., like the phrase "technicalities of the law," are too often invoked by counsel to express disapprobation of some proposition of law militating against their contention.

Numerous other points are presented upon which the views of this court are requested. Some of them, however, were disposed of in our former opinions herein, to which we still adhere, and those remaining, even though not specifically adverted to, are included in the above considerations.

The petition for rehearing is denied.

XXXV. Ex parte WAGNER

(95 Pacific Reporter, 435)

Supreme Court of Oklahoma. April 27, 1908.

1. CONSTITUTIONAL LAW — INITIATIVE AND REFERENDUM.

The initiative and referendum provisions in the Constitution (article 5, §§ 1, 2, 3, 4, 5, and article 18, §§ 4, 5) are not in conflict with the Constitution of the United States (section 4, art. 4) guaranteeing to every state a republican form of government.

2. SAME — ENFORCEMENT OF PROVISIONS.

Said provisions as contained therein are not self-executing, but are made effective by an act of the Legislature approved April 16, 1908.

3. MUNICIPAL CORPORATIONS — ORDINANCES — PETITION FOR REFERENDUM.

Until said provisions were made effective by legislation, a petition for a referendum filed with the chief executive officer of a municipality of the first class was of no effect.

4. HABEAS CORPUS — VIOLATION OF ORDINANCE — PETITION FOR REFERENDUM.

An ordinance having been passed and published, and thereafter a petition for referendum filed, with the mayor of Kingfisher, and afterwards said relator being convicted in said municipal court for an alleged violation after the filing of said petition, he is not entitled to be discharged from said conviction.

(Syllabus by the Court.)

Application of C. L. Wagner for a writ of habeas corpus. Writ denied.

On December 5, 1907, the mayor and council of the city of Kingfisher, Okl., passed an ordinance, No. 118, entitled "An ordinance providing for a levy and collection of a license tax on certain trades, occupations, callings, businesses and avocations, and regulating the same and providing penalties for violations thereof." The ordinance provided for the punishment of persons engaged in business without having paid a license tax as prescribed by said ordinance. On December 12, 1907, the ordinance was published in the official organ of said city. On December 18, 1907, a petition signed by 25 per cent of the qualified voters of said city, demanding a referendum vote on said ordinance, and requesting that same be held in abeyance until such election was held at which said ordinance could be voted upon and approved or rejected by the electors of said city, was filed with the mayor thereof. On December 20, 1907, relator, C. L. Wagner, was tried and found guilty of violating said ordinance, and adjudged to pay a fine and costs of the action. The relator refused to pay the fine, and for that reason was committed to the city jail by the respondent, George H. Brown, the marshal of said city, under a commitment issued by the police court on the judgment rendered against said relator. The relator alleges in his petition that ever since that date he has been restrained of his liberty under said commitment. Thereafter, on the 2d day of January, 1908, application was made to this court for a writ of habeas corpus for the purpose of determining whether or not he was lawfully restrained of his liberty, and the same was issued on said date, made returnable on the 11th day of January, 1908. The ordinance was in due form, and there is no allegation against its validity, but the contention is that by virtue of said petition filed for a referendum vote that the same was held in abeyance until the next city election. George H. Brown, marshal of said city, as respondent, made his return to said writ, showing that he held the relator under a commitment issued by the police court of said city on a judgment of conviction for the violation of said ordinance. The facts as heretofore set out were admitted on a hearing of this cause.

C. G. Horner and P. S. Nagle, for relator.

John T. Bradley, Jr., for respondent.

WILLIAMS, C. J. (after stating the facts as above). The question raised in this case is whether or not a petition demanding a referendum vote upon an ordinance duly passed by a city of the first class after the same had taken effect and was in force, such demand having been presented to and filed with the chief executive officer of such city after such ordinance had been published, suspends the force and effect of said ordinance until the next municipal election. Of course, the question necessarily arises as to whether or not the different sections in the Constitution providing for the initiative and referendum are valid, and were in force and effect or self-executing on the 18th day of December, A.D. 1907, the date on which the petition demanding a referendum on said ordinance was filed with the mayor of the city of Kingfisher. The initiative and referendum provisions, relating, not only to the affairs of the state, but also to counties and cities, are taken substantially from the Constitution of Oregon. The Supreme Court of that state, in the case of Kadderley v. Portland, 44 Or. 119, 74 Pac. 720, 75 Pac. 222, has held that the same are not in conflict with section 4, art. 4, Const. U. S., guaranteeing to every state a republican form of government.

The next question is: Were said provisions self-executing on the 18th day of December, A.D. 1907? The Supreme Court of Oregon, in the case of Stevens v. Benson (Or.), 91 Pac. 577, held that the initiative and referendum provisions as contained in the Oregon Constitution were self executing. The only difference between the provisions in that Constitution and those of this state is that in the former it is provided that, in submitting such petitions to the people, the Secretary of State and all other officers shall be guided by the general laws and the act submitting the initiative and referendum amendment to the people for adoption or rejection until legislation shall be especially provided therefor — clearly indicating that it was the intention in adopting the Oregon amendment that the same should then and there become self-executing. This clause does not appear in the Oklahoma Constitution. Substantially such provision was contained therein prior to the time that the constitutional convention reassembled after the proposed Constitution had been provided to be submitted to the people for adoption or rejection. When the convention reconvened, in order to obviate any possible objection that might be made by the President of the United States to the same, wherein it was required by section 4, art. 4, Const. U. S., and the terms of the enabling act (Act June 16, 1906, c. 3335, 34 St. 267) to be republican in form, and not in conflict with the provisions of said act, that part was eliminated, leaving it to the Legislature to carry same into effect. There was undoubted wisdom and precaution in that act. If the enemies of the principle of the initiative and referendum in popular government had been able to convince the department of justice of the federal government that such provisions of the initiative, and referendum, when adopted by a state, rendered such state government unrepublican in form, still it remained that until the Legislature acted that the principle was not self-executing in the Oklahoma Constitution. And, until the Legislature enacted measures carrying it into effect, the federal government had less right or reason to complain, and that was one of the reasons for such action assigned at the time; for, if that contention against the provisions of the Constitution or to the initiative and referendum had been sustained, yet, as the same were not self-executing in that Constitution, reason and consideration of the rights of the people of the proposed state should certainly have impelled the promulgation of the proclamation of the admission of the state into the Union. For, when the act of Legislature had been passed carrying same into effect, then the question could in due and proper time have been raised that such act was in conflict with section 4, art. 4, Const. U. S., and been declared void, and by such course preserved the supremacy of the Constitution of the United States, and at the same time vouchsafe the right of local self-government to over one million of citizens.

The Legislature, carrying out the intention of the constitutional convention with commendable fidelity, have enacted what is known as House Bill No. 174, entitled "An act to carry into effect the initiative and referendum powers reserved by the people in articles 5 and 18 of the Constitution of the state of Oklahoma, to regulate elections thereunder, and to punish violations thereof," which was approved by the Governor on the 16th day of April, A.D. 1908, thereby making absolutely complete and effective said provisions of said Constitution. See Reg. Sess. Laws Or. 1903, p. 244; Sess. Laws Or. 1907, p. 398. This is a very comprehensive act, providing fully for the forms of petition, both initiative and referendum, and for review of the action of the Secretary of State by the Supreme Court, whose judgment shall be final and binding upon such officer, and provisions in detail are contained for the holding of such election. Sections 17, 18, and 19 of the same act relate to municipalities. In said section 17 it is provided that in all cities, counties, and other municipalities which do not provide by ordinance or charter for the manner of exercising the initiative and referendum powers reserved by the Constitution to the whole people thereof, as to their municipal legislation, the duties required of the Governor and Secretary of State by this act, as to state legislation, shall be performed as to such municipal legislation by the chief executive and the chief clerk of such municipality; and the duties required in this act of the Attorney General shall be performed by the attorney for the county, district, or other municipality.

In the case of Taylor *v.* Hutchinson et al., 145 Ala. 207, 40 South, 109, the court says: —

"Our Constitution contains many instances of non-self-executing provisions. In these cases there is always some indication that something is left for the Legislature to do, or there is something in the nature of the provision that renders such legislation necessary."

In the case of Willis *v.* Mabon, 48 Minn. 140, 50 N. W. 1110, 16 L. R. A. 281, 31 Am. St. Rep. 626, discussing the question as to whether or not a provision of the Constitution of that state was self-executing, the court said: —

"The question in every case is whether the language of a constitutional provision is addressed to the courts or to the Legislature. Does it indicate that it was intended as a present enactment, complete in itself as definite legislation, or does it contemplate subsequent legislation to carry it into effect? This is to be determined both from a consideration of the language used and of the intrinsic nature of the provision itself. If the nature and extent of the right conferred and of the liability imposed is fixed by the provision itself, so that they can be determined by examination and construction of its own terms, and there is no language used indicating that the subject is referred to the Legislature for action, then the provision should be construed as self-executing."

See, also, Acme Dairy v. City of Astoria (Or.), 90 Pac. 153; Swift & Co. v. City of Newport News, 105 Va. 108, 52 S. E. 821, 3 L. R. A. (N. S.) 404; Logan et al. v. Parish of Ouachita, 105 La. 499, 29 South, 975. Section 3, art. 5, Const. (Bunn's Ed. § 55), relating to the initiative and referendum provision, provides that "The Legislature shall make suitable provision for carrying into effect the provisions of this article." This especially indicates that it was not the intention of the constitutional convention that said articles should become effective until made so by act of the Legislature. In determining whether or not a provision of the Constitution is self-executing, we would consider the language in the light of the surrounding circumstances and conditions under which it was adopted, with a view of ascertaining the intention of the parties framing it. We accordingly conclude that on the 18th day of December, A.D. 1907, the provisions in our Constitution relating to the initiative and referendum were not self-executing, and that they did not become effective until the 16th day of April, A.D. 1908, when the act of the Legislature heretofore referred to was approved by the Governor of the state.

It is evident that if the provisions of article 5, relating to the initiative and referendum, were not self-executing on December 18, 1907, that section 4, art. 18, was also not self-executing, and it results as a matter of course that the petition demanding a referendum vote on the ordinance, filed with the mayor of the city of

Kingfisher on the 18th day of December, A.D. 1907, was without effect, and did not operate to supersede or suspend any ordinance. The fact that since that date the Legislature of this state has enacted a comprehensive and valid law carrying into effect all of the provisions of the initiative and referendum as reserved and contained in the Constitution could not give any validity to such petition as that would have a retroactive effect or in the nature of an ex post facto law. Hence it is not necessary, in order properly to dispose of this case, to determine whether or not, after a city or municipality passes an ordinance and it becomes effective, a petition demanding the referendum on such ordinance thereafter being filed with the proper officer, in accordance with the charter or ordinance of said city, or with the general laws of the state, would have the effect to supersede or suspend the operation of such ordinance until the next municipal election. That question is not now properly before this court for determination; it being admitted that the ordinance under which this relator was prosecuted was properly enacted and published and otherwise valid. The only question before this court now is whether or not the demand for the referendum on such ordinance had the effect to supersede or suspend said ordinance. Having reached the conclusion that at the time such ordinance was passed and published the provisions in the Constitution relating to the initiative and referendum not being self-executing, although the same have since then been carried into effect by legislation, would not entitle the relator to the relief prayed for.

Writ of habeas corpus denied.

TURNER and DUNN, J. J., concur. KANE and HAYES, J. J., concur in the conclusion denying the writ.

XXXVI. BONNER *v.* BELSTERLING (138 Southwestern Reporter, 571)

(Supreme Court of Texas. June 23, 1911)

1. MUNICIPAL CORPORATIONS (§ 154[1]) — OFFICERS — "REMOVED" — RECALL.

A recall is a method of removal of officers, within Dallas city charter, providing that elective officers may be "removed" in a manner therein provided.

[Ed. Note. — For other cases, see Municipal Corporations, Cent. Dig. § 350; Dec. Dig. § 154.[1]

For other definitions, see Words and Phrases, vol. 7, pp. 6078-6081; vol. 8, p. 7784.]

2. MUNICIPAL CORPORATIONS (§ 211[1]) — MUNICIPAL OFFICERS — BOARD OF EDUCATION — REMOVAL.

The members of the board of education of the city of Dallas, created by the charter placing the control of the city public schools in a board of education, composed of a president and six members, who shall be elected and hold their office for a specified term and until their successors are elected and qualified, are officers of the city, and are not within Const. art. 5, § 24, authorizing the judges of the district court to remove enumerated county officers and other county officers and the Legislature may provide for the removal of the members of the board otherwise than by the judges of the district court.

[Ed. Note. — For other cases, see Municipal Corporations, Cent. Dig. §§ 567-570; Dec. Dig. § 211.[1]]

3. STATES (§ 1[1]) — MUNICIPAL CORPORATIONS (§ 64[1]) — REPUBLICAN FORM OF GOVERNMENT — GOVERNMENT OF CITIES.

Except as limited by the federal Constitution, the people of Texas may adopt any form of government, and, subject to the limitations of the federal and state Constitutions, the Legislature may confer on any municipality any power that it may see fit to give.

[Ed. Note. — For other cases, see States, Cent. Dig. § 1; Dec. Dig. § 1;[1] Municipal Corporations, Cent. Dig. §§ 156, 157; Dec. Dig. § 64.[1]]

---

[1] For other cases, see same topic and section number in Dec. Dig. & Am. Dig. Key No. Series & Rep'r. Indexes.

4. STATES (§ 4¹) — MUNICIPAL CORPORATIONS (§ 64¹) — RE-
"PUBLICAN FORM OF GOVERNMENT" — RECALL PROVISION IN
MUNICIPAL CHARTER.

A recall provision in a city charter, vesting the powers of government in the people and constituting all inhabitants of the city a body politic, is not violative of the Const. U. S. art. 4, § 4, guaranteeing to every state a "republican form of government," which merely means a government by the citizens in mass, acting directly, and not personally, according to the rules established by the majority.

[Ed. Note. — For other cases, see States, Cent. Dig. § 2; Dec. Dig. § 4;¹ Municipal Corporations, Cent. Dig. §§ 156, 157; Dec. Dig. § 64.¹

For other definitions, see Words and Phrases, vol. 8, p. 7785.]

5. CONSTITUTIONAL LAW (§ 43¹) — DUE PROCESS OF LAW — REMOVAL OF OFFICERS.

A city officer elected subject to the recall provision in the charter may not urge that his removal from office by a recall deprives him of the benefit of his term of office without due process of law; he not securing the right to hold the office contrary to the wishes of the people electing him.

[Ed. Note. — For other cases, see Constitutional Law, Cent. Dig. § 41; Dec. Dig. § 43.¹]

6. MUNICIPAL CORPORATIONS (§ 67¹) — OFFICERS — TERM OF OFFICE — LEGISLATIVE POWER.

Under Const. art. 16, § 30, declaring that the duration of office, not fixed by the Constitution, shall never exceed two years, the Legislature in creating a municipality need not make the term of office two years, but it may fix the term at any time not exceeding two years, and the Legislature may grant to the people of the municipality the right to remove by a recall any officer failing to discharge his duty in a manner satisfactory to the people of the municipality.

[Ed. Note. — For other cases, see Municipal Corporations, Cent. Dig. §§ 161–165; Dec. Dig. § 67.¹]

7. OFFICERS (§ 67¹) — REMOVAL — "OFFICERS OF THE STATE."

Const. art. 15, § 7, requiring the Legislature to provide for the trial and removal from office of all "officers of the state," when considered in connection with article 5, § 24, providing for the

---

[1] For other cases, see same topic and section number in Dec. Dig. & Am. Dig. Key No. Series & Rep'r. Indexes.

removal of county officers, relates only to state officers and does not prohibit the removal from office of an officer of a city by recall.

[Ed. Note. — For other cases, see Officers, Cent. Dig. §§ 161-165; Dec. Dig. § 67.]

Dibrell, J., dissenting.

Error from Court of Civil Appeals of Fifth Supreme Judicial District.

Actions by Shearon Bonner and by one Lefevre against E. L. Belsterling and others. There were judgments of the Court of Civil Appeals (137 S. W. 1154) affirming judgments for defendants in each case, and plaintiff in each case brings error. Affirmed.

Meador & Davis, A. B. Flanary, and E. G. Senter, for plaintiffs in error. Jas. J. Collins, Lee Richardson, and Lawther & Worsham, for defendants in error.

Brown, C. J. The city of Dallas has a population exceeding 10,000 and by special act of the Thirtieth Legislature of Texas (Sp. Acts 1907, c. 71), and by the amendment of its charter by the Thirty-First Legislature (Sp. Acts 1909, c. 93; Sp. Acts 1909 [2d Called Sess.] c. 14), it was created a municipal corporation. Section 1 of article 5 of the charter provides for a board of education in this language: —

"The city public schools shall be under the management and control of a board of education, composed of a president and six members, who shall be elected on the first Tuesday of April, 1908, and at a regular election to be held biennially thereafter on the first Tuesday of April, and shall hold their offices for two years and until their successors are elected and qualified. Any vacancy occurring in the board of education shall be filled by an election to be held by said board, and the person elected shall hold office for the unexpired term. The members of said board shall serve without compensation, shall have exclusive control of the public schools of the city of Dallas, and shall have full and ample authority, in accordance with the provisions hereof, to provide necessary school buildings and facilities, and to open and conduct a sufficient number of schools to meet the wants of the scholastic population of the city of Dallas, so far as they can do so by prudent and judicious application of the means made subject to their administration and management. Among the powers hereby conferred on said board of education, the following are for greater certainty enumerated: To contract for, lease and purchase lots, and to construct buildings for school purposes, and to make all needed repairs and alterations in same; to furnish said school buildings with all appropriate furniture, fixtures and apparatus; to sell or dispose of school property when the same is necessary or advisable; to lay off the city into such school districts as, in the judgment of the said board, shall be proper; to increase or diminish said districts, and to change the boundaries thereof at pleasure; to employ superintendents, teachers and such other persons as may be necessary, and to fix their compensation and prescribe their duties, and to establish all such regulations and rules deemed necessary by the board to provide and maintain an efficient system of public schools in the city of Dallas. The board of commissioners, when levying the annual tax for the fiscal year, shall levy an ad valorem tax of one-fourth of one per centum of the taxable value of the city of Dallas for that fiscal year, and said tax, when collected, shall be deposited with the city treasurer by the board of commissioners to the credit of the school fund, which said sum, together with all sums received from the state, county and other school funds, shall be held by the city treasurer subject to the order and disbursement of the board of education, and shall be paid out upon warrants issued by order of said board of education, audited by the city auditor and signed by the president and secretary of the board of education."

Article 9 of the charter provides: "The holder of an elective office may be removed at any time by the qualified voters of the city of Dallas. The procedure to effect the removal of an incumbent of an elective office shall be as follows: A petition signed by the qualified voters of said city, equal in number to at least 35 per cent of the entire vote cast for candidates for the office of mayor on the final ballot at the last preceding general municipal election, demanding the election of a successor of the person sought to be removed, shall be filed with the city secretary; provided, that the petition sent to the board of commissioners shall contain a general statement of the grounds for which removal is sought."

It is conceded that the recall election was conducted according to the charter, and it is therefore unnecessary to copy that portion which prescribes the manner of proceedings in such elections.

After the enactment of the charter and the amendment thereof, to wit, on the 5th day of April, 1910, an election was held under the terms of the charter for members of the board of education, and C. C. Lane was elected president; H. D. Audrey, Robert N. Watkin, Shearon Bonner, petitioner herein, L. K. Wright, John W. George, and John C. Mann were elected members of the said board, all of whom were duly installed according to the requirements of the law. On the 11th day of August, 1910, another election was held, and John W. George and J. C. Mann were removed from the said board, and J. D. Carter and J. B. McCraw were elected and installed as such, and thereafter, on the 4th day of April, 1911, there was another recall election held under and in compliance with the provisions of article 9 of the city charter, at which E. A. Belsterling was elected president, and J. D. Carter, John B. McCraw, M. A. Turner, W. A. Goode, and Frank Gilbert were chosen as members of the board of education to succeed those previously named, including the plaintiff Shearon Bonner.

Shearon Bonner instituted this suit against the appellees in the district court of Dallas county for the purpose of obtaining restoration to the office from which he had been removed by the recall, and also to obtain a mandatory injunction requiring the parties who were elected at the recall election to surrender their said offices. The judge of the district court sustained a general demurrer to the petition and dismissed the case, which judgment was affirmed by the Court of Civil Appeals of the Fifth district.

Counsel for the plaintiff in error assert that the recall provision of the charter of the city of Dallas is violative of the Constitution of the United States in many respects, and that it is also violative of the Constitution of the state of Texas in 15 particulars. We do not feel called upon to discuss separately each of the objections made to the validity of the charter. We have examined each one of them sufficiently to satisfy ourselves that they are not of sufficient importance to require a separate discussion; therefore we overrule such as are not distinctly treated in this opinion.

It is claimed that the recall is a method of removing the officers of the city of Dallas, and is violative of article 5, § 24, of the state Constitution, which reads as follows: "County judges, county attorneys, clerks of the district and county courts, justices of the peace, constables, and other county officers, may be removed by the judges of the district court for incompetency, official misconduct, habitual drunkenness, or other causes defined by law, upon the cause therefor being set forth in writing, and the finding of its truth by a jury."

[1] It is claimed that the members of the board of education of the city of Dallas are county officers, and that they are therefore embraced within the article of the Constitution above copied, and cannot be removed in the manner attempted. The language of article 9 of the charter distinctly says that all elective officers may be "removed" in the manner therein provided. We are of opinion that the recall is a method of removal, and, so regarding it, we will proceed to inquire whether the officers involved in this proceeding come within the provision of the Constitution above copied. If they are within the designation, "other county officers," the proceeding for removal provided by the Constitution might be held to be exclusive, and that the Legislature could not authorize such removal by the recall method, but it is not necessary to decide that question.

In Hendricks *v.* State, 20 Tex. Civ. App. 178, 49 S. W. 705, the Court of Civil Appeals for the First district held that a trustee of a school district was an officer of the county, within the meaning of section 24 of article 5 of the state Constitution, and subject to removal by the district court. In that case the district was a subdivision of a county, and the trustee derived his authority solely from the general law which applied to the county. He was therefore an officer in the county and of the county in the same sense as was a justice of the peace. The court properly held that he was subject to removal under the article above stated.

In Kimbrough v. Barnett, 93 Tex. 301, 55 S. W. 120, this court answered the following question, which was certified to it by the Court of Civil Appeals of the First district, "Is the position of superintendent of the public schools of the city of Houston an office for which a suit may be maintained in the district court?" To that question this court answered as follows: "We answer the first question in the affirmative. The position of superintendent of the free schools in the city of Houston is an office, and the lawful incumbent of it would have a right of action to recover it or its emoluments in case he was unlawfully deprived of the benefit. State v. Catlin, 84 Tex. 48 [19 S. W. 302]." It will be observed that the question to be answered embraced only one proposition; that is, Was the position of superintendent of public schools of the city of Houston an office for which suit might be maintained in the district court? The answer which is copied above fully and completely answered that question, and in the course of the discussion this court said: "We think there can be no doubt that a school trustee of an independent school district in this state is a county officer, as was held in the case of Hendricks v. State, 20 Tex. Civ. App. 178 [49 S. W. 705]."

[2] The board of education of the city of Dallas was created and its powers and duties prescribed by article 5 of the chapter of the said city hereinbefore copied. The board derives its existence and all of the authority it possesses from the charter, which operates only within the limits of the city. By the provisions of the charter, the board had entire control of the school fund and of the property; in fact, of everything pertaining

thereto. The auditor of the city is required to pass upon all accounts of the said board, and no act of the board has any reference whatever to the county or its officers. The relation of the board of education to the county is only incidental to its being a part of the system of free schools of the state. We therefore conclude that the members of the board of education are officers of the city of Dallas, and not of the county of Dallas. Gertum v. Board of Officers, 109 N. Y. 174, 16 N. E. 328; Throop on Public Officers, § 27. The members of the board of education being of the city were not within the terms of article 5, § 24, of the Constitution, and it was within the power of the Legislature to provide for their removal otherwise than by the judge of a district court.

[3] Except as limited by the Constitution of the United States, the people of Texas have the right to adopt any form of government which they may prefer, and, subject to the same limitations and such limitations as may be found in the state Constitution, the Legislature may confer upon any municipal government any power that it may see fit to give. Brown v. City of Galveston, 97 Tex. 1, 75 S. W. 488; Telegraph & Telephone Co. v. Dallas, 134 S. W. 321.

[4] But is is claimed that the recall provision of the city of Dallas is a violation of article 4, § 4, of the Constitution of the United States, which we here copy: "The United States shall guarantee to every state in this Union a republican form of government."

Counsel for the defendants in error have made an exhaustive research for authorities upon this question, and by the citations in their admirable brief have made the examination of the question comparatively easy.

As to the meaning of the phrase, "Republican form of government," there is no better authority than Mr. Jefferson, who, in discussing the matter, said: "Indeed, it must be acknowledged that the term 'republic' is of very vague application in every language. Were I to assign to this term a precise and definite idea, I would say, purely and simply, it means a government by its citizens in mass, acting directly and not personally, according to rules established by the majority; and that every other government is more or less republican in proportion as it has in its composition more or less of this ingredient of the direct action of the citizens. . . . On this view of the import of the term 'republic,' instead of saying, as has been said, that it may mean anything or nothing, we may say with truth and meaning that governments are more or less republican as they have more or less of the element of popular election and control in their composition; and believing, as I do, that the mass of the citizens is the safest depository of their own rights, and especially that the evils flowing from the duperies of the people are less injurious than those from the egotism of their agents, I am a friend to that composition of government which has in it the most of this ingredient."

We could quote and cite any number of authorities, using the brief of the learned counsel for the defendants in error, but we deem it unnecessary to multiply them, and will proceed to examine the provisions of the charter with a view of determining if it fulfills the definition given by Mr. Jefferson; and, if it does, it is not obnoxious to the provisions of the federal Constitution as above quoted.

In the charter of the city of Dallas, all of the powers of government — that is, the sovereignty of the municipality — are vested in the people, which powers are exercised by representatives of the people; that is, officers elected by the voters. The charter of the city of Dallas vests the power of government in the people by these words: "Section 1. Corporate Name. All inhabitants of the city of Dallas, Dallas county, Texas, as the boundaries and limits of said city are herein established or may be hereafter established, shall be a body politic, incorporated under, and to be known by, the name and style of the 'City of Dallas,' with such powers, rights and duties as herein provided."

It will be observed that the people who reside within the described limits of the city of Dallas constitute the city, and to them is intrusted the powers of government. The sovereignty of the municipal government, its powers by which its affairs are conducted, are vested in the masses of the people, just as is required to constitute a republican form of government, and the other requirements to fulfill the definition are met in the charter by the several provisions for the election of officers named therein. That the city of Dallas is strictly republican in form of government is not questioned, if the recall be eliminated. But it is said that with the recall provision, it ceases to be republican. How this can be is not made plain to us. With the recall provision in the charter, the people are still invested with the sovereign power of the municipality, and they are intrusted with the selection of their representatives, who are to administer the city government. It occurs to us that there is a greater degree of sovereignty with the people with the recall of their representatives than would otherwise be the case; in fact, the right of recall asserts in a larger degree the right of representation; that is, representation in fact of the will and wishes of the voters. This enlargement of the control of the masses does not make the government less republican.

The policy of reserving to the people such power as the recall, the initiative, and the referendum is a question for the people themselves in framing the government, or for the Legislature in the creation of municipal governments. It is not for the courts to decide that question. We are unable to see from our viewpoint how it can be that a larger measure of sovereignty, committed to the people by this method of government, and a more certain means of securing a proper representation in any way militates against its character as a republican form of government, and that it is thereby rendered in any sense obnoxious to the provision of the Constitution of the United States.

[5] Article 16, § 30, of the state Constitution reads: "The duration of all offices not fixed by the Constitution shall never exceed two years," etc. It is claimed that the recall by the citizenship

of a city deprives the officer of the benefit of his term of office without due process of law. If the officer had been elected to the office and the law were changed subsequently, there might be some ground for making such an argument, but in this case the law provided for the recall at the time the plaintiff in error was elected to his office, and he took it upon the condition that the people might remove him from office, and he cannot now be heard to say that he had been deprived of his office without due process of law, for, in fact, the proceeding is just what he contracted for when he accepted the office. It seems to be in the mind of some of the counsel that an officer has some kind of secured right to hold an office contrary to the will and wishes of the people he represents, but we are of opinion that he has no more right, as a matter of good morals, to hold such office under such circumstances than any employé or agent has to continue in the discharge of his duty for which he has been employed when he ceases to give satisfaction, except that under the Constitution and laws as they have heretofore existed in this state such an officer could not be removed upon a failure on his part to give satisfaction in the discharge of his duties, but must be guilty of some offense to justify the removal under the constitutional provisions which are in effect in this state.

[6] In the creation of the municipal corporation, the Legislature was not bound to make the term of office two years; it might have made it to extend to any time not exceeding two years; and we conclude what we have to say in expressing the view again, that we have so frequently stated, that the people of the city of Dallas were invested with the sovereign power of the city by virtue of the grant of the charter to them, and that the Legislature has the power to grant to them the right to remove, by process of the recall provision, any officer who failed to discharge his duty in a manner satisfatory to the people of that city.

[7] Section 7, art. 15, of the Constitution, reads: "The Legislature shall provide by law for the trial and removal from office

of all officers of this state, the modes for which have not been provided in this Constitution." It is objected that the removal by recall is violative of that section, because it does not provide for a trial of the officer. The section applies only to "officers of the state." In the connection in which it is used, the language must be held to refer to the class of officers treated of in that section, but omitted therefrom. We are of opinion that "officers of the state" have the same signification as "state officer." In article 5, § 24, the removal of all county officers had been provided for, and the language of section 7 of article 15 had the effect to include all state officers not included in that article. The objection is not sound, and is overruled.

The facts and questions of law are practically the same in cause No. 2,295, Lefevre *v.* Belsterling, this day decided, and this opinion applies to both cases.

It is ordered that the judgments of the district court and Court of Civil Appeals in each case be affirmed.

DIBRELL, J. I regret that I am not able to agree with a majority of the court in their disposition of this case, but, on account of the fact that the court is on the eve of adjournment, I will not have time to express my views on the questions involved. I consider the questions presented in this case of great importance, calling for a construction of more than one provision of the Constitution of this state, and affecting the form of our government.

I will reduce to writing my views for this dissent, and file later on.

VI. APPENDIX

THE PROPOSED OREGON SYSTEM[1]

[The following is a draft of a plan for a reform in the government of Oregon prepared by Mr. W. S. U'Ren and a group of Oregon citizens.]

There are 47 boards and commissions created to enforce the laws and manage the business of the State of Oregon. In addition to these we have the governor, secretary of state, state treasurer, superintendent of instruction, state printer, attorney-general, commissioner of labor, 34 sheriffs, unknown numbers of deputies, police, and constables, 11 district attorneys and 37 deputies. Every one is in a great degree independent of all others and of everybody else.

There is no one officer who is responsible to the people of the State for the enforcement of the state laws and the efficient management of the state business. The constitution says that the governor "shall take care that the laws of the State be faithfully executed," but gives him no power beyond that of making recommendations. No successful private business is conducted so carelessly as American public business and it is generally admitted that the state and county governments are seldom successful either in enforcing the laws or giving the taxpayers good value for their money.

At some general elections in Oregon the voters must choose from 20 to 39 officers. The number varies in different counties and districts and at different elections. The offices range in importance from county surveyor to governor and United States Senator. The usual number of candidates varies from about 80 to 170. In such a crowd is it any wonder that many grafters and incompetents are elected? The average citizen is compelled to vote according to his party brand because he cannot possibly have knowledge of the unfit among so many candidates for so many offices.

The plan herein proposed contemplates the election of only the most important officers. After the general election in 1914 the lowest

---

[1] *Senate Document*, No. 603; 61st Cong., 2d Sess., pp. 145 ff.

number to be voted for by any elector at a general election would be 5, including United States Senator and Representatives in Congress, and the highest number at any general election would be 8; the subordinates, clerks, and other employees would be appointed by the chief officers so elected by the people.

The plan is criticised by some Americans, who say it is "equivalent to a monarchical form of government," in that it provides for appointment of the secretary of state, treasurer, and other cabinet officers, and of the sheriffs and district attorneys by the governor; also for the abolition of 46 of the 47 commissions now supposed to govern Oregon.

The President appoints the United States marshals and district attorneys; all the United States judges and officers of the Army and the Navy; the postmasters, local customs and internal-revenue collectors, and a host of others. Not counting soldiers and sailors, the President directly or indirectly appoints and controls more than 350,000 officers and employees of the United States.

Another says that the governor might build a political machine. That is as much as to say that the people of Oregon are too ignorant or too selfish for self-government.

Ten years ago the people of Oregon were in bondage to the political parties, bosses, and machines. It was commonly charged that nominations were bought from convention delegates, as well as elections from legislators. It was not denied that the highest offices were shamelessly sold for money and political favors. Within that ten years the citizens of Oregon have conquered from the political parties and bosses the power to make their constitution, laws, and ordinances; to directly nominate candidates for elective public office; to order a recall election and discharge any public officer. The people of the United States have none of these powers. It is unthinkable that the men of Oregon will submit to machine government or official tyranny. No punishment has been invented to fit the cowardly crime of men having these powers who would yet allow their public servants to rob them of liberty.

If the people of Oregon cannot protect their liberties with the direct powers they have, then, where is the boasted freedom of the American people? They have none of those great powers possessed by the voters of Oregon.

If the national plan of one elective chief executive would be bad for

Oregon, then the state plan ought to be good for the nation. How would it do to require the people to elect the United States marshals, the postmasters, the Secretary of War, the national Secretary of State, and all the other officers, and then make each one of them as independent of the President and of each other, as our sheriffs, district attorneys, state treasurer, secretary of state, and all our other state and county officers, are independent of the governor and of each other.

But the State of Oregon, besides its political duty to protect the life and liberty of every citizen, is also a great business corporation. Every citizen is a stockholder owning one share in the corporation of Oregon. The management of a private corporation is important to its stockholders because it controls a part of their property and is supposed to return them a cash dividend every year. But the government business corporation of Oregon in its various forms is of infinitely greater importance, because every year its officers take in taxes on average of about one thirty-third of all the property of all its citizens. The tax payment increases every year.

Under the present system the taxpayers get the maximum of politics and the minimum of business. The proposed plan is intended to produce the maximum of business and the minimum of politics for the public money. There has been little or no improvement in the business system of Oregon's state and county governments for fifty years past.

It is written that "there is safety in a multitude of counselors," and the people of Oregon have applied this principle by giving to every citizen an equal vote by the initiative and referendum in making or rejecting state and local laws. But no one has ever said there is victory in a multitude of generals, or business success in a crowd of general managers.

As to public business, "a crowd of general managers" is no dream. Every elected officer is practically a general manager in his own department. Every state institution buys its own supplies and keeps its own accounts. Most of the elected county officers buy the supplies for their offices; even the road supervisors are practically supreme in their districts, and in very many cases absorb more than half of the road tax for themselves and their familes and teams. Discussing this phase of the subject recently, a farmer said that our state and county governments are like a farm without a foreman, but with half a dozen hired men, each practically safe from discharge for two or four years, and every one doing as he pleases in his own department and getting good wages all the time, no matter how much the farm loses every year.

In all the forms of coöperation for the general welfare in business, when the stockholders and directors have made the rules or approved the plans, the execution is intrusted wholly to one man, the president or general manager of the corporation. When the pioneers were traveling across the plains, every train elected a wagon boss or captain, and so long as he held his office it was his sole duty to enforce the train rules, and he was intrusted with power sufficient for that purpose.

The President and Congress spent much time and money deciding on the kind of canal to be built and whether it should be at Panama or Nicaragua, but when their decision was made there was no question about whether one chief engineer or a dozen should have charge of the construction work.

Suppose the stockholders of the Southern Pacific Railroad should decide to run the railroad business by electing their president, general passenger agent, and other heads of departments, making each one supreme in his office and independent of all others, and make a complete change every four years like the people of Oregon do with nearly all their public officers and employees. When would the Southern Pacific stockholders get a dividend? When would the bondholders get their interest? Probably about as soon as the Oregon citizens will get low taxes and good roads under the present system of state and county governments.

It is not the fault of the public officers in Oregon. Most of them are honest and fairly competent. But the law does not organize them for "team work" for the common good. Faithful and competent work is no promise of promotion or of continuance in the public service, because the "system" nearly always turns them out after a two or four years' term.

But the Oregon citizen in his private business and private corporations organizes for intelligently directed "team work," and when he gets a first-class hired man keeps and promotes him as long as possible. The American citizen in his private business and corporation is among the most successful of men.

Why would it not be good to apply the principles of American private business to the business of American state and county government?

This plan centralizes the state executive power toward the people. If the governor proves unfit for his office, recall him. If the appropriations are extravagant, the governor and the people will be to blame, because he, or they, could have ordered the referendum if the legislature raised his estimates. If the state business is badly or wastefully managed, it will be the governor's fault, because he can remove the ignorant or extravagant officers. If the state laws are not faithfully executed, the governor will be responsible, because he will be able to appoint and can remove the sheriffs and district attorneys. And the governor can be discharged at any time by the people.

If the legislature is ignorant, vicious, or unfaithful, the voters will be able to discharge the whole body, or either house, or any guilty members.

If the county business is badly managed, one man will be responsible, the county business manager. If the plans for county business are not good, the voters of the county will be able to recall any or all of the county board of directors.

If the governor fails, or refuses to remove an insolent or unfaithful officer, the people of his district can discharge the officer and the people of the State can discharge the governor.

The people have struggled through the centuries for efficient methods as well as the right to govern themselves, but even the seers have not dreamed of a people's automatic government that would be always efficient, honest, and free. Eternal vigilance is the price of liberty, and American experience proves it is also the price of success for the taxpayers on the business side of the Government.

FURTHER EXPLANATION

The people of Oregon pay more than $8,500,000 in taxes every year. It is an average of more than $68 for every registered voter. For this we get state government, county government, city government, and schools. Do we pay too much for what we get? Nearly every one says we do, but why and where is the money wasted? No one knows, exactly. We have no people's inspectors of government; no regular examinations of public offices; no well-informed, unselfish, or non-partisan criticism of any department of the government; no plain, comprehensive system of brief reports delivered to our citizens. We do not have these things for any office or department of our state, county, or city governments. Could a railroad or any other great business corporation be run successfully in this slipshod manner?

The legislative assembly is often spoken of on the street and in the press as though it was a sort of public enemy. The courts are by no means free from criticism. Every department of our Government is commonly believed to be extravagant and wasteful in the use of public money. And yet, with all this complaint, the citizens and taxpayers have no authentic information; no exact knowledge, nor any practical means of informing themselves about the doings of their public officers. A remedy for this evil must be found and applied.

We hold that it would be economy for the taxpayers to furnish every registered voter, at frequent intervals and in readable form, the fullest possible authentic information concerning every office and every department of the state and local governments. Every voter should have knowledge and interest every day and all the time in his government; a great interest for three or four weeks of a "hot campaign" once in two or four years is not enough, because he cannot possibly inform himself in so short a time.

It is commonly believed that the average farmer and business man, and even the average private corporation, gets as much value in business for from 40 to 60 cents as our state and local governments get for $1. It is not unusual to hear a man of experience say, in speaking of the county, "I could take half the money and get better results if I could run it on business principles like I do my own affairs."

There is experience to justify this opinion. In the period from January to July, 1902, when the business that is now done by the county clerk's office in Multnomah County was done in three departments by an elected recorder of conveyances, an elected clerk of the circuit court, and an elected county clerk, the receipts were $13,968.50; expenses, $23,928.97. It cost $1.71 to do a dollar's worth of clerical work and get the money. In the period from January to June, 1908, with the three offices consolidated in one, the receipts were $31,355; the expenses were $20,200.51. It cost 64 cents for the county to do the work and get in one dollar under Mr. Field's management of the business of the three departments consolidated in one.

Multnomah County is getting more work for 38 cents than it used to get under the old system for $1. The direct nomination law, by elimination of the party bosses and of the machines, is in some degree responsible for the saving, but we believe it is in equal degree due to the concentration of executive responsibility and power in the hands of one man. Of course we do not overlook the fact that the county clerk is a very able man and thoroughly loyal to the public interest.

We believe the general principles of the executive department of our National Government furnish the best form yet devised for American use, and if applied to our state executive department, with some additions taken from the British plan, we think Oregon would get very much better results than from the present form.

Because the people of Oregon now have the initiative, the referendum, and the recall, and thereby have supreme, direct, and effective control over all their public servants and the making of all but the national laws, there need be no fear that executive officers can destroy or reduce our political rights and liberties. We can protect our liberties for ourselves.

AS TO PUBLIC INFORMATION. — We propose a board of three people's inspectors of government, to be elected by the people, and to be as nearly nonpartisan as judges of the supreme court. Let them edit an official gazette and mail it to every registered voter in the State. Let the gazette be devoted wholly to the science of government, but especially to its administration in the Oregon state and local governments. Let it publish the inspectors' reports on every department and office of the state and local governments, general reports of chief officers, letters from the people and the public servants and news of government in other states and nations. It would cost about 60 cents per year for each registered voter. It should not accept commercial advertising.

LEGISLATOR'S RIGHT TO QUESTION GOVERNOR AND CABINET. — Members of the legislature may question the governor and cabinet officers concerning any part of the administration of the government and execution of the laws. Answers must be given. This is the parliamentary practice, and one of the results is that our American legislative whitewashing investigation committees are practically unknown.

EMERGENCY AND REFERENDUM ON EMERGENCY MEASURES. — The legislative assembly has abused its power to repeal initiative laws and use the emergency clause on bills. Our amendment would require three-fourths of all the members elected to vote for the emergency clause on a roll call separate from the passage of the bill; it also allows the filing of a referendum petition against the bill; also a three-fourths vote to amend or repeal any measure approved by vote of the people; it also allows filing a referendum petition against a bill notwithstanding the emergency clause; in that case the bill would be in operation until the next regular general election, when, if the people should vote "no," the bill would be repealed. These new limitations on the power of the legislature apply also to city councils.

LOGROLLING. — We offer an amended oath of office pledging the members against the practice. An action is authorized by any ten citizen freeholders against any bill alleging that it was passed by logrolling, or secret methods, and if the jury renders a verdict that they believe from the evidence the bill was passed by such prohibited schemes and trades, it cannot take effect unless it is approved by referendum vote of the people at the next general election. The complaint must be filed in the court within ten days after the bill is passed.

The governor and his cabinet are given seats on the floor of both houses with the right to speak and introduce measures, and especially general appropriation bills for the maintenance of the state government and existing institutions. Very much of the logrolling is now centred about the appropriation bills. The foregoing, with the people's inspectors on duty in each house and reporting to the people; the open committee rooms; longer term of six years for members; the dissolution power in the hands of the people, and election of persons for speaker of the house and president of the senate who are not members, and whose principal duty and power is to preside, we believe ought to greatly reduce the evil of logrolling and trading votes.

HASTY LEGISLATION. — Another of the principal causes that justify criticism of the legislature is the hasty, crude, heedless, and unconsidered character of much of its work, especially the rush to pass bills in the last few days of the session. We think this evil will be greatly reduced by the following provisions: The long term of members with the experience thereby gained; the annual sessions; bills introduced after the tenth day of the session not to be passed at that session; the public committee meetings and hearings during the session as well as in the vacations, and written notice of meetings to every one who has notified the committee of a desire to be heard on the measure; the $10 deduction from any member's salary for every time he is not present at roll call.

ANNUAL SALARY FOR SENATORS AND REPRESENTATIVES. — The State should not permit any citizen to serve in any office without reasonable wages. It is now deprived of all opportunities for legislative services from many farmers, laborers, mechanics, school teachers, and others of Oregon's best and most thoughtful citizens. These men cannot aspire to the office of senator or representative without great sacrifices, because the wages are not sufficient to pay the legitimate and necessary expenses of the campaign and of living during the session. The wages should be sufficient to enable any person who earns $5 a day in his own business to serve and pay all necessary expenses and the wages of a substitute in his business at home, and have his own wages while he serves in the legislative work. For that reason we propose a salary of $350 a year.

NO GERRYMANDERING. — We propose a system of proportional representation of parties and independents in the election of members of the legislature, combining general local distribution of the nominations, with an accurate allotment to each political party of a number of members which bears the same proportion to the whole number of senators and representatives that the votes of the party bear to the whole number of votes cast in the State. The plan is equally fair to all independent candidates. If this system had been in operation at the general election in 1908, and each of the political parties had cast the same number of votes in the different counties for representative in the legislative assembly that were cast for representatives in Congress, the distribution of seats would have been 37 to the Republicans, 16 to the Democrats, 4 to the Socialists, and 3 to the Prohibitionists, and the same proportion of the seats in the state senate. The distribution of seats to the different counties would have been almost exactly as it was in 1908, but each party would have had its fair share for the State.

EXECUTIVE. — We suggest giving the governor the power to appoint and remove his cabinet and all subordinate officers through whom he must execute the laws. The President of the United States has this power for the nation and as to district attorneys and marshals. We do not require that his appointments or removals be confirmed by the senate, because experience has proven that it takes a very large part of a senator's time, often gets up very ugly and bitter local contests, and is of no real value in securing competent officers. Thus the governor will be wholly responsible. Require the appointment of a state business manager, subject to the governor, whose duty it shall be to see that the dollars and cents business of the State is done on business principles. Allow the people of any county the right by recall petition and special election to order the recall of any sheriff or district attorney appointed to serve in their county.

GOVERNOR MAY ORDER REFERENDUM ON HIS BILLS. — The recommendations of the President to Congress as well as of the governor to the legislature are often treated with contempt. The experience of President Roosevelt and of Governor Hughes are recent examples. Therefore we propose to take away the veto power and give the governor and cabinet seats on the floor of both houses; give the governor the right to introduce measures, and especially the general appropriation bills for the maintenance of the state government and existing state institutions; allow the governor and the cabinet officers to speak on administration measures and the governor the right to order the referendum on any measure he introduces which does not pass. If the legislature passes a bill for the same subject differing from the governor's, give him the right to order the referendum on both measures, so that the people may choose between them. The governor is not allowed to succeed himself. This will help him to give all his time to public business.

CIVIL SERVICE. — Except the governor's cabinet, no appointed officer shall be transferred, promoted, or removed at any time for personal, political, or partisan reasons. The purpose is to have appointed public servants hold their positions as long as they are competent, efficient, and faithful, just as they do in private business.

COUNTY GOVERNMENT. — Elect a board of three directors. Require that they hire a business manager for the county and that he shall do all the business of the county under their supervision. Do not elect any other county officers except the county judge. Allow the county business manager to hold his office while his services are satisfactory to the board. Let his salary be in the discretion of the board, subject to reduction on referendum vote by the people of the county. The legislature is not given power to change salaries of county officers. That is left to the county board of directors and the voters of the county.

We believe we have briefly stated the important changes offered, without going into the details, for which the measures must be carefully studied.

Appendix 359

CREATION OF A BOARD OF PEOPLE'S INSPECTORS OF GOVERNMENT, ETC.

A Bill for an act to create a board of people's inspectors of government; to provide for the publication and circulation of an official gazette; to fix the salaries and define the powers and duties of said board of inspectors, and making an appropriation.

Be it enacted by the people of the State of Oregon: —

SECTION 1. THREE INSPECTORS OF STATE AND LOCAL GOVERNMENT — OFFICIAL GAZETTE. — A board of three "people's inspectors of government," which shall be their official title, is hereby established and by virtue of their office they shall be the editors of the Oregon Official Gazette. The official gazette shall be published by the State from the state printing office not later than the second Friday of every second month, beginning with January, A.D. 1911, with extra numbers when necessary, and in such form as to be entitled to entry under the postal laws and transmission through the United States mails as second-class matter.

SEC. 2. DUTY OF INSPECTORS TO INVESTIGATE. — It is the duty of the board of inspectors to have at least one of their number present at all times of every session in each house of the legislative assembly; to be watchful for any defect or imperfection in the state and local systems of government; to investigate the management of every public office and of every institution supported wholly or partly by public funds, and every department of the state and local governments, as often as may be necessary. They shall conduct all these inspections and investigations and perform all the duties of their offices, and report through the gazette, solely for the information of the citizens, without motive or desire for personal or partisan advantage.

SEC. 3. DUTY OF INSPECTORS AS EDITORS OF GAZETTE. — The inspectors shall publish in the gazette, without unnecessary delay, their own reports; brief and comprehensive reports furnished by the governor concerning the affairs of the different departments of the state government; similar reports concerning the county government by the chief executive county officers; similar reports for cities by the mayors; reports from local district officers that the editors may consider of local or general interest; letters and communications from citizens and public officers on all matters of common interest relating to government; letters and information concerning our National Government and law-making and the action of our Representatives and Senators in Congress; the results of important experiments and developments in the science of government by other nations, States, counties, and cities; all publications which may be required by law to be mailed to every registered voter, which publishing shall be a sufficient compliance with such laws; other matters which they believe will advance the general welfare. If any citizen or officer shall offer a communication which the board does not consider of sufficient interest for publication, he may pay at reasonable column rates, to be fixed by the board, for the publication of not exceeding three columns in any issue. The board shall not publish any malicious, libelous, or personally abusive communications. The board shall so edit the gazette that only matters of general interest shall be published in the edition that is mailed to all voters, and that matters of local interest shall be included in the editions going only to the locality interested.

SEC. 4. SUBSCRIBERS TO GAZETTE — WHO SHALL BE CONSIDERED. — The head of every family who is a registered voter, every registered voter who is not a member of a family, and every Oregon taxpayer shall be considered subscribers to the gazette, and it shall be mailed to them at public expense. The gazette shall not be a commercial enterprise nor a general newspaper, and its editors shall not seek to give the general news, nor accept commercial advertising. The subscription price to be paid by those who wish the gazette and are not Oregon registered voters or taxpayers shall be $1 per year, payable in advance. As nearly as practicable, the editors shall correct the list of addresses from month to month and sell printed copies thereof to any person at cost on demand.

SEC. 5. ELECTION OF INSPECTORS — DUTY OF LEGISLATURE TO PROVIDE FOR. — If this bill shall be approved by the people it shall be the duty of the legislative assembly to forthwith provide for the election of said three inspectors from the State at large. The method of election shall be such that any candidate who is the choice of so many as one-third of the electors of the State actually voting for inspectors shall thereby be elected. The voter shall be authorized to write on his ballot the figure 1 opposite the name of the candidate who is his first choice, the figure 2 opposite the name of the candidate who is his second choice, and the figure 3 opposite the name of the candidate who is his third choice, and so on in the order of his preference for the said office of inspector. It is intended that, if practicable, every ballot shall be effective in the election of one candidate who is the personal preference of the elector who cast the ballot. The board shall be chosen at the regular general election in A.D. 1912 to serve two years and at the regular general election in A.D. 1914, and thereafter said inspectors shall be chosen when the governor is elected and for the same term for which he shall be elected.

SEC. 6. SALARIES AND APPOINTMENT OF FIRST THREE INSPECTORS. — Said inspectors shall receive a salary of $3,000, per annum and all necessary traveling expenses, payable quarterly. If this bill shall be approved by the people, within thirty days thereafter the Order of Grangers and Patrons of Husbandry of Oregon, the Federated Trades Convention of Oregon representing organized labor, and the assembled presidents of the boards of trade and chambers of commerce in Oregon may severally, for each organization, recommend to the governor the names of three persons for appointment to said office of inspector to serve until their successors are elected and qualified as provided herein. The governor shall appoint one of each three of the persons so recommended, if any. If either of such organizations shall fail within said time to recommend three persons for such office the governor shall immediately thereafter make an appointment without such recommendation.

SEC. 7. INSPECTORS' AUTHORITY, EXPENSES, AND APPROPRIATION. — The inspectors shall devote their time exclusively to the public service and the performance of their official duties. The bills for the expenses and salaries of said board and the bills for the publication of the gazette shall be audited by the secretary of state or state auditor and shall be paid from the general fund. The total amount to be paid for any year shall not exceed a sum equal to $1 for each registered voter in Oregon. Said inspectors shall have authority to demand the production for their examination of all public books, documents, cash and securities in the possession or under the control of any public officer at all reasonable hours and without previous notice. The board is hereby authorized to expend such sums as may be necessary, not exceeding $15,000 yearly for expert accountants and other assistance in making investigations. If such sum is not sufficient the board is hereby authorized to apply to the people, by initiative petition, for such amount as they believe they need. The board shall not apply to the legislative assembly for any appropriation. It is intended that these inspectors shall be independent of all other officers and powers except the sovereign people of Oregon; that they shall not receive official favors nor incur official obligations to any public servant nor any private citizen or corporation.

SUGGESTED AMENDMENTS TO THE CONSTITUTION OF OREGON

Article IV of the constitution of the State of Oregon shall be, and the same hereby is, amended to read as follows: —

Article IV

SEC. 1. LEGISLATIVE AUTHORITY. — The legislative authority of the State shall be vested in the legislative assembly, consisting of a senate and house of representatives, but the people reserve to themselves the power to propose legislative measures, resolutions, laws, and amendments to the constitution, and to enact or reject the same at the polls, independent of the legislative assembly, and also reserve power, at their own option, to approve or reject at the polls any act, item, section, or part of any resolution, act, or measure passed by the legislative assembly.

SEC. 1a. INITIATIVE. — The first power reserved by the people is the initiative, and not more than 8 per cent, nor in any case more than 50,000, of the legal voters shall be required to propose any measure by such petition, and every such petition shall include the full text of the measure so proposed. Initiative petitions for all but municipal legislation shall be filed with the secretary of state not less than four months before the election at which they are to be voted upon. If conflicting measures submitted to the people shall be approved by a majority of the votes severally cast for and against the same, the one receiving the highest number of affirmative votes shall thereby become law as to all conflicting provisions. Proposed amendments to the constitution shall in all cases be submitted to the people for approval or rejection.

SEC. 1b. REFERENDUM. — The second power is the referendum, and it may be ordered on any measure or resolution passed by the legislative assembly, either by petition signed by the required percentage of the legal voters, or by the legislative assembly as other bills are enacted. Not more than 5 per cent, nor at any time more than 30,000, of the

Appendix

legal voters shall be required to sign and make a valid referendum petition.

SEC. 1C. EMERGENCY. — If it is necessary for the immediate preservation of the public peace, health, or safety that a law or ordinance shall become effective without delay, such necessity shall be stated in one section, and if upon yea-and-no vote three-fourths of all the members elected to each house or city council, as the case may be, shall vote on a separate roll call in favor of the measure going into instant operation because it is necessary for the immediate preservation of the public peace, health, or safety, such law shall become operative upon being filed in the office of the secretary of state. It shall be necessary to state in such section the facts which constitute the emergency. If a referendum petition be filed against such emergency measure, it shall be a law until it is voted upon by the people, and if it is then rejected by a majority of those voting upon the question, such emergency measure shall be thereby repealed. No statute, ordinance, or resolution approved by vote of the people shall be amended or repealed by the legislative assembly or any city council except by three-fourths vote of all the members elected. The provisions of this section apply to city councils.

SEC. 1d. LOCAL INITIATIVE AND REFERENDUM. — The initiative and referendum powers of the people are hereby further reserved to the legal voters of each municipality and district as to all local, special, and municipal legislation of every character in or for their respective municipalities and districts. In case of laws chiefly of local interest, as the creation of new counties or of new or additional judges or other officers or offices, referendum by petition shall be for approval or rejection by the people of the district interested. Cities and towns may provide for the manner of exercising the initiative and referendum powers as to their municipal legislation. Not more than 10 per cent of the legal voters may be required to order the referendum nor more than 15 per cent to propose any measure by the initiative in any city or town.

SEC. 1e. GENERAL PROVISIONS. — The filing of a referendum petition against one or more items, sections, or parts of any act, legislative measure, resolution, or ordinance shall not delay the remainder of the measure from becoming operative. Referendum petitions against measures passed by the legislative assembly shall be filed with the secretary of state not later than ninety days after the final adjournment of the session of the legislative assembly which passed the measure on which the referendum is demanded. Referendum petitions shall be filed in like manner on adjournment of the legislative assembly at any time for a period longer than ninety days. The veto power of the governor or mayor shall not extend to measures initiated by or referred to the people. All elections on general, local, and special measures referred to the people of the State or any locality shall be had at the biennial regular general elections, except when the legislative assembly shall order a special election; but counties, cities, and towns may provide for special elections on their municipal legislation proposed by their citizens or local legislative bodies. Any measure initiated by the people or referred to the people as herein provided shall take effect and become the law if it is approved by a majority of the votes cast thereon, and not otherwise. Such measure shall be in operation on and after the thirtieth day after the election at which it is approved. The style of all bills shall be "Be it enacted by the people of the State of Oregon," and of ordinances "Be it ordained by the people of" (name of municipality). The style of charter amendments shall be similar to that used for constitutional amendments. This section shall not be construed to deprive any member of the legislative assembly or of a city council of the right to introduce any measure. The whole number of electors who voted for justice of the supreme court at the regular election last preceding the filing of any petition for the initiative or for the referendum shall be the basis on which the number of legal voters necessary to sign such petition shall be counted. Petitions and orders for the initiative and referendum shall be filed with the secretary of state, or in municipal elections such other officers as may be provided by law. In submitting the same to the people he and all other officers shall be guided by the general laws until additional legislation shall be especially provided therefor. This section is self-executing, but legislation may be enacted especially to facilitate its operation.

SEC. 2. NUMBER OF SENATORS, REPRESENTATIVES, AND TERM OF OFFICE. — The senate shall consist of 30 members, and the house of representatives of 60 members and no more. They shall be nominated, apportioned, and elected in such manner and from such districts as may be provided by law, but districts shall be composed of contiguous territory. The term of office for senators shall be six years, and the term of office for representatives shall be six years, both beginning with the general election of 1912, at which time all such offices shall be vacant, and 30 senators and 60 representatives shall be chosen. The term shall begin the day next after their general election.

SEC. 3. PEOPLE MAY RECALL LEGISLATIVE ASSEMBLY AND ELECT NEW. — The people reserve the right to recall either or both houses of the legislative assembly, and at the same time to elect a new house or senate, or both, as the case may be.

SEC. 3a. PETITION FOR RECALL OF LEGISLATIVE ASSEMBLY — SPECIAL ELECTION. — If at any time a petition shall be filed with the secretary of state signed by a number of legal voters equal to not less than 25 per cent of the whole number of electors who voted for justice of the supreme court at the last preceding general election, and such petition shall demand the recall of the legislative assembly, or either house thereof, stating the reasons therefor in not more than two hundred words, the secretary of state shall immediately order a special general election throughout the State, to take place in not less than sixty nor more than ninety days from the date of filing said petition.

SEC. 3b. PURPOSE OF SPECIAL ELECTION FOR RECALL OF LEGISLATIVE ASSEMBLY. — Such election shall be to decide whether the legislative assembly or the house against which the petition is filed shall be recalled, and also to choose the senators and representatives of a new legislative assembly, or of a new house or senate, as the case may be, if a majority of those voting vote for such recall.

SEC. 3c. WHAT SHALL BE PRINTED ON RECALL SPECIAL BALLOTS. — There shall be printed on the ballots for such election, first, the usual forms and instructions to voters; second, a statement of the reasons offered by the petitioners for said recall in not exceeding two hundred words; third, a statement, if any is offered by the legislative assembly, of the reasons against said recall in not exceeding two hundred words; fourth, the question and answers: —

"Shall the legislative assembly, house of representatives, senate, as the case may be, be dissolved?

"Yes."

"No."

The names of candidates for senators and representatives shall be printed on the ballot in like manner as at the regular election, including the names of the sitting members who do not refuse to be candidates. If a recall petition shall be filed against one or more members for the same cause from the same nominating district, the election shall be in that district only unless the reason given for the recall petition is refusal to obey an instruction from the State.

SEC. 3d. LEGISLATIVE ASSEMBLY RECALLED IF MAJORITY VOTE YES. — If a majority of the whole number of the electors who vote on the question vote "Yes," the legislative assembly, or either house thereof, as the case may be, shall be thereby recalled and the newly elected senators and representatives shall take their seats in the new legislative assembly to fill the unexpired term of the one recalled. If a majority vote "No," the sitting senators and representatives are thereby continued in office.

SEC. 3e. FILING RECALL PETITION SUSPENDS LEGISLATIVE FUNCTIONS — EXCEPTION. — The filing of such a recall petition shall operate as a complete suspension from office of all the senators and representatives against whom it is filed, and of all the powers of said legislative assembly, except as herein provided. Said legislative assembly shall not, nor any of its members, meet or pretend to do any business whatever, and shall have no power to meet or to do any business whatever, unless the returns of the special election as canvassed shall show that it, or the house against which the petition was filed, is continued in office by the people; except only, that in case of emergency, caused by war, insurrection, or great national calamity, the governor may convene the members of the said legislative assembly in special session, to act on questions arising by reason of said emergency, but they shall have no power or authority to act on any other question or subject. This section is self-executing, but laws may be enacted to facilitate its operation.

SEC. 4. HOW SENATORS AND REPRESENTATIVES TO BE CHOSEN. — Senators and representatives shall be chosen by the legal electors, by such method of proportionate representation of all the voters that, as nearly as may be practicable, any one-sixtieth of all the citizens of the State voting for one person for representative shall insure his election, and any one-thirtieth of the citizens of the State voting for one person for senator shall insure his election; until otherwise provided by law the method shall be as follows: —

SEC. 4a. NOMINATIONS — PETITIONS — PARTY NAME ON PLEDGES ON BALLOTS. — Candidates for the office of senator or representative shall be nominated in districts now provided for their election, but they shall be elected by the electors from the State at large. Each candidate's name shall be printed on the official ballot in the district or districts where he is nominated, but in no other. Any elector in any district may vote for a candidate in any other district by writing or sticking on his ballot the name and political party, position, or pledge of the candidate voted for. No candidate for nomination shall circulate his petition nor pay for its circulation outside of the nominating district where he resides. Every candidate for senator or representative at the general election has the right to have printed with his name on the official ballot not exceeding twelve words to state his political party, position, or pledges to the people on any questions of public policy. Every qualified elector may vote for one candidate for representative and one candidate for senator in the legislative assembly.

SEC. 4b. COUNT, CANVASS, AND RETURN OF VOTES. — The votes for the election of senators and representatives in the legislative assembly shall be counted, canvassed, and returned in like manner as such votes are now counted, canvassed, and returned in the election of senators and representatives from districts composed of two or more counties.

SEC. 4c. NUMBER OF VOTES NECESSARY TO INSURE MEMBERS' ELECTION. — The whole number of votes cast in the State for all candidates for representative shall be divided by sixty, being the number to be chosen, and the quotient will be the number of votes necessary to insure the election of one representative.

SEC. 4d. SEATS — HOW DIVIDED AMONG PARTY AND INDEPENDENT CANDIDATES. — The whole number of votes received in the State by all the candidates of each party and by independent candidates for representative shall be severally divided by said quota of election; the quotients will be the number of representative seats to which each party is entitled, and that number of the party candidates who have received, each for himself the full quota or nearest to the full quota of voters, shall be thereby elected. Any independent candidate who receives for himself a quota of votes shall be thereby elected. The seat or seats which cannot be allotted to any party or independent candidates for full quotas shall be given to the several political parties or independent candidates having the highest remainders, in the order of such high remainders, until the sixty seats are filled.

SEC. 4e. VOTE FOR SENATORS DIVIDED BY THIRTY FOR QUOTA. — The votes for candidates for senators in the legislative assembly shall be treated in like manner as the votes for representatives, save only that the whole number of votes cast in the State for candidates for senators shall be divided by thirty to obtain the quota necessary to insure the election of a senator. This section is self-executing, but laws may be enacted to facilitate its operation.

SEC. 5. VACANCIES IN LEGISLATIVE ASSEMBLY. — HOW FILLED. — If any vacancy shall occur in the office of senator or representative in the legislative assembly, it shall be filled by seating the qualified candidate from the same party as that of the retiring officer who received for himself nearer to the quota of votes than any candidate of his party who was not seated, except vacancies created by recall.

SEC. 6. QUALIFICATIONS OF SENATORS OR REPRESENTATIVES. — No person shall be a senator or representative who is not a citizen of the United States at the time of his election, nor unless he shall be at least 21 years of age, and a resident of the State at least five years before the election.

SEC. 7. MEMBERS' RIGHT OF INTERPELLATION. — Every member shall have the right to question the governor or any officer of the cabinet concerning any act, plan, measure, or contemplated act or plan of the administration, and the governor or cabinet officer shall be obliged to answer without unnecessary delay, except in case that immediate answer in the opinion of the governor might be prejudicial to the public interest or the public service, and upon such statement the answer may be delayed until the danger is past.

SEC. 8. WHEN AND WHAT PART OF APPROPRIATIONS IMMEDIATELY AVAILABLE. — Appropriations for the maintenance of the state government and all existing public institutions, and all institutions aided by state funds, not exceeding the amount of any previous appropriation for the same purpose, shall take effect and be available at once, but any increase in any such appropriation shall be subject to the referendum by petition, except in the emergency of war, insurrection, or great natural calamity.

SEC. 9. MEMBERS — WHEN FREE FROM ARREST — WORDS UTTERED IN DEBATE. — Senators and representatives in all cases, except for treason, felony, or breaches of the peace, shall be privileged from arrest during the session of the legislative assembly, and in going to and returning from the same; and shall not be subject to any civil process during the session of the legislative assembly, nor during the fifteen days next before the commencement thereof. Nor shall a member, for words uttered in debate in either house, be questioned in any other place.

SEC. 10. ANNUAL SESSIONS OF LEGISLATIVE ASSEMBLY. — The sessions of the legislative assembly shall be held annually at the capital of the State, commencing at such dates as may be provided by law.

SEC. 11. ELECTION OF OFFICERS — JUDGE OF QUALIFICATIONS, ETC. — PRESIDING OFFICERS NOT MEMBERS. — Each house, when assembled, shall choose its own officers, judge of the election, qualifications and returns of its own members, determine its own rules of proceeding, and sit upon its own adjournment; but neither house shall, without the concurrence of the other, adjourn for more than two days, nor to any other place than that in which it may be sitting. The presiding officers shall not be members nor hold any other office at the same time, and shall be chosen by their respective houses. They shall not appoint standing committees, and shall have no voice or vote on legislative business. They shall preside over the sessions of the body by which they are chosen, shall hold office during its pleasure, and shall have such powers as may be conferred upon them by their respective houses not contrary to the provisions of this article.

SEC. 12. QUORUM — TIME FOR ORGANIZATION. — Two-thirds of each house shall constitute a quorum to do business, but a smaller number may meet, adjourn from day to day, and compel the attendance of absent members. A quorum being in attendance, if either house fail to effect an organization within the first five days thereafter, the members of the house so failing shall be entitled to no compensation from the end of the said five days until an organization shall have been effected.

SEC. 13. JOURNAL — WHEN YEAS AND NAYS TO BE ENTERED. — Each house shall keep a journal of its proceedings. The yeas and nays on any question, shall, at the request of any two members, be entered, together with the names of the members demanding the same, on the journal: *Provided*, that on a motion to adjourn, it shall require one-tenth of the members present to order the yeas and nays.

SEC. 14. WHEN SESSIONS AND COMMITTEE MEETINGS MAY BE SECRET. — The doors of each house and all committees shall be kept open except only in such cases as in the opinion of either house require secrecy, but in every such case the yeas and nays shall be entered on the journal. Committees may sit during vacation and shall be liberal in allowing public hearings on measures; the chairman shall notify in writing all persons who advise the committee of their desire to be heard on any measure in its charge.

SEC. 15. PUNISHMENT OF MEMBERS. — Either house may punish its members for disorderly behavior, and may, with the concurrence of two-thirds, expel a member, but not a second time for the same cause.

SEC. 16. PUNISHMENT OF A PERSON NOT A MEMBER. — Either house, during its session, may punish by imprisonment any person not a member, who shall have been guilty of disrespect to the house, by disorderly or contemptuous behavior in its presence, but such imprisonment shall not at any time exceed twenty-four hours.

SEC. 17. GENERAL POWERS. — Each house shall have all powers necessary for a branch of the legislative department of a free and independent State.

SEC. 18. BILLS — WHERE TO ORIGINATE. — Bills may originate in either house, but may be amended or rejected in the other, except that bills for raising revenue shall originate in the house of representatives.

SEC. 19. READING OF BILLS — VOTE ON FINAL PASSAGE — FILED WITH SECRETARY OF STATE. — Every bill shall be read by sections, on three several days in each house, unless, in case of emergency, two-thirds of the house where such bill may be pending shall, by a vote of yeas and nays, deem it expedient to dispense with this rule; but the reading of a bill by sections on its final passage shall in no case be dispensed with, and the vote on the passage of every bill or joint resolution shall be taken by yeas and nays. Every measure, when finally passed, shall be filed in the office of the secretary of state.

SEC. 20. SUBJECT AND TITLE OF ACT. — Every act shall embrace but one subject and matters properly connected therewith, which subjects shall be expressed in the title. But if any subject shall be embraced in an act which shall not be expressed in the title, such act shall be void only as to so much thereof as shall not be expressed in the title.

SEC. 21. ACT TO BE PLAINLY WORDED. — Every act and joint resolution shall be plainly worded, avoiding, as far as practicable, the use of technical terms.

SEC. 22. MODE OF REVISION AND AMENDMENT. — No act shall ever be revised or amended by mere reference to its title, but the act revised or section amended shall be set forth and published at full length.

SEC. 23. WHAT LOCAL AND SPECIAL LAWS PROHIBITED. — The legislative assembly shall not pass special or local laws in any of the following enumerated cases — that is to say: —

1. Regulating the jurisdiction and duties of justices of the peace and of constables.
2. For the punishment of crimes and misdemeanors.
3. Regulating the practice in courts of justice.
4. Providing for changing the venue in civil and criminal cases.
5. Granting divorces.
6. Changing the names of persons.
7. For laying, opening, and working on highways, and for election or appointment of supervisors.
8. Vacating roads, town plats, streets, alleys, and public squares.
9. Summoning and impaneling grand and petit jurors.
10. For the assessment and collection of taxes for state, county, township, or road purposes.
11. Providing for supporting common schools, and for the preservation of school funds.
12. In relation to interest on money.
13. Providing for opening and conducting the elections of state, county, or township officers, and designating the places of voting.
14. Providing for the sale of real estate belonging to minors or other persons laboring under legal disabilities by executors, administrators, guardians, or trustees.
15. When a general law can be made applicable.

SEC. 24. SUITS AGAINST THE STATE. — Provision may be made by general law for bringing suit against the State, as to all liabilities originating after or existing at the time of the adoption of this constitution; but no special act authorizing such suit to be brought, or making compensation to any person claiming damages against the State, shall ever be passed.

SEC. 25. MAJORITY NECESSARY TO PASS A BILL — BILL TO BE SIGNED BY PRESIDING OFFICERS. — A majority of all the members elected to each house shall be necessary to pass every bill or joint resolution; and all bills and joint resolutions so passed shall be signed by the presiding officers of the respective houses.

SEC. 26. PROTEST BY MEMBER. — Any member of either house shall have the right to protest, and have his protest, with his reasons for dissent, entered on the journal.

SEC. 27. WHAT STATUTES PUBLIC LAWS. — Every statute shall be a public law unless otherwise declared in the statute itself.

SEC. 28. WHEN ACT TO TAKE EFFECT. — No act shall take effect until ninety days from the end of the session at which the same shall have been passed, except in cases of emergency, which shall be declared as provided in section 1c of this article.

SEC. 29. COMPENSATION OF MEMBERS. — Members of the legislative assembly shall receive for their services an annual salary of $350, payable at the end of each regular session. Each member shall receive the amount of necessary fares he shall actually pay in going to and returning from the place of meeting on the most usual route. The presiding officers of the legislative assembly shall receive $500 per annum, with a member's allowance for travel.

SEC. 30. MEMBERS NOT ELIGIBLE TO OTHER OFFICES. — No senator or representative shall, during the time for which he may have been elected, be eligible to any office the election to which is vested in the legislative assembly; nor shall he be appointed to any civil office of profit which shall have been created, or the emoluments of which have been increased during such term, but this latter provision shall not be construed to apply to any officer elective by the people.

SEC. 31. OATH OF MEMBERS — PLEDGE AGAINST LOGROLLING. — The members of the legislative assembly shall, before they enter on the duties of their respective offices, take and subscribe the following oath of office or affirmation : —

"I do solemnly swear (or affirm, as the case may be) that I will support the Constitution of the United States and of the State of Oregon, and that I will faithfully discharge the duties of senator (or representative, as the case may be) according to the best of my ability. I do further affirm and promise the voters of the State of Oregon that during my term of office in acting or voting as such officer upon any measure I will always vote solely on my judgment that the bill or resolution will or will not advance the general welfare and without reference to the vote, action, or caucus of members on that or any other measure, and without any understanding (except my public pledges to the people or instructions from the people) in any form with any member or person that I will aid or be friendly to a measure in which he is interested because he will or may be inclined to aid one in which I am interested." Such oath may be administered by the governor or a judge of the supreme court.

SEC. 32. TIME WHEN BILLS MAY BE PASSED — WHAT BILLS NOT TO BE PASSED AT THE SAME SESSION THEY ARE INTRODUCED. — When a bill is introduced it shall be placed upon the calendar and may be acted upon any time during the life of that legislative assembly, except that bills introduced after the tenth day of any session shall not be passed at that session, unless they are emergency measures.

SEC. 33. PUNISHMENT FOR MEMBER FAILING TO VOTE ON ROLL CALL. — Ten dollars shall be deducted from the salary of any member for every time he fails to vote on a roll call unless excused by yea-and-nay vote of a majority of all the members of his house.

SEC. 34. CLERKS AND STENOGRAPHERS FOR LEGISLATIVE ASSEMBLY. — The presiding officer shall make requisition from day to day on the secretary of state or the state business manager for such clerical and stenographic assistance as his house may need. This shall not apply to the reading and calendar clerks.

SEC. 35. MAJORITY OF MEMBERS MAY CALL SPECIAL SESSION. — A majority of the members elected to each house may at any time unite in calling a special session of the legislative assembly.

SEC. 36. SEATS IN EACH HOUSE FOR PEOPLE'S INSPECTORS. — Seats and desks shall be provided on the floor of each house for the people's inspectors of government, if such shall be created by law.

SEC. 37. CITIZENS' ACTION AGAINST BILL PASSED BY TRADING OR LOGROLLING — PROCEEDINGS — REFERENDUM. — Any ten citizen freeholders shall have the right to unite in bringing an action in the circuit court at the seat of government against any measure within ten days after it is passed by the legislative assembly, alleging that the same was passed by bargaining, trading, logrolling, or other forms of undue influence. Summons and a copy of the complaint shall be served upon the attorney-general and the presiding officers of both houses as other process is served. The attorney-general shall defend the action, but senators and representatives may employ assistant counsel. The case shall be advanced on the docket if necessary and tried within twenty days after the close of the session. The verdict of the jury shall be on preponderance of evidence. If the jury finds from the evidence that they believe the bill was passed by any undue influence, that verdict shall be filed with the secretary of state; and as to such measure the verdict shall have the same effect as a petition for the referendum; said bill shall be referred to the people by the secretary of state for approval or rejection at the next regular general election. Senators, representatives, officers, and other persons may be subpœnaed and compelled to testify after the close of the session, but they shall not be prosecuted criminally or civilly for any action to which they shall testify.

SEC. 38. REPEAL OF CONFLICTING PROVISIONS. — Any provisions of the constitution and laws of Oregon in conflict with this amended article are hereby repealed in so far as they conflict herewith.

Article V of the constitution of the State of Oregon shall be, and the same hereby is, amended to read as follows: —

ARTICLE V

SECTION 1. EXECUTIVE POWER — ONE TERM ONLY — QUALIFICATIONS — DECISION ON TIE ELECTION. — The chief executive power of the State shall be vested in the governor, who shall hold his office for the term of six years and shall not be eligible to succeed himself. The governor shall be elected by the qualified electors of the State in such manner as may be provided by law, at the regular general election A.D. 1914, and every six years thereafter. The legislative assembly shall pass upon the election returns and declare the result. Contested elections for governor shall be determined by the legislative assembly in such manner as may be provided by law. The governor shall take his office on the first Monday after the organization of the legislature in January following the election. If two or more persons shall have an equal and the highest number of votes for governor, the two houses of the legislative assembly at the next regular session thereof shall forthwith in joint session by a majority vote proceed to elect one of said persons governor. The governor shall devote his time exclusively to the public service.

SEC. 2. WHO NOT ELIGIBLE FOR GOVERNOR. — No person except a citizen of the United States shall be eligible to the office of governor nor unless he shall have attained the age of 30 years and have been a resident of the State of Oregon five years next preceding his election. Except as may be otherwise provided in this constitution, no person shall hold any other office and at the same time fill the office of governor.

SEC. 3. VACANCY IN OFFICE — FILLED BY LEGISLATIVE ASSEMBLY.— In case of removal of the governor from his office or of his death, resignation, or inability to perform the duties of his office for any cause except a recall by the people, the secretary of state shall be governor until the office is filled by the legislative assembly, which shall forthwith convene and in joint session choose a governor by a majority vote, who shall hold the office until the next regular general biennial election, when the people shall elect a governor to fill the unexpired term, except when that is the regular election to choose the governor for a full regular term.

SEC. 4. GOVERNOR COMMANDER IN CHIEF MILITARY AND NAVAL FORCES. — The governor shall be the commander in chief of the military and naval forces of this State and may call out such forces to execute the laws, to suppress insurrection, or to repel invasion.

SEC. 5. APPOINTS SHERIFFS AND DISTRICT ATTORNEYS — MUST TAKE CARE THAT LAWS ARE FAITHFULLY EXECUTED. — The governor shall take care that the laws of this State be faithfully executed. He shall be commander in chief of all the forces maintained to protect the State and enforce its laws. He shall appoint a sheriff and district attorney for each county at a total cost for salaries, including deputies, not exceeding that now paid in the State, until such time as an increase may be allowed by law. He shall have power to suspend or remove any officer he appoints and such suspension or removal shall not be subject to appeal; but in every such case he shall file his order of suspension or removal with the secretary of state, and also the reasons therefor upon written demand of the person suspended or removed, or he may do so without such demand. All local officers appointed by the governor shall be subject to recall petition and a special election for their discharge by the people of their county or district in like manner as though they were elected. In case of such recall by election, the governor shall make another appointment, and shall not reappoint the recalled officer to any position.

SEC. 6. GOVERNOR APPOINTS CABINET OFFICERS — STATE AUDITOR TO BE ELECTED. — The governor shall appoint the attorney-general, the secretary of state, state treasurer, state printer, superintendent of public instruction, secretary of labor, and the state business manager, who shall constitute the cabinet, together with such other cabinet officers as may be provided by law. They shall hold office during the governor's pleasure. These officers shall perform such duties as may be required by this constitution and the general laws, or ordered by the governor. A state auditor shall be chosen by the legal voters of the State at the general election in November, A.D. 1912, to serve two years. At the general election in November, A.D. 1914, a state auditor shall be elected for a term of six years. The auditor's regular term of office shall be six years and his duties, powers, and salary shall be fixed by law. No person who has not had at least five years' experience as accountant or auditor shall be eligible or allowed to file his petition as a candidate for that office.

SEC. 7. SALARIES OF GOVERNOR AND CABINET OFFICERS. — The governor and the members of the cabinet shall receive such annual salaries as may be allowed by law, but no such salary shall be increased by a law with the emergency declaration. The state printer's salary shall be $4000 a year, until otherwise provided by law. They shall be citizens of the United States and of Oregon and shall have resided in the State not less than five years before their appointment, except that the governor shall not be limited to citizens of Oregon in employing the state business manager.

NOTE. — Judges of the supreme court are allowed by law $4,500 a year, governor $5,000, secretary of state $4,500, state treasurer $4,500, attorney-general $3,600, superintendent of public instruction $3,000, commissioner of labor statistics $3,000 a year. The state printer does not receive a salary, but is supposed to make a great deal more than any other officer in the State.

SEC. 8. STATE BUSINESS MANAGER — DUTIES — SALARY. — The state business manager, subject always to the governor's approval, shall so organize, consolidate, supervise, direct, and manage the business departments and affairs of the State (these being such as deal largely with money and money's worth) as to obtain the highest possible efficiency in the State's service and full value for the public money. He shall give counsel as to business matters when called upon by the chief officers of counties and other local governments. He shall advise the governor in writing of all possible opportunities and practical plans for the betterment of the public service, business, and the methods and laws of its administration, both for the state and local governments. The governor is authorized to make such rules and regulations as may be expedient to obtain these results, subject always to the constitution and laws of Oregon, and the decisions of the courts that any such rule or regulation is in contravention of the constitutional rights and liberties of citizens. The state business manager shall perform such other duties as may be required by law or ordered by the governor. The governor is authorized from time to time to allow and agree to such salary for the state business manager as will be sufficient to get the best man for the position, but subject always to reduction by the people on referendum vote.

SEC. 9. BOARDS AND COMMISSIONS ABOLISHED — GOVERNOR RESPONSIBLE — MAY MAKE RULES FOR CONDUCT OF BUSINESS. — From time to time, and before the first day of September, 1911, the governor shall complete taking over the control of the organization and management of all state institutions, state business, and public functions now wholly or partly governed or managed by boards or commissions. He may retain and continue such boards and commissions as he desires as counselors and advisers, but he shall have full power to manage and organize and shall be wholly and alone responsible to the people for results. No new boards or commissions shall be created by law to assume or have any power or responsibility for the faithful execution of any laws of the State, unless the law creating such new board or commission shall first be approved by the people on referendum vote. That the governor may be enabled promptly and successfully to perform the duties required by this article, all statutes creating such boards, commissions, and state institutions, or that provide for their management, are hereby declared to have only the force of rules and regulations, which the governor is authorized to change from time to time during recess of the legislative assembly until the end of the year 1912, in accordance with the provisions of section 8 of this article, as to rules and regulations for the management of state business. The board of railroad commissioners shall be excepted from the provisions of this article.

SEC. 10. GOVERNOR'S POWER TO APPOINT AND REMOVE OFFICERS AND EMPLOYEES — REASONS FOR. — Appointment, transfer, promotion, or removal of any officer or employee because of personal preference or dislike or for political or party advantage, or because of membership in a party, or for any reasons of partisanship is hereby prohibited. All the governor's cabinet officers except the state business manager are excepted from this section. On every appointment, transfer, promotion, or removal of a public officer or employee the officer making the same shall certify that he makes it wholly for the good of the public service, and not because of personal preference, friendship, favor, or dislike, nor because of or for the advantage of any political party, faction, or association; nor on account of membership or political activity in any political party or organization.

SEC. 11. GOVERNOR AND CABINET SEATS IN BOTH HOUSES LEGISLATIVE ASSEMBLY — DUTIES — GOVERNOR MAY ORDER REFERENDUM IN CERTAIN CASES. — The governor and his cabinet shall have seats on the floor of both houses of the legislative assembly, and when that body is sitting it shall be his duty and that of the members of the cabinet, but not necessarily together, to attend at least one session of each house each week. The governor shall have the right to introduce any measure or resolution in the house of representatives. It shall be his duty to introduce the appropriation bills for the maintenance of the state government and of existing state institutions. These measures shall be known as administration measures. The governor and members of the cabinet shall have the right to speak and to move for administration measures. The governor may appeal from the action or failure of the legislative assembly to act on any administration measure to a referendum vote of the people, and he is hereby authorized at his option to order the referendum in such cases at the next ensuing regular general election, that the voters may choose between the governor's and the legislature's measure. The governor and the members of his cabinet shall, when in attendance on either house, answer all questions that may be put to them in writing by members concerning the administration of the government or any department thereof, save that when such answers, if made public, might give information that would be prejudicial to the public interest upon the governor's statement of that fact the answer may be withheld until the emergency is past.

SEC. 12. GOVERNOR MAY CONVENE LEGISLATURE. — The governor may, on extraordinary occasions, convene the legislative assembly by proclamation, and shall state to both houses when assembled the purpose for which they shall have been convened.

SEC. 13. GOVERNOR TRANSACTS BUSINESS WITH OFFICERS — MAY REQUIRE INFORMATION. — He shall transact all necessary business with the officers of government and may require information in writing from them upon any subject relating to the duties of their various offices.

SEC. 14. REPRIEVE, PARDONS, ETC. — He shall have power to grant reprieves, commutations, and pardons, after conviction, for all offenses except treason, subject to such regulations as may be provided by law. Upon conviction for treason he shall have power to suspend the execution of the sentence until the case shall be reported to the legislative assembly at its next meeting, when the legislative assembly shall either grant a pardon, commute the sentence, direct the execution of the sentence, or grant a further reprieve. He shall have power to remit fines and forfeitures, under such regulations as may be prescribed by law; and shall report to the legislative assembly at its next meeting each case of reprieve, commutation, or pardon granted and the reasons for granting the same; and also the names of all persons in whose favor remission of fines and forfeitures shall have been made and the several amounts remitted.

SEC. 15. POWER TO FILL CERTAIN VACANCIES BY APPOINTMENT. — When, during the recess of the legislative assembly, a vacancy shall happen in any office, the appointment to which is vested in the legislative assembly; or when at any time a vacancy shall have occurred in any other state office, or in the office of judge of any court, the governor shall fill such vacancy by appointment, which shall expire when a successor shall have been elected and qualified.

SEC. 16. COMMISSIONS. — All commissions shall issue in the name of the State, shall be signed by the governor, sealed with the seal of the State, and attested by the secretary of state.

SEC. 17. WHEN THIS AMENDMENT TAKES EFFECT — REPEAL OF CONFLICTING PROVISIONS. — If this amendment shall be adopted, the secretary of state, state treasurer, state printer, attorney-general, superintendent of public instruction, labor commissioner, whose title shall be secretary of labor, who shall be chosen at the general election in November, A.D. 1910, shall be members of the governor's cabinet during the time for which they shall be elected; but in all other respects this amendment shall be in force from the thirtieth day after its adoption by the people. Any provisions of this constitution or of the laws of Oregon in conflict herewith are hereby repealed in so far as they conflict with this amendment.

Article VI of the constitution of the State of Oregon shall be, and the same hereby is, amended to read as follows: —

Article VI

SECTION 1. COUNTY BUSINESS — BOARDS OF DIRECTORS — COMPENSATION — TERM OF OFFICE — RECALL. — The legal voters of each county shall choose a board of three directors of county business to serve for four years. Their official title shall be the "Board of directors for the county of ———." The first election of directors shall be at the November election, A.D. 1912, for four years; thereafter their term of office shall be six years, beginning with the board to be elected in November, 1916, subject always to recall petition. More than one of the members may be included in one recall petition if the causes of complaint are the same. The legislative assembly shall forthwith provide by law for the election of the board from the county at large. The method of election shall be such that any candidate who is the choice of so many as one-third of the electors of the state actually voting for directors shall thereby be elected. The voter shall be authorized to write on his ballot the figure 1 opposite the name of the candidate who is his first choice, the figure 2 opposite the name of the candidate who is his second choice, and the figure 3 opposite the name of the candidate who is his third choice, and so on in the order of his preference, for said office of director. It is intended that, if possible, every ballot shall be effective in the election of one candidate who is the personal preference of the elector who cast the ballot. The directors shall receive such compensation as is now paid to the county commissioners until that shall be changed by the voters of the county.

SEC. 2. DUTY OF DIRECTORS — POWER — COUNTY BUSINESS MANAGER. — It is the duty of the board of directors to plan and order all the public affairs and interests of the county. The board shall make all expedient rules and regulations for the successful, efficient, and economic management of all county business and property, subject to the constitution and laws, and subject also to the vote of the people of the county. The board shall employ a county business manager, who shall be the chief executive of the county. He shall be a citizen of the United States, but the board shall not be limited to Oregon in seeking a man for the position.

SEC. 3. SALARY OF COUNTY BUSINESS MANAGER AND OTHER EMPLOYEES — FIXED BY DIRECTORS, SUBJECT TO VOTE OF PEOPLE. — The salary of the county business manager and of all other county employees shall be in the discretion of the board of directors except in so far as the same may be fixed from time to time by the legal voters of the county. No salaries of county officers shall be fixed by the legislative assembly. All subordinate officers and employees of the county shall be employed by the county business manager, except only that the board shall either audit the county bills or appoint a county auditor. The county business manager shall not be a member of the board. The county judge, justices of the peace, and constables, so long as the law provides for such officers, shall not be within the jurisdiction of the county business manager, nor of the board of directors, and their compensation shall be as now provided by law until changed by vote of the people of the county.

SEC. 4. COUNTY AND OTHER LOCAL OFFICERS AND EMPLOYEES. — State, district, county, township, precinct, and city officers and employees shall be such as may be provided by law, and vacancies shall be filled in such manner as may be required by law.

SEC. 5. WHEN THIS AMENDMENT TAKES EFFECT. — If this amendment shall be adopted, the county officers who are in office or are elected at the November election, 1910, may perform the duties of their offices until the end of that two-year term, but they shall do so under the direction of the county business manager. This amendment shall be in force as to all matters save the election, employment, and discharge by the county business manager of such officers as may be in office or elected by the people at the general election, 1910.

SEC. 6. REPEAL OF CONFLICTING PROVISIONS. — All provisions of the constitution and laws of Oregon in conflict with this article are hereby abrogated in so far as they conflict herewith.

Article VII of the constitution of the State of Oregon shall be, and the same hereby is, amended to read as follows: —

Article VII

Section 1. Judicial power of State — In whom vested. — The judicial power of the State shall be vested in one supreme court and in such other courts as may from time to time be created by law. The judges of the supreme and other courts shall be elected by the legal voters of the State or of their respective districts for a term of six years, and shall receive such compensation as may be provided by law, which shall not be diminished during the term for which they are elected.

Sec. 2. Courts and judicial system. — The courts, jurisdiction, and judicial system of Oregon, except so far as expressly changed by this amendment, shall remain as at present constituted until otherwise provided by law. But the supreme court may take original jurisdiction in mandamus, quo warranto, and habeas corpus proceedings.

Sec. 3. Legislative assembly not to declare emergency on certain bills — Salaries of judicial officers. — The legislative assembly shall not declare an emergency on any bill creating or abolishing any judicial office, or increasing the number of judges, or increasing or diminishing the salaries, or changing the term of any judicial officer.

Sec. 4. Appeals — Decision of supreme court. — Upon appeal of any case to the supreme court, either party may have attached to the bill of exceptions the whole testimony, the instructions of the court to the jury, and any other matter material to the decision of the appeal. If the supreme court shall be of opinion, after consideration of all the matters thus submitted, that the judgment of the court appealed from was such as should have been rendered in the case, such judgment shall be affirmed, notwithstanding any error committed during the trial; or if, in any respect, the judgment appealed from should be changed, and the supreme court shall be of opinion that it can decide on what judgment should have been entered in the court below, it shall direct such judgment to be entered in the same manner and with like effect as decrees are now entered in equity cases on appeal to the supreme court.

Sec. 5. Opinions of supreme court — What shall be printed. — Only such opinions of the supreme court shall be printed as decide new questions of law, or the meaning and construction of the statutes and the constitution of Oregon and of the United States, or that reverse former decisions of the court.

SEC. 6. JURORS — GRAND JURY. — In civil cases three-fourths of the jury may render a verdict. The legislative assembly shall so provide that the most competent of the permanent citizens of the county shall be chosen for jurors; and out of the whole number in attendance at the court, seven shall be chosen by lot as grand jurors, five of whom must concur to find an indictment. But provision may be made by law for drawing and summoning the grand jurors from the regular jury list at any time, separate from the panel of petit jurors, and for the sitting of the grand jury during vacation as well as session of the court, as the judge may direct. No person shall be charged in any circuit court with the commission of any crime or misdemeanor defined or made punishable by any of the laws of this State, except upon indictment found by a grand jury: *Provided, however*, That any district attorney may file an amended indictment whenever an indictment has, by a ruling of the court, been held to be defective in form.

SEC. 7. OFFICIAL DELINQUENCIES. — Public officers shall not be impeached; but incompetency, corruption, malfeasance, or delinquency in office may be tried in the same manner as criminal offenses, and judgment may be given of dismissal from office, and such further punishment as may have been prescribed by law.

SEC. 8. OATH OF OFFICE. — Every judge of the supreme court, before entering upon the duties of his office, shall take and subscribe, and transmit to the secretary of state, the following oath : —

"I, —— —— , do solemnly swear (or affirm) that I will support the Constitution of the United States, and the constitution of the State of Oregon, and that I will faithfully and impartially discharge the duties of a judge of the supreme and circuit courts of said State, according to the best of my ability, and that I will not accept any other office, except judicial offices, during the term for which I have been elected."

BALLOT TITLES FOR THE INITIATIVE AND
REFERENDUM MEASURES IN OREGON,
ELECTION OF NOVEMBER 8, 1910.

Women's taxpaying suffrage amendment, granting to taxpayers, regardless of sex, the right of suffrage.
Vote YES or NO.

300.	Yes.	35,270
301.	No.	59,065

An act authorizing the purchase of a site for and the construction and maintenance of a branch insane asylum to be located, in the discretion of the board of trustees of the Oregon State Insane Asylum, at or within five miles of either of the following cities, to-wit: Baker City, Pendleton, or Union, in Eastern Oregon, to be called "The Eastern Oregon State Hospital."
Vote YES or NO.

302.	Yes.	50,134
303.	No.	41,504

An act to elect, on the first Monday in June, 1911, delegates to a constitutional convention, to be held on the second Monday in October, 1911, for revising the Constitution of the State, and providing for submission of the proposed Constitution, so revised, to the legal voters of the State for adoption or rejection on the first Monday in April, 1912.
Vote YES or NO.

304.	Yes.	23,143
305.	No.	59,974

For amendment of Sections 6 and 7, Article IV, of the Constitution of this state, to provide a separate district for the election of each State Senator and each State Representative.
Vote YES or NO.

306.	Yes.	24,000
307.	No.	54,252

For an amendment of Section 32, Article I, of the Constitution of Oregon, by omitting the words, "and all taxation shall be equal and uniform," and inserting in lieu thereof, the words, "taxes shall be levied and collected for public purposes only, and the power of taxation shall never be surrendered, suspended, or contracted away."
Vote YES or NO.

308.	Yes.	37,619
309.	No.	40,172

For amendment of the Oregon Constitution, Article IX (XIX) authorizing the creation of railroad districts and the purchase and construction of railroads, or other highways by the State, counties, municipalities, and railroad districts, creation of liens upon property or levying taxes for the payment of the same.
Vote YES or NO.

310.	Yes.	32,844
311.	No.	46,070

For amendment of Section 1 of Article IX of the Constitution of the State of Oregon, directing a uniform rule of taxation "except on property specifically taxed," authorizing the levy and collection of taxes for State purposes and for county and other municipal purposes upon different classes of property, and apportioning State taxes among the several counties as county obligations.
Vote YES or NO.

312.	Yes.	31,629
313.	No.	41,692

An act providing for the payment of $1000 annually to the Judge of the Eighth Judicial District, by Baker county, in addition to the annual salary of $3000 received by him from the State.
Vote YES or NO.

314.	Yes.	13,161
315.	No.	71,503

A bill for an act to create the County of Nesmith out of a portion of the northern part of Douglas county and the southern part of Lane county; providing for its organization, fixing the salaries of the officers thereof, and for adjusting finances between the three counties.
Vote YES or NO.

316.	Yes.	22,866
317.	No.	60,951

A bill for a law to provide for the permanent support and maintenance of Oregon Normal School at Monmouth, Polk county, Oregon, by levying an annual tax of one-twenty-fifth of a mill on the dollar upon all the taxable property within the State of Oregon.
Vote YES or NO.

318.	Yes.	50,191
319.	No.	40,044

A bill for a law creating the County of Otis, Oregon, out of territory now included in the counties of Harney, Malheur and Grant, providing for its organization and for the adjustment of finances and transferring of records between the several counties affected by the proposed law.
Vote YES or NO.

320.	Yes.	17,426
321.	No.	62,016

A bill for a law to annex a portion of the northern part of Clackamas county, Oregon, to Multnomah county, Oregon, and providing for transcribing and transferring the records of the territory proposed to be annexed, and for adjustment of finances between the two counties.
Vote YES or NO.

322.	Yes.	16,250
323.	No.	69,002

A bill for an act to create the County of Williams out of a portion of Lane and Douglas counties, Oregon; providing for its organization; fixing the salaries of the officers thereof; and for adjustment of finances between the three counties.
Vote YES or NO.

324.	Yes.	14,508
325.	No.	64,090

For constitutional amendment providing for the people of each county to regulate taxation and exemptions within the county, regardless of constitutional restrictions or State statutes, and abolishing poll or head tax.
Vote YES or NO.

326.	Yes.	44,171
327.	No.	42,127

For constitutional amendment giving to cities and towns exclusive power to license, regulate, control, suppress, or prohibit the sale of intoxicating liquors within the municipality.
Vote YES or NO.

328.	Yes.	53,321
329.	No.	50,779

Ballot Titles

A bill for a law requiring protection for persons engaged in hazardous employment, defining and extending the liability of employers, and providing that contributory negligence shall not be a defense.
Vote YES or NO.

330.	Yes.	56,258
331.	No.	33,943

A bill for an act to create the County of Orchard out of the northeastern portion of Umatilla county, Oregon; providing for its organization; fixing the salaries of the officers thereof; and for adjustment of the finances between the two counties.
Vote YES or NO.

332.	Yes.	15,664
333.	No.	62,712

A bill for an act to create the County of Clark out of the northern portion of Grant county, Oregon; providing for its organization; fixing the salaries of the officers thereof; and for adjustment of finances between the two counties.
Vote YES or NO.

334.	Yes.	15,613
335.	No.	61,704

A bill for a law providing for the permanent support and maintenance of the Eastern Oregon State Normal School at Weston, Umatilla county, Oregon, by levying an annual tax of one-twenty-fifth of a mill on the dollar upon all the taxable property within the State of Oregon.
Vote YES or NO.

336.	Yes.	40,898
337.	No.	46,201

A bill for a law to annex a portion of the territory in the eastern part of Washington county, Oregon, to Multnomah county, Oregon, and providing for a transcript of the records of the territory annexed to be made and recorded in Multnomah county.
Vote YES or NO.

338.	Yes.	14,047
339.	No.	68,221

A bill for a law providing for the permanent support and maintenance of the Southern Oregon State Normal School at Ashland, Jackson county, Oregon, by levying one-twenty-fifth of a mill on the dollar on all taxable property in the State of Oregon therefor, and limiting instruction therein to those subjects promoting efficiency in the art of teaching.
Vote YES or NO.

340.	Yes.	38,473
341.	No.	48,655

An amendment of Section 35 of Article I of the Constitution of the State of Oregon, prohibiting the manufacture and sale of intoxicating liquors and the traffic therein within the State of Oregon, on and after the first day of July, A.D. 1911, excepting for medicinal, scientific, sacramental, and mechanical purposes.
Vote YES or NO.

342.	Yes.	43,540
343.	No.	61,221

A bill for a law to prohibit, prevent, and suppress the manufacture, sale, possession, exchange, or giving away of intoxicating liquors within the State of Oregon, except for specific purposes; to govern the shipment of the same, declaring what is intoxicating liquor within the State of Oregon, and providing penalty for violation of the act.
Vote YES or NO.

344.	Yes.	42,651
345.	No.	63,564

A bill for an act creating a Board of Commissioners of nine members to examine the subject of employees' indemnity for injuries sustained in the course of their employment, and to prepare a measure to be presented to the legislature governing the same, and report to the Governor of the State on or before the 1st day of February, 1911, and appropriating $1000 for purposes of the act.
Vote YES or NO.

346.	Yes.	32,224
347.	No.	51,719

A bill for an act prohibiting the taking of fish from the waters of Rogue River, or of any of its tributaries, by any means, except with hook and line, commonly called angling.
Vote YES or NO.

348.	Yes.	49,712
349.	No.	33,397

A bill for a law to create the County of Deschutes, Oregon, out of the northwest portion of Crook county, Oregon; providing for its organization, the salaries of its officers, and settlement of the finances between the proposed county and Crook county.
Vote YES or NO.

350.	Yes.	17,592
351.	No.	60,486

A bill for an act providing for the creation of new towns, counties and municipal districts (excepting drainage and irrigation districts of less than one county) or changing the boundaries of existing counties by a majority vote of the legal voters of the territory within the boundaries of the proposed municipality, and providing that 30 per cent of the number of legal voters within such territory may petition for the creation of a new municipal corporation, and providing for the appointment of officers and adjustment of the finances of the new corporation, and the method of procedure to create the same.
Vote YES or NO.

352.	Yes.	37,129
353.	No.	42,327

An amendment of Section 10 of Article XI of the Constitution of the State of Oregon, permitting counties to incur indebtedness beyond $5000 to build permanent roads, and providing that debts for permanent roads may be incurred on approval of a majority of those voting on the question.
Vote YES or NO.

354.	Yes.	51,275
355.	No.	32,906

A bill for a law to amend the direct primary law by extending its provisions to presidential nominations, allowing voters to designate their choice for their party candidate for President and Vice-President; for direct nomination of party candidates for presidential electors; for election by party voters of delegates to their party national nominating conventions, each voter voting for one delegate; for payment of delegates' actual traveling expenses, not exceeding two hundred dollars for each delegate, and extending the publicity rights of candidates in the State nominating and general election campaign books.
Vote YES or NO.

356.	Yes.	43,353
357.	No.	41,624

A bill for a law creating a board of people's inspectors of government, providing for publication of an official State magazine, said board to be the editors and publishers thereof, the printing to be done by the State Printer; all books of public officials subject to examination by the board of inspectors and reports thereof published in said magazine; all expenses of the board for printing and publication of magazine salaries, etc., not to exceed one dollar for each registered voter in the State; the magazine shall be mailed every two months to each registered voter at public expense.
Vote YES or NO.

358.	Yes.	29,955
359.	No.	52,538

Ballot Titles

For an amendment of Article IV, Constitution of Oregon, increasing initiative, referendum, and recall powers of the people; restricting use of emergency clause and veto power on State and municipal legislation; requiring proportional election of members of Legislative Assembly from the State at large, annual sessions, and increasing members' salaries and terms of office; providing for election of Speaker of House and President of Senate, outside of members, restricting corporate franchises to twenty years; providing ten dollars penalty for unexcused absence from any roll call, and changing form of oath of office to provide against so-called legislative logrolling.

Vote YES or NO.

360.	Yes.		37,031
361.	No.		44,366

For amendment to the Constitution of the State of Oregon, providing for verdict by three-fourths of jury in civil cases, authorizing grand juries to be summoned separate from the trial jury, permitting change of judicial system by statute, prohibiting retrial where any evidence to support verdict; providing for affirmance of judgment on appeal notwithstanding error committed in lower court, directing Supreme Court to enter such judgment as should have been entered in lower court; fixing terms of Supreme Court; providing judges of all courts be elected for six years, and increasing jurisdiction of Supreme Court.

Vote YES or NO.

362.	Yes.		44,538
363.	No.		39,399

INDEX

Adams, John, on meaning of word "democracy," p. 27.
Amendments, constitutional, evolution of in states, p. 18; by initiative and refereudum, *see* Initiative and Referendum.
Arizona, debate on admission of, pp. 55 ff.; initiative and referendum provisions, pp. 23 ff.; recall provisions proposed by constitutional convention, pp. 244 f.; recall provisions stipulated by Congress, pp. 263 f.; resolution for admission, pp. 256 ff.; veto of constitution, pp. 245 ff.
Arkansas, initiative and referendum amendment, p. 180.
Australian ballot, p. 11.

Ballot, increase in complexity of, p. 15; effect of recall on, p. 68.
Bicameral system in cities, p. 10.
Bills, drafting of, p. 33.
Blackstone on woman's position, p. 13.
Bonner *v.* Belsterling, pp. 337 ff.
Bradford, Gamaliel, criticism of legislature, p. 7.
Bryce, James, state politics, p. 14.

California, adopted constitutional amendments, initiative and referendum, pp. 184 ff.; recall, pp. 264 ff.
Cases cited, *see* Judicial Decisions.
Chamberlain, Senator, on recall of judges, pp. 60 ff.
Choate, Rufus, on independence of judges, p. 67.
Colorado, initiative and referendum constitutional amendment adopted, pp. 181 ff.
Commisson government, cause of growth, p. 10; in Iowa, pp. 280 ff.; in New Jersey, pp. 285 ff.
Constitution, federal, power of minority under, p. 64; ratification of, p. 15; reverence for, p. 25.

Constitutional convention (federal), debate on meaning of word "republican," p. 25; Dickinson on suffrage, p. 13.
Constitutionality of initiative and refereudum, pp. 29 ff., 291 ff.
Constitutions, limitations on power of legislatures in, p. 6; ratification of, pp. 15, 17.
County government, proposed Oregon plan, pp. 358 ff., 380 ff.
Courts, Taft on delays of, p. 117.
Cullop, Rep., on recall of judges, p. 62.

Declaration of Independence, p. 17.
Delegates to National Convention, expenses of, in Oregon, p. 99.
Democracy, compared with Old World conditions, p. 14; Hamilton on, p. 14; humanizing influences of, p. 14; success of, p. 15.
"Denver Municipal Facts," p. 114.
Des Moines, Iowa, commission government law, pp. 280 ff.
Dickinson on suffrage, p. 13.
Direct legislation, *see* Initiative.
Direct primary, cause of agitation for, p. 12; importance of, p. 104; presidential, pp. 101 ff., 119 ff.; presidential in Oregon, pp. 95 ff.

Emergency clause in acts, abuse and proposed remedy in Oregon, p. 106.
Executive, confidence in, p. 7; early fear of, p. 3; power, in Oregon proposed plan, pp. 349 ff., 357, 374 ff.; veto power of, in New York, p. 3; without veto power in North Carolina, p. 7.
Ex parte Wagner, pp. 330 ff.

Federal constitution, *see* Constitution.
Federalist, The, on meaning of "democracy," pp. 26 ff.
Federal judiciary, *see* Judiciary.

391

Index

Gazette, proposed in Oregon, pp. 113 ff., 115, 360.
Gerrymander, proposed plan to prevent, in Oregon, p. 357.
Goodnow, F. J., on the function of the judiciary, p. 60.
Gorham, on republican government, p. 27.
Government, plan for efficient, p. 69.
Governor, *see* Executive.
Governors, cause of popularity, p. 7.

Hamilton, Alexander, on republican government, pp. 28, 65.
Harlan, Justice, on judicial legislation, p. 62.
Harmon, Judson, supporter of Ohio plan, pp. 274 ff.
House of Commons, p. 108.

Idaho, initiative and referendum amendment proposed, pp. 200 ff.; recall amendment proposed, p. 271.
Illinois, public opinion law, pp. 238 ff.
Impeachment, p. 63.
Initiative, competing measure by legislature, p. 37; definition of, p. 20; drafting of bills, p. 34; illustrations of, pp. 94 ff.; use of, as compared with referendum, p. 47; *see* Initiative and Referendum.
Initiative and Referendum, Arizona provisions, pp. 230 ff.; Arkansas provisions, p. 180; California provisions, pp. 184 ff.; Colorado provisions, pp. 181 ff.; commission government provisions, pp. 28 ff. 287 ff.; constitutionality of, pp. 29 ff., 304 ff.; effect on minority legislation, p. 40; effect on representative government, pp. 22 ff.; experience limited, p. 13; extent of adoption, pp. 1 ff.; forms of, pp. 20 ff.; Idaho proposed provisions, pp. 205 ff.; Iowa provisions for, in commission government, p. 281; lack of danger in, p. 69; map of, *see* frontispiece; Maine provisions, pp. 162 ff.; Michigan provisions, pp. 178 ff.; Montana provisions, pp. 126 ff.; municipal government provisions, pp. 274 ff.; Nebraska proposed provisions, pp. 195 ff.; Nevada provisions, pp. 120 ff.; New Jersey provisions for, in commission government, pp. 287 ff.; North Dakota proposed provisions, pp. 210 ff.; number of signatures, p. 37; Oklahoma provisions, pp. 137, 139, 159, 161; opinions of founders of government as to, p. 29; Oregon provisions, pp. 79, 81 ff.; publicity of bills, p. 41; solicitors for signatures, p. 36; South Dakota provisions, pp. 70, 73; Utah provisions, p. 78; vote under, pp. 38 ff.; in Oregon, p. 43; in South Dakota, p. 49; Washington proposed provisions, pp. 191 ff.; Wisconsin proposed provisions, pp. 206 ff.; Wyoming proposed provisions, pp. 201 ff.
Inspector of government, proposed Oregon plan, pp. 114, 359 ff.
Interpellation, in proposed Oregon plan, p. 368.
Iowa commission government law, pp. 280 ff.

Jefferson on republican government, p. 344.
Journalism, p. 115.
Judicial decisions, Bonner *v.* Belsterling, pp. 337 ff.; case pending in United States Supreme Court, p. 310. *Ex parte* Wagner, pp. 330 ff.; Kadderly *v.* City of Portland, pp. 304 ff.; Kiernan *v.* City of Portland, pp. 314 ff.; Luther *v.* Borden, pp. 291 ff.; State *v.* Pacific States Telephone and Telegraph Co., pp. 310 ff.
Judicial legislation, Harlan on, p. 62.
Judiciary, advantages in the Oregon plan, p. 117; debate in Congress, pp. 55 ff.; federal, pp. 65, 68; Goodnow on, p. 60; Harlan on, p. 62; independence of, p. 67; proposed Oregon plan, pp. 382 ff.; recall of, pp. 55 ff.; Roosevelt on, p. 66.
Jury, in Oregon, p. 117.

Kadderly *v.* City of Portland, pp. 304 ff.
Kentucky, abuses by legislature in, p. 5.
Kiernan *v.* City of Portland, pp. 31, 314 ff.

Index 393

Legare, Rep., on the judiciary, p. 56.

Legislation, judicial, p. 62; proposed Oregon plan to prevent hasty legislation, p. 112; requirements of, p. 33.

Legislature, abuses by, in Kentucky, p. 5; constitutional limitations on power of, pp. 5 ff.; contest with the convention, p. 4; effect of Australian ballot on, pp. 11 ff.; history of decrease of confidence in, pp. 3 ff.; lack of judgment of members of, pp. 48, 62; New York legislatures of 1910 and 1911, and New York *Times* on, p. 8; proposed Oregon plan, pp. 108, 362 ff.; reasons for lack of confidence in, pp. 12 ff.

Lincoln, Abraham, on the judiciary, p. 55.

Littleton, Martin W., on recall of judges, pp. 58 ff.

Logrolling, proposed Oregon plan to prevent, pp. 113, 356, 373.

Luther *v.* Borden, pp. 29 ff., 293 ff.

Madison, James, on representative government, pp. 26 ff.

Maine, initiative and referendum amendment adopted, pp. 162 ff.; sample ballot, 1910, p. 162.

Michigan, initiative and referendum constitutional provisions, pp. 178 ff.

Missouri, initiative and referendum amendment adopted, pp. 168 ff.

Montana, initiative and referendum constitutional provisions, pp. 126 ff.

Municipal government, pp. 9 ff.; initiative and referendum in, pp. 274 ff.

"Municipal Report," San Francisco, p. 114.

National convention, delegates to, under Oregon plan, p. 99.

Nebraska, initiative and referendum amendment, pp. 195 ff.

Nevada, initiative and referendum provisions, pp. 121 ff.; proposed recall amendment, p. 272.

New Jersey, commission government law, pp. 285 ff.

New Mexico, amendment scheme proposed by Congress, pp. 258 ff.; joint resolution for admission, pp. 256 ff.; proposed provisions, pp. 234 ff.; veto of constitution, pp. 245 ff.

New York, power of veto in executive, p. 3.

New York City, Board of Estimate and Apportionment, p. 10.

New York *Evening Post*, on necessity for an Official Gazette, p. 115.

New York *Times*, on New York legislature of 1911, p. 8.

Nominations, *see* Direct Primary.

North Carolina, veto power, p. 7.

North Dakota, proposed amendments for initiative and referendum, pp. 210 ff.; for recall, pp. 210, 221 ff.

Official publications, "Denver Municipal Facts," p. 114; Oregon publicity pamphlet, p. 94; Oregon Gazette, proposed, pp. 113 ff., 360 ff.; "Municipal Report," San Francisco, p. 114.

Ohio, statute for initiative and referendum in cities, pp. 274 ff.

Oklahoma, constitutional provisions for initiative and referendum, pp. 137 ff.; elaborating acts, pp. 139, 153, 161; *Ex parte* Wagner, pp. 330 ff.

Oregon, initiative and referendum provisions, pp. 79 ff., 81 ff.; judiciary system, p. 107; jury procedure, p. 117; Kadderly *v.* City of Portland, pp. 304 ff.; Kiernan *v.* City of Portland, pp. 314 ff.; political results of reforms, p. 50; presidential primary, pp. 95 ff.; publicity pamphlet, pp. 41, 94 ff.; ballot titles, 1910, pp. 384 ff.; State *v.* Pacific States Telephone and Telegraph Co., pp. 310 ff.; vote on measures since 1904, p. 42; U'Ren's proposed plan, — county government, pp. 358, 380 ff., executive functions, pp. 357, 374 ff., Gazette, p. 360, inspectors of government, pp. 114, 359 ff., judiciary, pp. 382 ff., prevention of abuse of emergency clause, p. 112, prevention of gerrymander, p. 357, prevention of hasty legislation, p. 112, prevention of logrolling, pp. 113, 356, and 373, punishment for legislators' failure to vote, p. 373, Speaker not member of House, p. 112.

Owen, Senator, on recall of judges, p. 62.

Pickett, Rep., on the judiciary, p. 56.
Popular election, theory of, p. 53.
President, Oregon plan for, nomination pp. 99 ff.
Presidential direct primary, pp. 95 ff., 101 ff., 119 ff.
Primaries, see Direct Primary.
Proportional representation, a preventative of the gerrymander, p. 357.
Proposed Oregon plan, see Oregon.
Publications, see Official.
Publicity pamphlet, in Oregon, pp. 41 ff., 94 ff.
Public opinion law in Illinois, p. 238.

Randolph, on what is representative government, p. 27.
Ratification of constitutions, pp. 15 and 17.
Recall, and the short ballot, p. 54; Arizona proposed provision, pp. 244 ff.; Arizona provision inserted by Congress, pp. 263 ff.; California provision, pp. 264 ff.; commission government plan in Iowa, pp. 280 ff.; commission government plan in New Jersey, pp. 285 ff.; constitutionality of, pp. 337 ff.; debate in Congress on, pp. 55 ff.; effect on ballot, p. 68; efficiency of, with long term, p. 108; Idaho proposed provision, p. 271; Iowa commission government provisions, pp. 280 ff.; judges, pp. 55 ff., 245 ff.; danger in, considered p. 69; Legare on, p. 56; Littleton on, p. 58; movement for, pp. 52 ff.; Nevada proposed provision, p. 272; New Jersey commission government provisions, p. 285; North Dakota proposed provisions, pp. 210 ff., 221 ff.; Oregon provisions, p. 242; Pickett on, p. 56; Roosevelt on, p. 66; Taft's veto message, pp. 245 ff.
Referendum, definition of, p. 20; see Initiative and Referendum.
Republican government, defined in *The Federalist*, pp. 25 ff.; evolution of, p. 3; failure in the early state and municipal governments, pp. 3 ff., 9 ff.; initiative and referendum under, pp. 24 ff.; opinions of Madison, Randolph, Gorham, Wilson, and Adams on, pp. 26 ff.; practice of, p. 32; theory of, p. 32; *The Federalist* on, pp. 25 ff.
Roosevelt, Theodore, on the recall, p. 66.

Sample ballots, Maine, p. 162; Oregon, p. 79.
San Francisco, "Municipal Report," p. 114.
Saunders, Rep., on the recall, p. 65.
Short ballot, necessity for, p. 54.
South Dakota, experience with initiative and referendum, p. 49; amendment providing for initiative and referendum, p. 70; elaborating law, statewide, p. 71; elaborating law, local, pp. 73 ff.
Speaker, powers of in Oregon proposed plan, p. 112.
State v. Pacific States Telephone and Telegraph Co., pp. 310 ff.
Statutory law, comparison with constitutional law, p. 19.
Suffrage, effect of its extension, pp. 12 ff.; Dickinson on, p. 13; opinion of founders of the government on, p. 13.

Taft, W. H., on judicial procedure, p. 117; recall veto, pp. 245 ff.
Texas, Bonner v. Belsterling, pp. 337 ff.; statute for party initiative, p. 240.

U'Ren, W. S., see Oregon, proposed plan for, pp. 349 ff.
Utah, initiative and referendum amendment adopted, p. 78.

Veto power of executive, in New York, p. 3; in North Carolina, p. 7.
Vote in Oregon, p. 42.
Voters, interest of, pp. 37 ff.; judgment of, p. 48.

Washington, initiative and referendum amendment proposed, pp. 191 ff.
Wilson, Woodrow, author of New Jersey plan, pp. 285 ff.
Wisconsin, initiative and referendum amendment proposed, pp. 206 ff.
Wyoming, initiative and referendum amendment proposed, pp. 201 ff.

THE following pages contain advertisements of a few of the Macmillan publications by the same author and on kindred subjects.

By CHARLES A. BEARD

Professor of History in Columbia University, author of
"Introduction to the English Historians."

Readings in American Government and Politics

A collection of interesting material illustrative of the different periods in the history of the United States, prepared for those students who desire to study source writings.

Cloth, crown 8vo. Now Ready, $1.90 net

"An invaluable guide for the student of politics, setting forth in an illuminating way the many phases of our political life." — *Critic.*

American Government and Politics

Cloth, 776 pages, 12mo, index, $2.10 net

A work designed primarily for college students, but of considerable interest to the general reader. A special feature is the full attention paid to topics that have been forced into public attention by the political conditions of the present time.

By WILLIAM ARCHIBALD DUNNING, PH.D.

Professor of History in Columbia University

A History of Political Theories

2 Volumes

I — ANCIENT AND MEDIEVAL
II — FROM LUTHER TO MONTESQUIEU

Cloth, 8vo, each $2.50 net

The successive transformations through which the political consciousness of men has passed from early antiquity to modern times are stated in a clear, intelligible manner, and to aid in a fuller study of the subject references are appended to each chapter covering the topics treated therein. At the end of each volume has been placed an alphabetical list containing full information as to all the works referred to, together with many additional titles.

PUBLISHED BY

THE MACMILLAN COMPANY

64-66 Fifth Avenue, New York

A GREAT WORK INCREASED IN VALUE

The American Commonwealth
By JAMES BRYCE

New edition, thoroughly revised, with four new chapters
Two 8vo volumes $4.00 net

"More emphatically than ever is it the most noteworthy treatise on our political and social system." — *The Dial.*

"The most sane and illuminating book that has been written on this country." — *Chicago Tribune.*

"What makes it extremely interesting is that it gives the matured views of Mr. Bryce after a closer study of American institutions for nearly the life of a generation." — *San Francisco Chronicle.*

"The work is practically new and more indispensable than ever." — *Boston Herald.*

"In its revised form, Mr. Bryce's noble and discerning book deserves to hold its preëminent place for at least twenty years more." — *Record-Herald*, Chicago, Ill.

The American Commonwealth

Abridged Edition, for the use of Colleges and High Schools. Being an Introduction to the Study of the Government and Institutions of the United States. By JAMES BRYCE.

One volume.   Crown 8vo, xiii + 547 pages, $1.75 net

"It is a genuine pleasure to commend to our readers the abridged edition of 'The American Commonwealth' just issued by the Macmillan Company. Mr. Bryce's book, which has heretofore been issued only in two volumes, has no peer as a commentary upon American political institutions." — *Public Opinion.*

PUBLISHED BY

THE MACMILLAN COMPANY
64-66 Fifth Avenue, New York

COMMISSION GOVERNMENT IN AMERICAN CITIES

By

ERNEST S. BRADFORD, Ph.D.

Member National Municipal League; Sometime Research Scholar in Political Science, University of Wisconsin; Fellow in Political Science, University of Pennsylvania; Author of "Municipal Gas Lighting," etc.

Half Leather, 12mo, $1.25 net; by mail, $1.35

Of the recent developments in the field of municipal politics, none has attracted more attention than the introduction and rapid spread of the commission form of city government, so called from the commission or board which constitutes the governing body.

Under this plan, the organization of a city is similar to that of a business corporation. This popular study of one of the greatest issues to-day before the American people contains an account of the rise and spread of the commission form of government and the results of its operation in Galveston, Houston, Des Moines, Cedar Rapids, Huntington, Haverhill and elsewhere.

Accompanying this there is a critical comparison of the various types of commission government so far standing, the principles involved, a list of the cities that rejected the plan, as well as those which have adopted it, and finally a discussion of the limitations and objections urged against commission government. There is thus presented in this work the most complete and up-to-date history of this form of government and of its recent marvelous development in American municipal life.

PUBLISHED BY

THE MACMILLAN COMPANY

64–66 Fifth Avenue, New York

By M. OSTROGORSKI

Democracy and the Party System in the United States

A Study in Extra-constitutional Government

Cloth, 478 pp., index, 12mo, $1.75 net; by mail, $1.88

"Students of government, the world over, will turn to this book for exact information and critical discussion of its most vital problem." — *The Dial*, Chicago.

"It would be an astonishing book had it been written by an Englishman or an American who had spent a lifetime in the study and practice of politics. Coming as it does from the pen of a foreign student, it is simply an amazing embodiment of minute observation and extraordinary knowledge." — *Manchester Guardian.*

"It should stand beside Mr. Bryce's great work, as a book which will avail as much for instruction and correction in righteousness. The gratitude of democracy to its accomplished author should be great; republics in the end are *not* ungrateful." — *The Literary World*, Boston.

"The work of M. Ostrogorski, great in every respect, continues and completes the work of Tocqueville, Sumner, Maine, Lecky, and Bryce." — *L'Année Sociologique*, Paris.

"This is a work, a great work, which claims the attention of the politician and of the citizen, speaks of his rights, as well as of the philosopher and the historian. It makes an epoch in the history of political thought as did, in their time, the 'Esprit des lois' by Montesquieu, and 'Democracy in America,' by Tocqueville." — *Le Temps*, Paris.

"This is a great work such as has not yet even been published." — *Revue du droit public*, Paris.

"It is one of the most notable books which has been written about the workings of democratic institutions. It goes beyond the forms, and . . . it gets at the reality of things." — *New York Tribune.*

"The author's style is such that it is no hardship to follow him from beginning to end of his discussion." — *New York Times.*

"The remarkable work by Mr. Ostrogorski . . . is undoubtedly one of the most notable books in political science that has appeared in many years. . . . The author merits great praise for his industry in gathering facts and his skill in making so long and elaborate a work so readable." — *Springfield Republican.*

PUBLISHED BY

THE MACMILLAN COMPANY

64–66 Fifth Avenue, New York

The American Federal State

A Text-Book in Civics for High Schools and Colleges

By ROSCOE LEWIS ASHLEY

New edition, illustrated, cloth, 12mo, $2.00 net

The important changes in this new edition are chiefly in Part III on Policies and Problems, while Part I on Historical Development and Part II on Government are substantially the same as in the old edition. In Part II, however, the chapters on Executive Departments and Some Phases of State Activity have been rewritten, so as to include developments of the last decade. In Part III a new chapter has been added on Natural Resources, while the chapter on Commerce, Industry, and Labor is practically new, because of increased regulation of industry and railroads, and new phases of labor protection. A large number of new references has been added throughout the book.

If every American youth were led through a conscientious study of American civics as set forth in this book, there would be no more ignorant voting, no more unintelligent support of party politicians, no more "railroad legislation" because of ignorant party followers; every citizen of the coming generation would know, definitely and clearly, the how and the why of every phase of governmental machinery.

Although this book contains more material and outlines a more complete study of civics than most text-books on the subject, the author has arranged a plan by which more cursory study may be made, using only parts of the book. High school and even grammar school teachers will find this plan of unusual merit.

PUBLISHED BY

THE MACMILLAN COMPANY

64-66 Fifth Avenue, New York

Lightning Source UK Ltd.
Milton Keynes UK
UKHW05f0104040918
328269UK00018B/771/P